FUN Family

By Benjamin Frisch

The Fun Family © 2016 Benjamin Frisch.

Published by Top Shelf Productions, PO Box 1282, Marietta, GA 30061-1282, USA. Top Shelf Productions is an imprint of IDW Publishing, a division of Idea and Design Works, LLC. Offices: 2765 Truxtun Road, San Diego, CA 92106. Top Shelf Productions®, the Top Shelf logo, Idea and Design Works®, and the IDW logo are registered trademarks of Idea and Design Works, LLC. All Rights Reserved. With the exception of small excerpts of artwork used for review purposes, none of the contents of this publication may be reprinted without the permission of IDW Publishing. IDW Publishing does not read or accept unsolicited submissions of ideas, stories, or artwork.

Editor-in-Chief: Chris Staros.
Designed by Benjamin Frisch and Chris Ross.
Edited by Chris Staros with Zac Boone.

Visit our online catalog at www.topshelfcomix.com.

Printed in Korea.

ISBN 978-1-60309-344-6

19   18   17   16   5   4   3   2   1

To My Parents

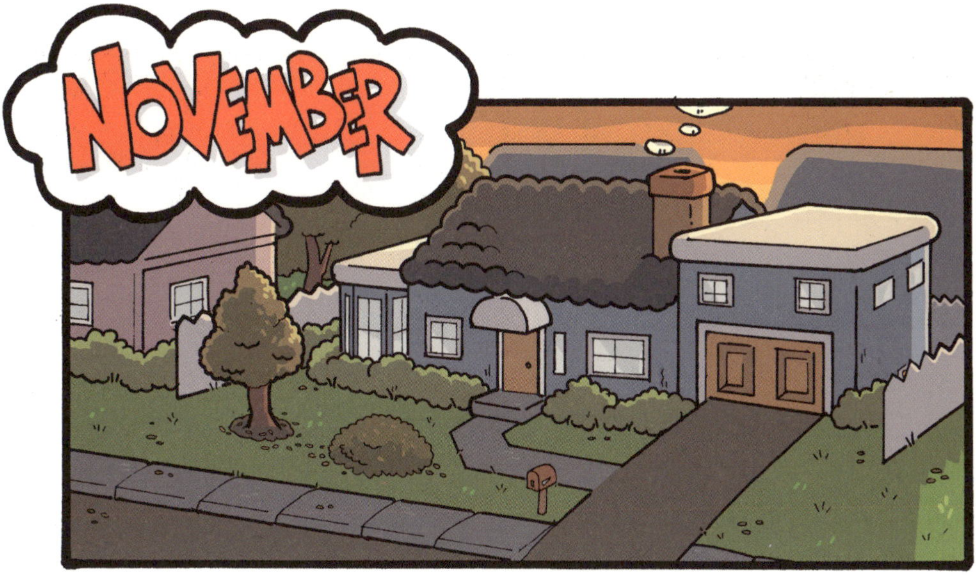
NOVEMBER

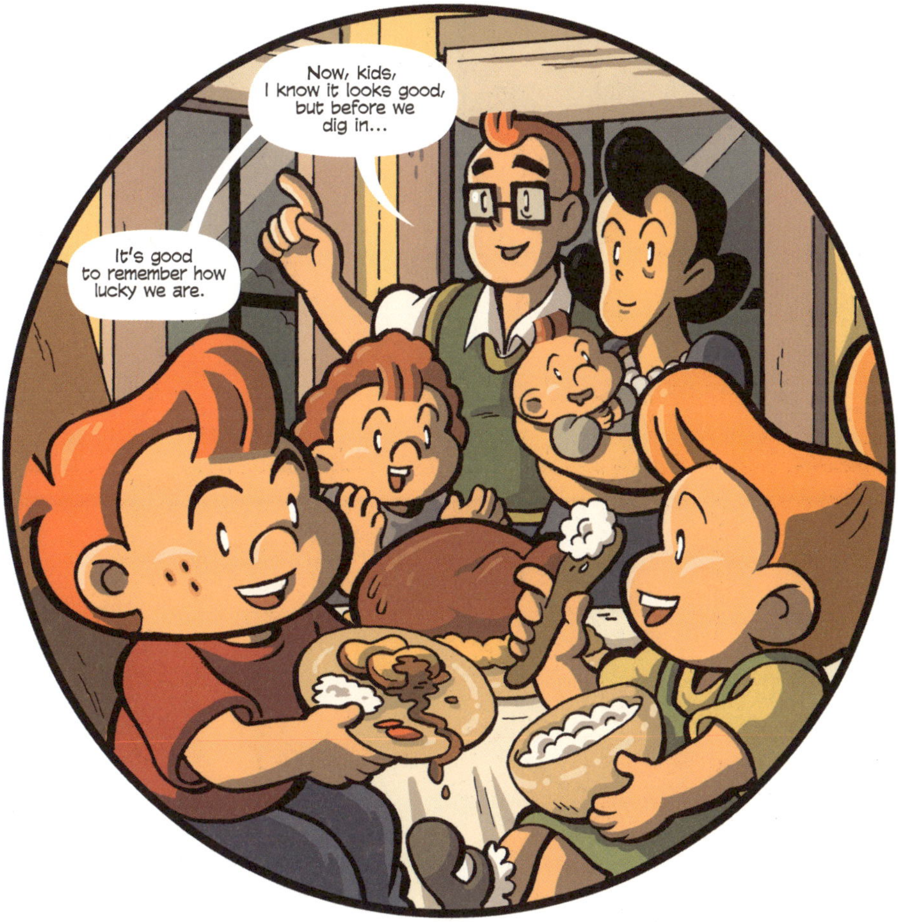
Now, kids, I know it looks good, but before we dig in...
It's good to remember how lucky we are.

Let's go around the table and say what we're thankful for!

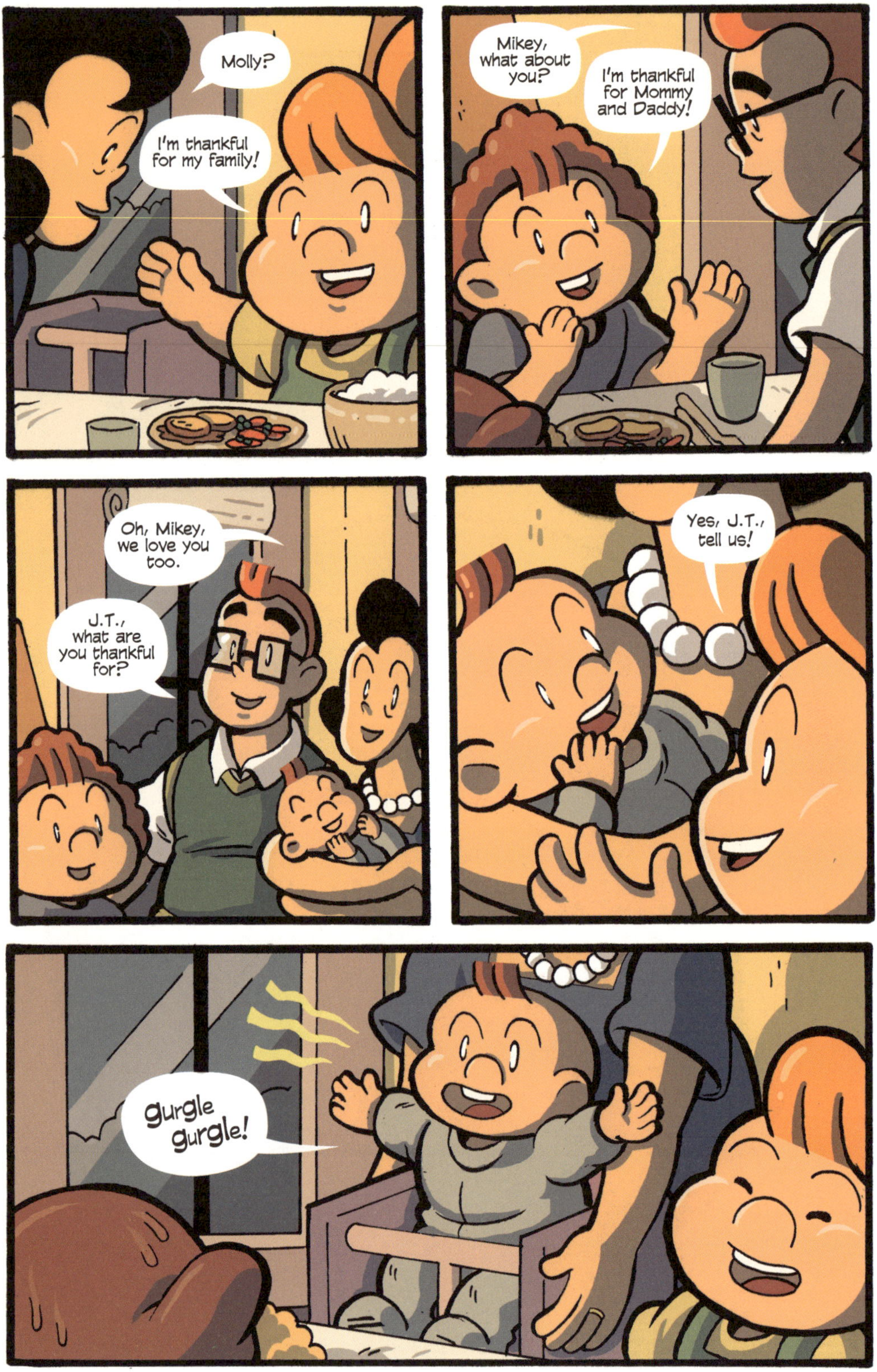

Molly?
I'm thankful for my family!
Mikey, what about you?
I'm thankful for Mommy and Daddy!
Oh, Mikey, we love you too.
J.T., what are you thankful for?
Yes, J.T., tell us!
gurgle gurgle!

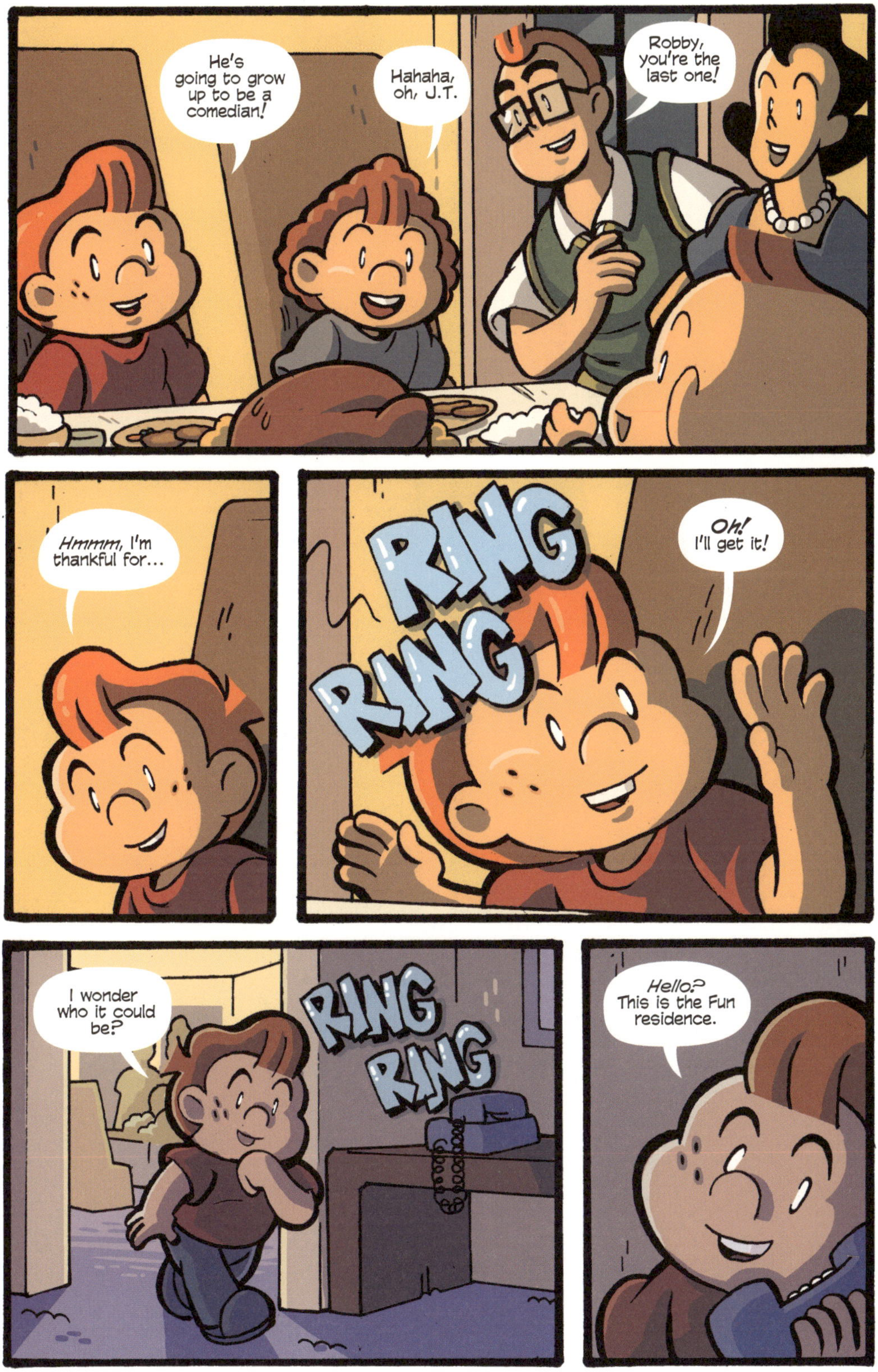
He's going to grow up to be a comedian!
Hahaha, oh, J.T.
Robby, you're the last one!
Hmmm, I'm thankful for...
RING RING
Oh! I'll get it!
I wonder who it could be?
RING RING
Hello? This is the Fun residence.

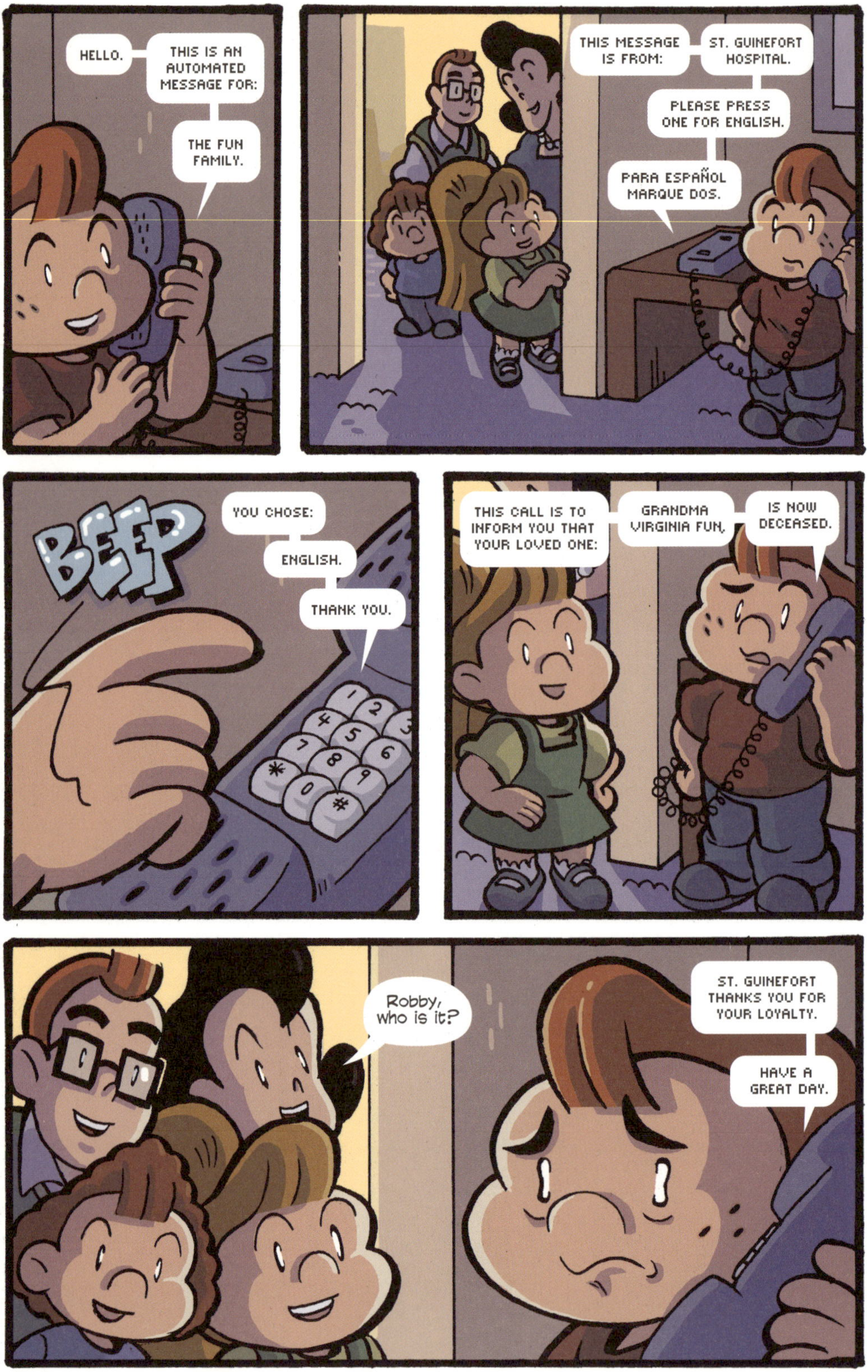
HELLO.
THIS IS AN AUTOMATED MESSAGE FOR:
THE FUN FAMILY.
THIS MESSAGE IS FROM:
ST. GUINEFORT HOSPITAL.
PLEASE PRESS ONE FOR ENGLISH.
PARA ESPAÑOL MARQUE DOS.
BEEP
YOU CHOSE:
ENGLISH.
THANK YOU.
THIS CALL IS TO INFORM YOU THAT YOUR LOVED ONE:
GRANDMA VIRGINIA FUN,
IS NOW DECEASED.
Robby, who is it?
ST. GUINEFORT THANKS YOU FOR YOUR LOYALTY.
HAVE A GREAT DAY.

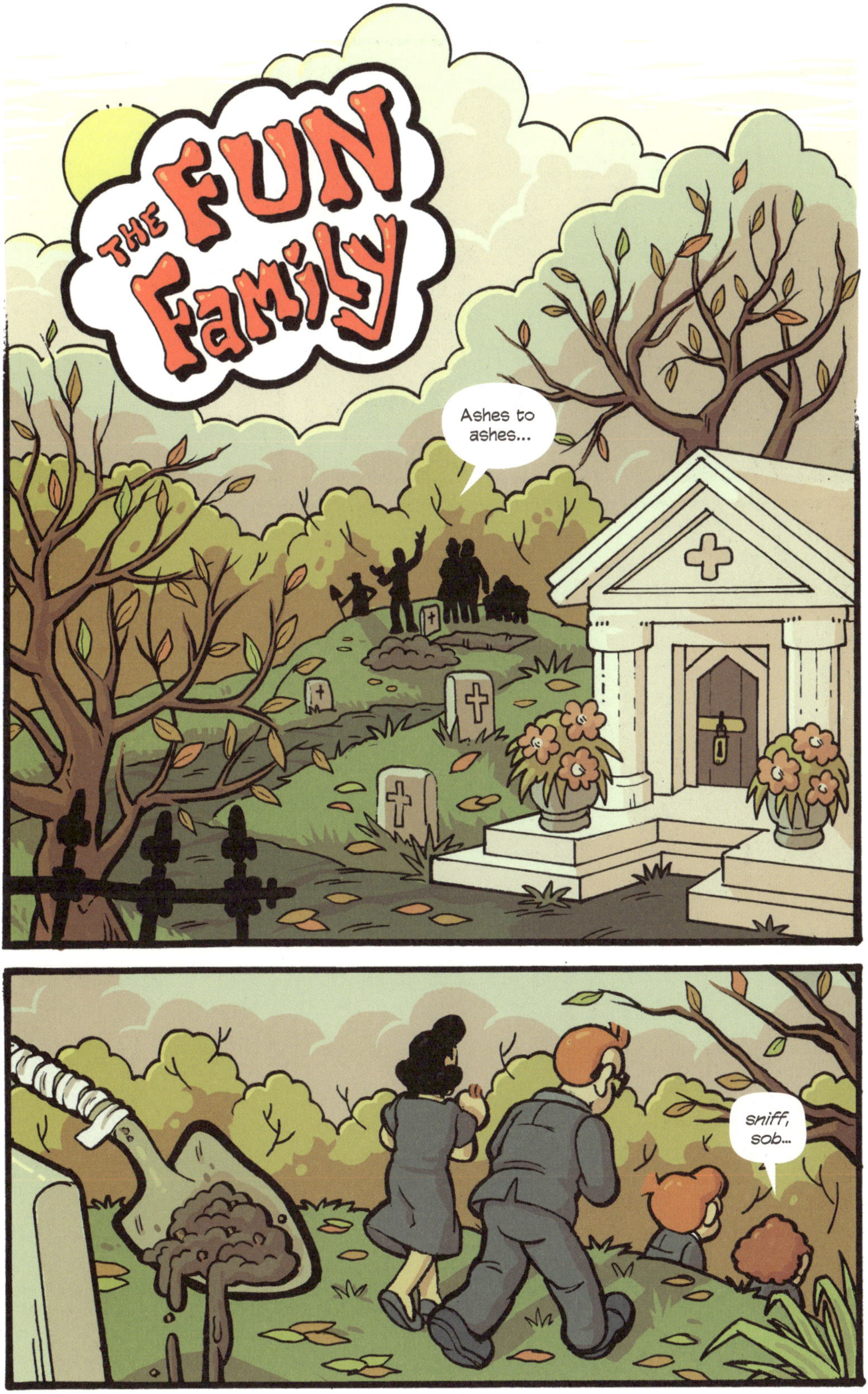
THE FUN Family
Ashes to ashes...
sniff, sob...

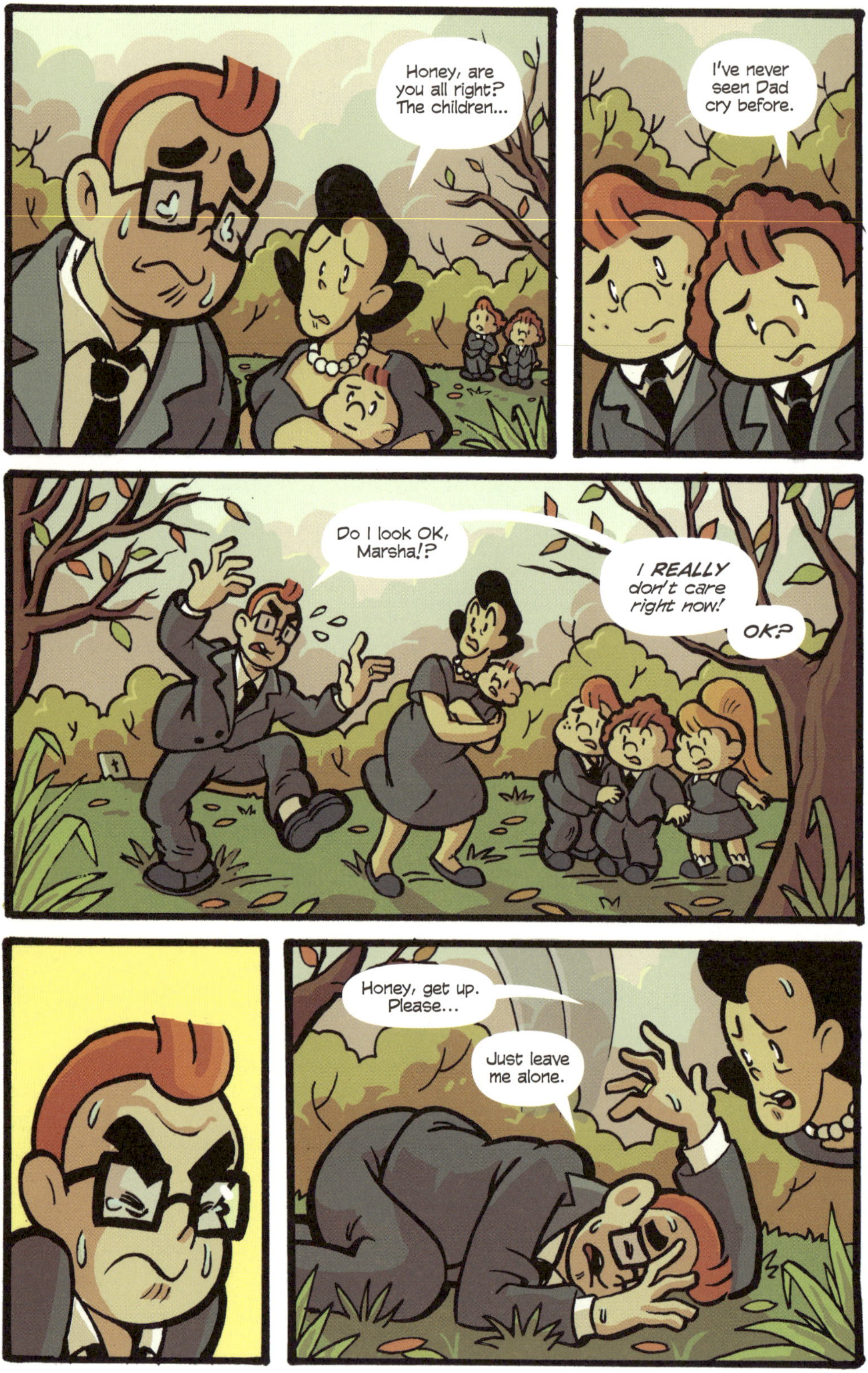
Honey, are you all right? The children...
I've never seen Dad cry before.
Do I look OK, Marsha!?
I REALLY don't care right now!
OK?
Honey, get up. Please...
Just leave me alone.

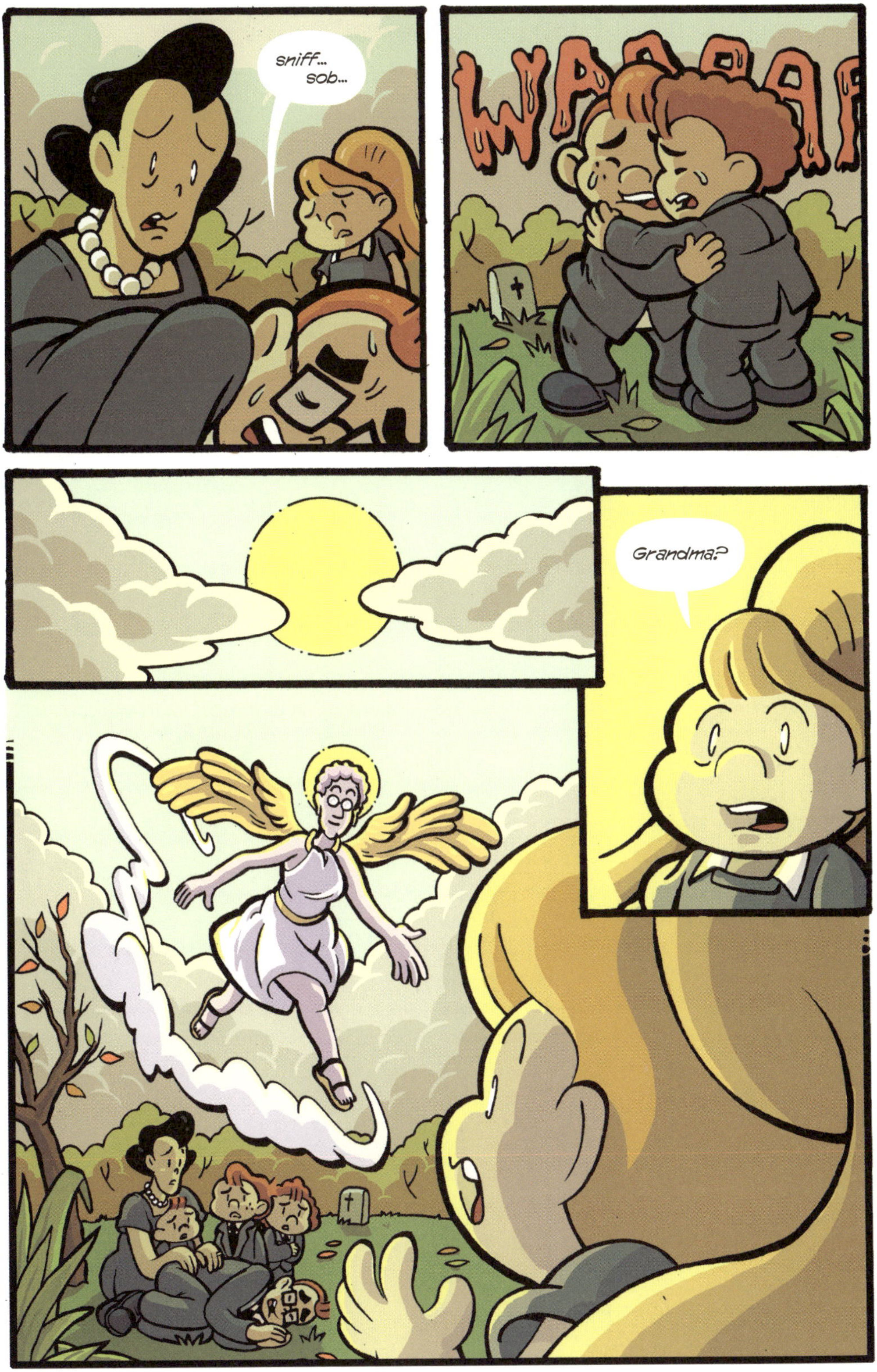
sniff... sob...
Grandma?

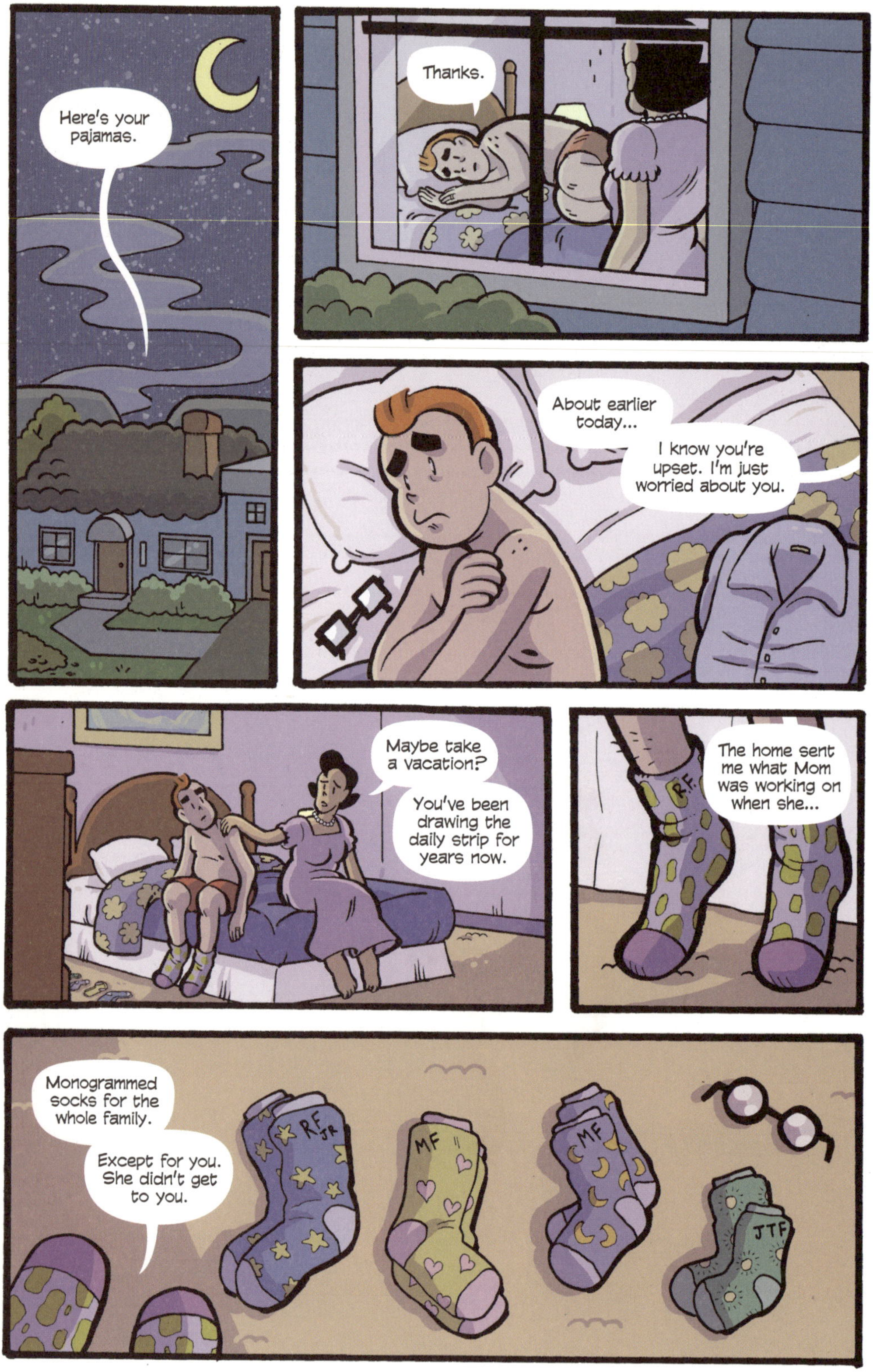
Here's your pajamas.
Thanks.
About earlier today...
I know you're upset. I'm just worried about you.
Maybe take a vacation?
You've been drawing the daily strip for years now.
R.F.
The home sent me what Mom was working on when she...
Monogrammed socks for the whole family.
Except for you. She didn't get to you.
RF JR
MF
MF
JTF

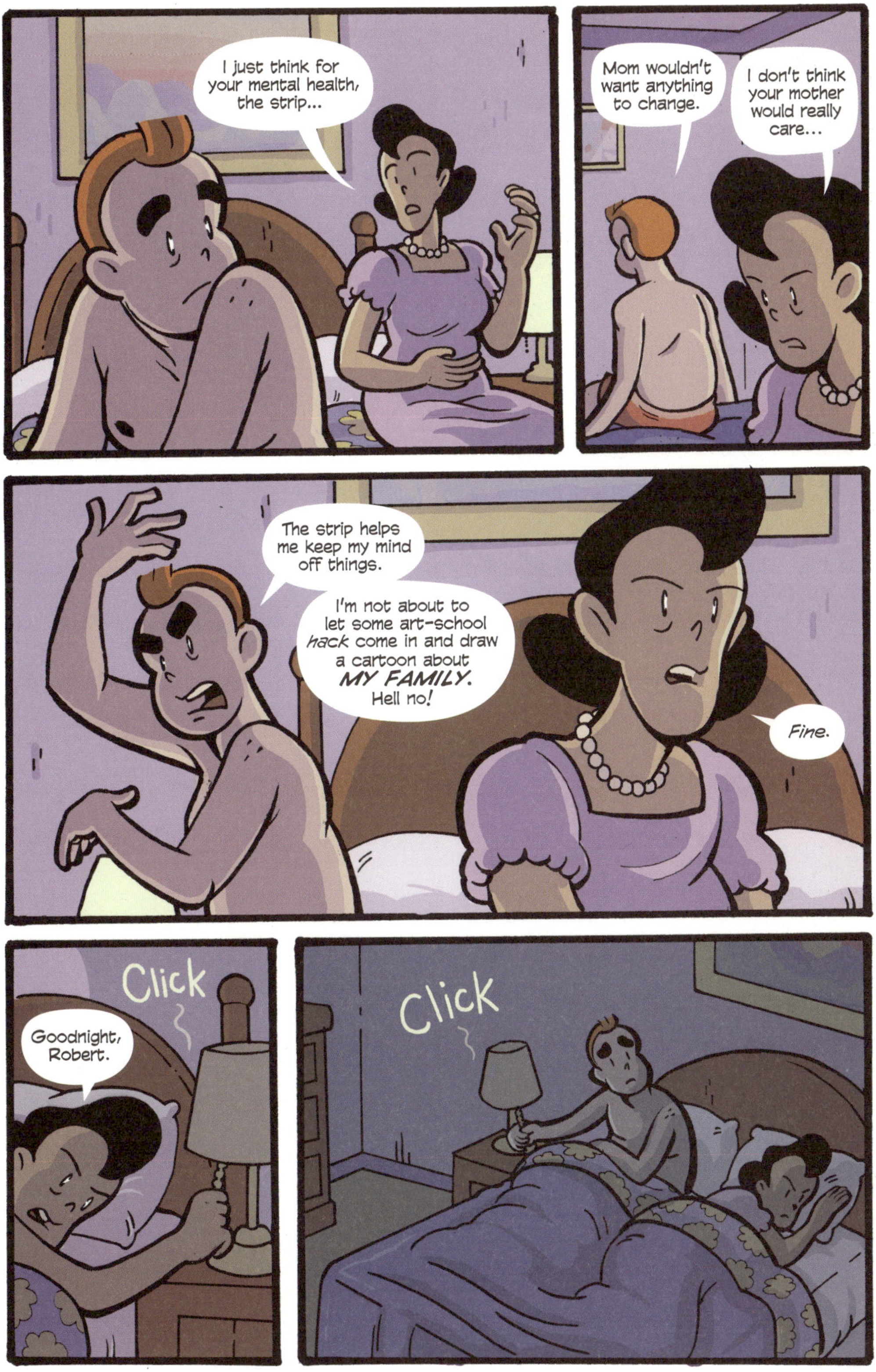
I just think for your mental health, the strip...
Mom wouldn't want anything to change.
I don't think your mother would really care...
The strip helps me keep my mind off things.
I'm not about to let some art-school *hack* come in and draw a cartoon about ***MY FAMILY.*** Hell no!
Fine.
Click
Goodnight, Robert.
Click

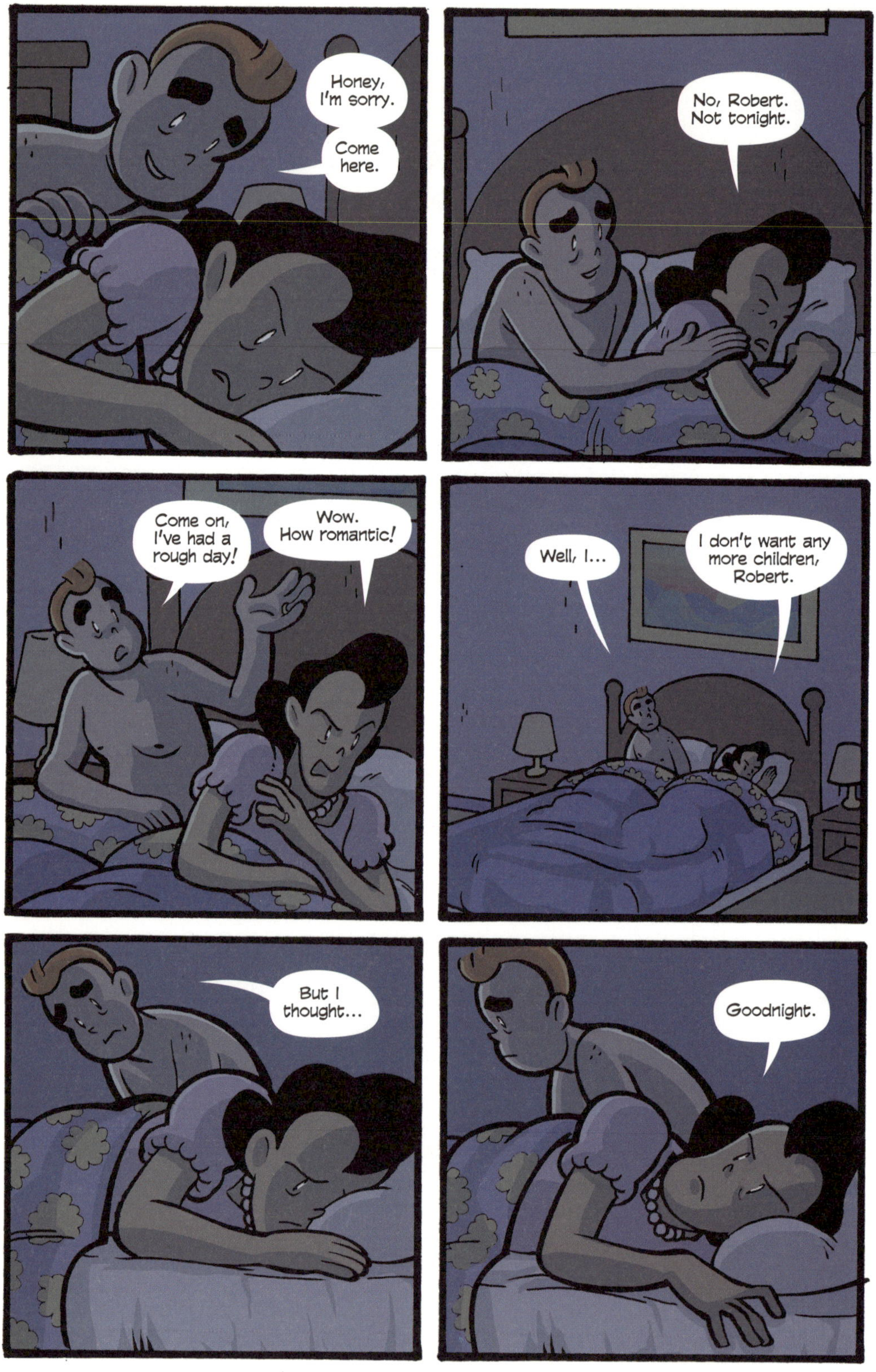
Honey, I'm sorry.
Come here.
No, Robert. Not tonight.
Come on, I've had a rough day!
Wow. How romantic!
Well, I...
I don't want any more children, Robert.
But I thought...
Goodnight.

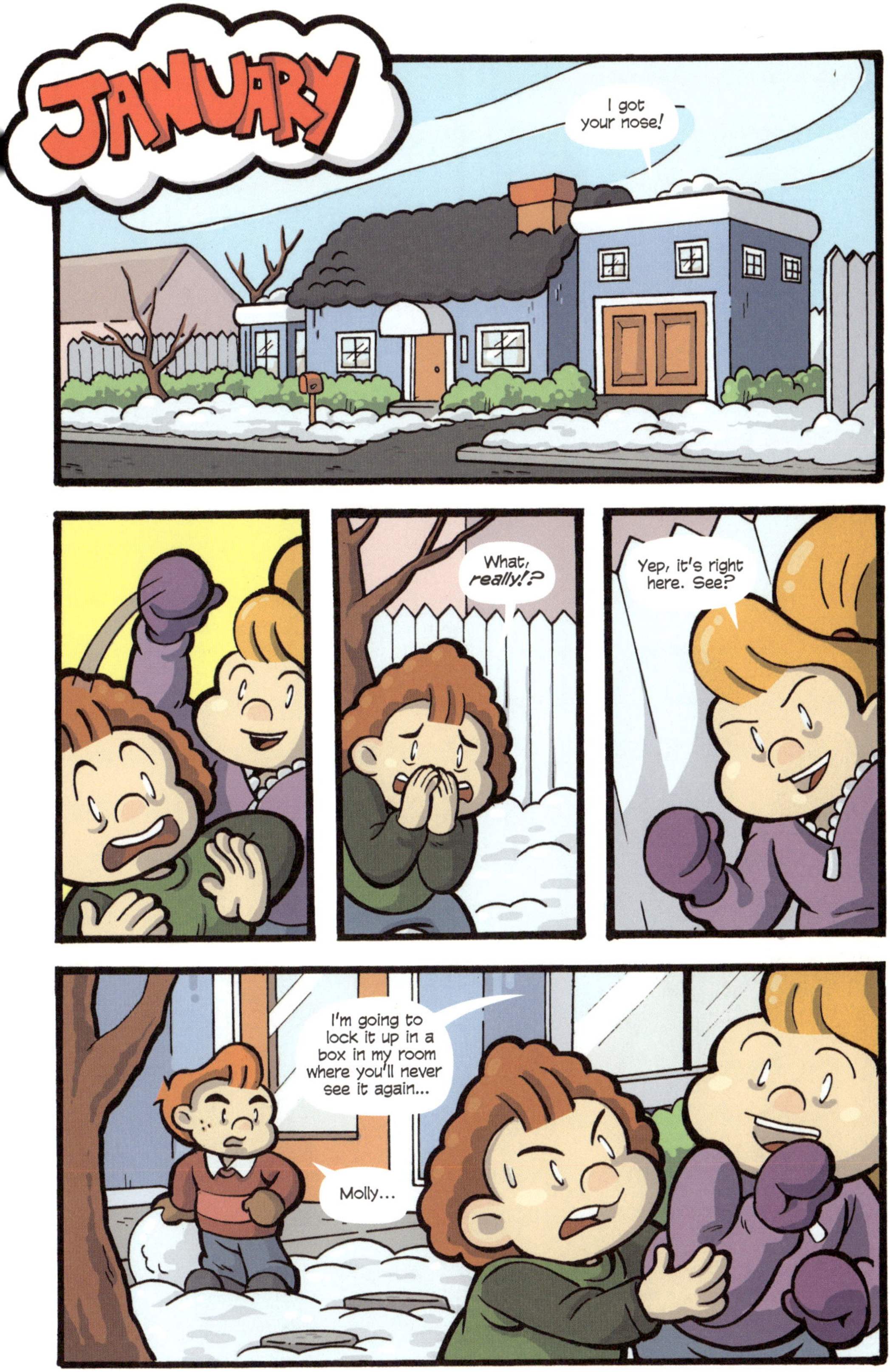
JANUARY
I got your nose!
What, *really!?*
Yep, it's right here. See?
I'm going to lock it up in a box in my room where you'll never see it again...
Molly...

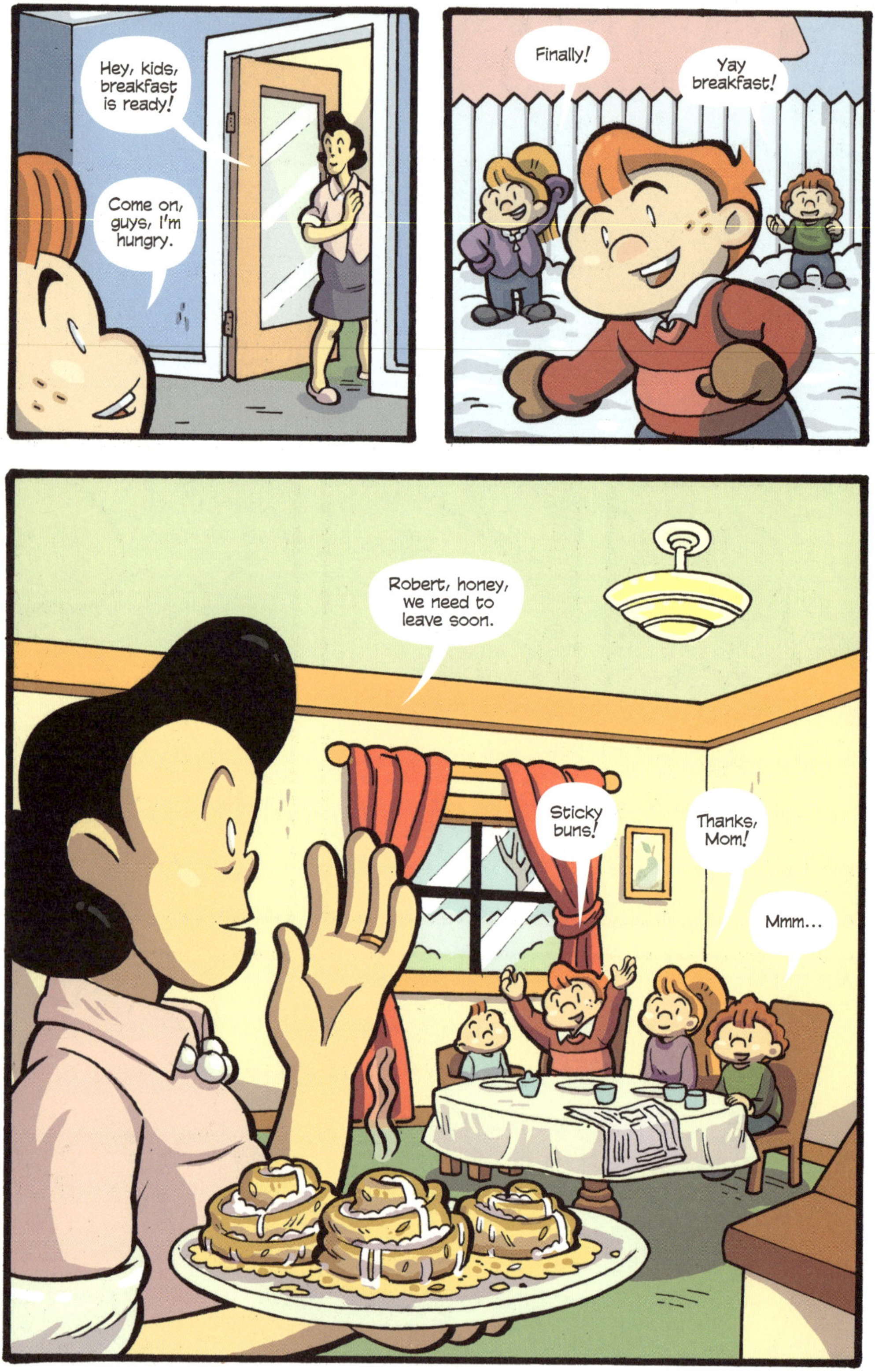
Hey, kids, breakfast is ready!
Come on, guys, I'm hungry.
Finally!
Yay breakfast!
Robert, honey, we need to leave soon.
Sticky buns!
Thanks, Mom!
Mmm...

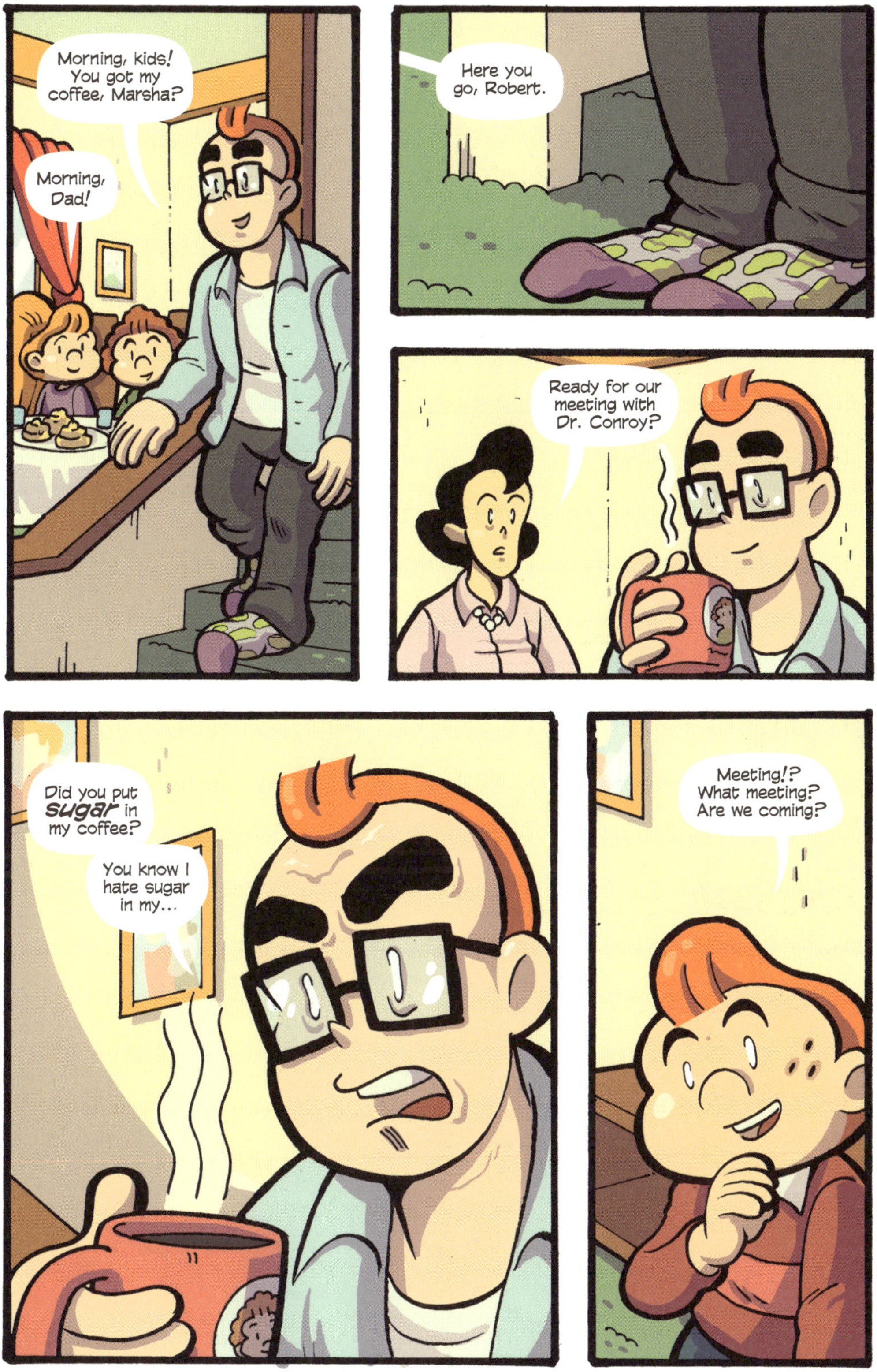
Morning, kids! You got my coffee, Marsha?
Morning, Dad!
Here you go, Robert.
Ready for our meeting with Dr. Conroy?
Did you put sugar in my coffee?
You know I hate sugar in my...
Meeting!? What meeting? Are we coming?

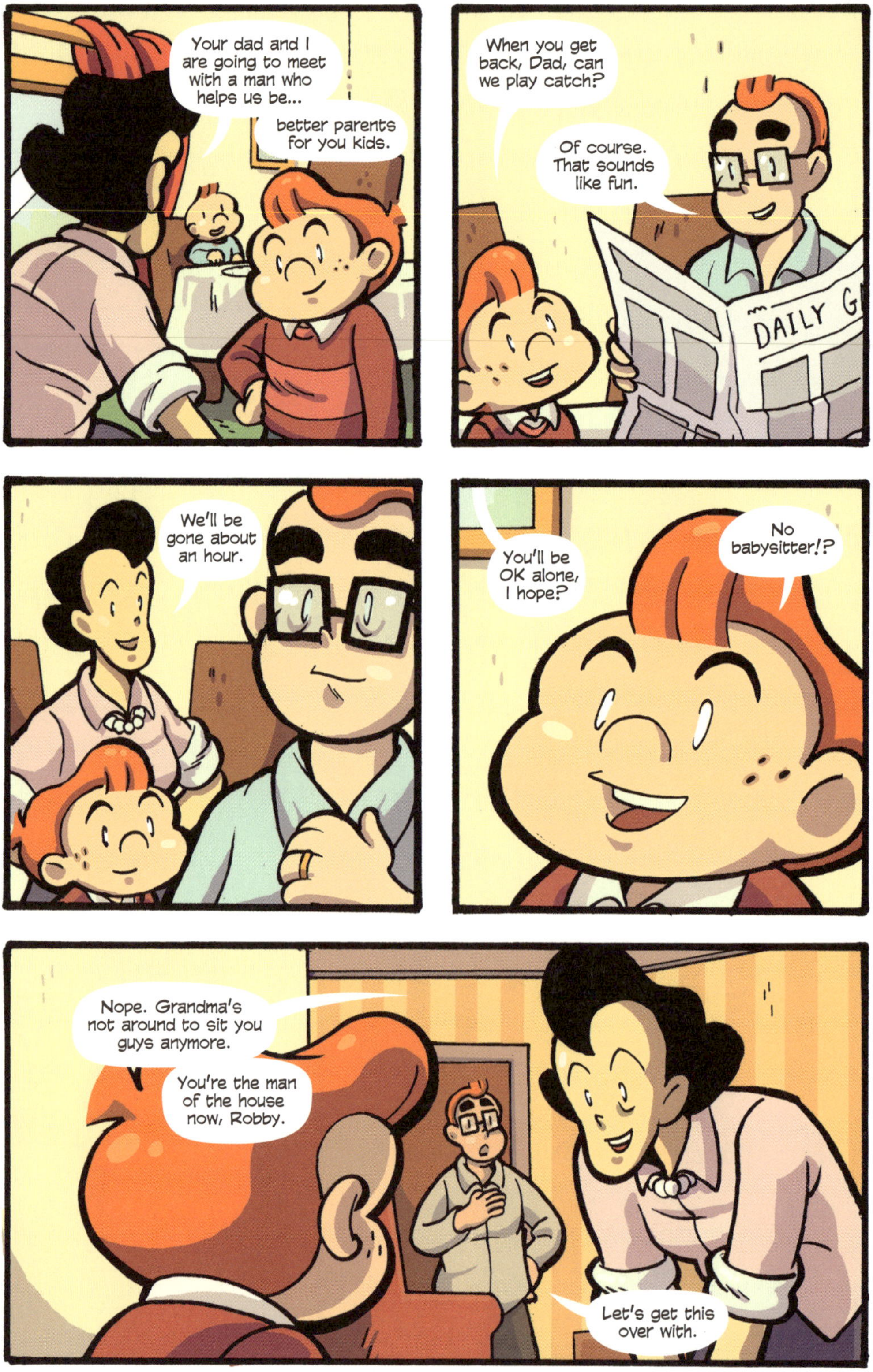
Your dad and I are going to meet with a man who helps us be...
better parents for you kids.
When you get back, Dad, can we play catch?
Of course. That sounds like fun.
DAILY G
We'll be gone about an hour.
You'll be OK alone, I hope?
No babysitter!?
Nope. Grandma's not around to sit you guys anymore.
You're the man of the house now, Robby.
Let's get this over with.

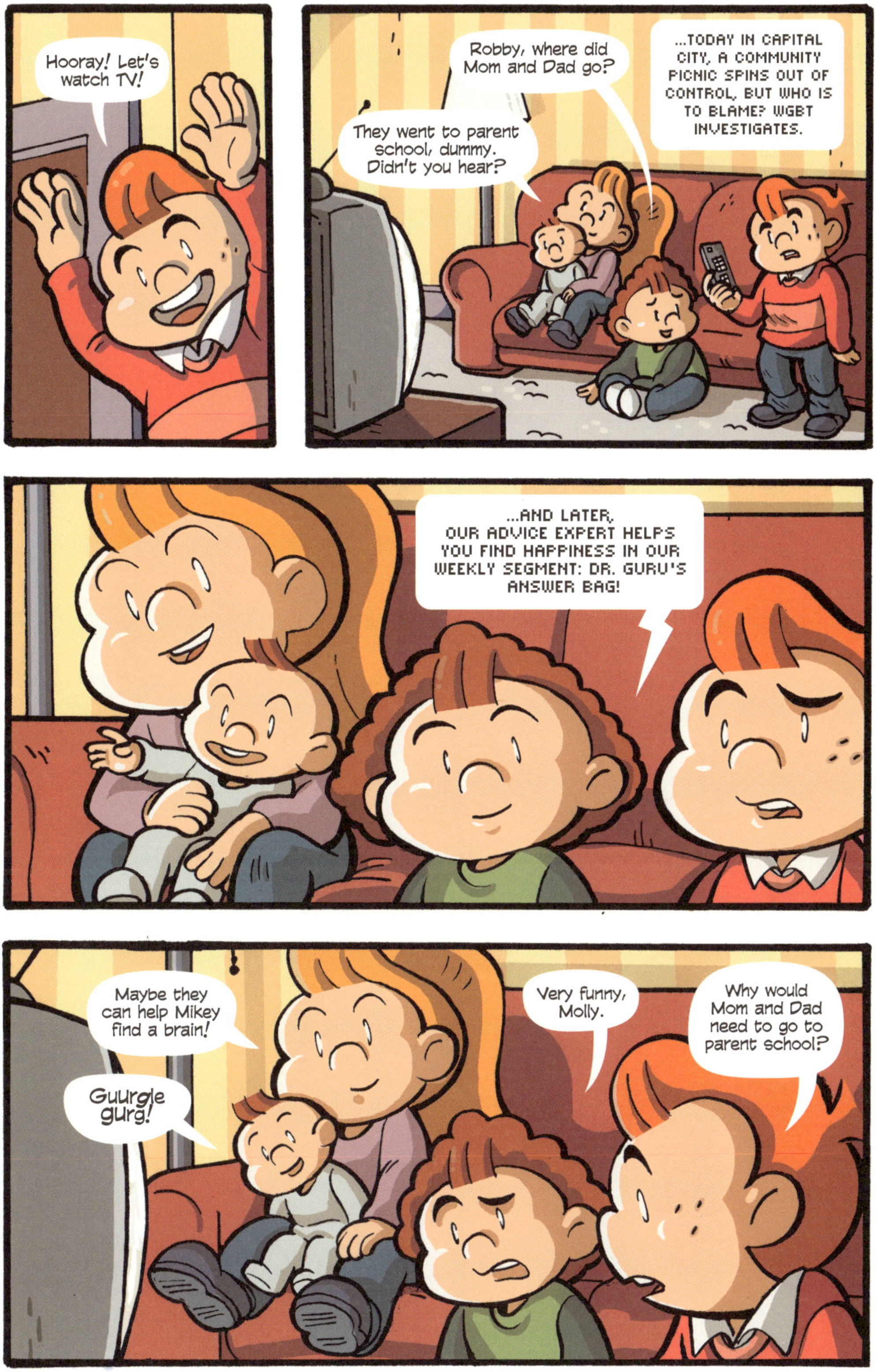
Hooray! Let's watch TV!
Robby, where did Mom and Dad go?
...TODAY IN CAPITAL CITY, A COMMUNITY PICNIC SPINS OUT OF CONTROL, BUT WHO IS TO BLAME? WGBT INVESTIGATES.
They went to parent school, dummy. Didn't you hear?
...AND LATER, OUR ADVICE EXPERT HELPS YOU FIND HAPPINESS IN OUR WEEKLY SEGMENT: DR. GURU'S ANSWER BAG!
Maybe they can help Mikey find a brain!
Guurgle gurg!
Very funny, Molly.
Why would Mom and Dad need to go to parent school?

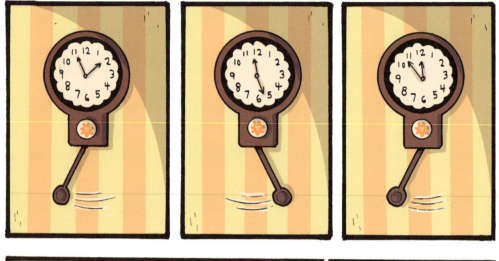

CHICK CHICK CHICK

It's the garage door! Turn it off!

They're home!

I just think Dr. Conroy has a good point.

He came highly recommended...

It's all a crock if you ask me.

I'm going to get some work done.

I'll be in the studio.

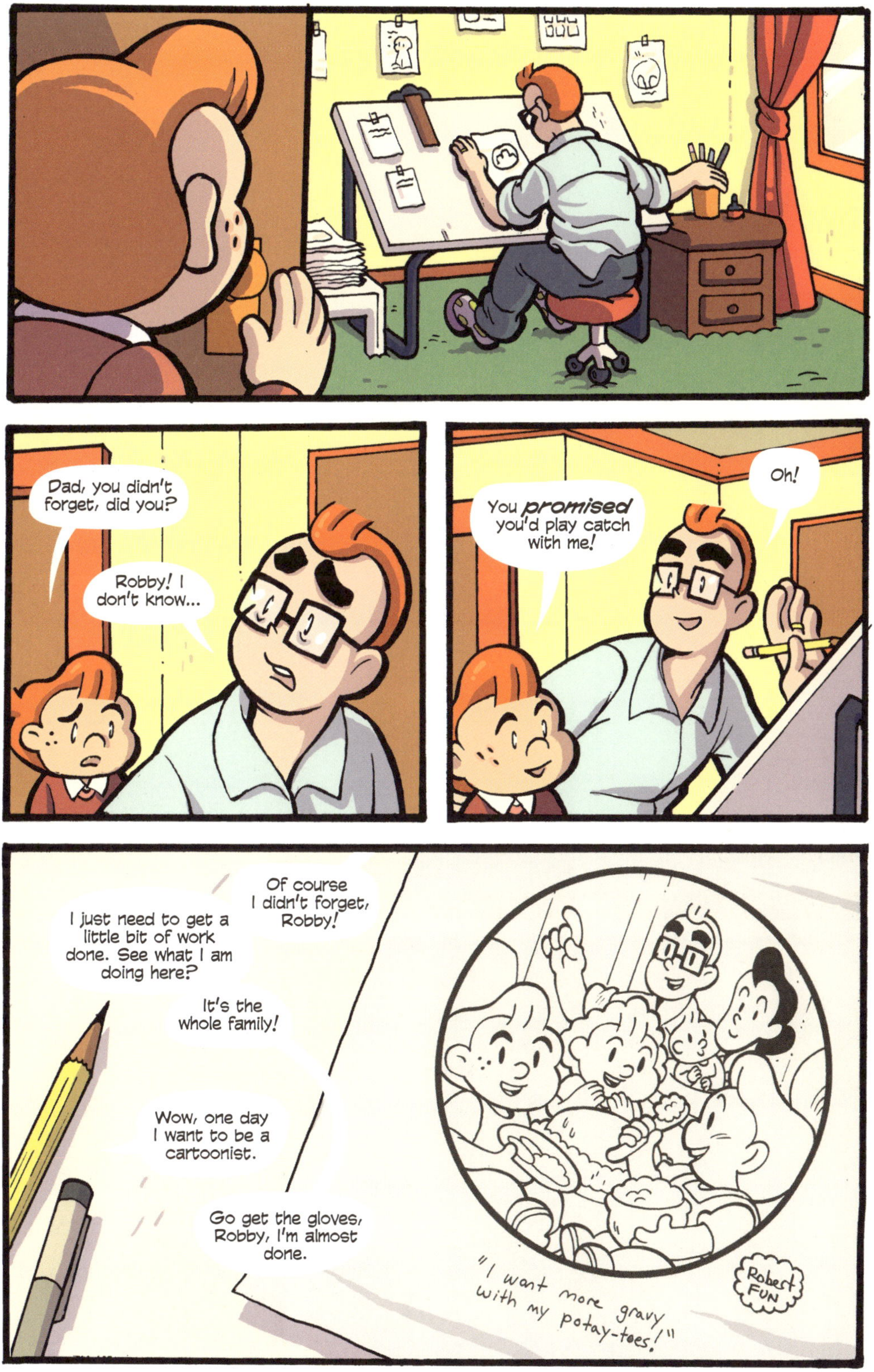
Dad, you didn't forget, did you?
Robby! I don't know...
You *promised* you'd play catch with me!
Oh!
Of course I didn't forget, Robby!
I just need to get a little bit of work done. See what I am doing here?
It's the whole family!
Wow, one day I want to be a cartoonist.
Go get the gloves, Robby, I'm almost done.
"I want more gravy with my potay-toes!"
Robert FUN

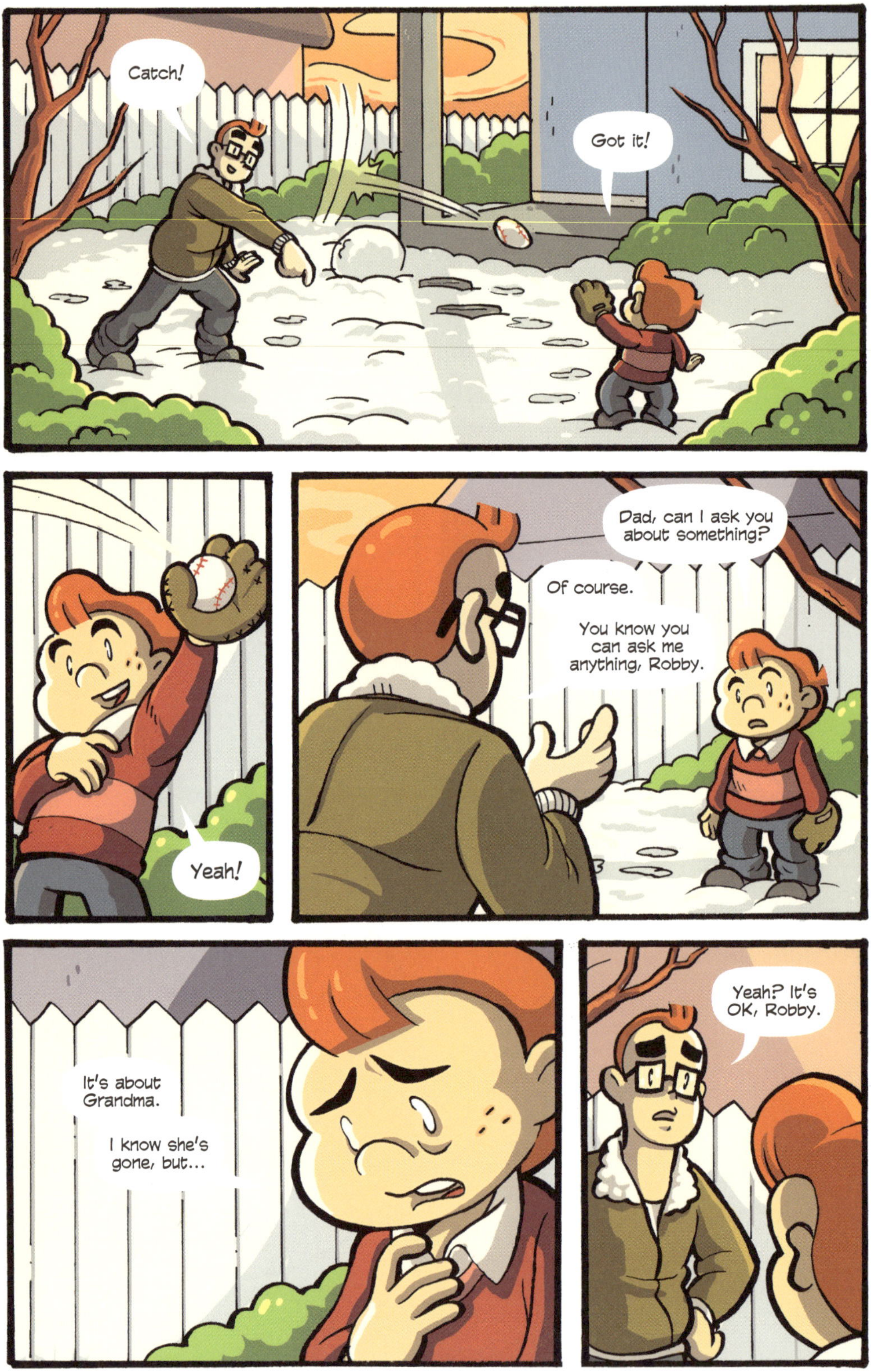
Catch!
Got it!
Yeah!
Dad, can I ask you about something?
Of course.
You know you can ask me anything, Robby.
It's about Grandma.
I know she's gone, but...
Yeah? It's OK, Robby.

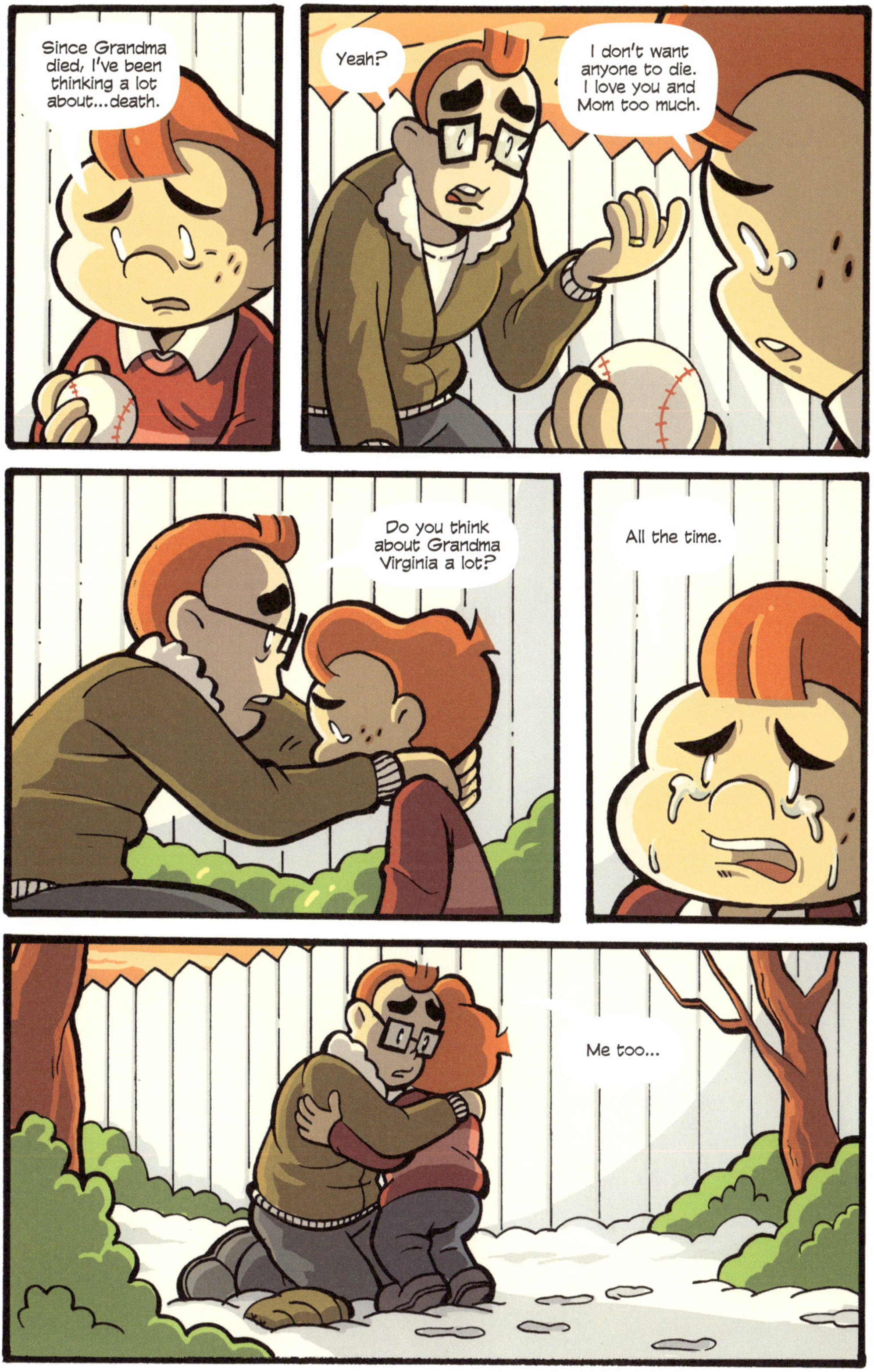
Since Grandma died, I've been thinking a lot about...death.
Yeah?
I don't want anyone to die. I love you and Mom too much.
Do you think about Grandma Virginia a lot?
All the time.
Me too...

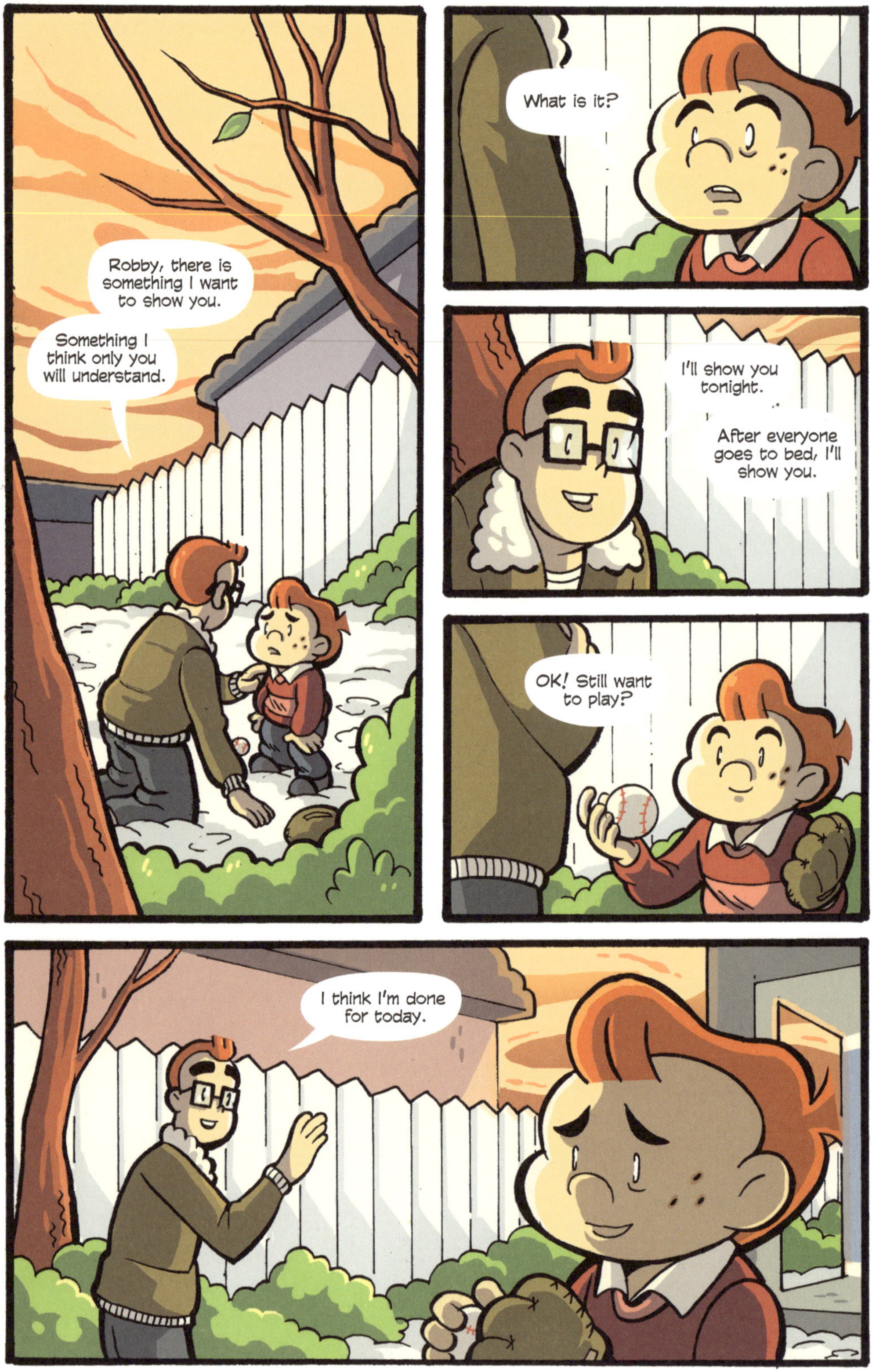
Robby, there is something I want to show you.
Something I think only you will understand.
What is it?
I'll show you tonight.
After everyone goes to bed, I'll show you.
OK! Still want to play?
I think I'm done for today.

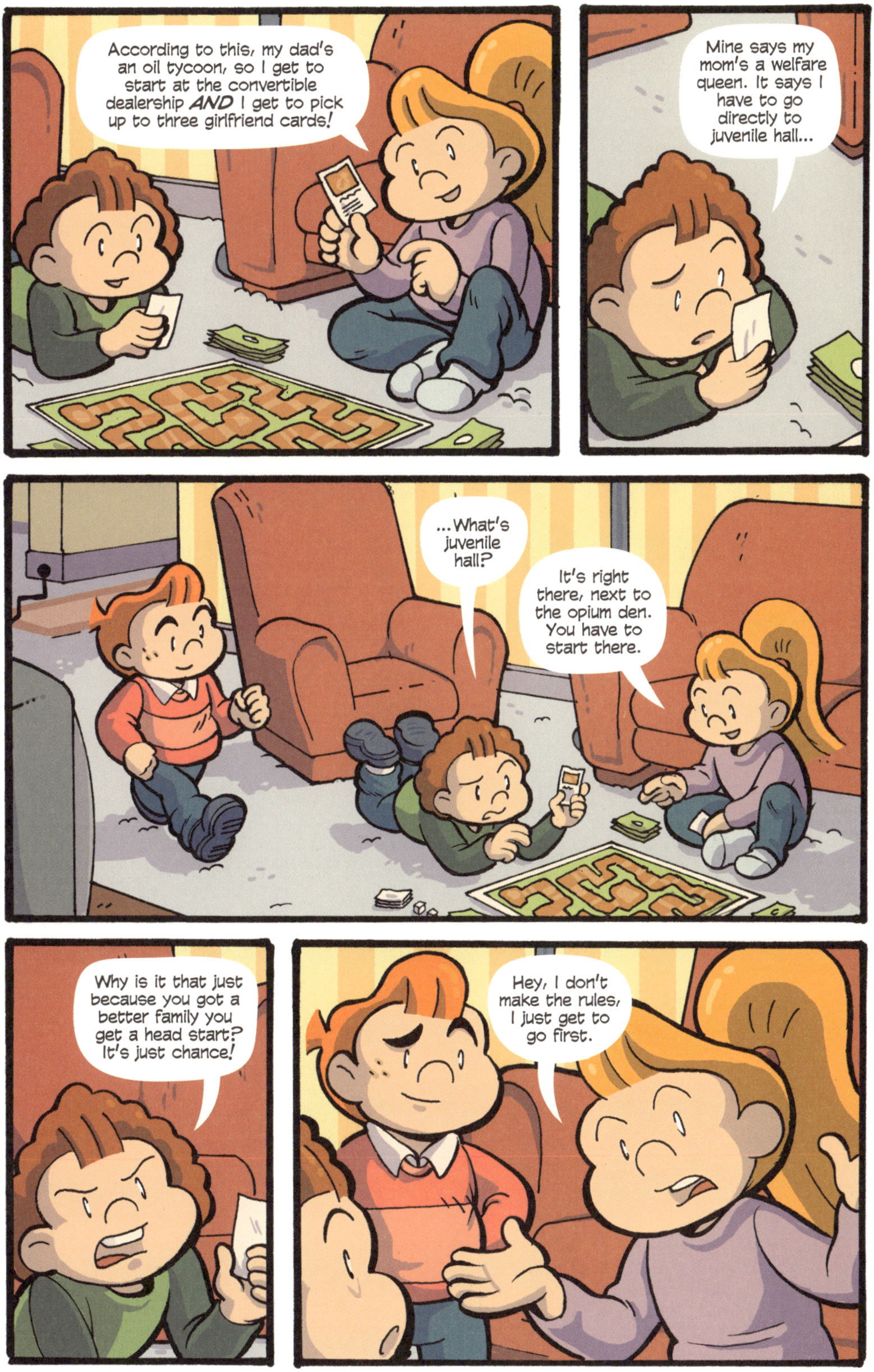

According to this, my dad's an oil tycoon, so I get to start at the convertible dealership AND I get to pick up to three girlfriend cards!
Mine says my mom's a welfare queen. It says I have to go directly to juvenile hall...
...What's juvenile hall?
It's right there, next to the opium den. You have to start there.
Why is it that just because you got a better family you get a head start? It's just chance!
Hey, I don't make the rules, I just get to go first.

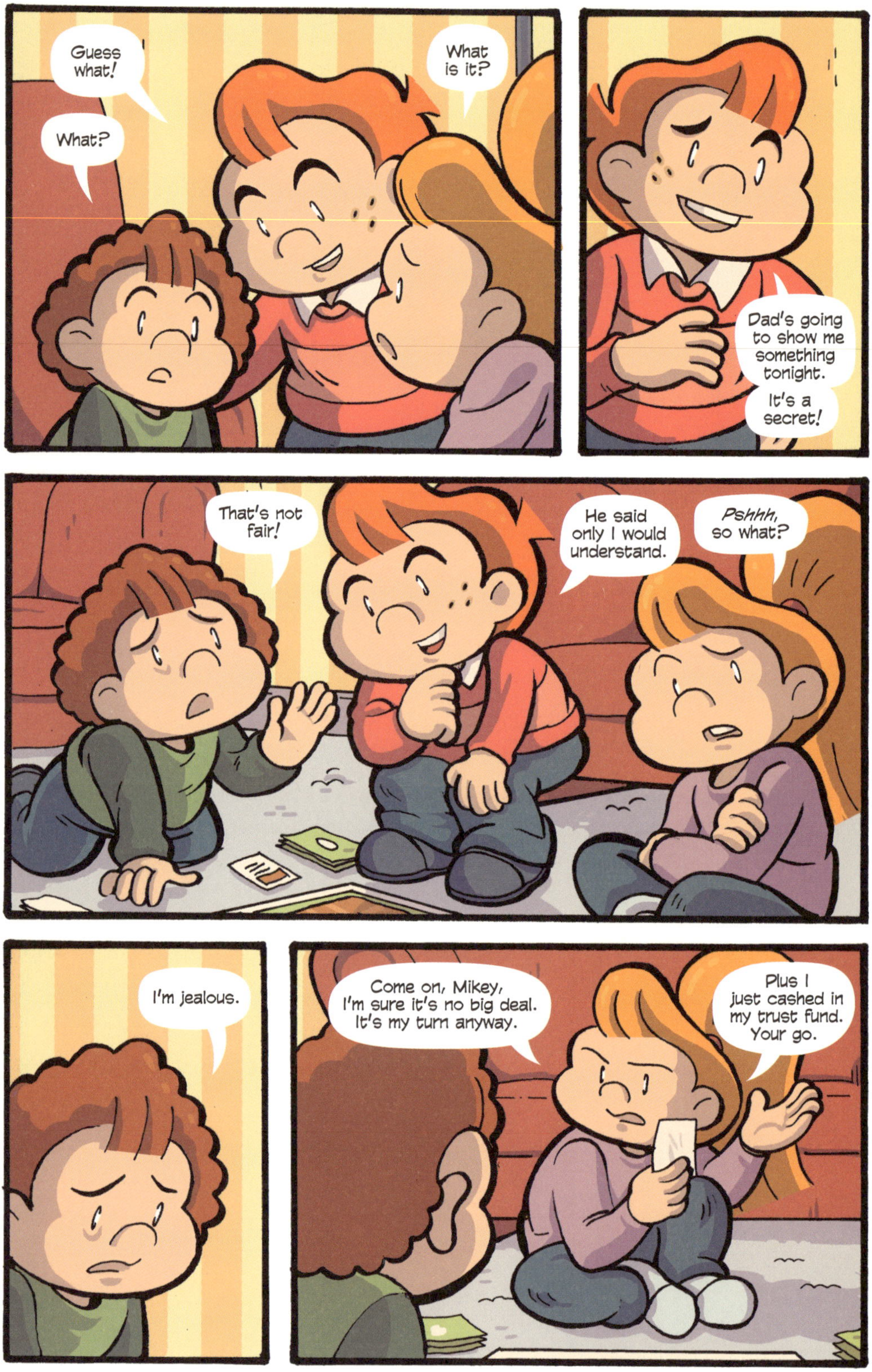

Guess what!
What?
What is it?
Dad's going to show me something tonight.
It's a secret!
That's not fair!
He said only I would understand.
Pshhh, so what?
I'm jealous.
Come on, Mikey, I'm sure it's no big deal. It's my turn anyway.
Plus I just cashed in my trust fund. Your go.

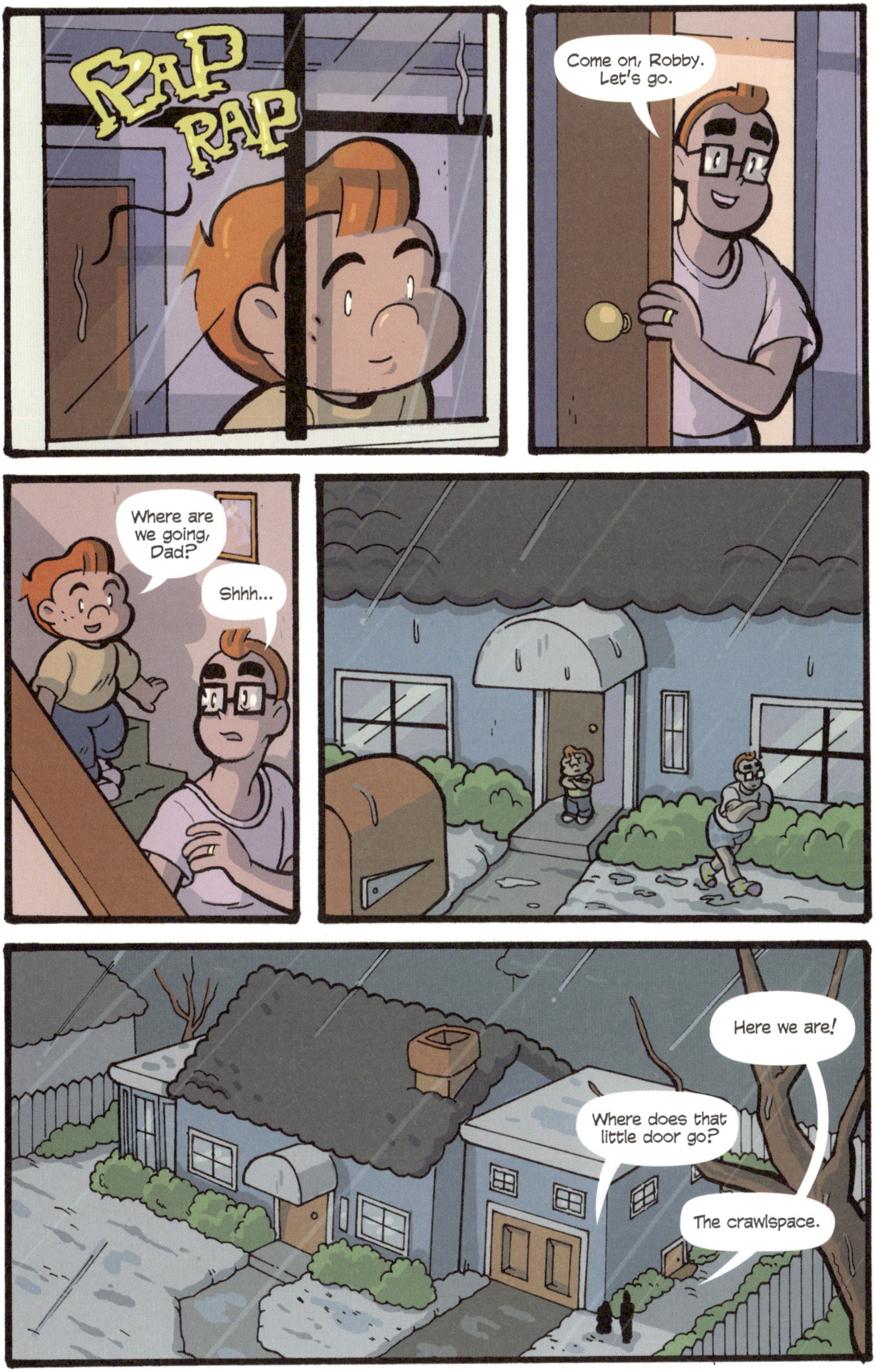
RAP RAP
Come on, Robby. Let's go.
Where are we going, Dad?
Shhh...
Here we are!
Where does that little door go?
The crawlspace.

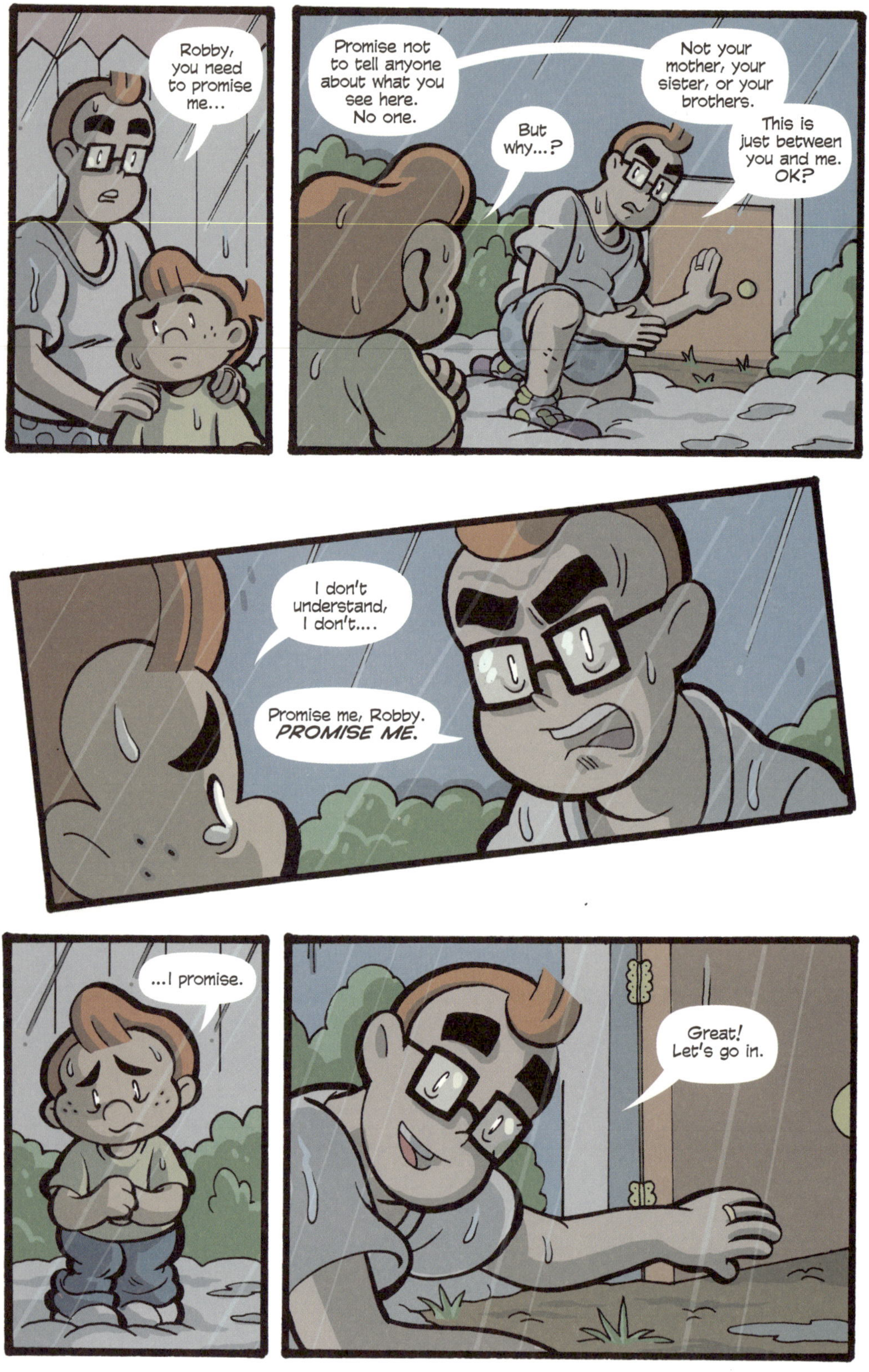

Robby, you need to promise me...
Promise not to tell anyone about what you see here. No one.
Not your mother, your sister, or your brothers.
But why...?
This is just between you and me. OK?
I don't understand, I don't....
Promise me, Robby. PROMISE ME.
...I promise.
Great! Let's go in.

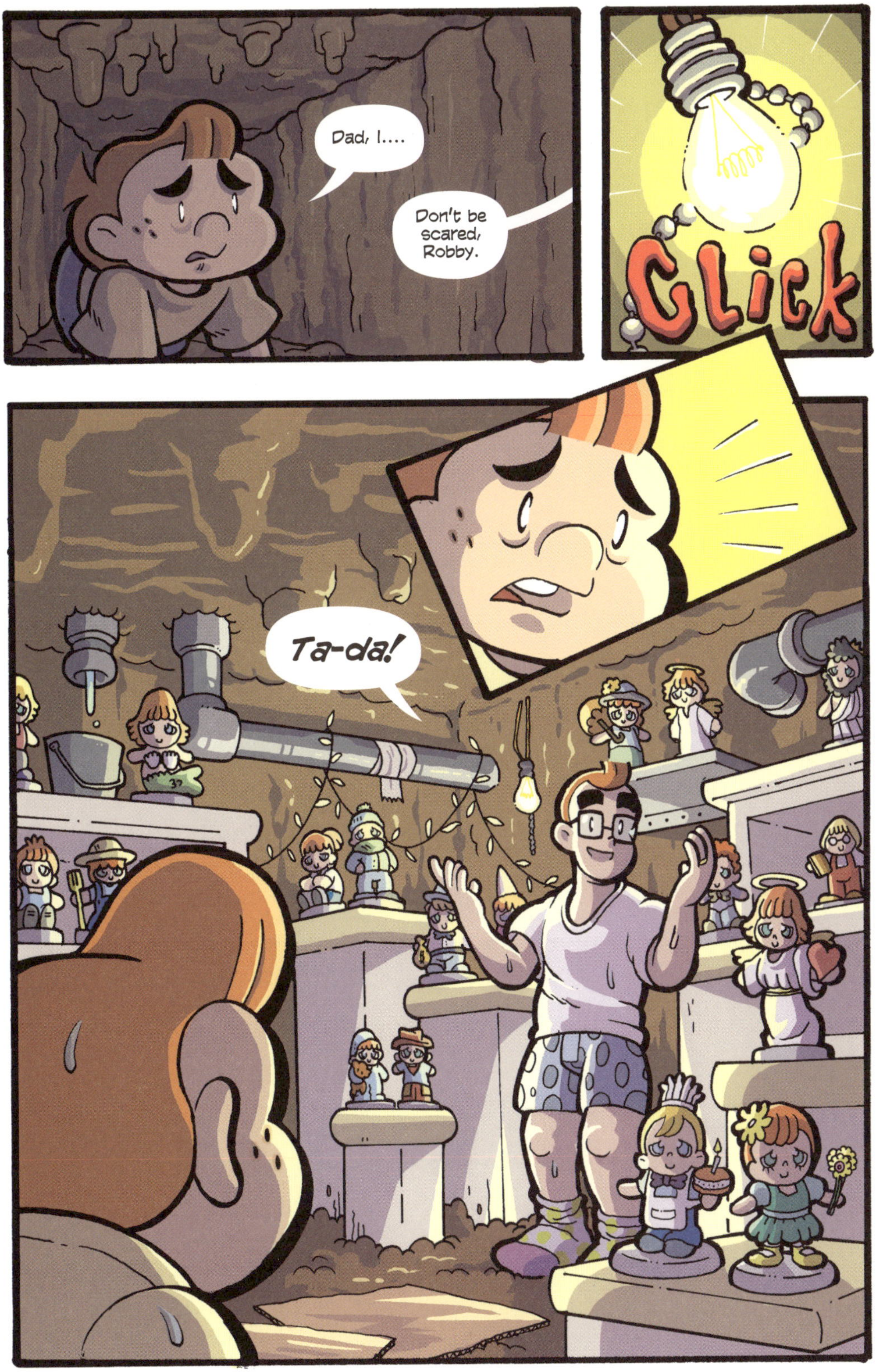
Dad, I....
Don't be scared, Robby.
CLICK
Ta-da!

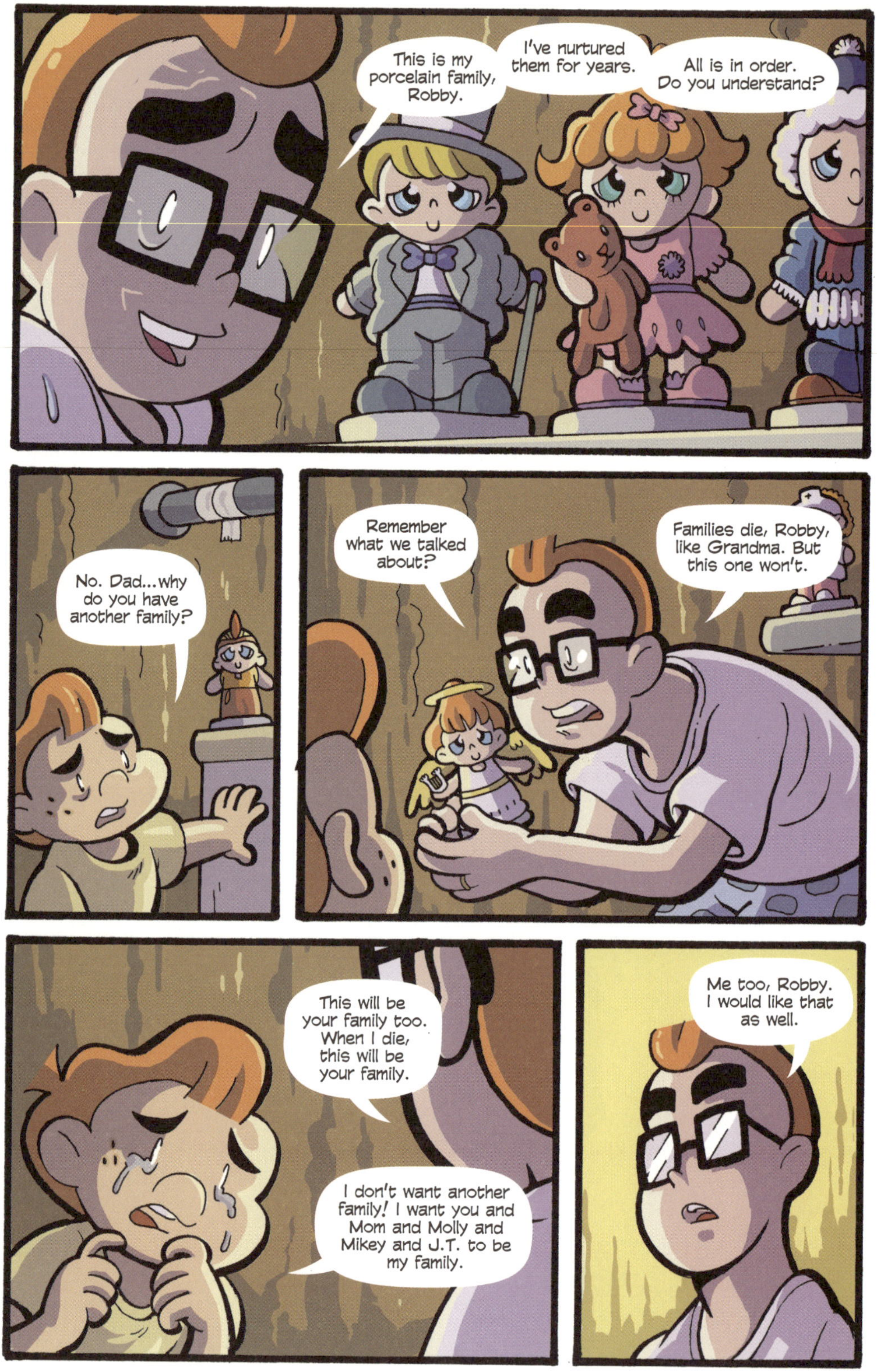
This is my porcelain family, Robby.
I've nurtured them for years.
All is in order. Do you understand?
No. Dad...why do you have another family?
Remember what we talked about?
Families die, Robby, like Grandma. But this one won't.
This will be your family too. When I die, this will be your family.
I don't want another family! I want you and Mom and Molly and Mikey and J.T. to be my family.
Me too, Robby. I would like that as well.

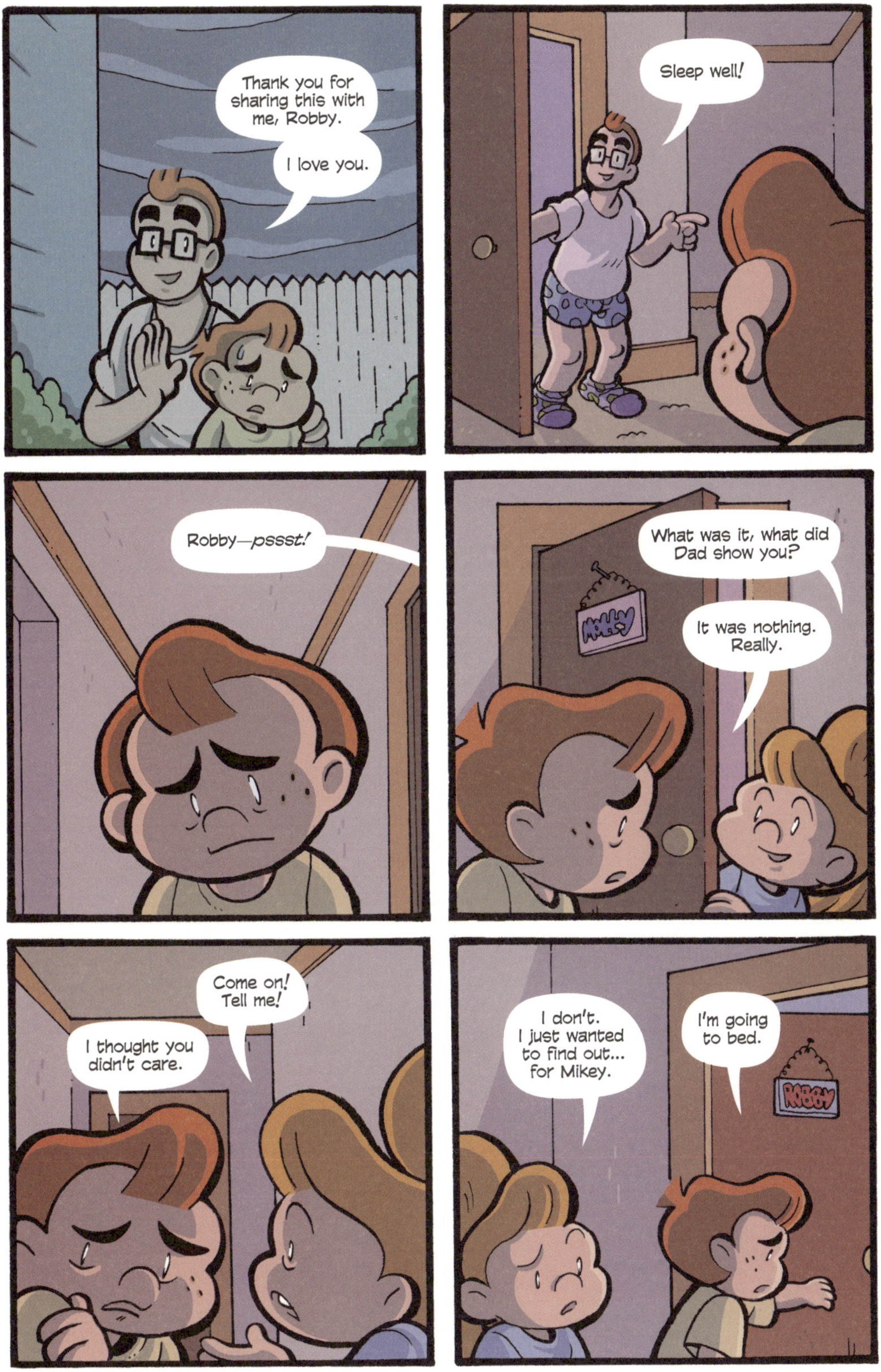
Thank you for sharing this with me, Robby.
I love you.
Sleep well!
Robby—psssst!
What was it, what did Dad show you?
It was nothing. Really.
MOLLY
Come on! Tell me!
I thought you didn't care.
I don't. I just wanted to find out... for Mikey.
I'm going to bed.
ROBBY

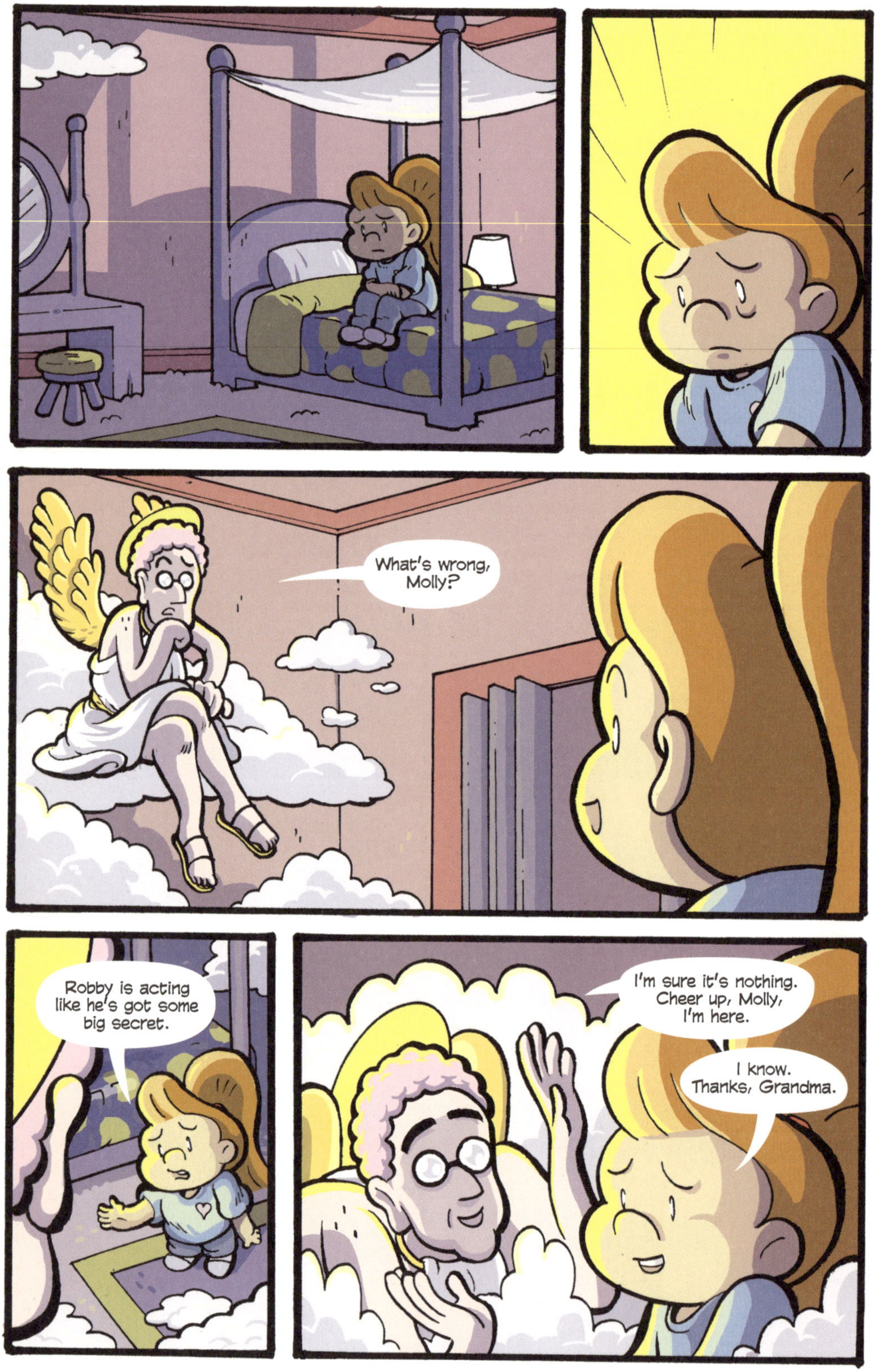
What's wrong, Molly?
Robby is acting like he's got some big secret.
I'm sure it's nothing. Cheer up, Molly, I'm here.
I know. Thanks, Grandma.

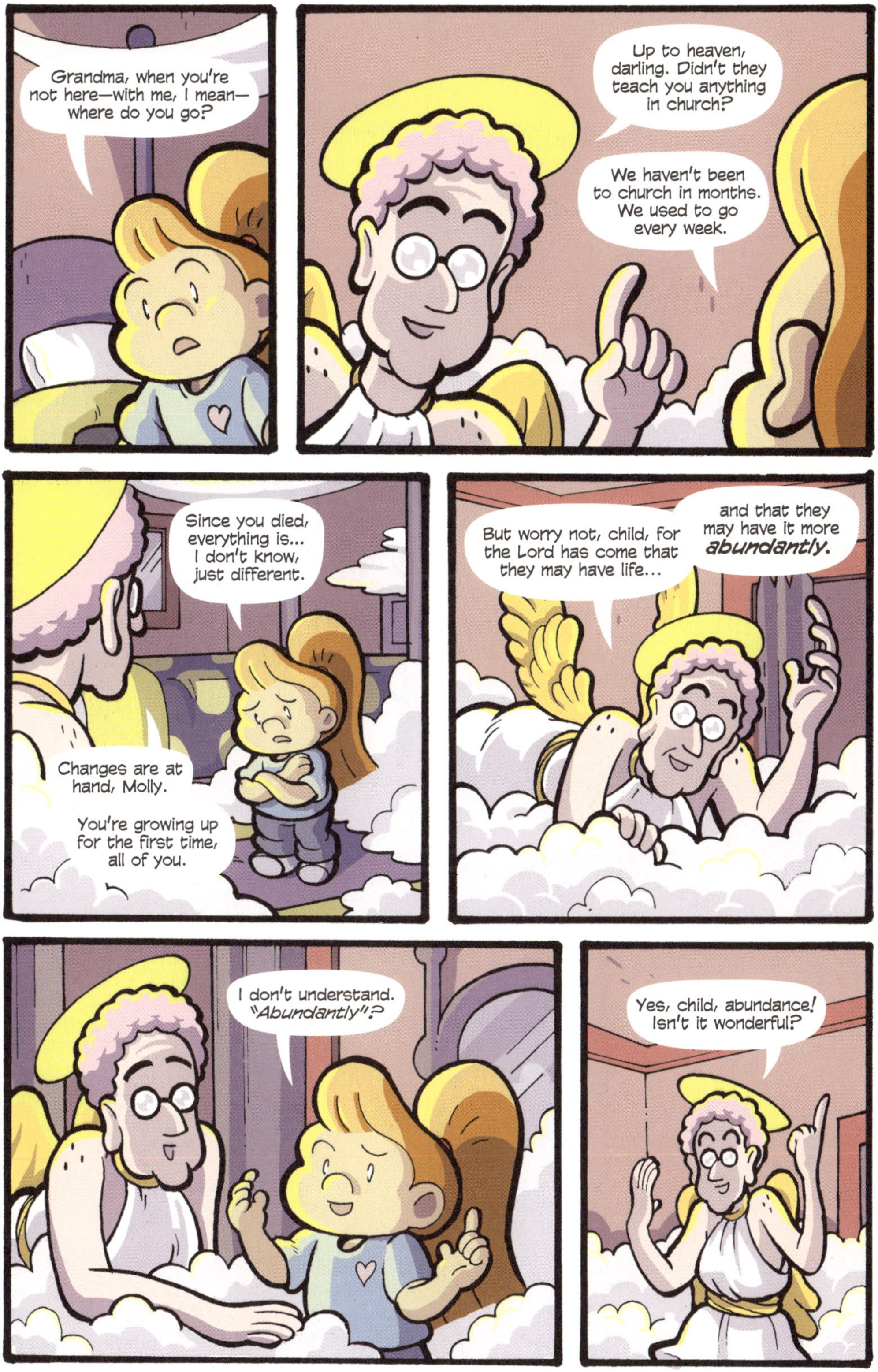
Grandma, when you're not here—with me, I mean—where do you go?
Up to heaven, darling. Didn't they teach you anything in church?
We haven't been to church in months. We used to go every week.
Since you died, everything is... I don't know, just different.
Changes are at hand, Molly.
You're growing up for the first time, all of you.
But worry not, child, for the Lord has come that they may have life...
and that they may have it more ***abundantly.***
I don't understand. *"Abundantly"?*
Yes, child, abundance! Isn't it wonderful?

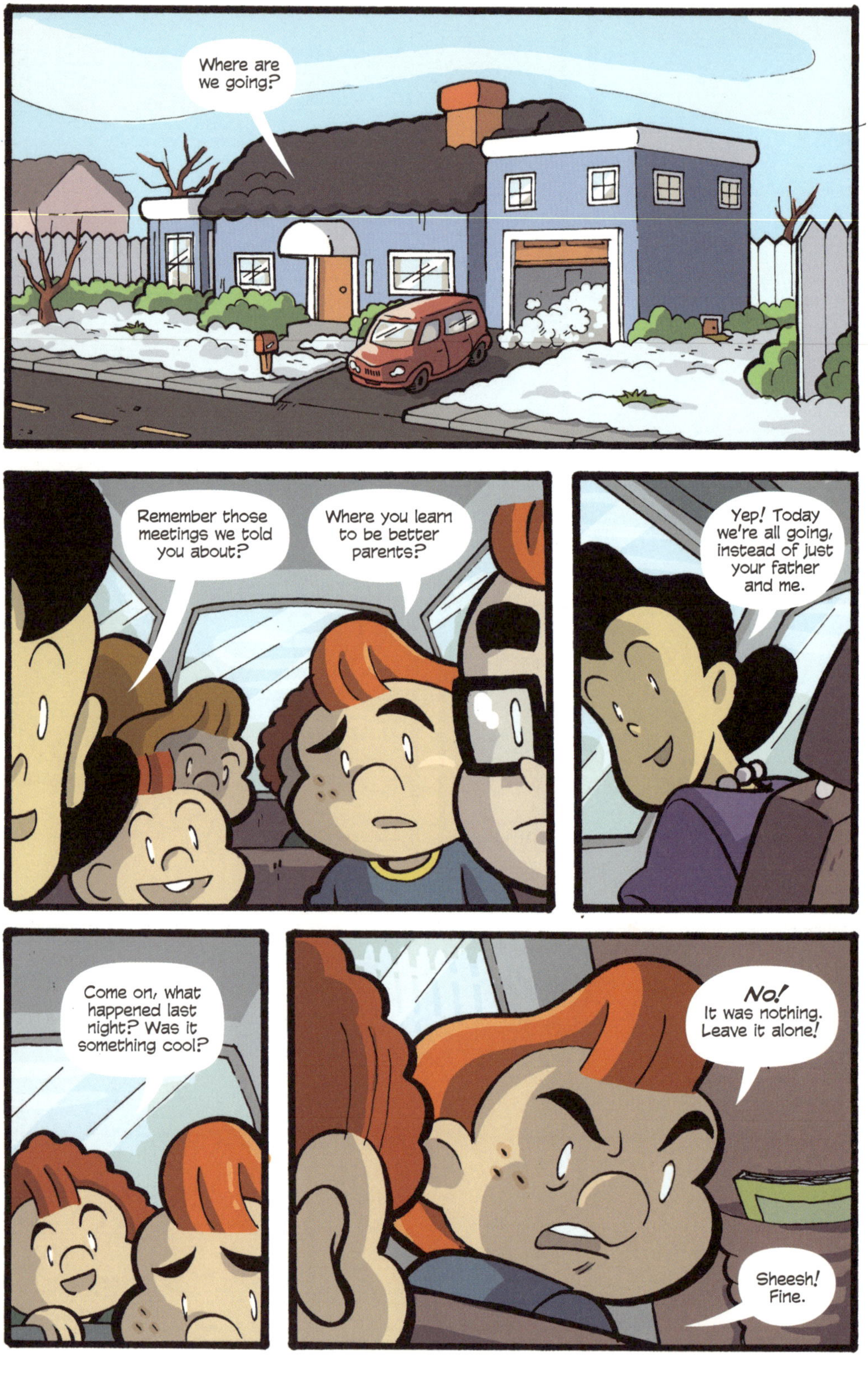
Where are we going?
Remember those meetings we told you about?
Where you learn to be better parents?
Yep! Today we're all going, instead of just your father and me.
Come on, what happened last night? Was it something cool?
No! It was nothing. Leave it alone!
Sheesh! Fine.

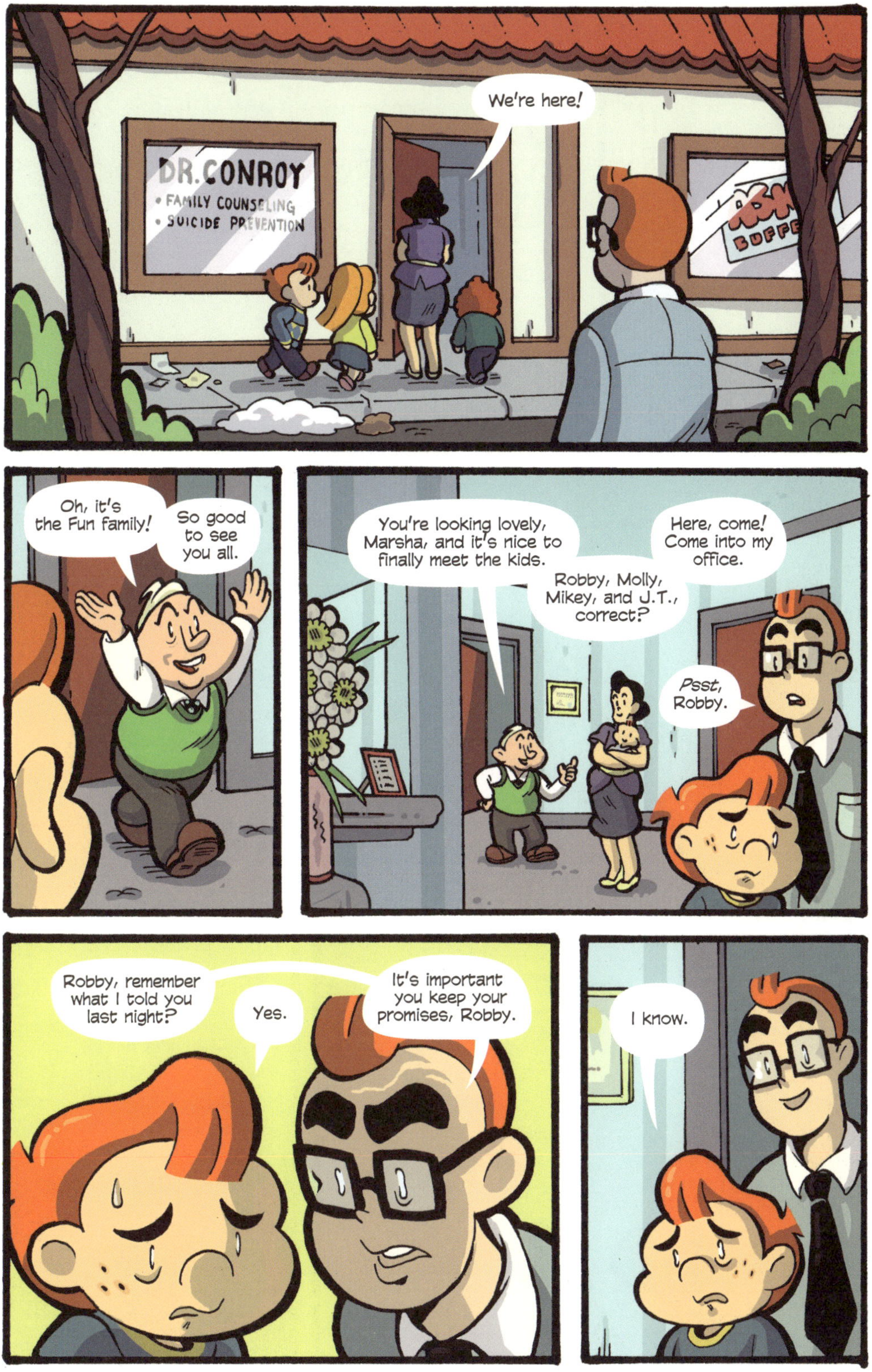

DR. CONROY
• FAMILY COUNSELING
• SUICIDE PREVENTION
We're here!
BUFFE
Oh, it's the Fun family!
So good to see you all.
You're looking lovely, Marsha, and it's nice to finally meet the kids.
Robby, Molly, Mikey, and J.T., correct?
Here, come! Come into my office.
Psst, Robby.
Robby, remember what I told you last night?
Yes.
It's important you keep your promises, Robby.
I know.

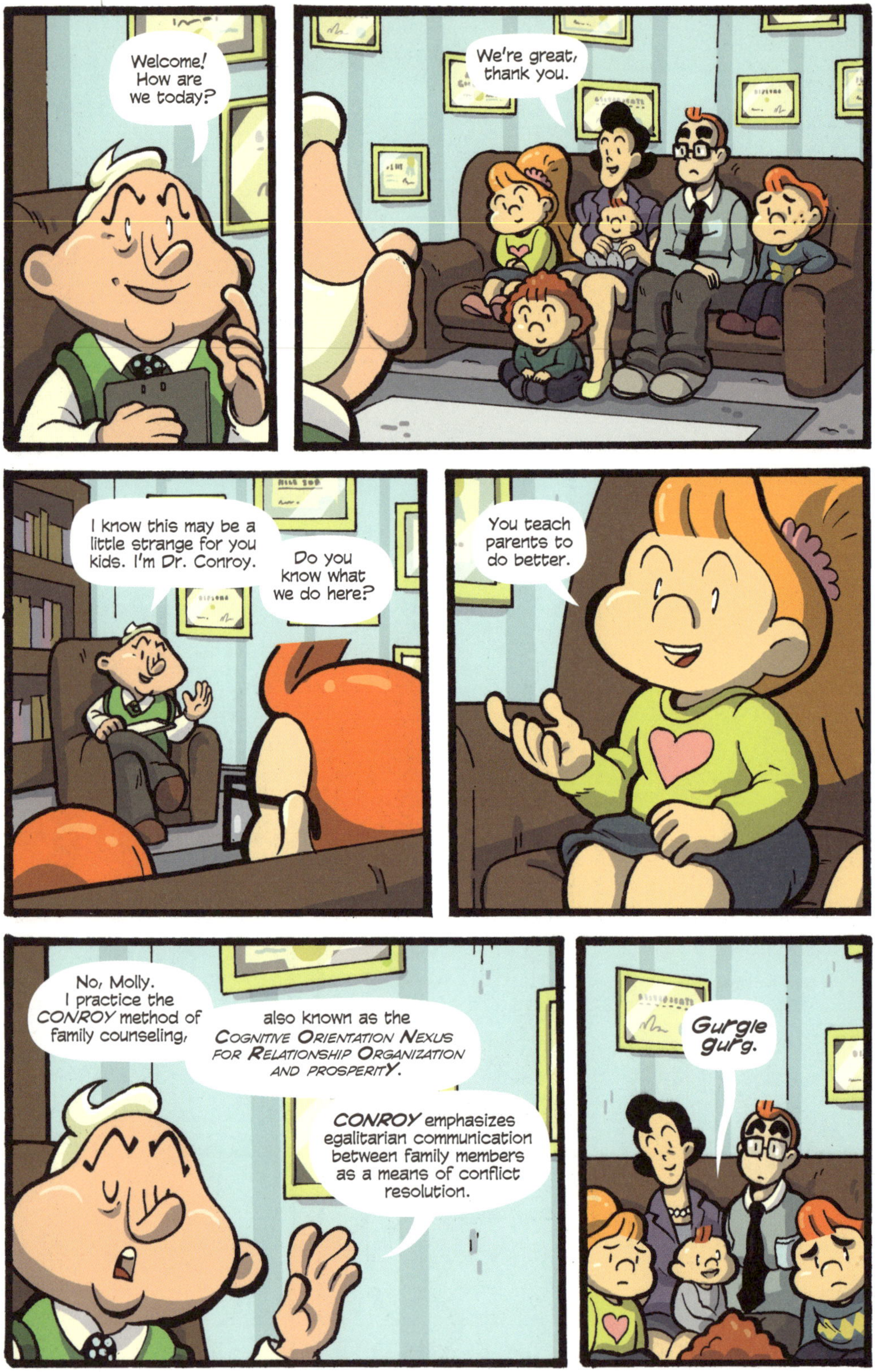
Welcome! How are we today?
We're great, thank you.
I know this may be a little strange for you kids. I'm Dr. Conroy.
Do you know what we do here?
You teach parents to do better.
No, Molly. I practice the CONROY method of family counseling,
also known as the COGNITIVE ORIENTATION NEXUS FOR RELATIONSHIP ORGANIZATION AND PROSPERITY.
CONROY emphasizes egalitarian communication between family members as a means of conflict resolution.
Gurgle gurg.

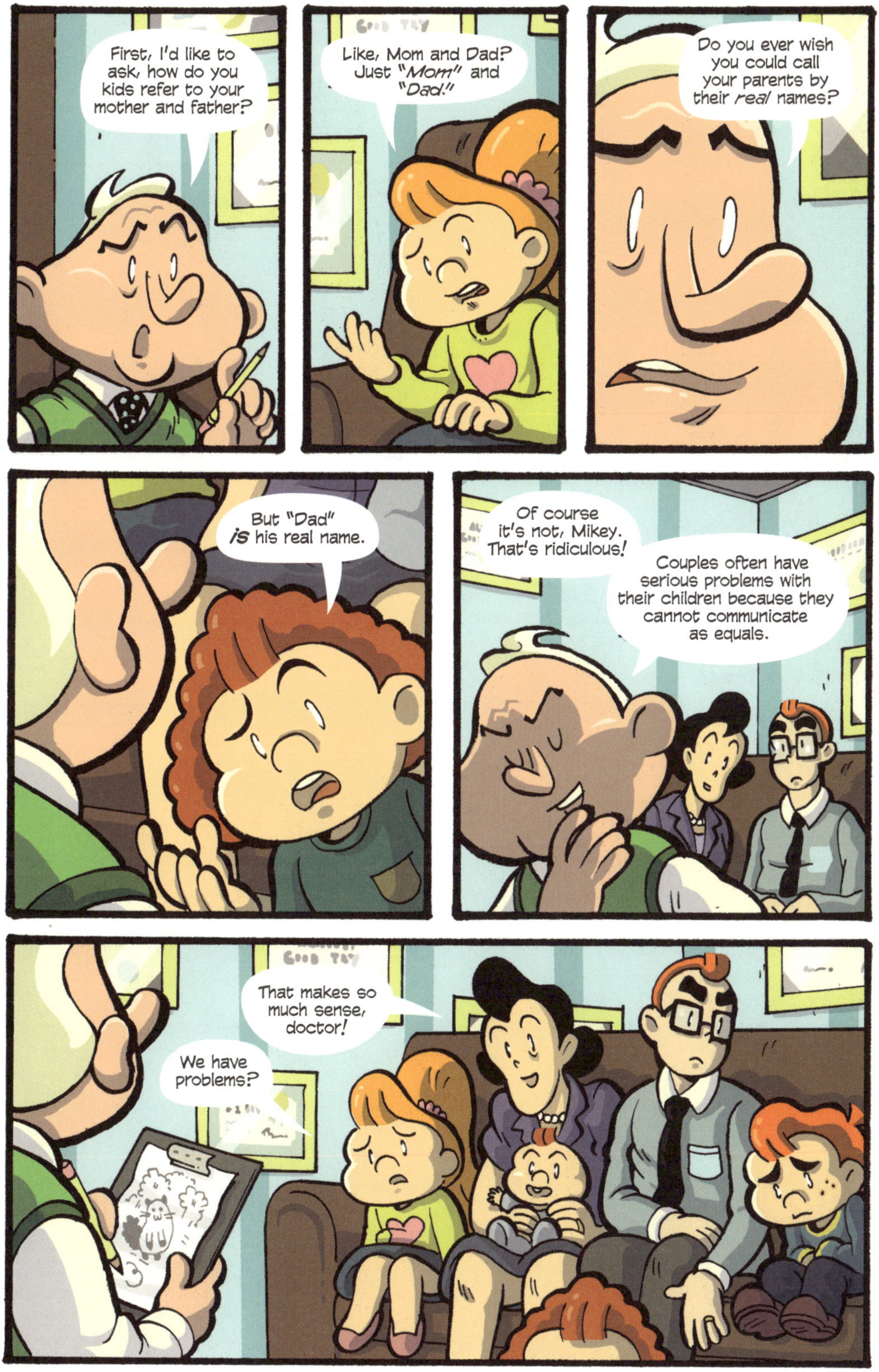
First, I'd like to ask, how do you kids refer to your mother and father?
Like, Mom and Dad? Just "Mom" and "Dad."
Do you ever wish you could call your parents by their real names?
But "Dad" is his real name.
Of course it's not, Mikey. That's ridiculous!
Couples often have serious problems with their children because they cannot communicate as equals.
That makes so much sense, doctor!
We have problems?

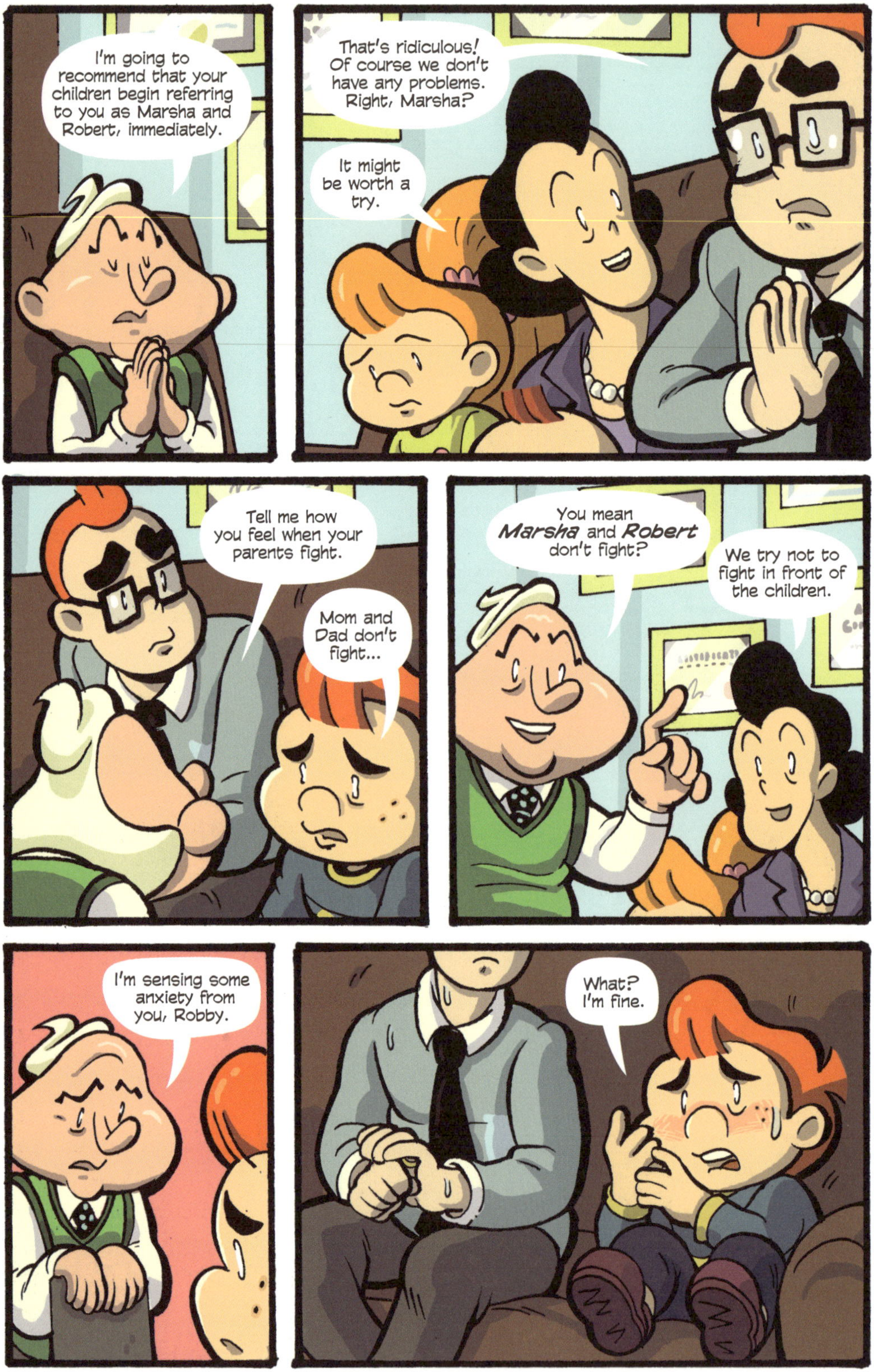
I'm going to recommend that your children begin referring to you as Marsha and Robert, immediately.
That's ridiculous! Of course we don't have any problems. Right, Marsha?
It might be worth a try.
Tell me how you feel when your parents fight.
Mom and Dad don't fight...
You mean *Marsha* and *Robert* don't fight?
We try not to fight in front of the children.
I'm sensing some anxiety from you, Robby.
What? I'm fine.

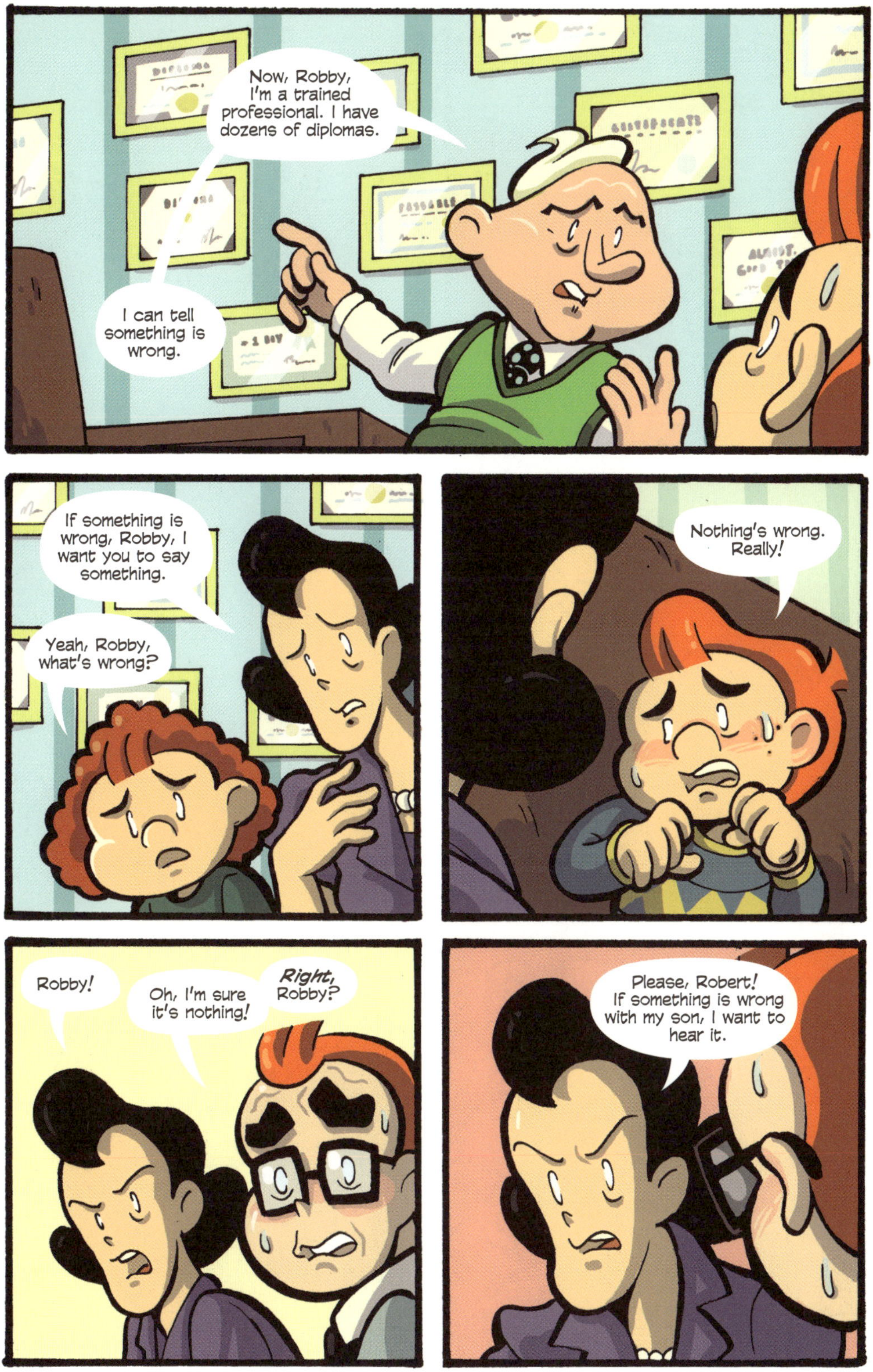
Now, Robby, I'm a trained professional. I have dozens of diplomas.
I can tell something is wrong.
If something is wrong, Robby, I want you to say something.
Yeah, Robby, what's wrong?
Nothing's wrong. Really!
Robby!
Oh, I'm sure it's nothing!
Right, Robby?
Please, Robert! If something is wrong with my son, I want to hear it.

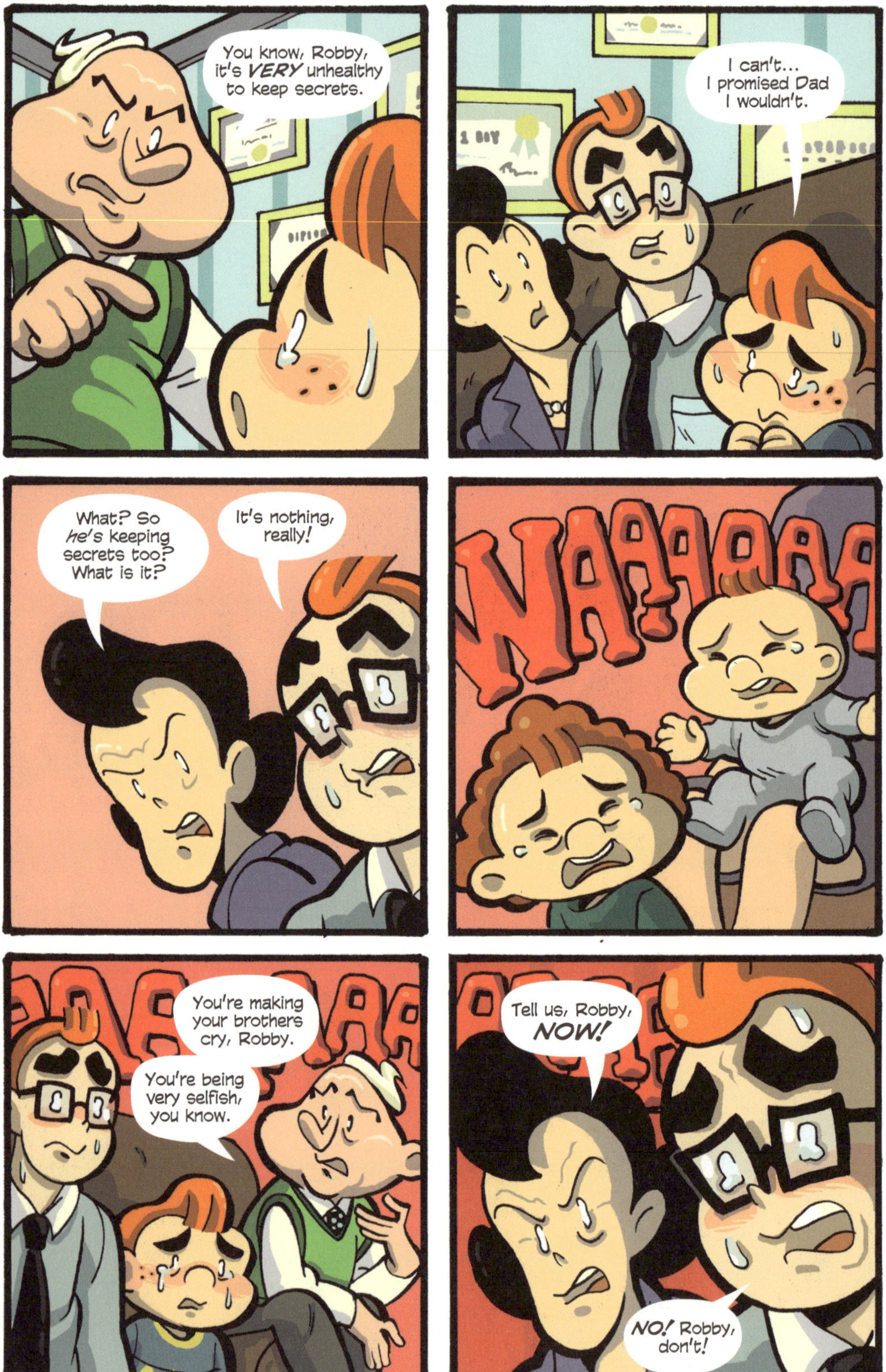
You know, Robby, it's VERY unhealthy to keep secrets.
I can't... I promised Dad I wouldn't.
What? So he's keeping secrets too? What is it?
It's nothing, really!
WAAAAAA
You're making your brothers cry, Robby.
You're being very selfish, you know.
Tell us, Robby, NOW!
NO! Robby, don't!

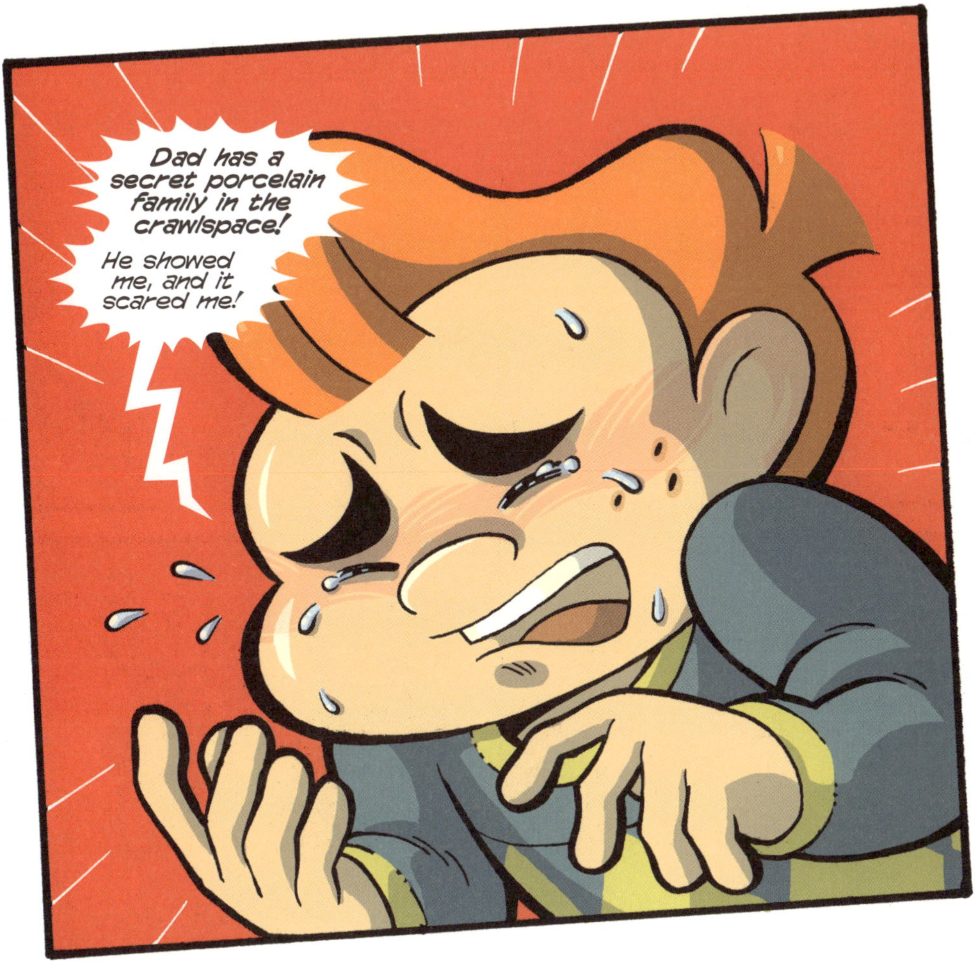
Dad has a secret porcelain family in the crawlspace!
He showed me, and it scared me!

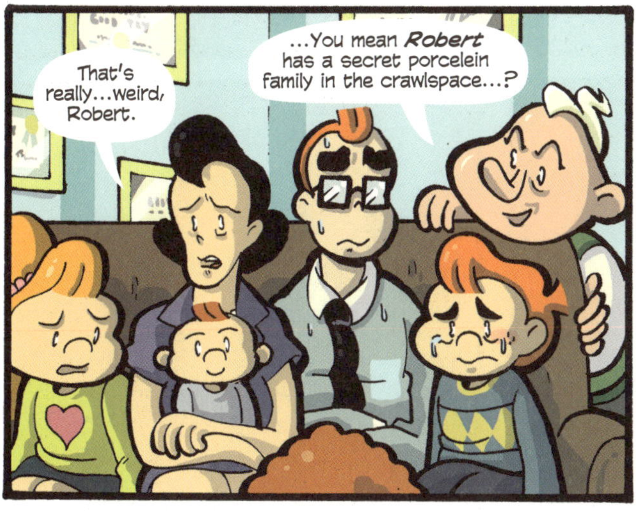
That's really...weird, Robert.
...You mean *Robert* has a secret porcelein family in the crawlspace...?

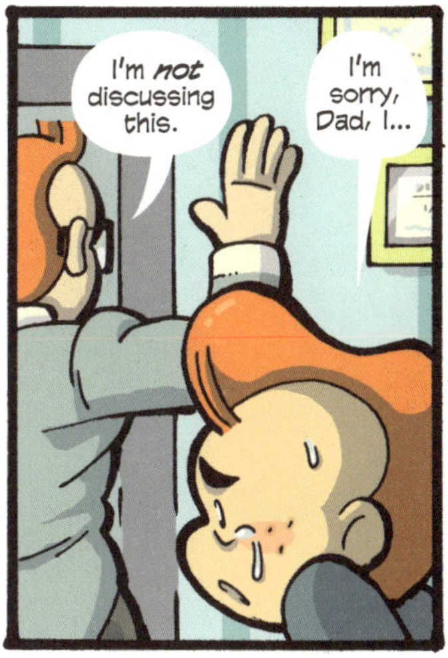
I'm sorry, Dad, I...
I'm *not* discussing this.

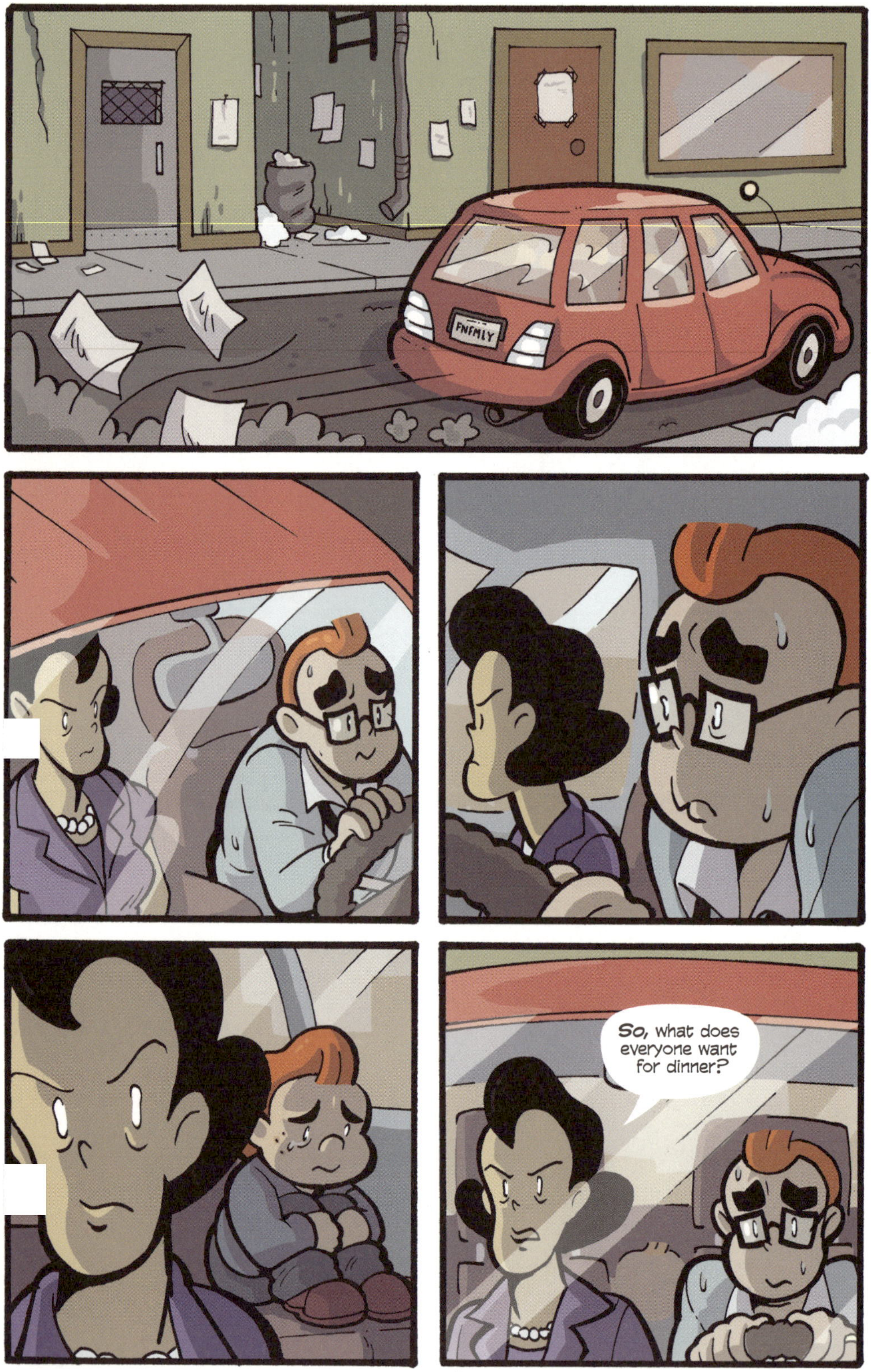
FNFMLY
So, what does everyone want for dinner?

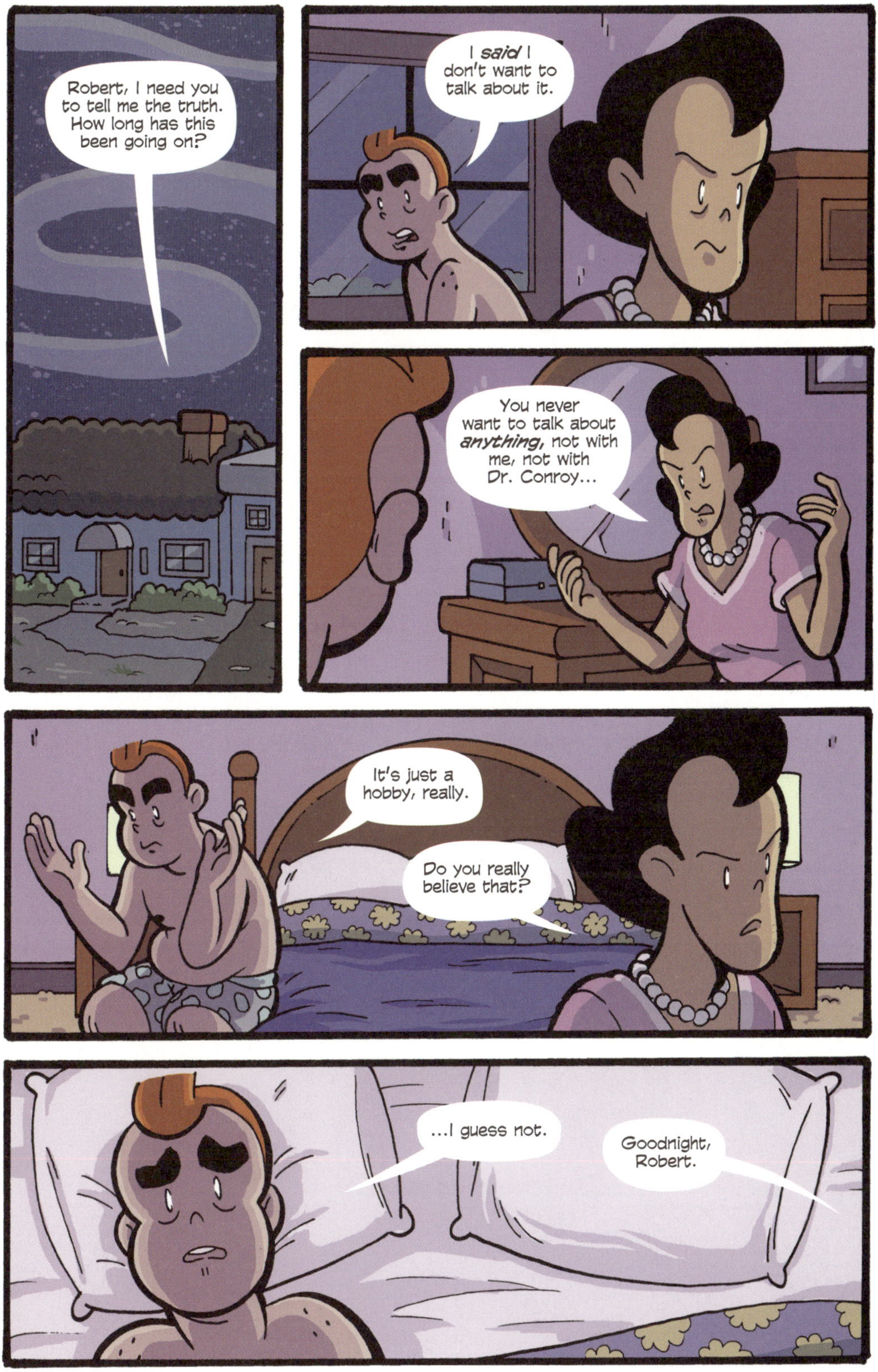
Robert, I need you to tell me the truth. How long has this been going on?
I *said* I don't want to talk about it.
You never want to talk about *anything*, not with me, not with Dr. Conroy...
It's just a hobby, really.
Do you really believe that?
...I guess not.
Goodnight, Robert.

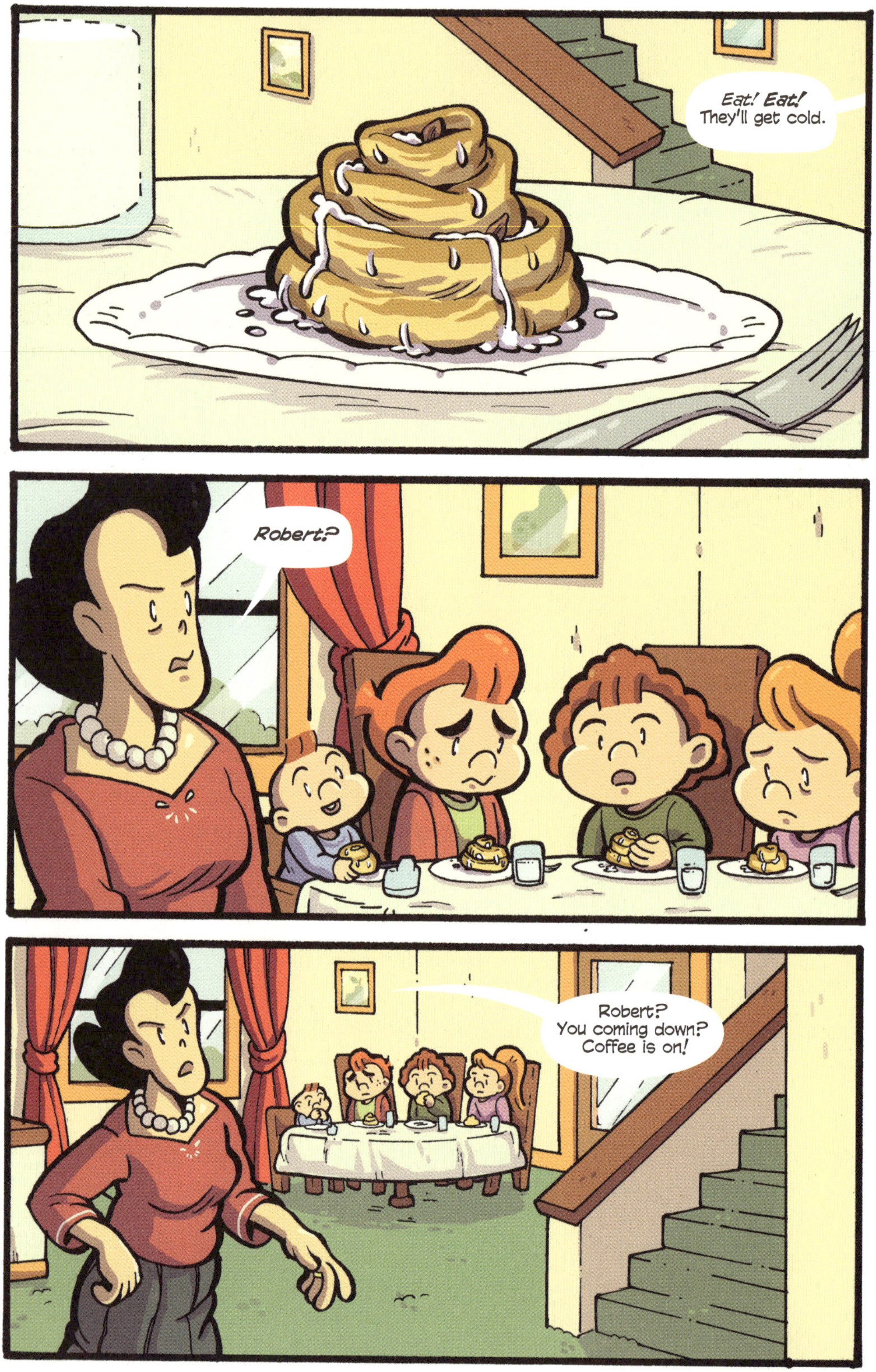

Eat! Eat! They'll get cold.
Robert?
Robert? You coming down? Coffee is on!

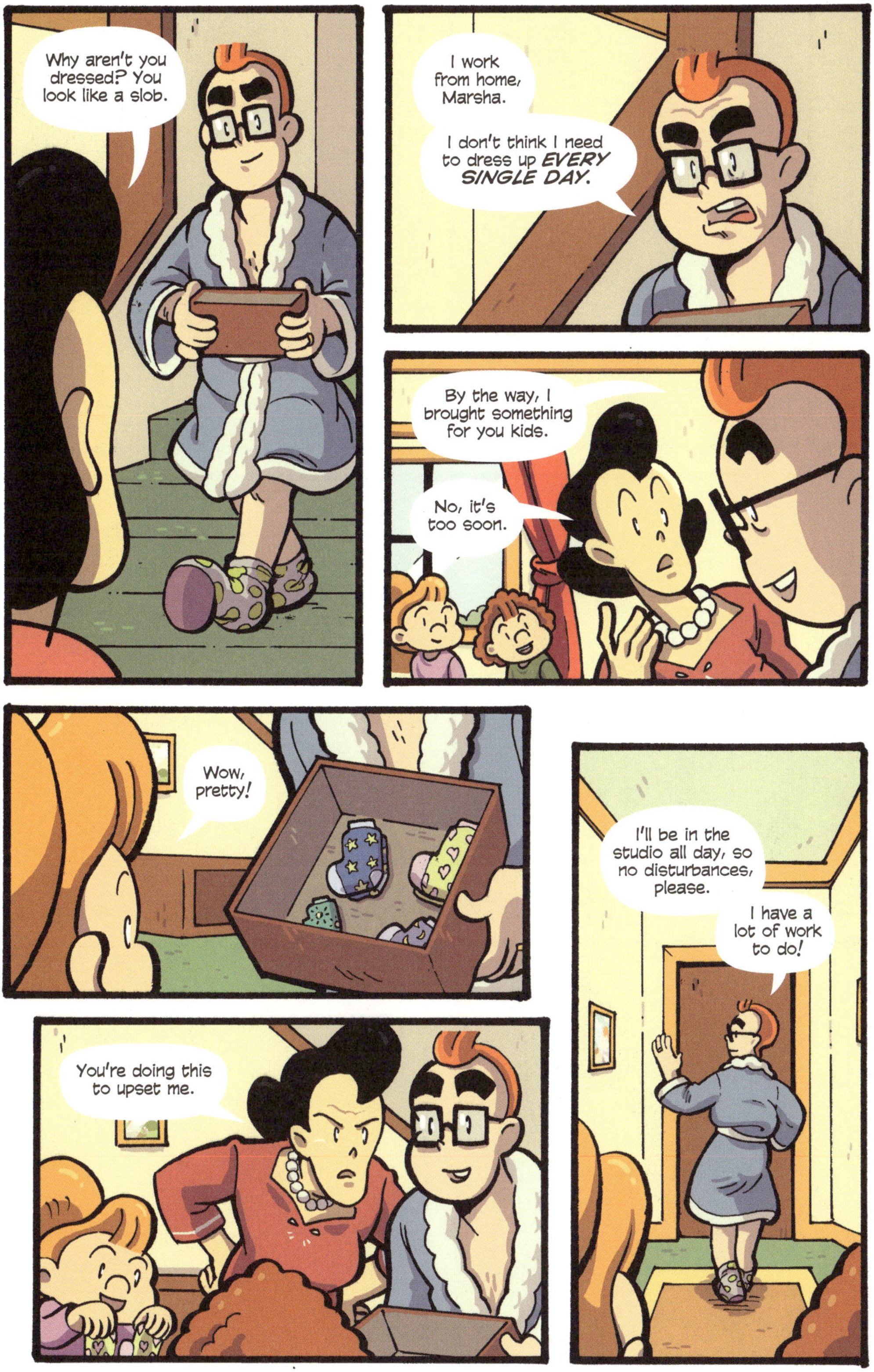
Why aren't you dressed? You look like a slob.
I work from home, Marsha.
I don't think I need to dress up EVERY SINGLE DAY.
By the way, I brought something for you kids.
No, it's too soon.
Wow, pretty!
You're doing this to upset me.
I'll be in the studio all day, so no disturbances, please.
I have a lot of work to do!

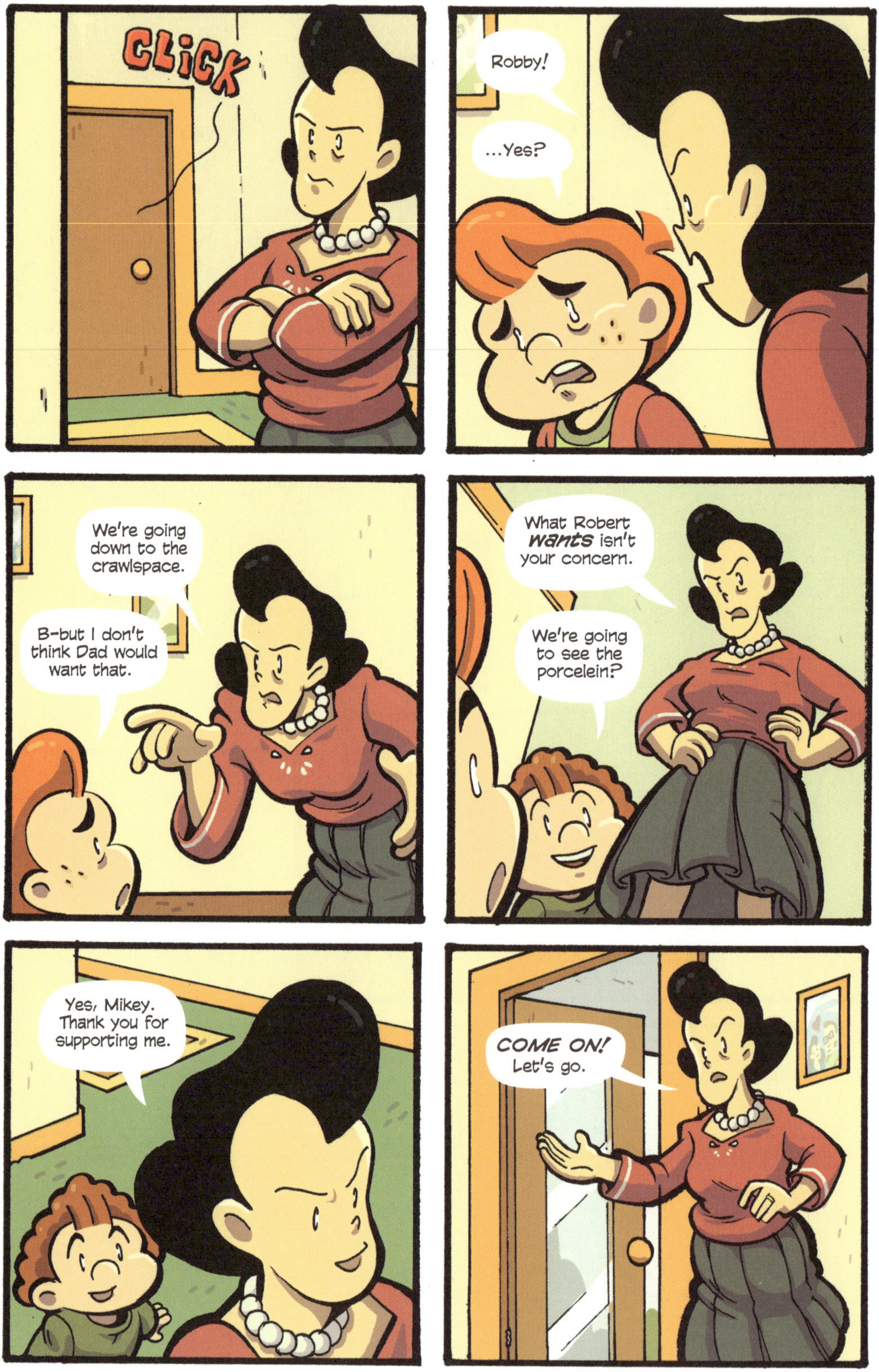
CLICK
Robby!
...Yes?
We're going down to the crawlspace.
B-but I don't think Dad would want that.
What Robert **wants** isn't your concern.
We're going to see the porcelein?
Yes, Mikey. Thank you for supporting me.
COME ON! Let's go.

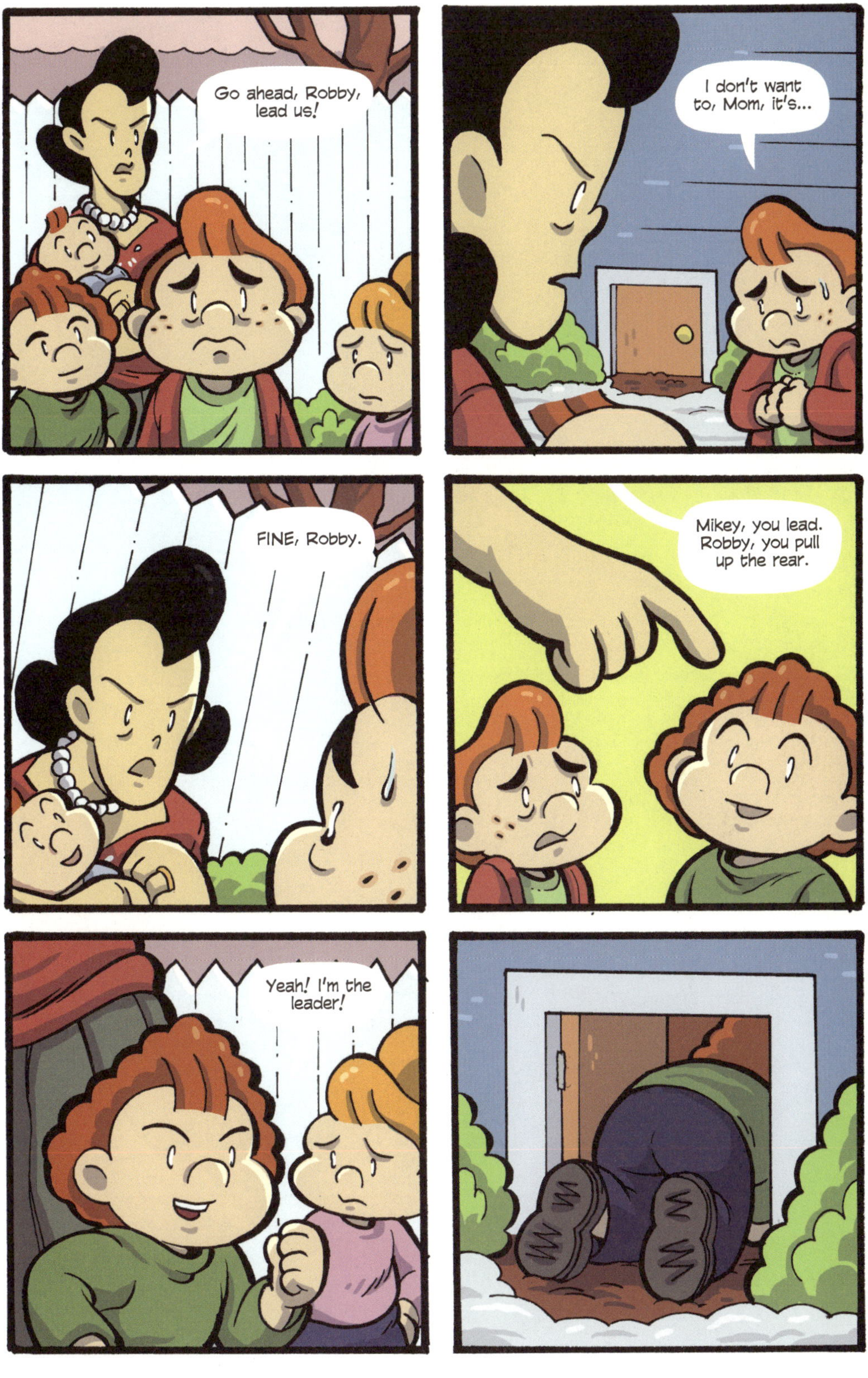
Go ahead, Robby, lead us!
I don't want to, Mom, it's...
FINE, Robby.
Mikey, you lead. Robby, you pull up the rear.
Yeah! I'm the leader!

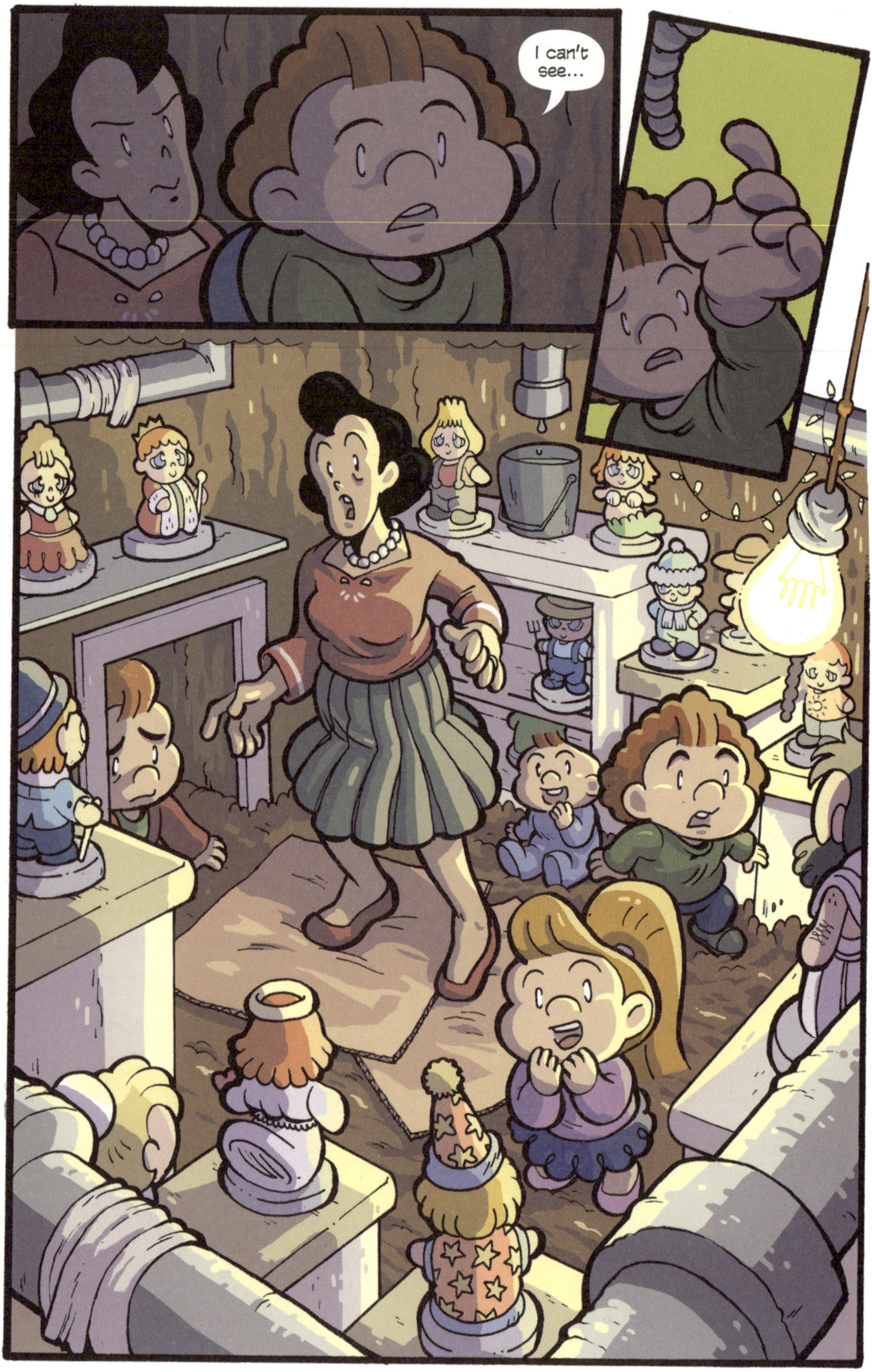
I can't see...

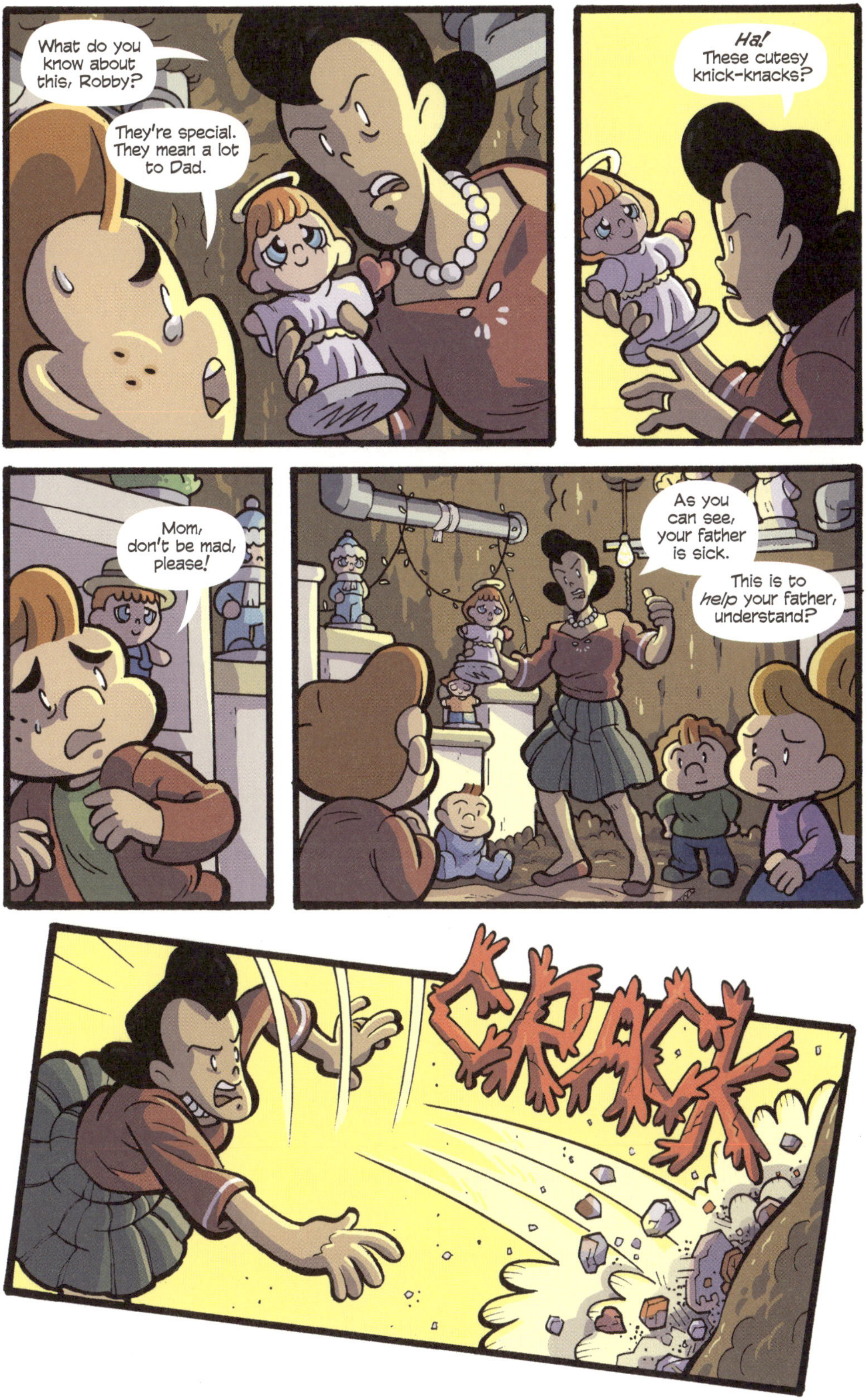
What do you know about this, Robby?
They're special. They mean a lot to Dad.
Ha! These cutesy knick-knacks?
Mom, don't be mad, please!
As you can see, your father is sick.
This is to help your father, understand?
CRACK

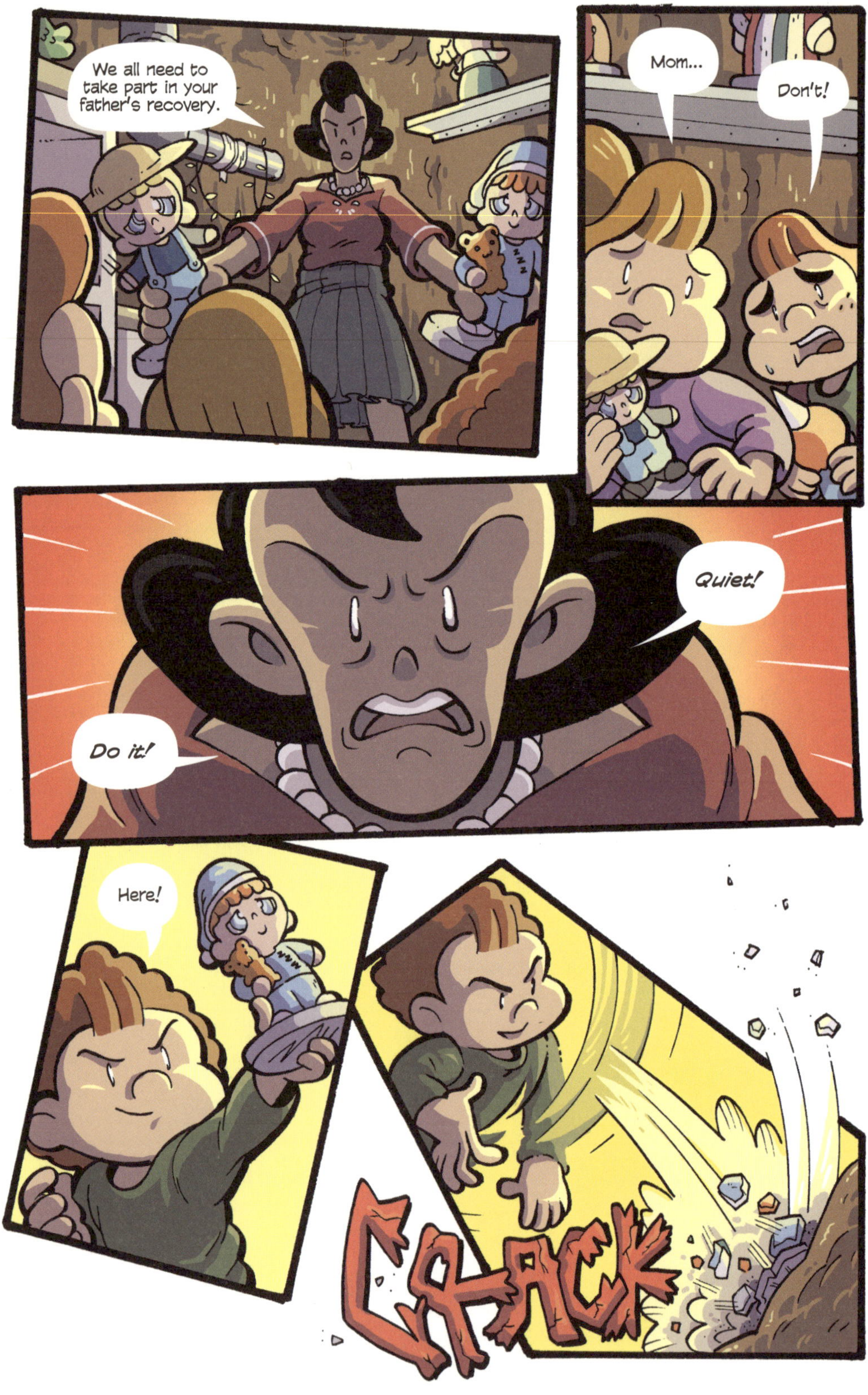
We all need to take part in your father's recovery.
Mom...
Don't!
Quiet!
Do it!
Here!
CRACK

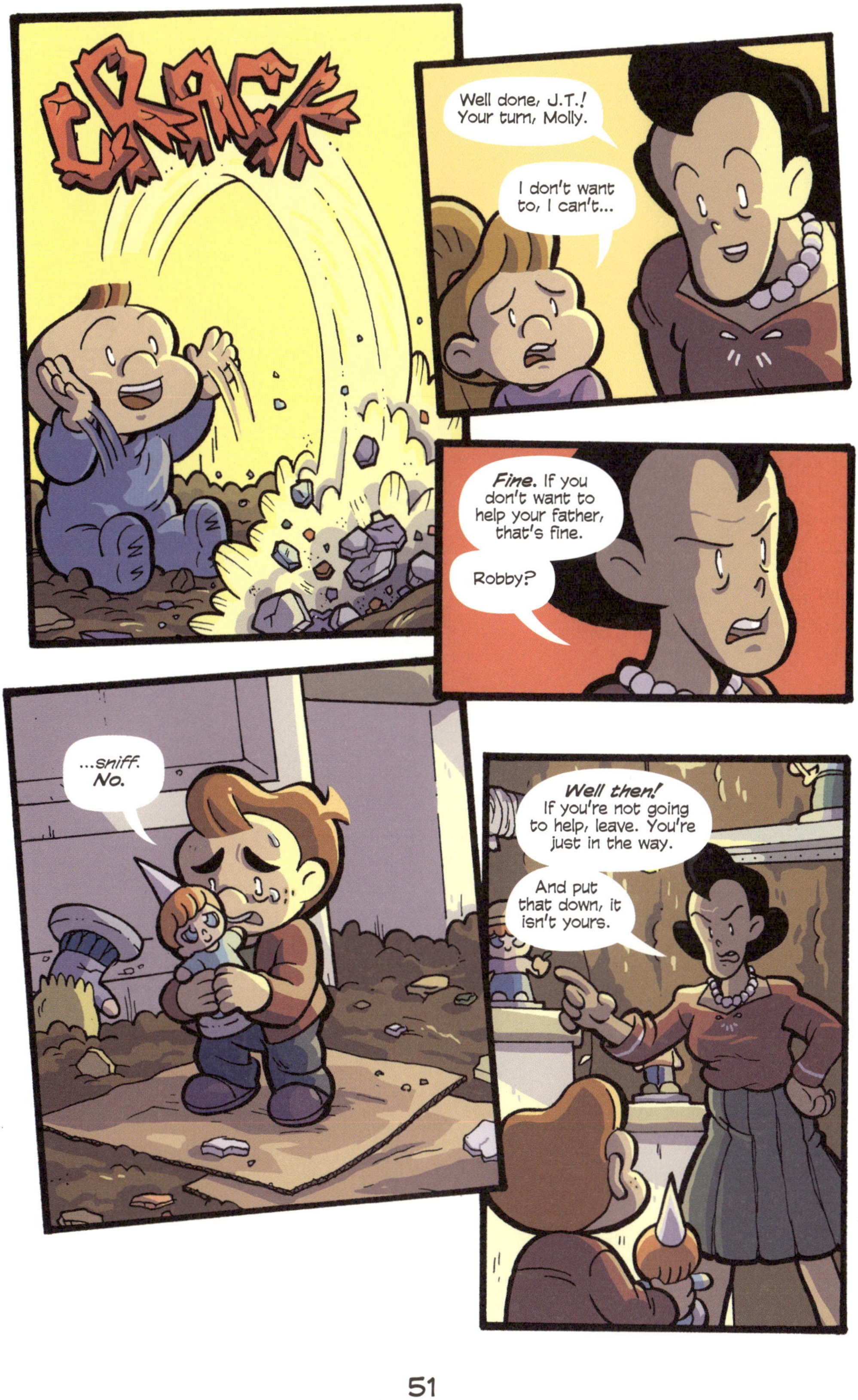
CRACK
Well done, J.T.! Your turn, Molly.
I don't want to, I can't...
Fine. If you don't want to help your father, that's fine.
Robby?
...sniff. *No.*
Well then! If you're not going to help, leave. You're just in the way.
And put that down, it isn't yours.

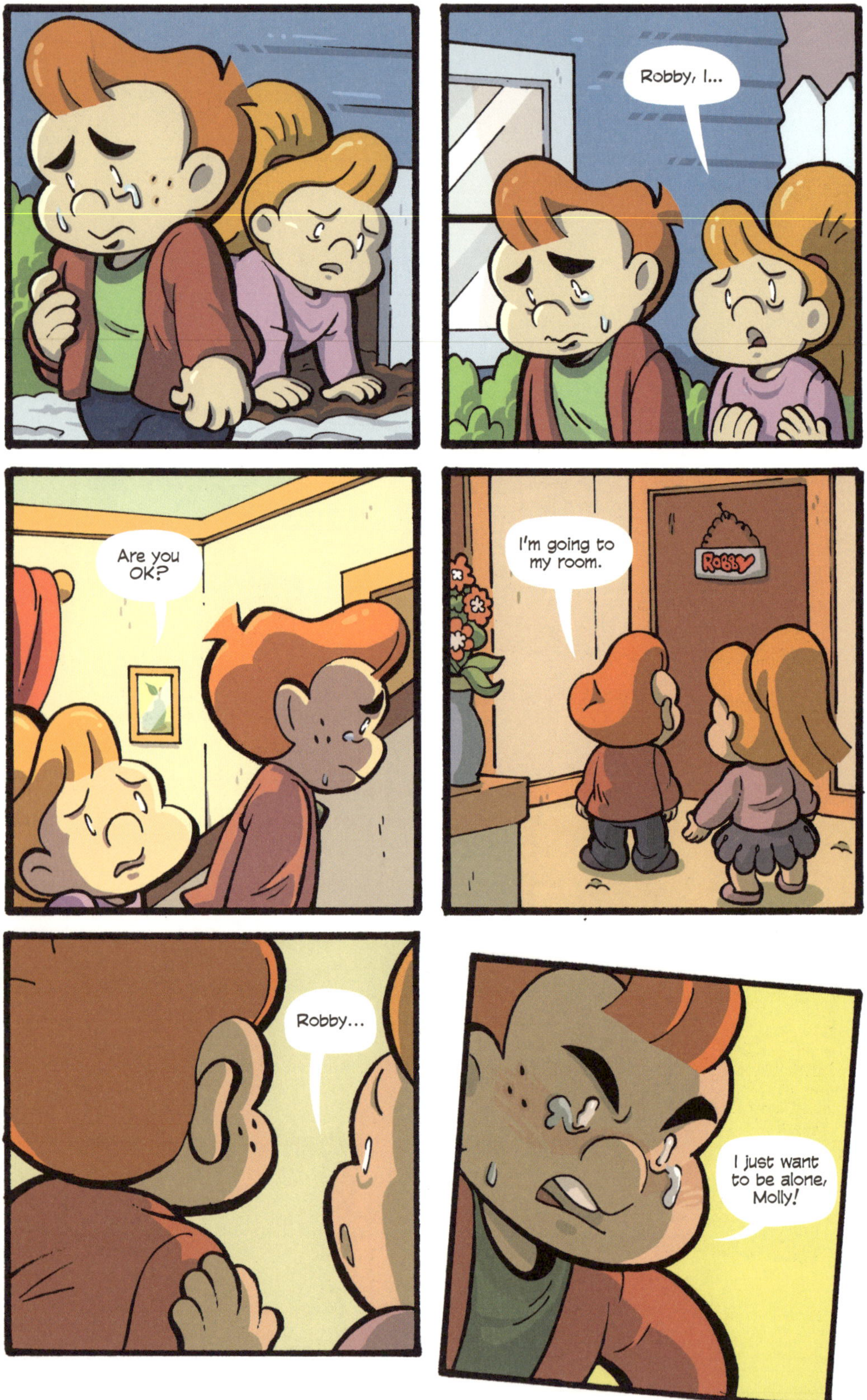

Robby, I...
Are you OK?
I'm going to my room.
ROBBY
Robby...
I just want to be alone, Molly!

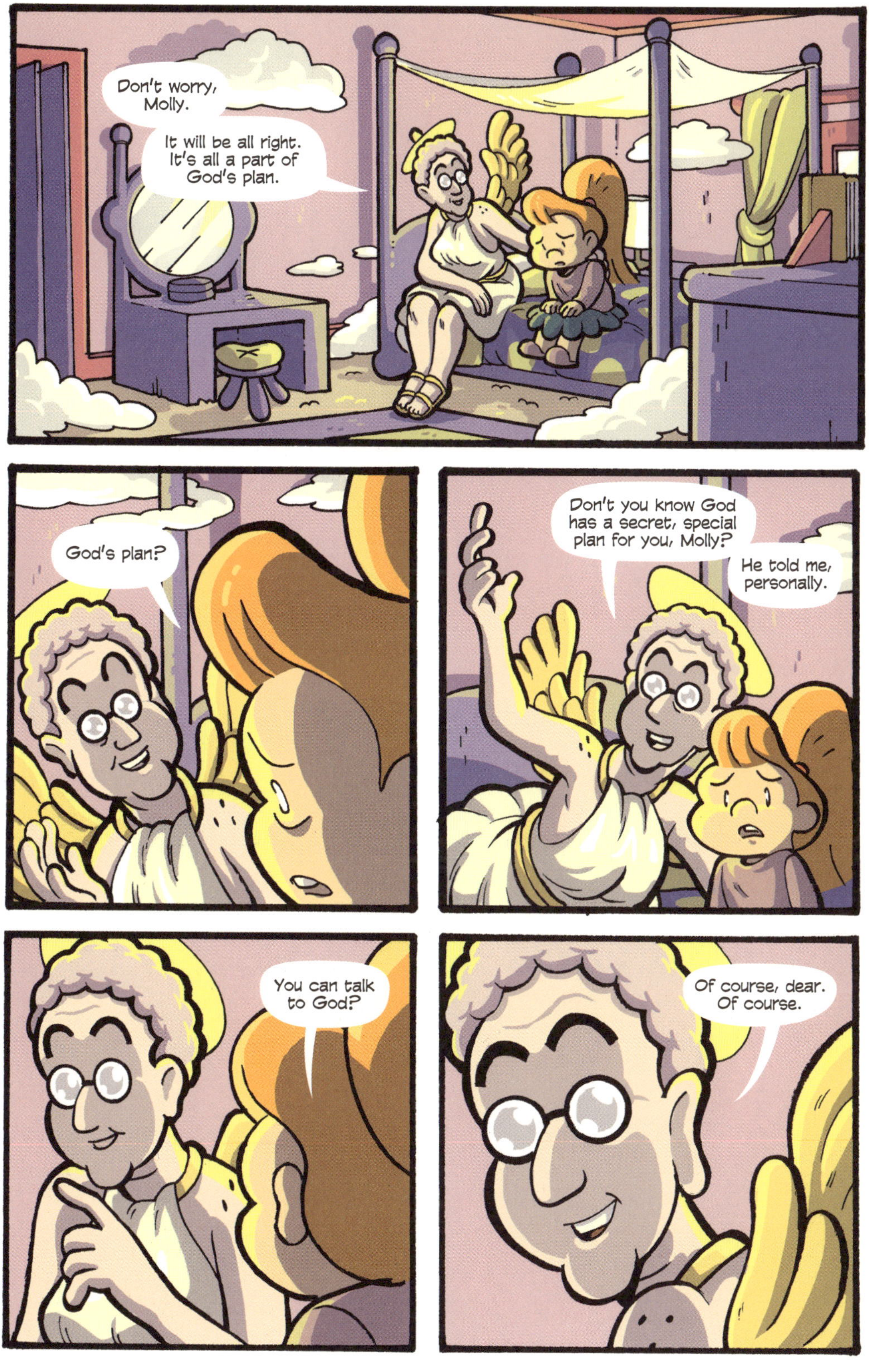
Don't worry, Molly.
It will be all right. It's all a part of God's plan.
God's plan?
Don't you know God has a secret, special plan for you, Molly?
He told me, personally.
You can talk to God?
Of course, dear. Of course.

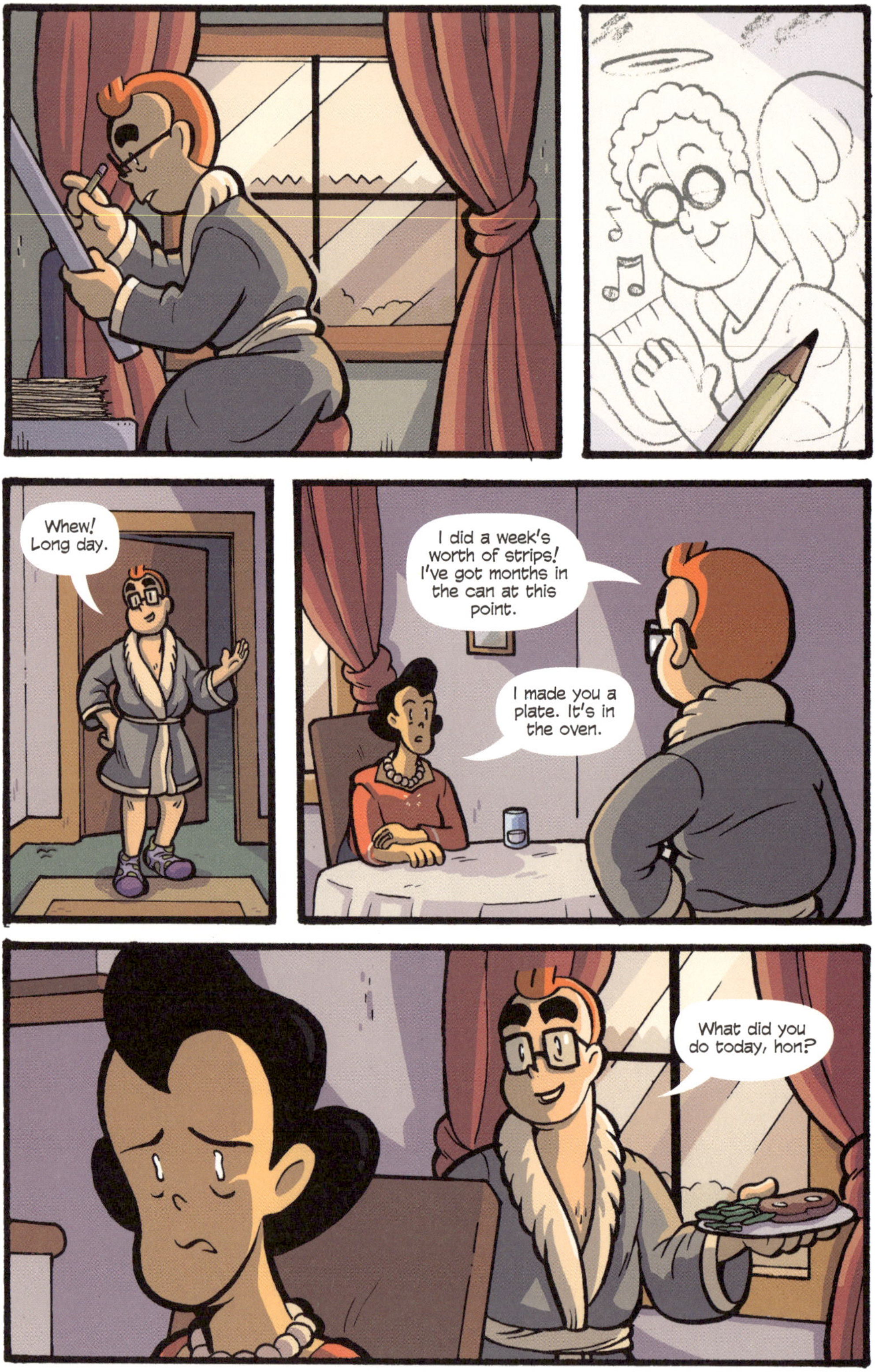
Whew! Long day.
I did a week's worth of strips! I've got months in the can at this point.
I made you a plate. It's in the oven.
What did you do today, hon?

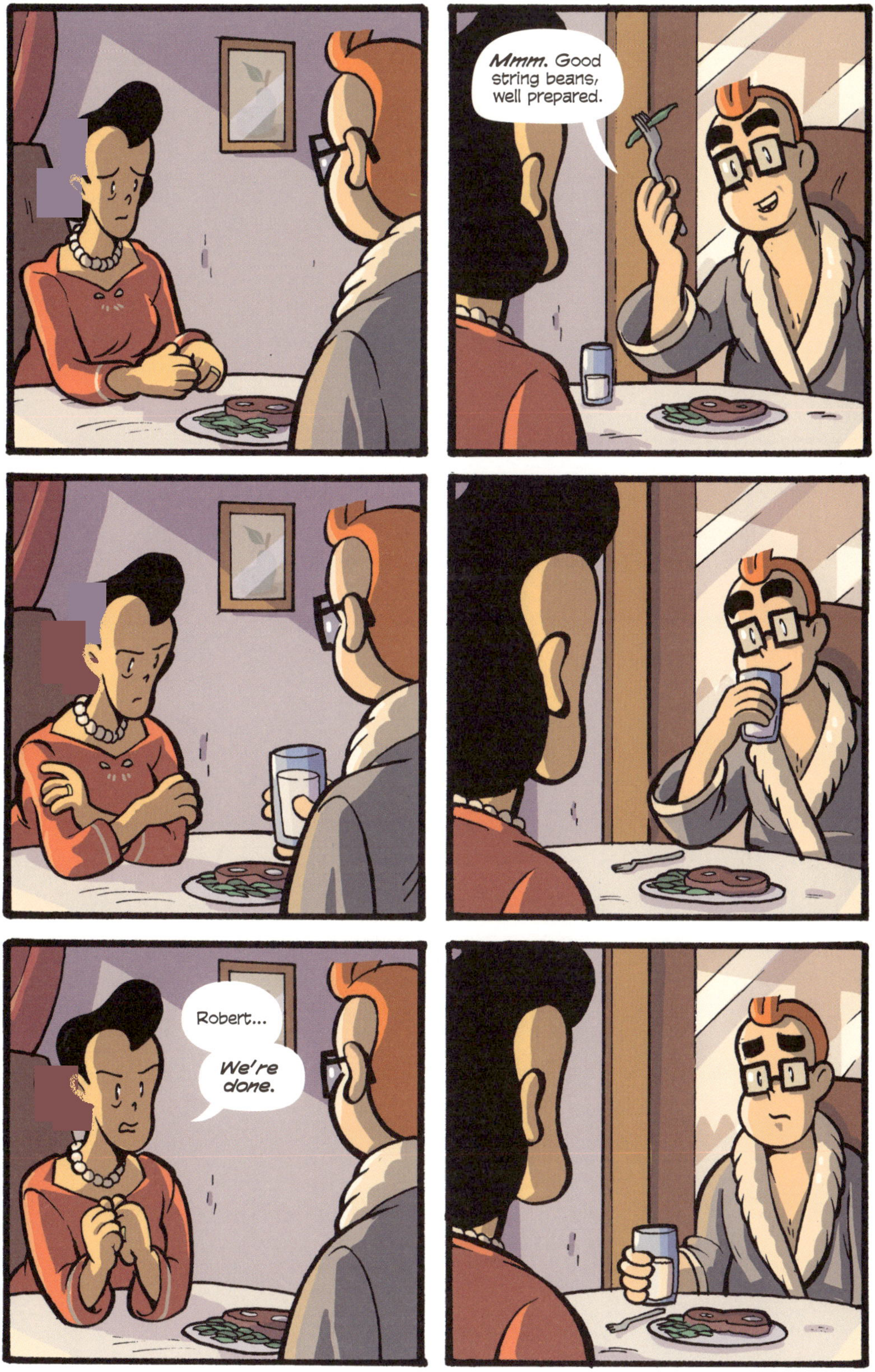
Mmm. Good string beans, well prepared.
Robert...
We're done.

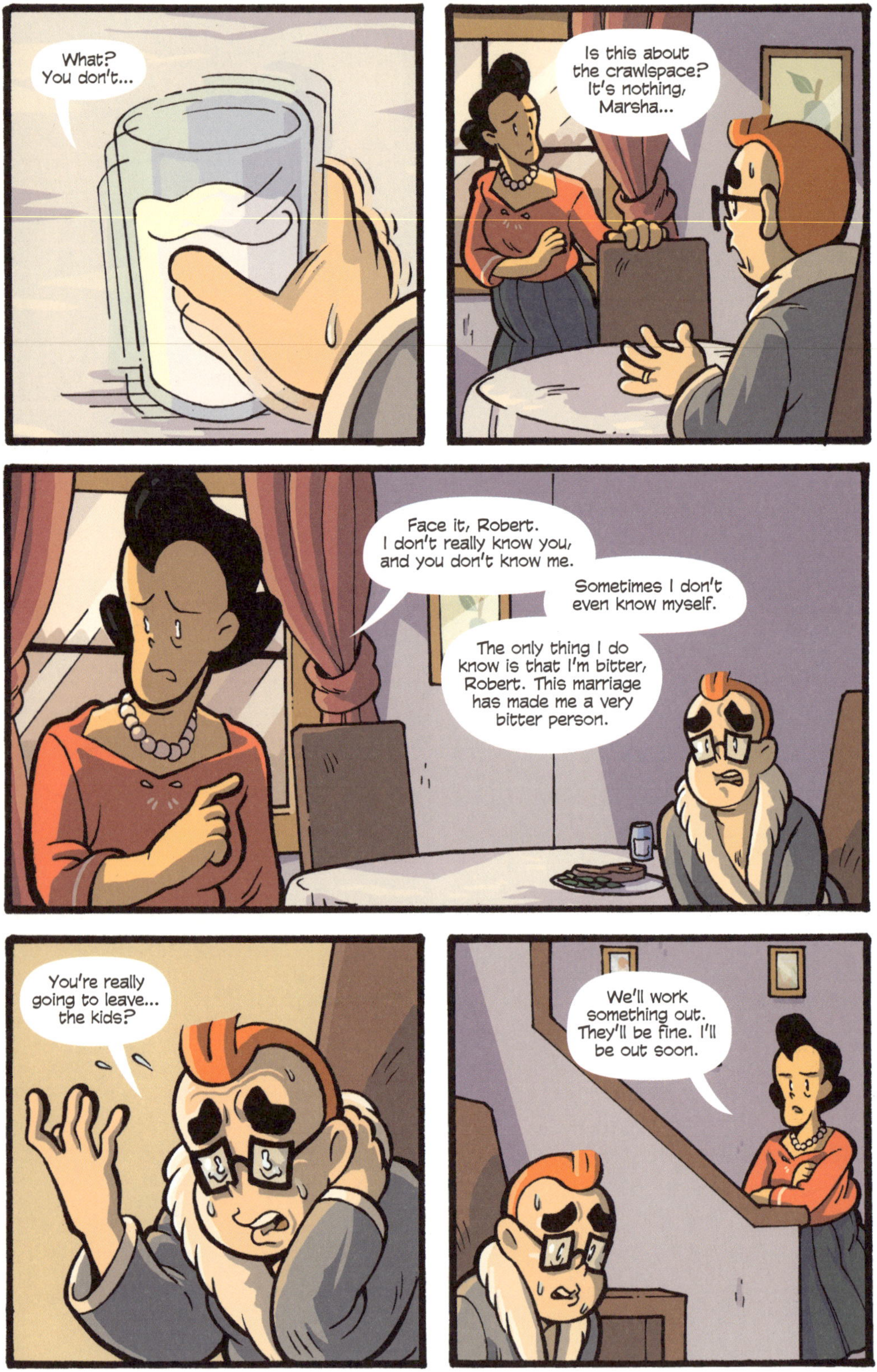
What? You don't...
Is this about the crawlspace? It's nothing, Marsha...
Face it, Robert. I don't really know you, and you don't know me.
Sometimes I don't even know myself.
The only thing I do know is that I'm bitter, Robert. This marriage has made me a very bitter person.
You're really going to leave... the kids?
We'll work something out. They'll be fine. I'll be out soon.

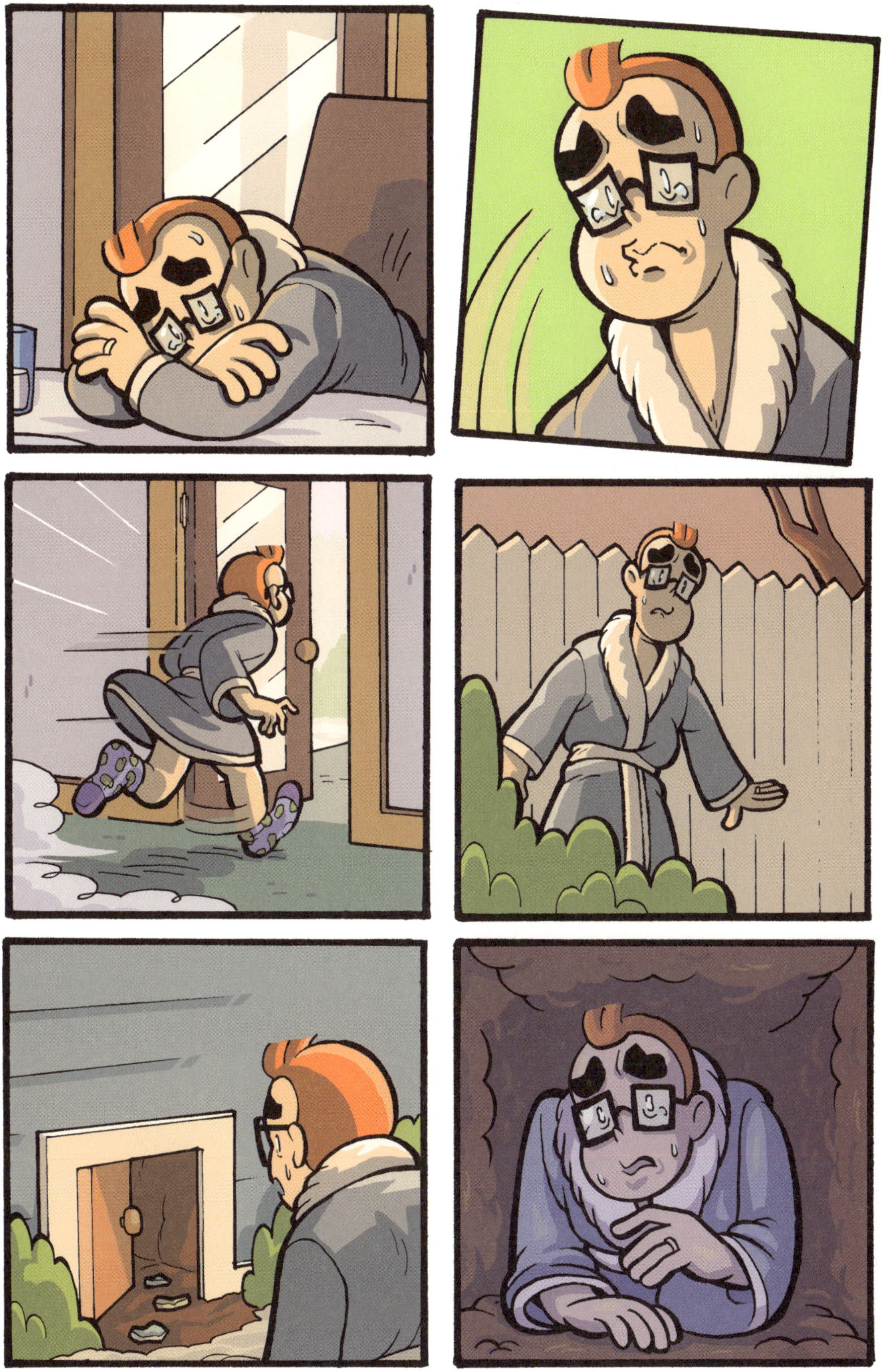

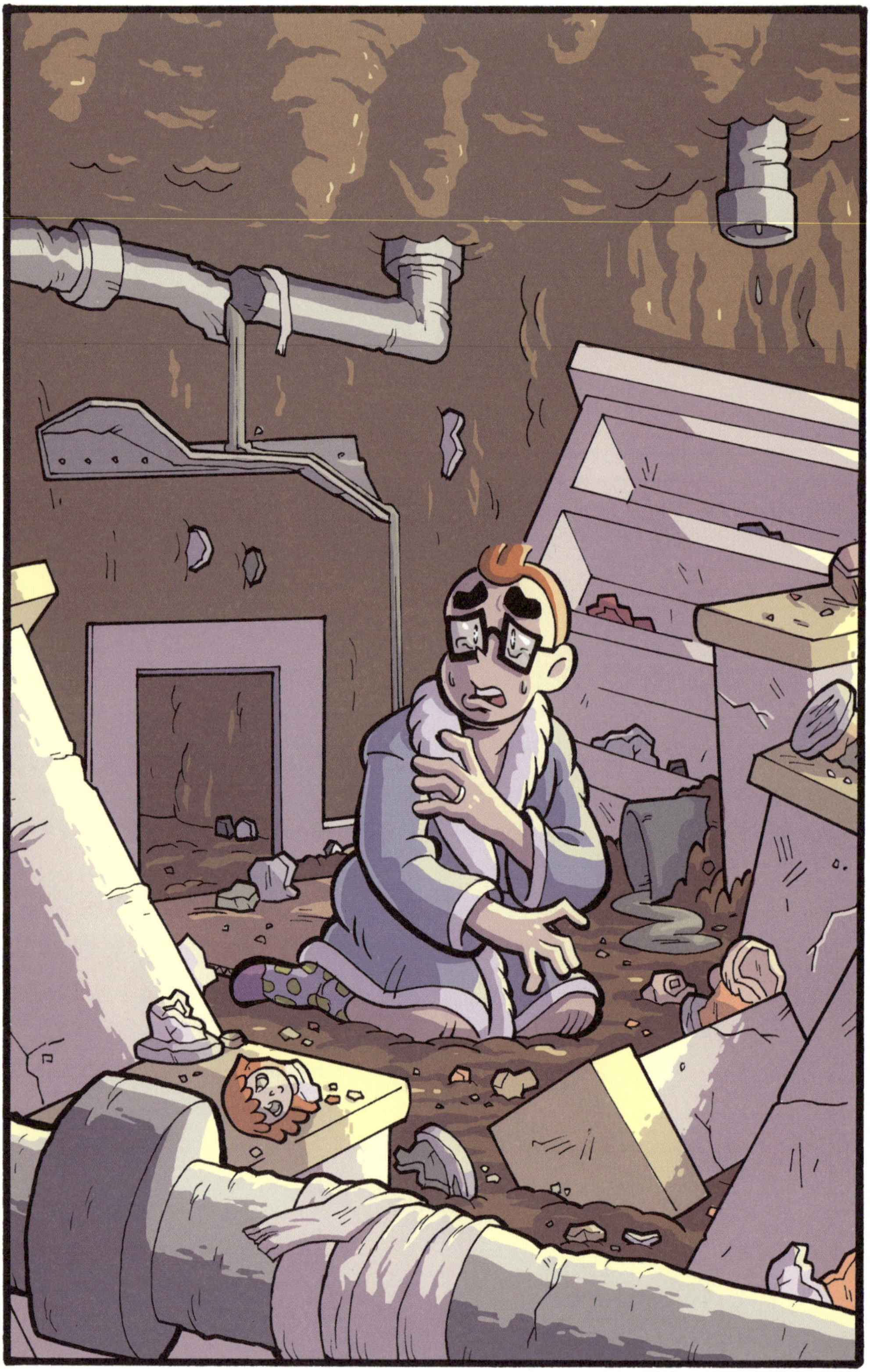

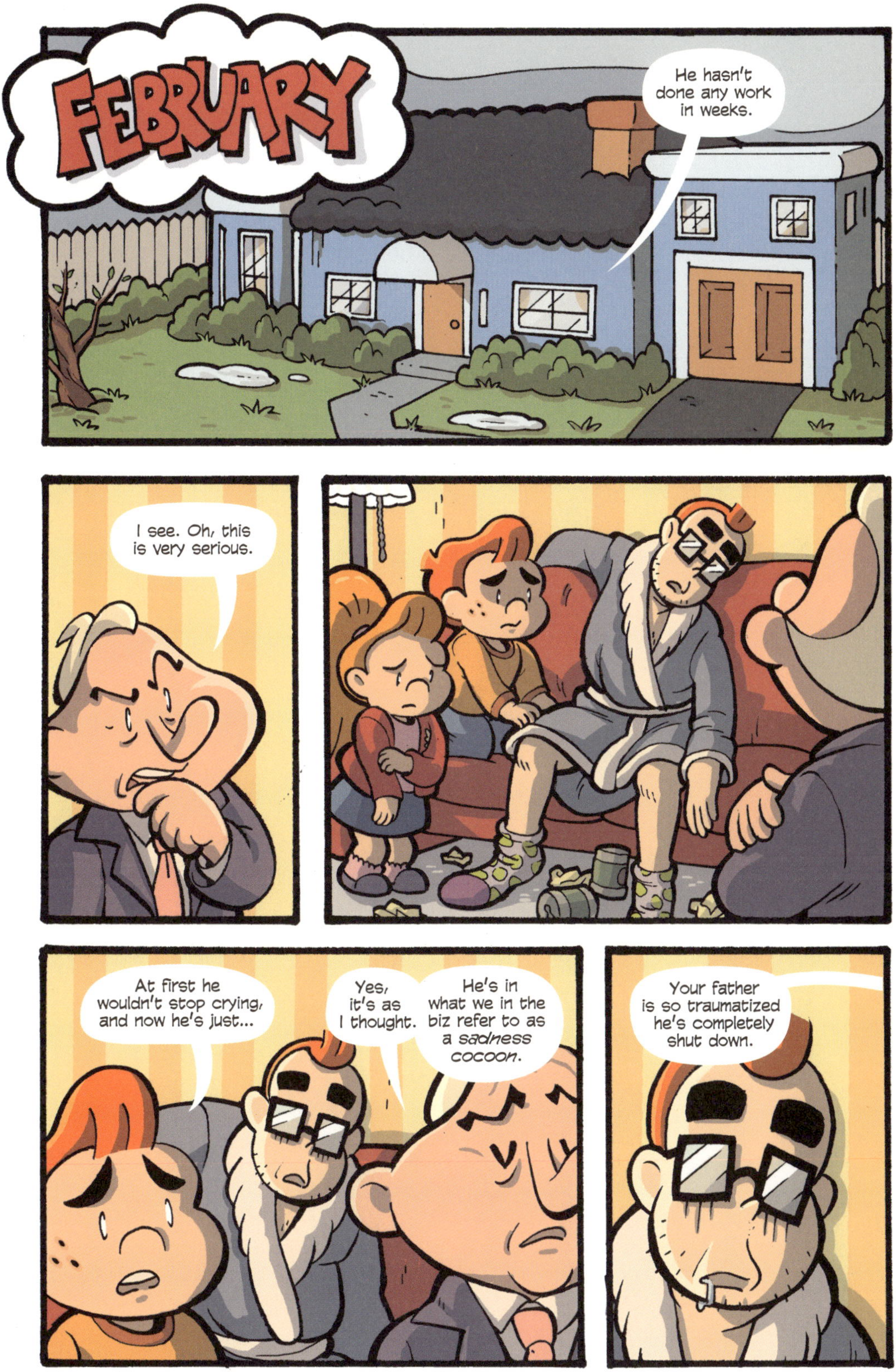
FEBRUARY
He hasn't done any work in weeks.
I see. Oh, this is very serious.
At first he wouldn't stop crying, and now he's just...
Yes, it's as I thought.
He's in what we in the biz refer to as a *sadness cocoon*.
Your father is so traumatized he's completely shut down.

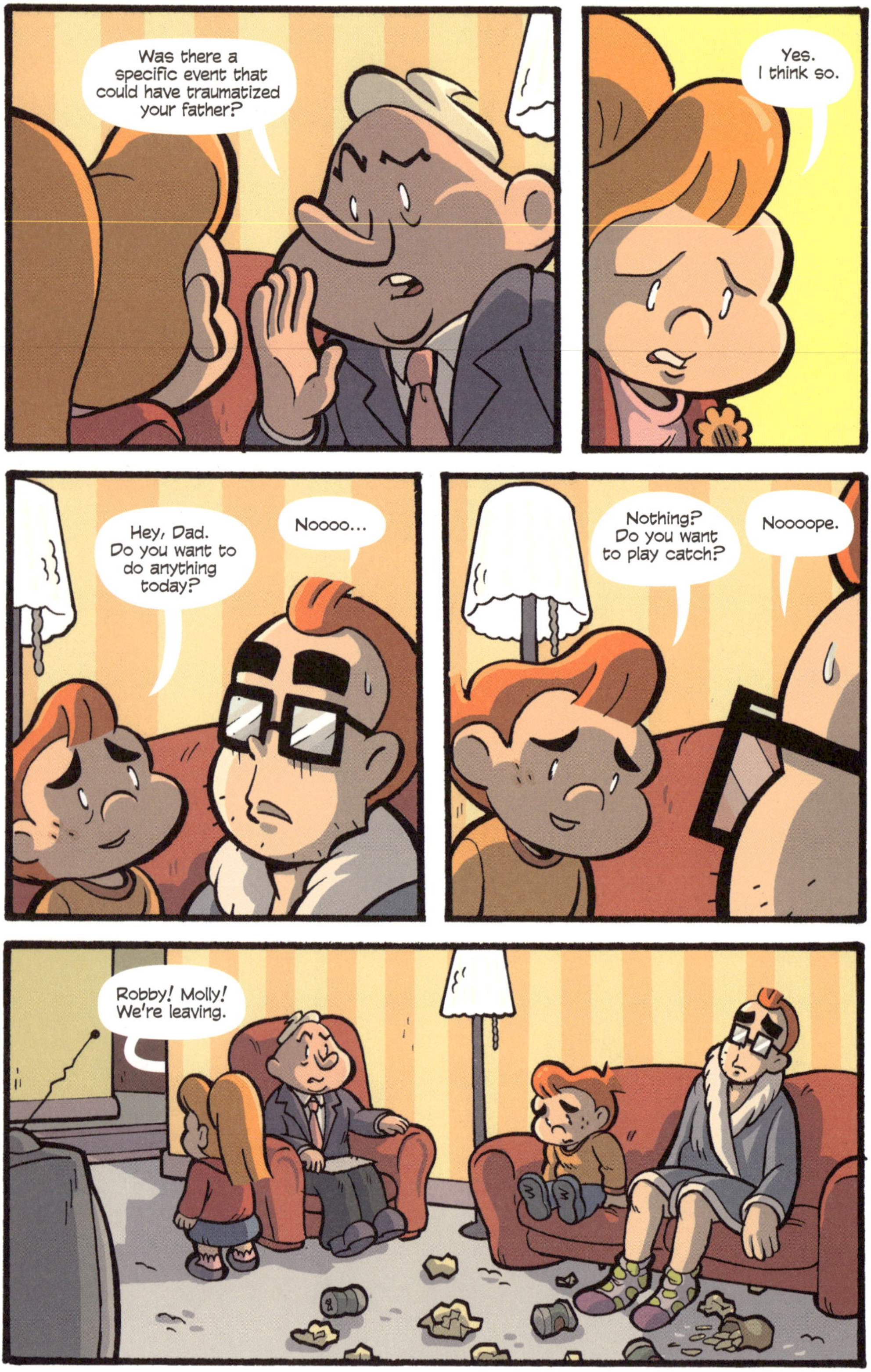
Was there a specific event that could have traumatized your father?
Yes. I think so.
Hey, Dad. Do you want to do anything today?
Noooo...
Nothing? Do you want to play catch?
Noooope.
Robby! Molly! We're leaving.

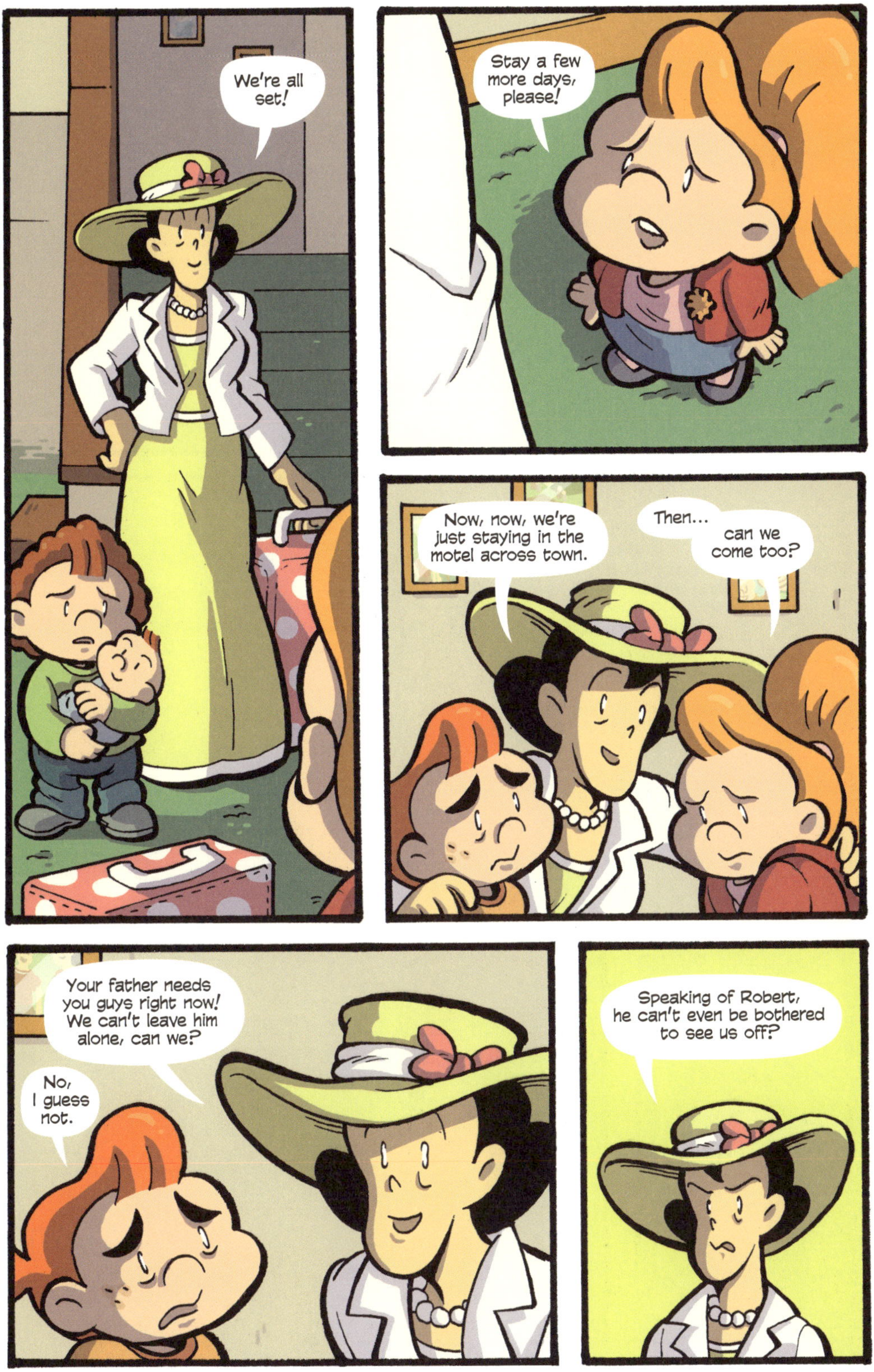
We're all set!
Stay a few more days, please!
Now, now, we're just staying in the motel across town.
Then...
can we come too?
Your father needs you guys right now! We can't leave him alone, can we?
No, I guess not.
Speaking of Robert, he can't even be bothered to see us off?

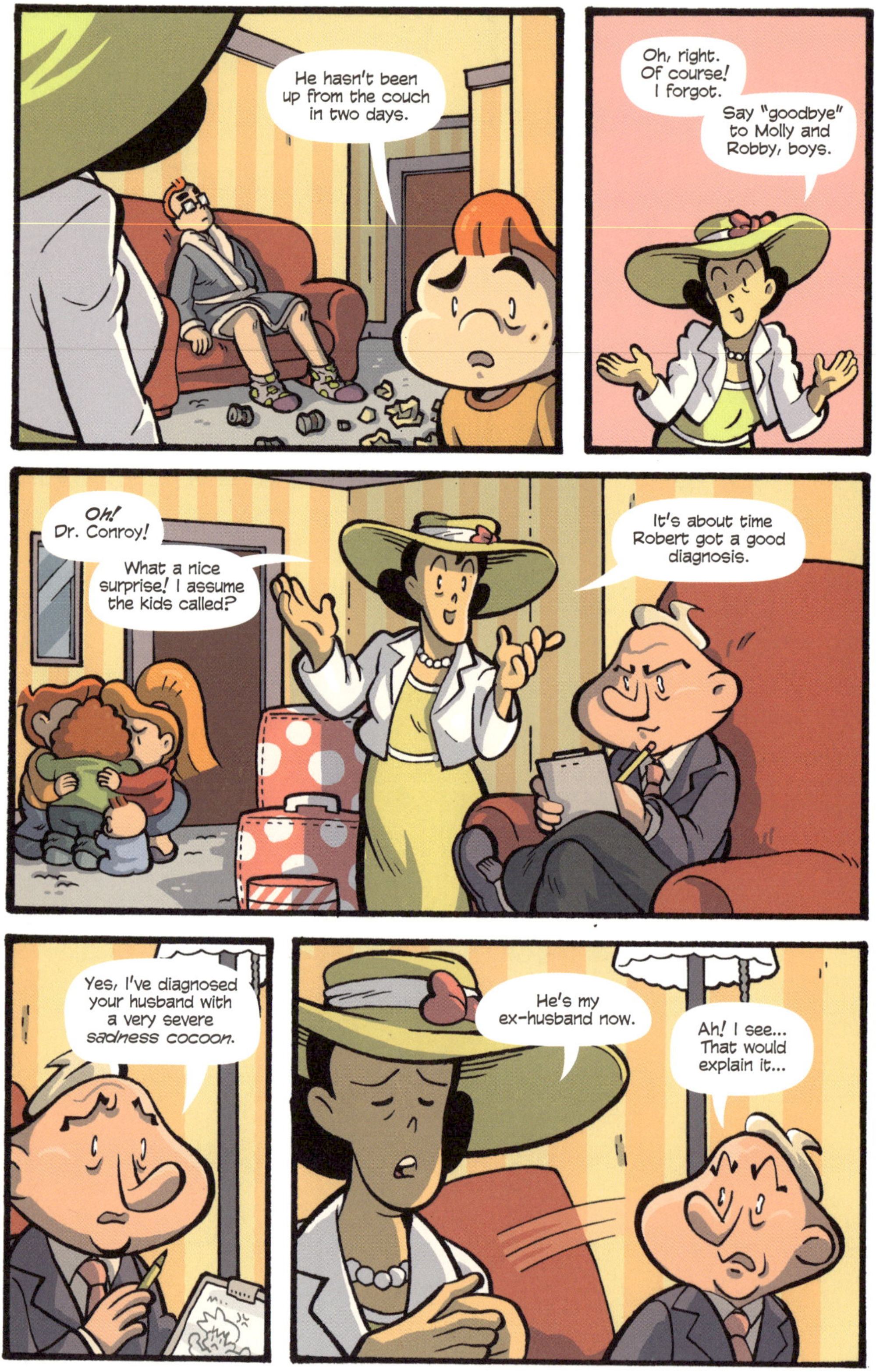
He hasn't been up from the couch in two days.
Oh, right. Of course! I forgot.
Say "goodbye" to Molly and Robby, boys.
Oh! Dr. Conroy!
What a nice surprise! I assume the kids called?
It's about time Robert got a good diagnosis.
Yes, I've diagnosed your husband with a very severe *sadness cocoon.*
He's my ex-husband now.
Ah! I see... That would explain it...

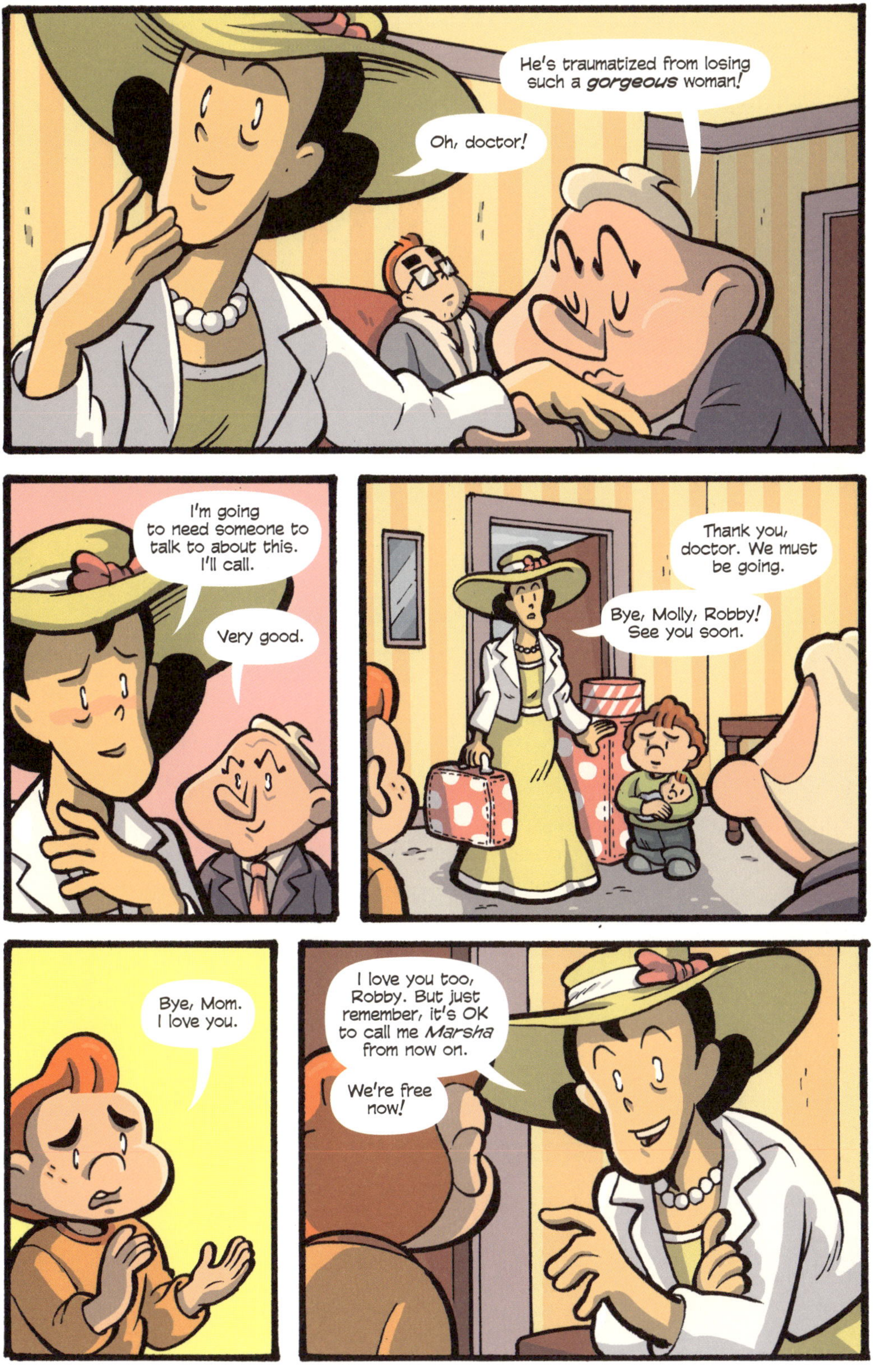
He's traumatized from losing such a *gorgeous* woman!
Oh, doctor!
I'm going to need someone to talk to about this. I'll call.
Very good.
Thank you, doctor. We must be going.
Bye, Molly, Robby! See you soon.
Bye, Mom. I love you.
I love you too, Robby. But just remember, it's OK to call me *Marsha* from now on.
We're free now!

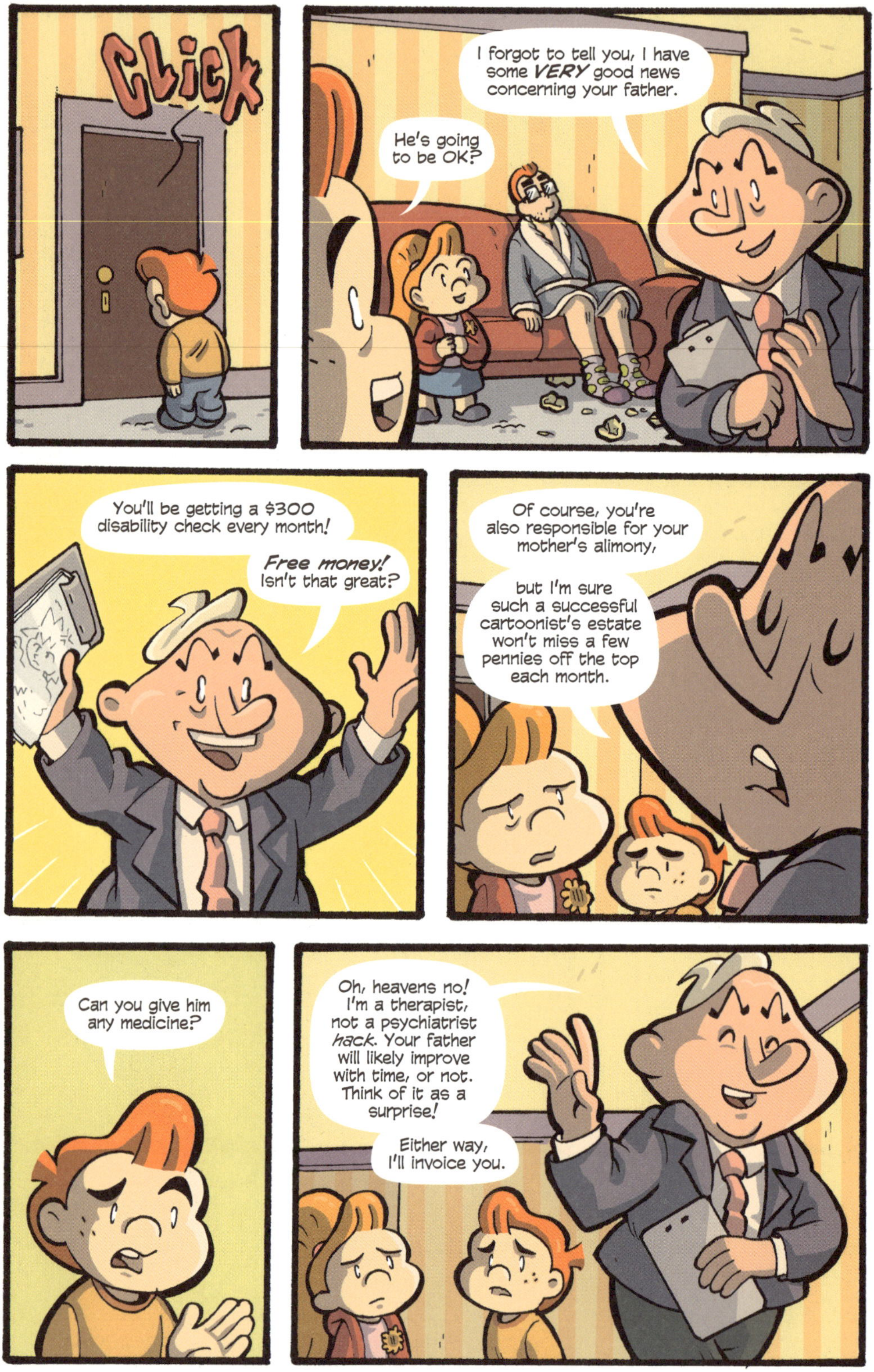

CLICK
I forgot to tell you, I have some VERY good news concerning your father.
He's going to be OK?
You'll be getting a $300 disability check every month!
Free money! Isn't that great?
Of course, you're also responsible for your mother's alimony,
but I'm sure such a successful cartoonist's estate won't miss a few pennies off the top each month.
Can you give him any medicine?
Oh, heavens no! I'm a therapist, not a psychiatrist hack. Your father will likely improve with time, or not. Think of it as a surprise!
Either way, I'll invoice you.

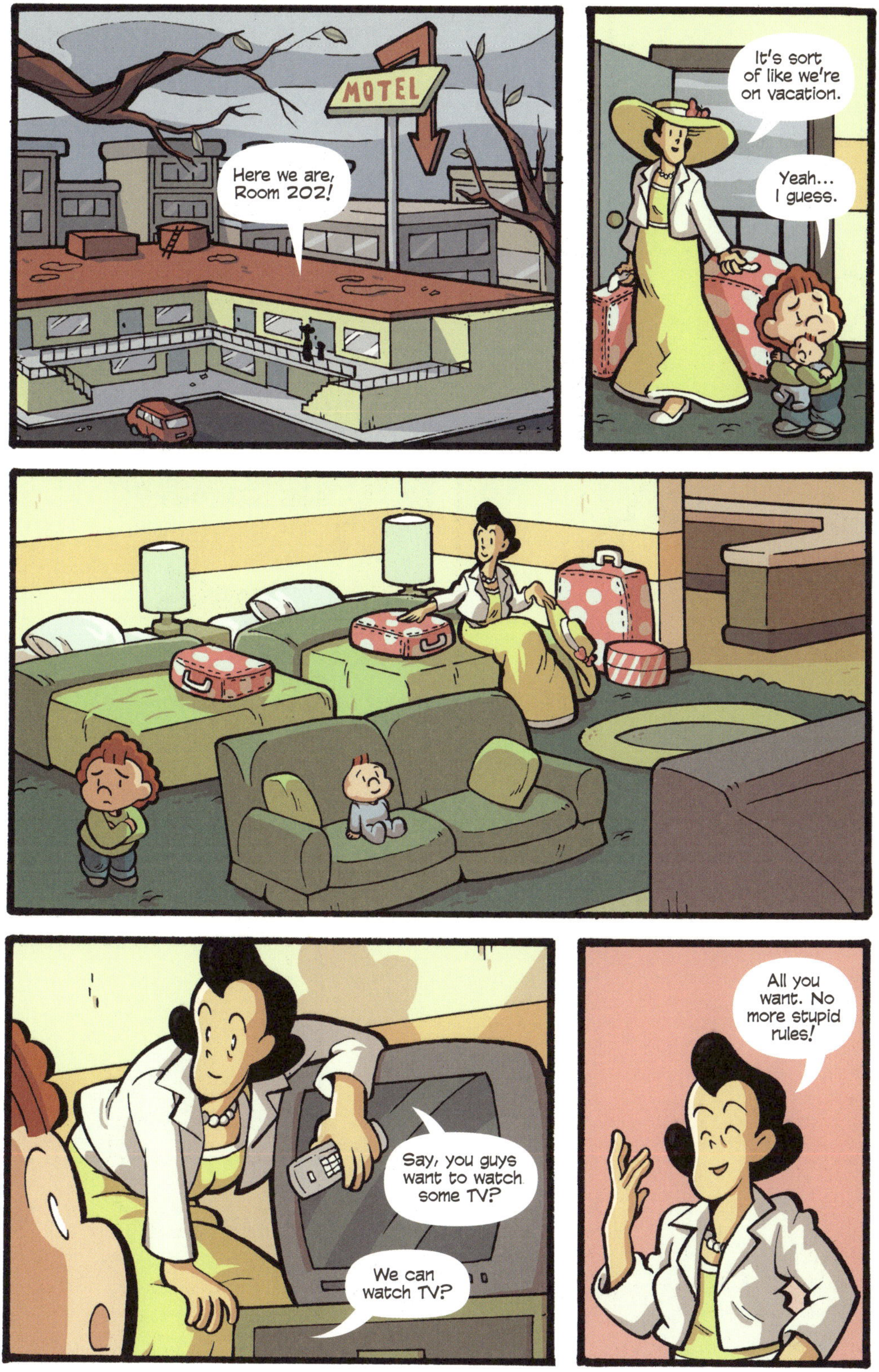
MOTEL
Here we are, Room 202!
It's sort of like we're on vacation.
Yeah... I guess.
Say, you guys want to watch some TV?
We can watch TV?
All you want. No more stupid rules!

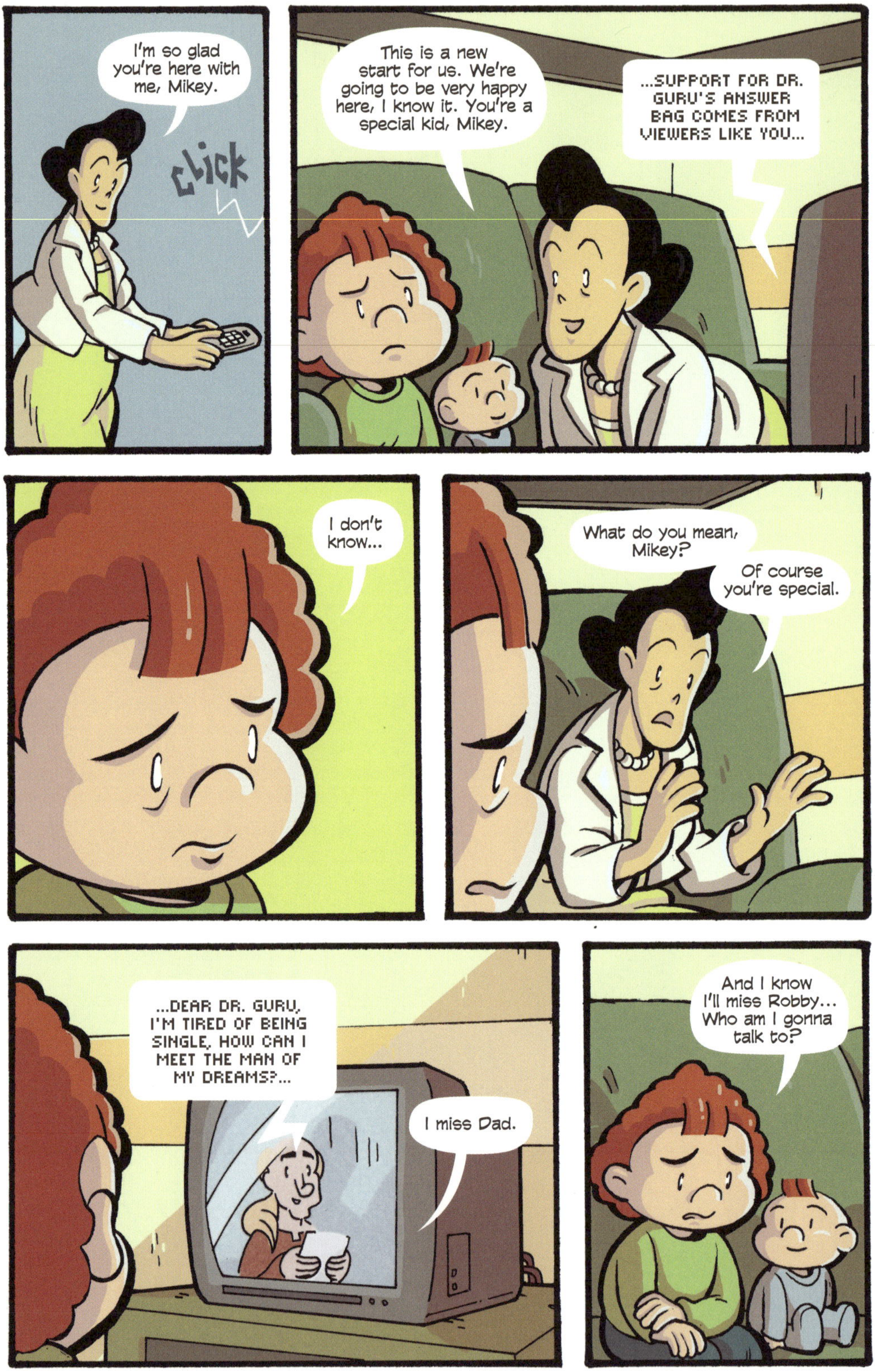
I'm so glad you're here with me, Mikey.
CLICK
This is a new start for us. We're going to be very happy here, I know it. You're a special kid, Mikey.
...SUPPORT FOR DR. GURU'S ANSWER BAG COMES FROM VIEWERS LIKE YOU...
I don't know...
What do you mean, Mikey?
Of course you're special.
...DEAR DR. GURU, I'M TIRED OF BEING SINGLE. HOW CAN I MEET THE MAN OF MY DREAMS?...
I miss Dad.
And I know I'll miss Robby... Who am I gonna talk to?

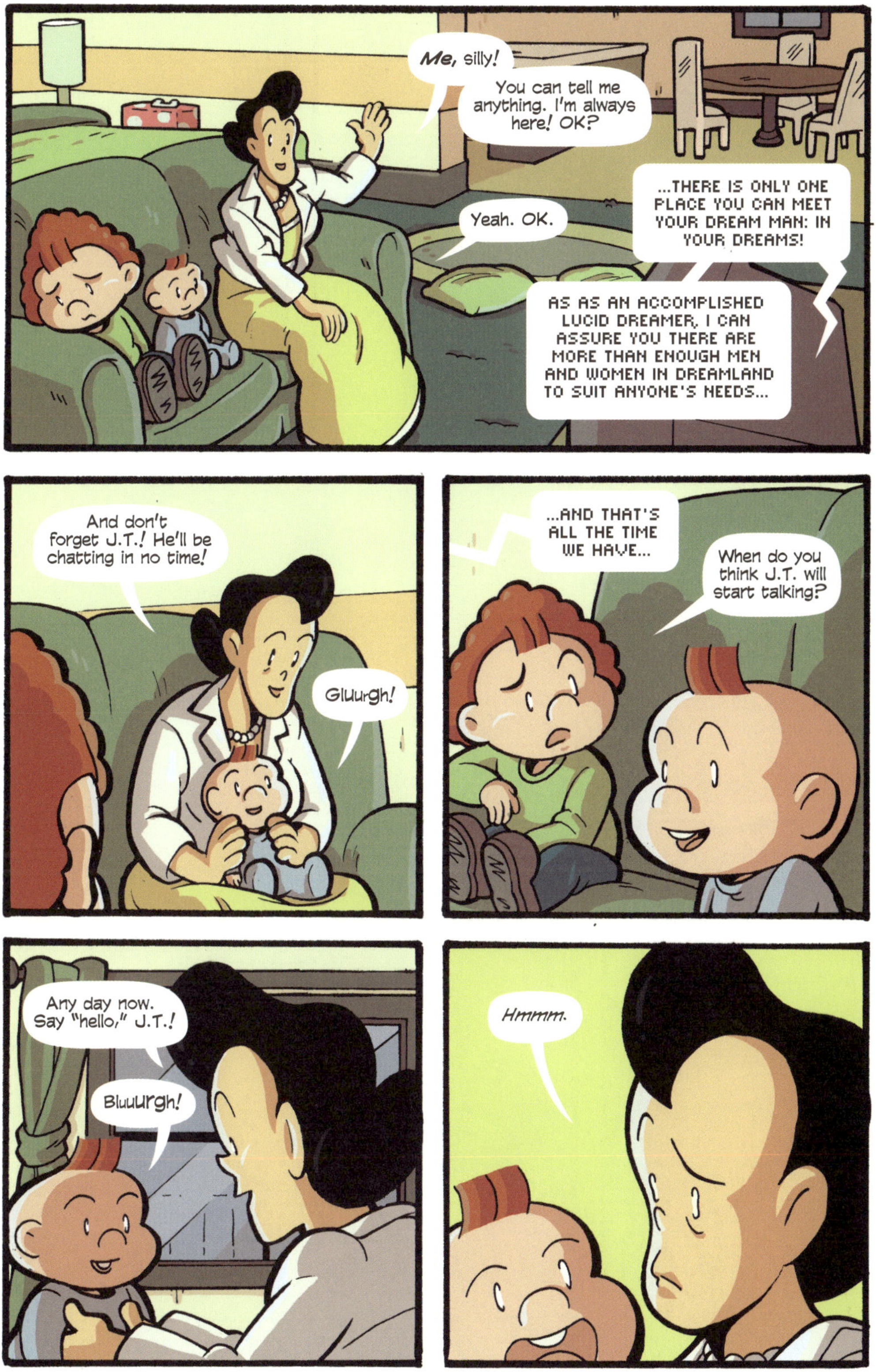

Me, silly!
You can tell me anything. I'm always here! OK?
Yeah. OK.
...THERE IS ONLY ONE PLACE YOU CAN MEET YOUR DREAM MAN: IN YOUR DREAMS!
AS AS AN ACCOMPLISHED LUCID DREAMER, I CAN ASSURE YOU THERE ARE MORE THAN ENOUGH MEN AND WOMEN IN DREAMLAND TO SUIT ANYONE'S NEEDS...
And don't forget J.T.! He'll be chatting in no time!
Gluurgh!
...AND THAT'S ALL THE TIME WE HAVE...
When do you think J.T. will start talking?
Any day now. Say "hello," J.T.!
Bluuurgh!
Hmmm.

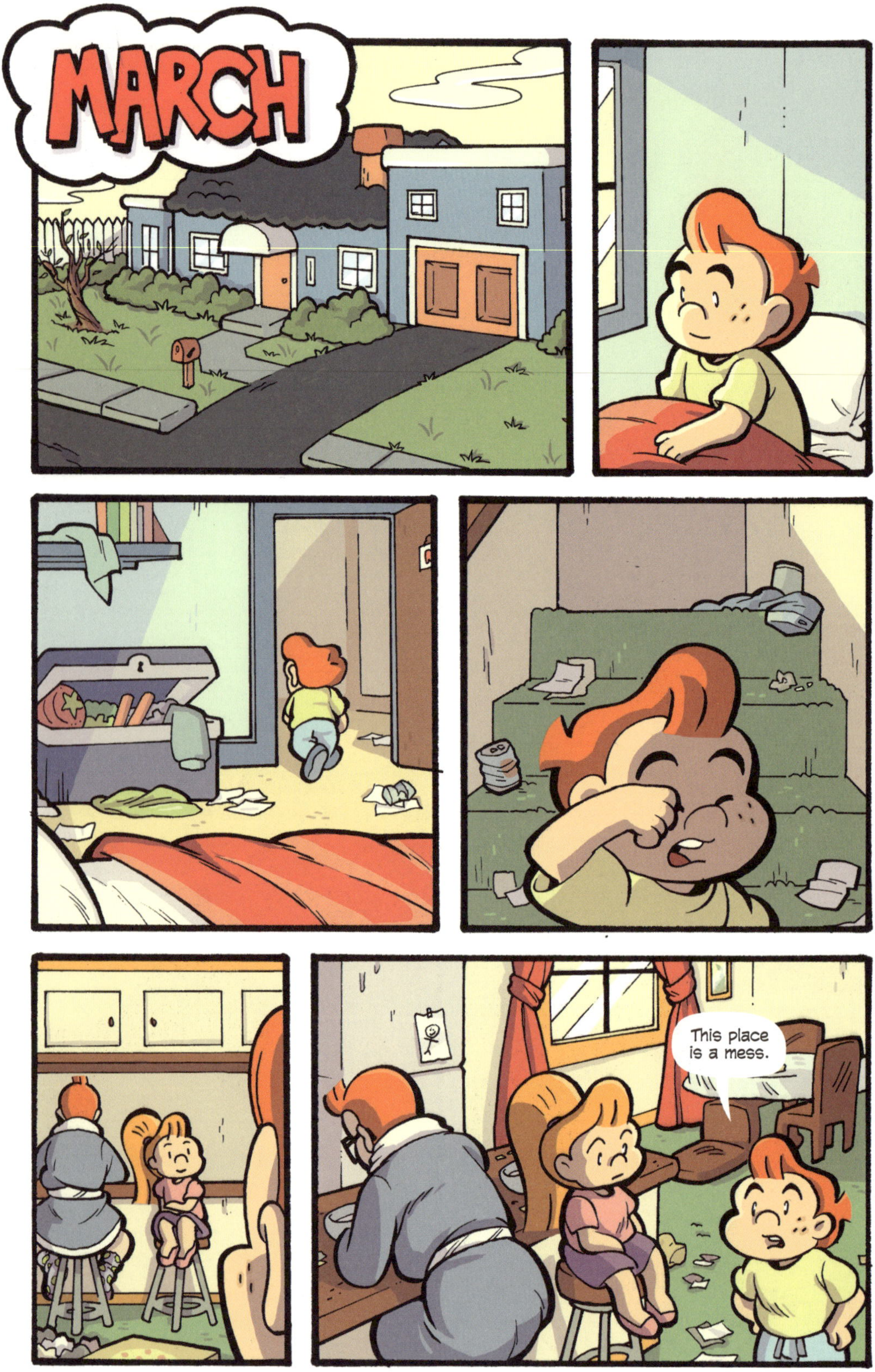
MARCH
This place is a mess.

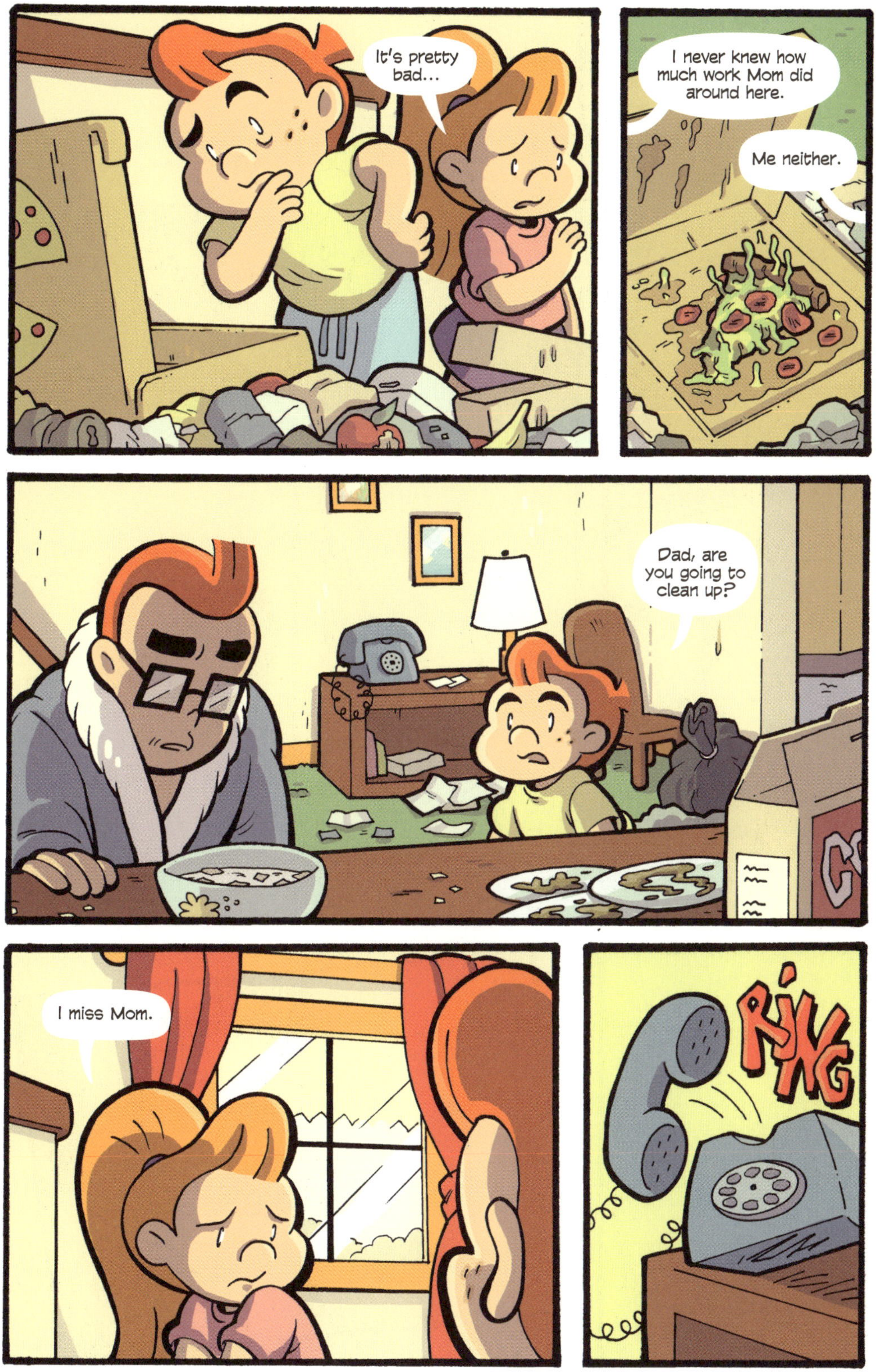
It's pretty bad...
I never knew how much work Mom did around here.
Me neither.
Dad, are you going to clean up?
I miss Mom.
RING

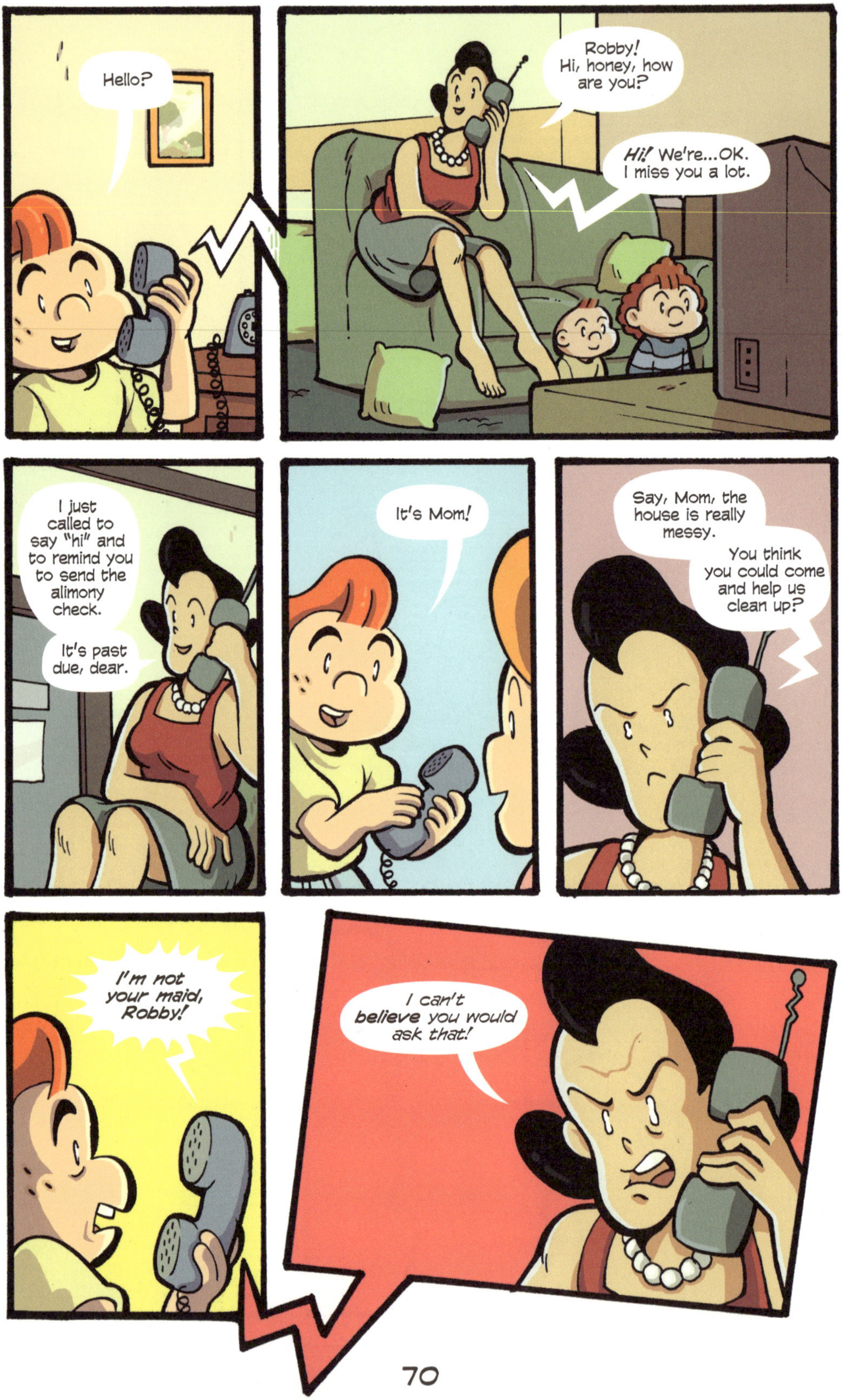
Hello?
Robby! Hi, honey, how are you?
Hi! We're...OK. I miss you a lot.
I just called to say "hi" and to remind you to send the alimony check.
It's past due, dear.
It's Mom!
Say, Mom, the house is really messy.
You think you could come and help us clean up?
I'm not your maid, Robby!
*I can't **believe** you would ask that!*

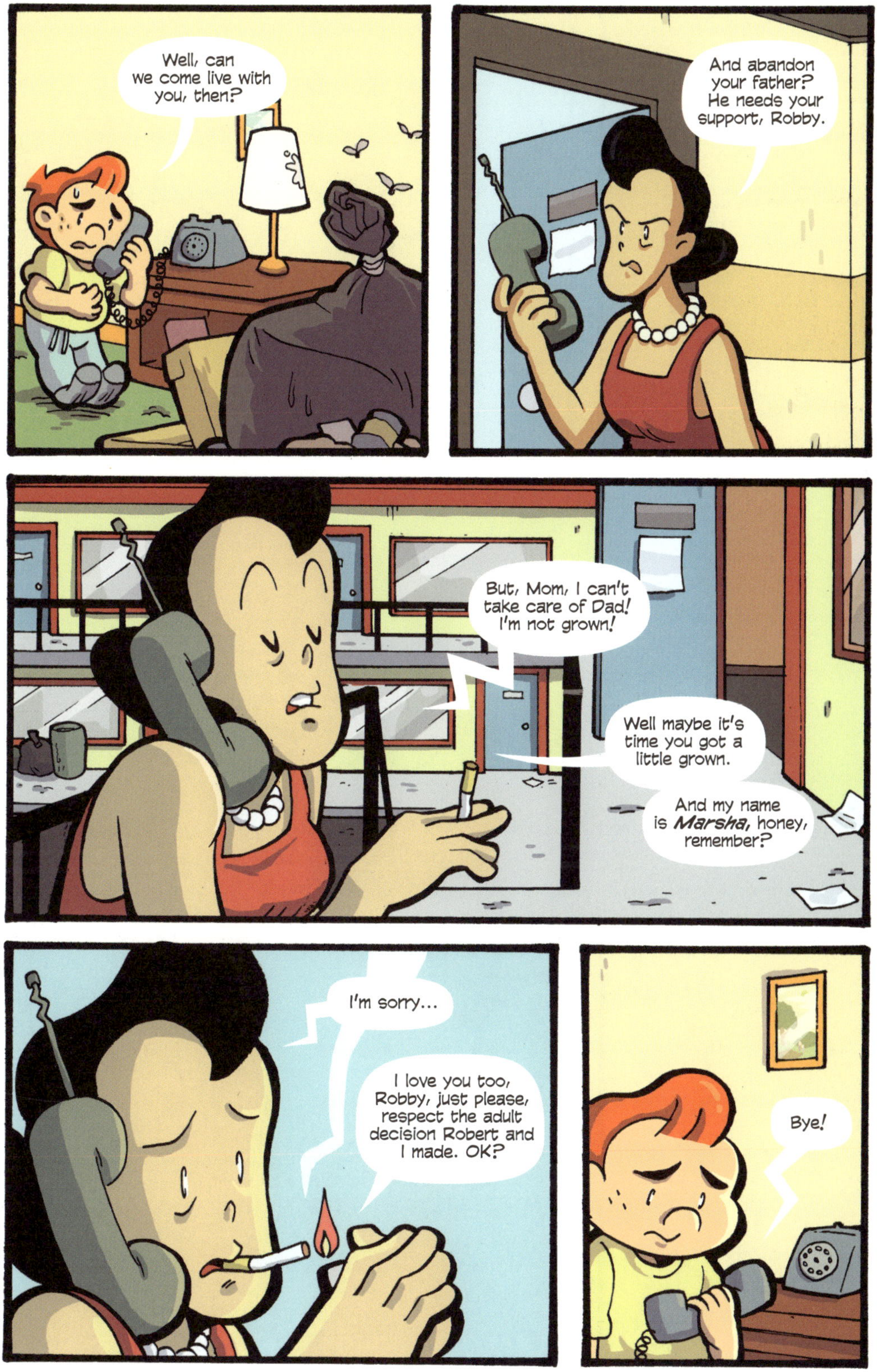
Well, can we come live with you, then?
And abandon your father? He needs your support, Robby.
But, Mom, I can't take care of Dad! I'm not grown!
Well maybe it's time you got a little grown.
And my name is *Marsha,* honey, remember?
I'm sorry...
I love you too, Robby, just please, respect the adult decision Robert and I made. OK?
Bye!

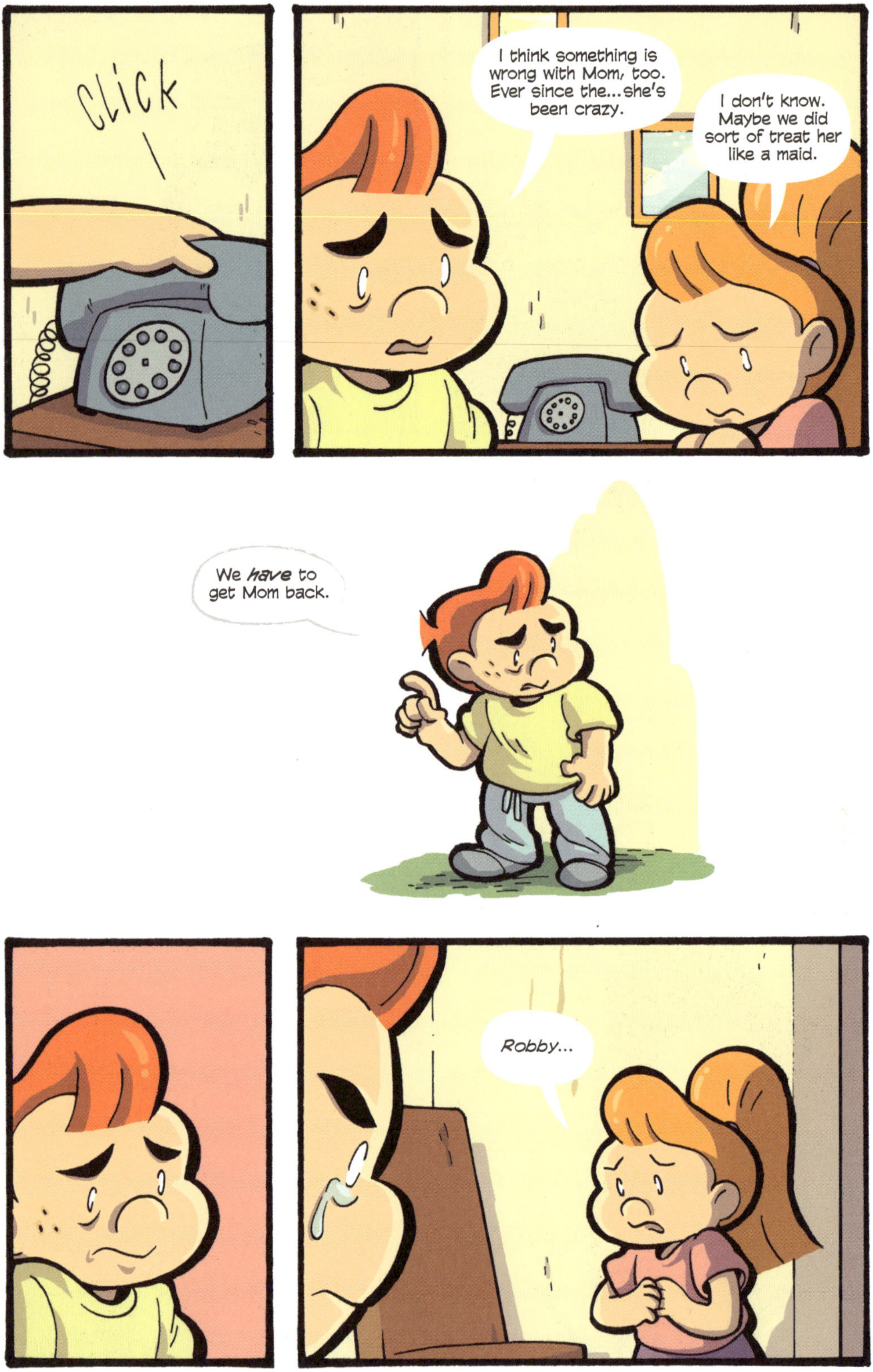
CLICK
I think something is wrong with Mom, too. Ever since the...she's been crazy.
I don't know. Maybe we did sort of treat her like a maid.
We *have* to get Mom back.
Robby...

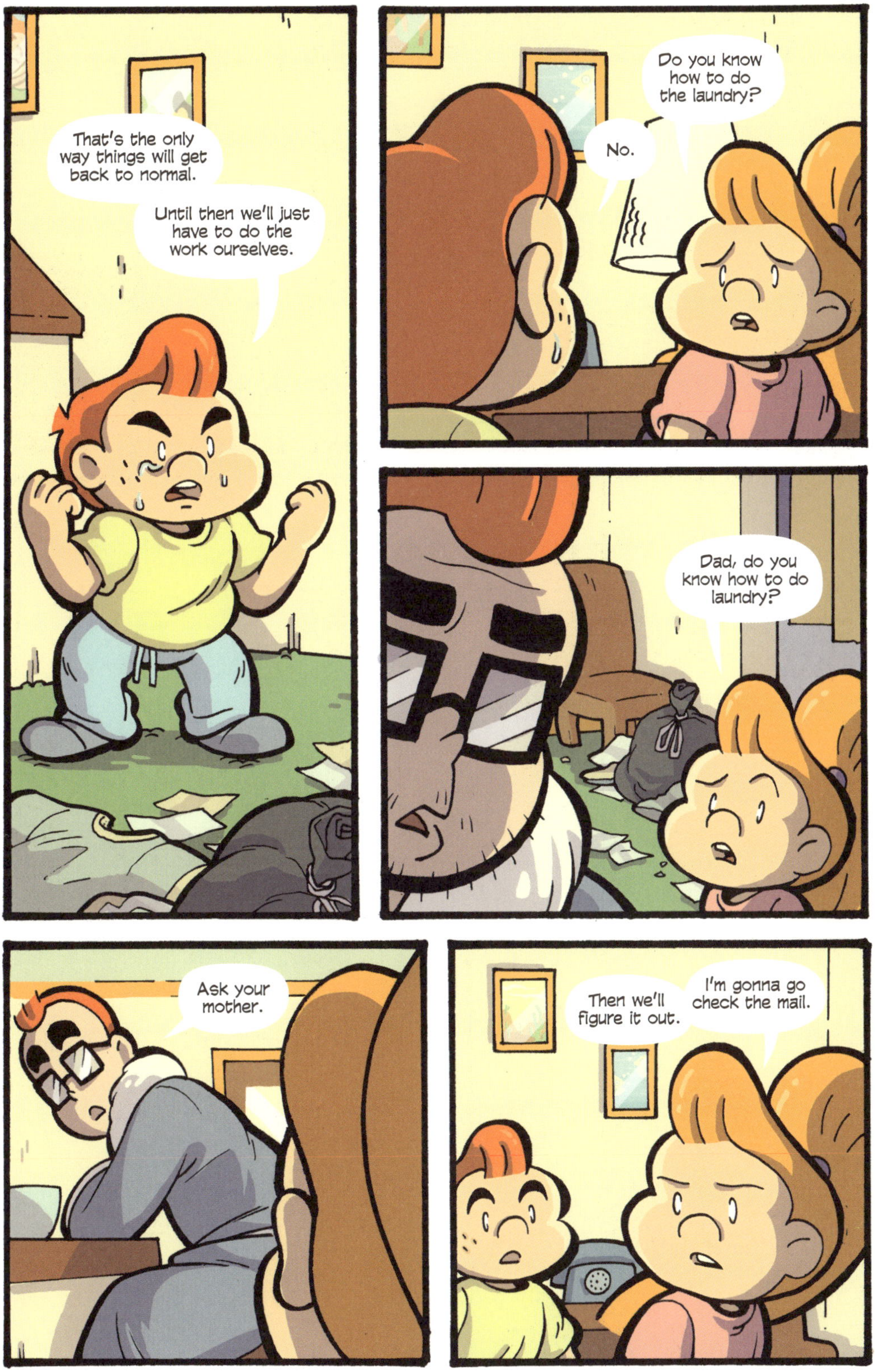
That's the only way things will get back to normal.
Until then we'll just have to do the work ourselves.
Do you know how to do the laundry?
No.
Dad, do you know how to do laundry?
Ask your mother.
I'm gonna go check the mail.
Then we'll figure it out.

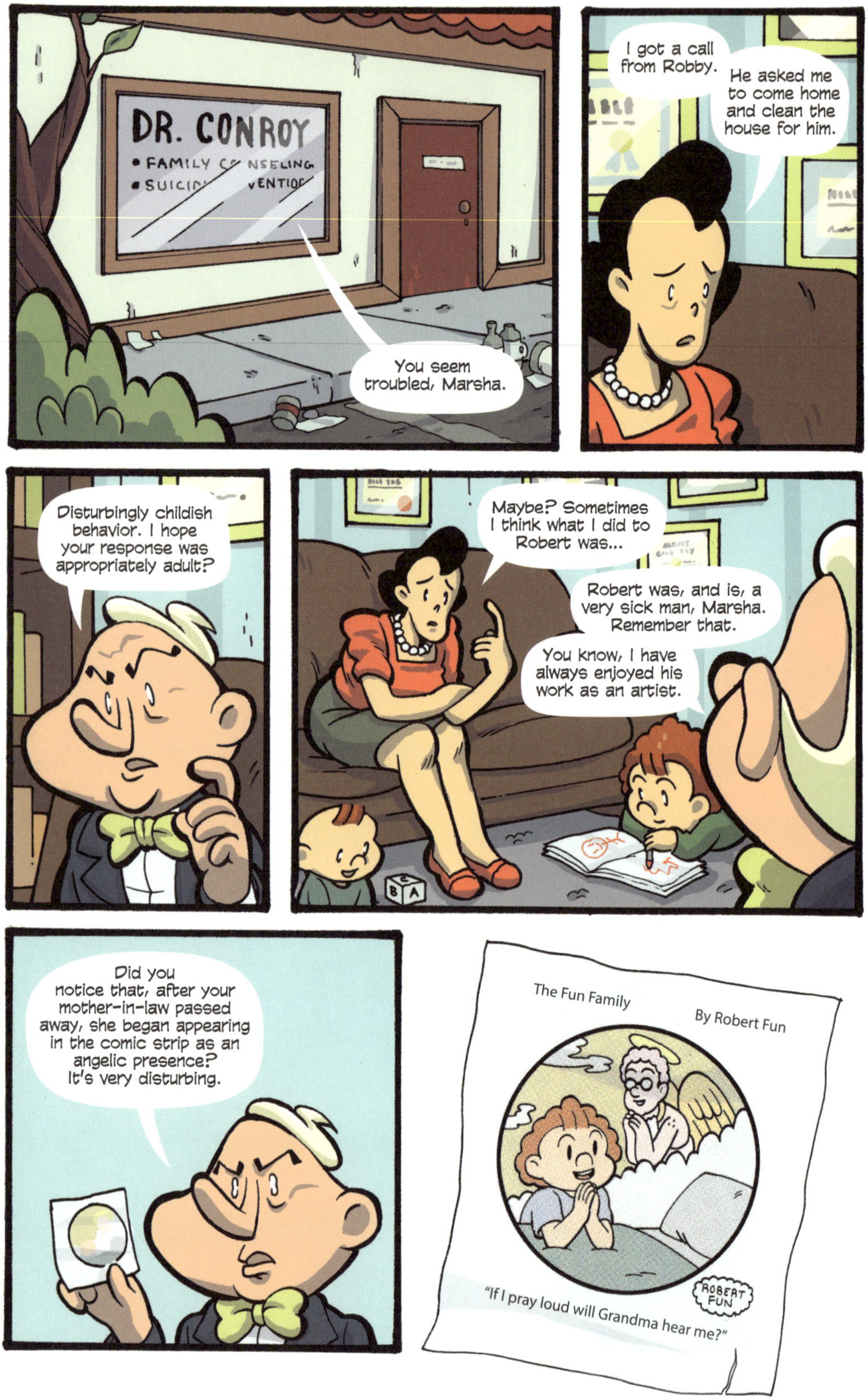
DR. CONROY
• FAMILY C NSELING
• SUICI VENTIO
You seem troubled, Marsha.
I got a call from Robby.
He asked me to come home and clean the house for him.
Disturbingly childish behavior. I hope your response was appropriately adult?
Maybe? Sometimes I think what I did to Robert was...
Robert was, and is, a very sick man, Marsha. Remember that.
You know, I have always enjoyed his work as an artist.
Did you notice that, after your mother-in-law passed away, she began appearing in the comic strip as an angelic presence? It's very disturbing.
The Fun Family
By Robert Fun
ROBERT FUN
"If I pray loud will Grandma hear me?"

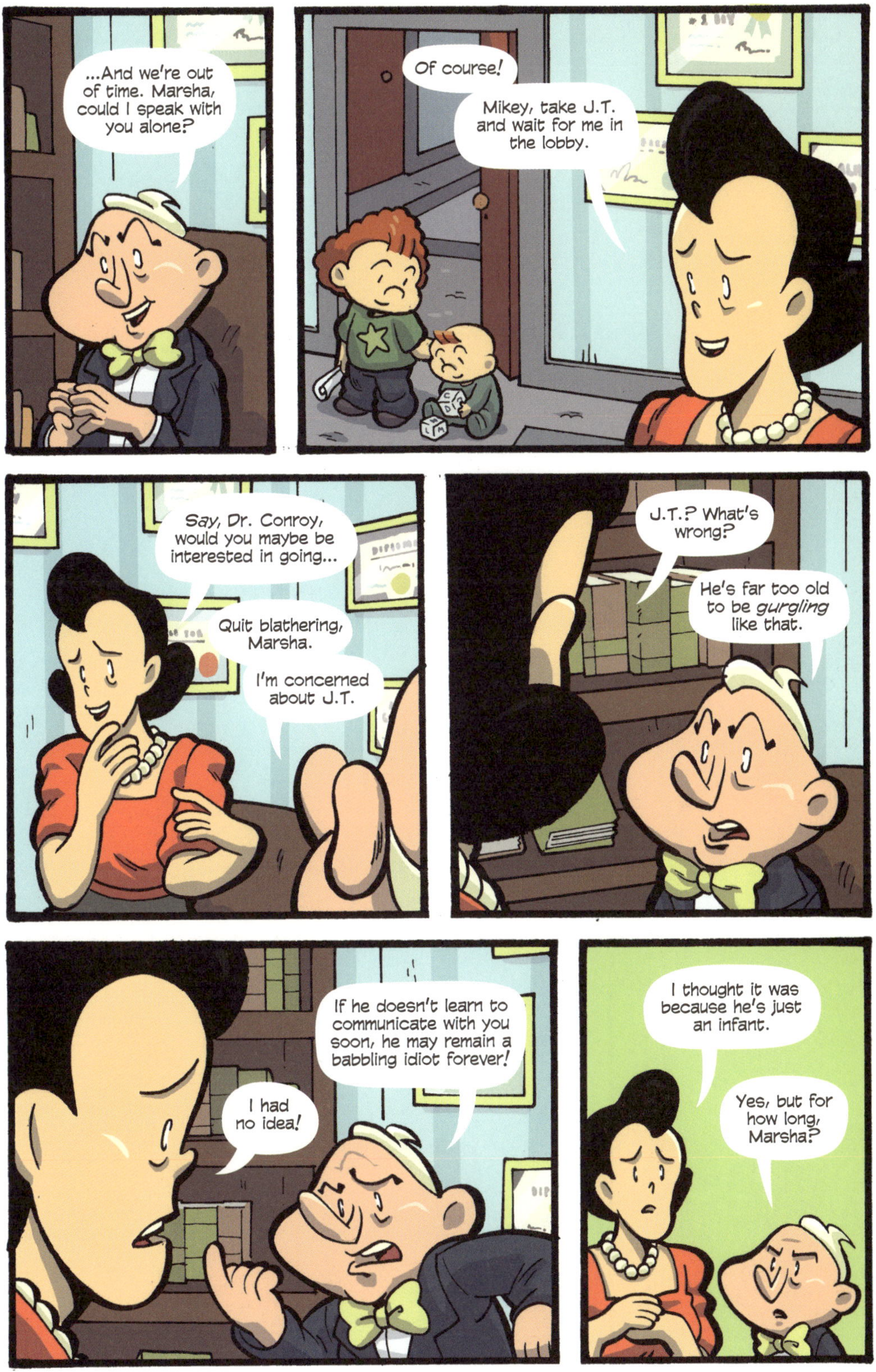
...And we're out of time. Marsha, could I speak with you alone?
Of course!
Mikey, take J.T. and wait for me in the lobby.
Say, Dr. Conroy, would you maybe be interested in going...
Quit blathering, Marsha.
I'm concerned about J.T.
J.T.? What's wrong?
He's far too old to be *gurgling* like that.
If he doesn't learn to communicate with you soon, he may remain a babbling idiot forever!
I had no idea!
I thought it was because he's just an infant.
Yes, but for how long, Marsha?

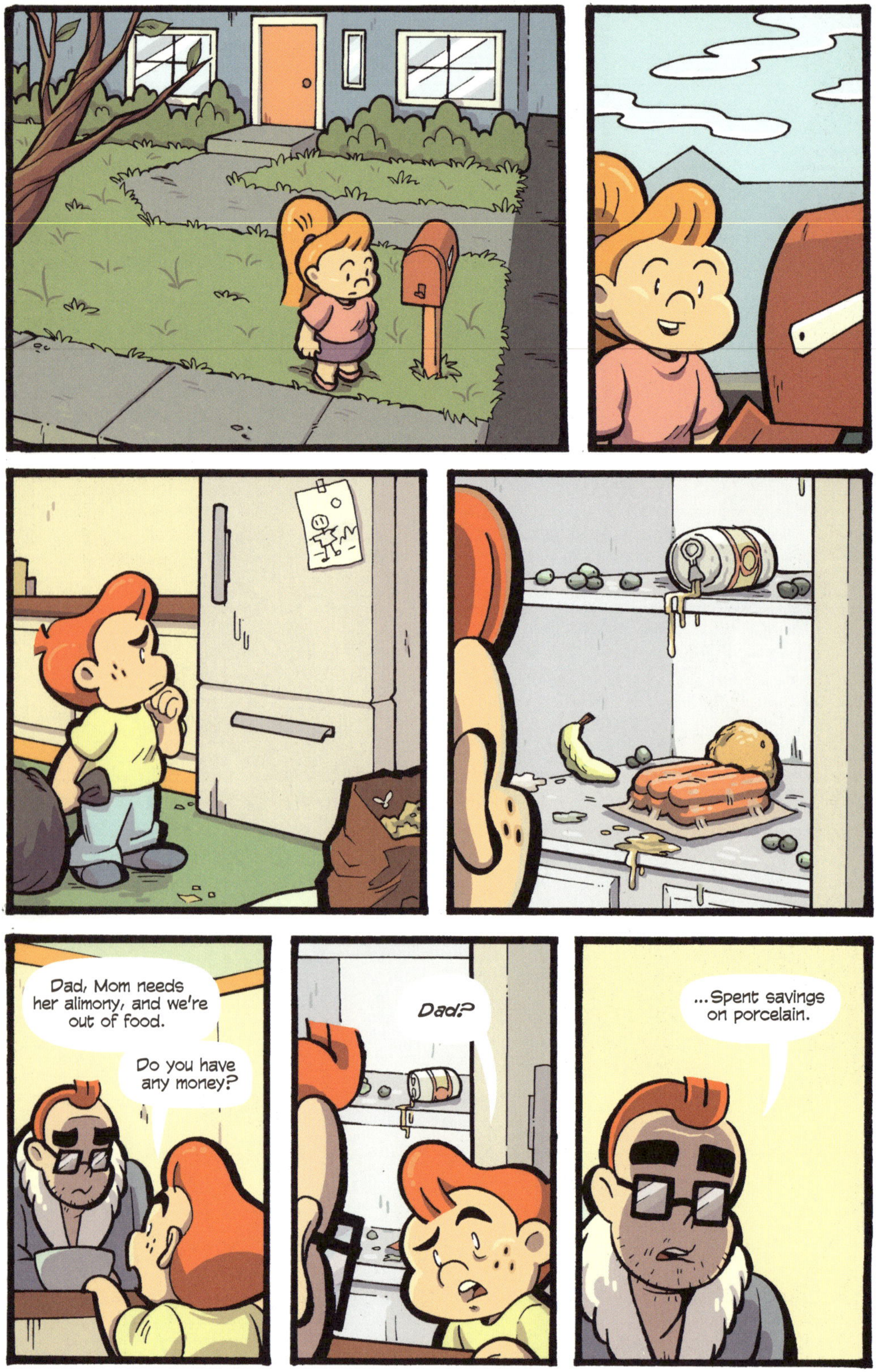

Dad, Mom needs her alimony, and we're out of food.
Do you have any money?
Dad?
...Spent savings on porcelain.

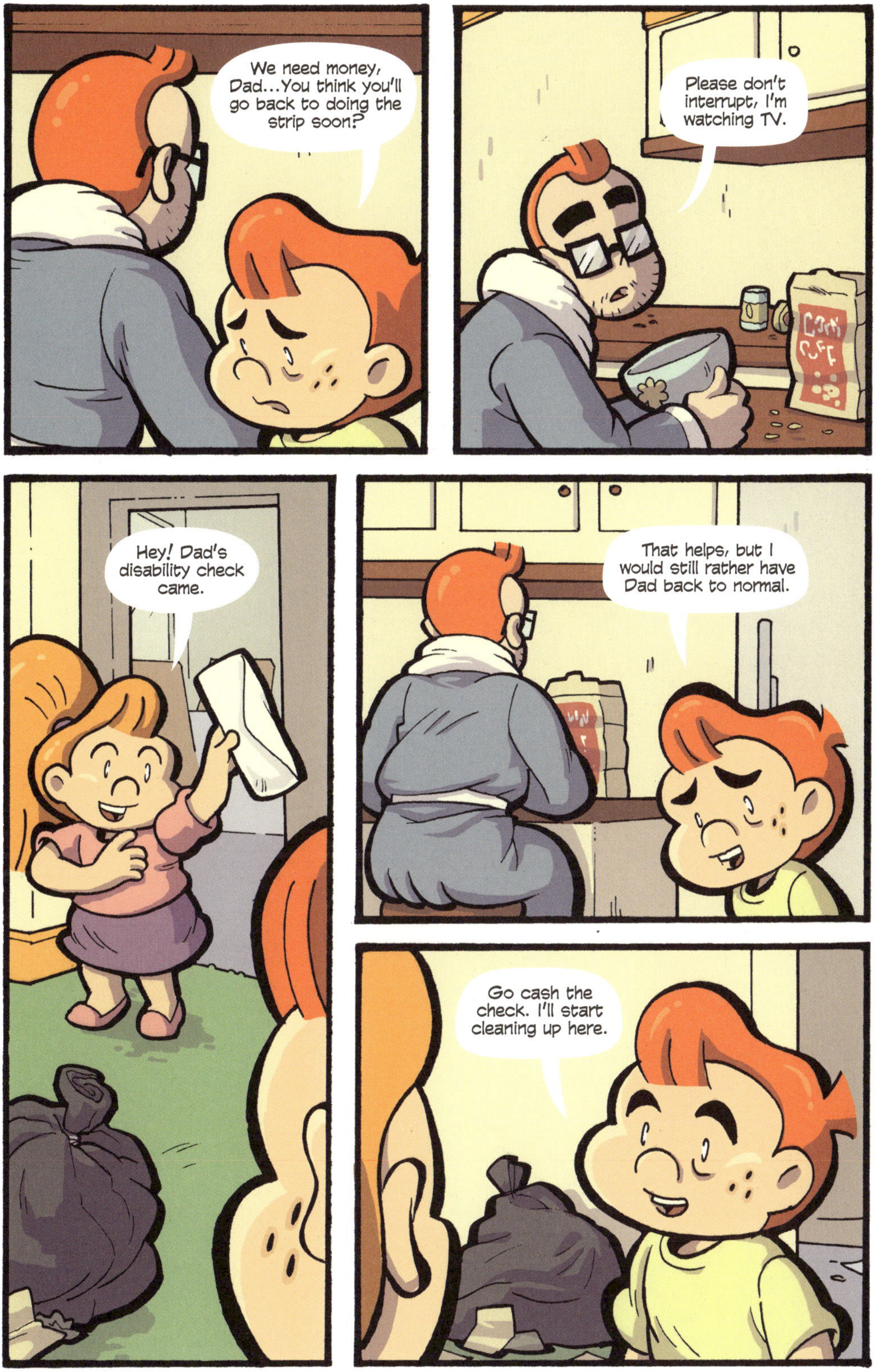
We need money, Dad...You think you'll go back to doing the strip soon?
Please don't interrupt, I'm watching TV.
Hey! Dad's disability check came.
That helps, but I would still rather have Dad back to normal.
Go cash the check. I'll start cleaning up here.

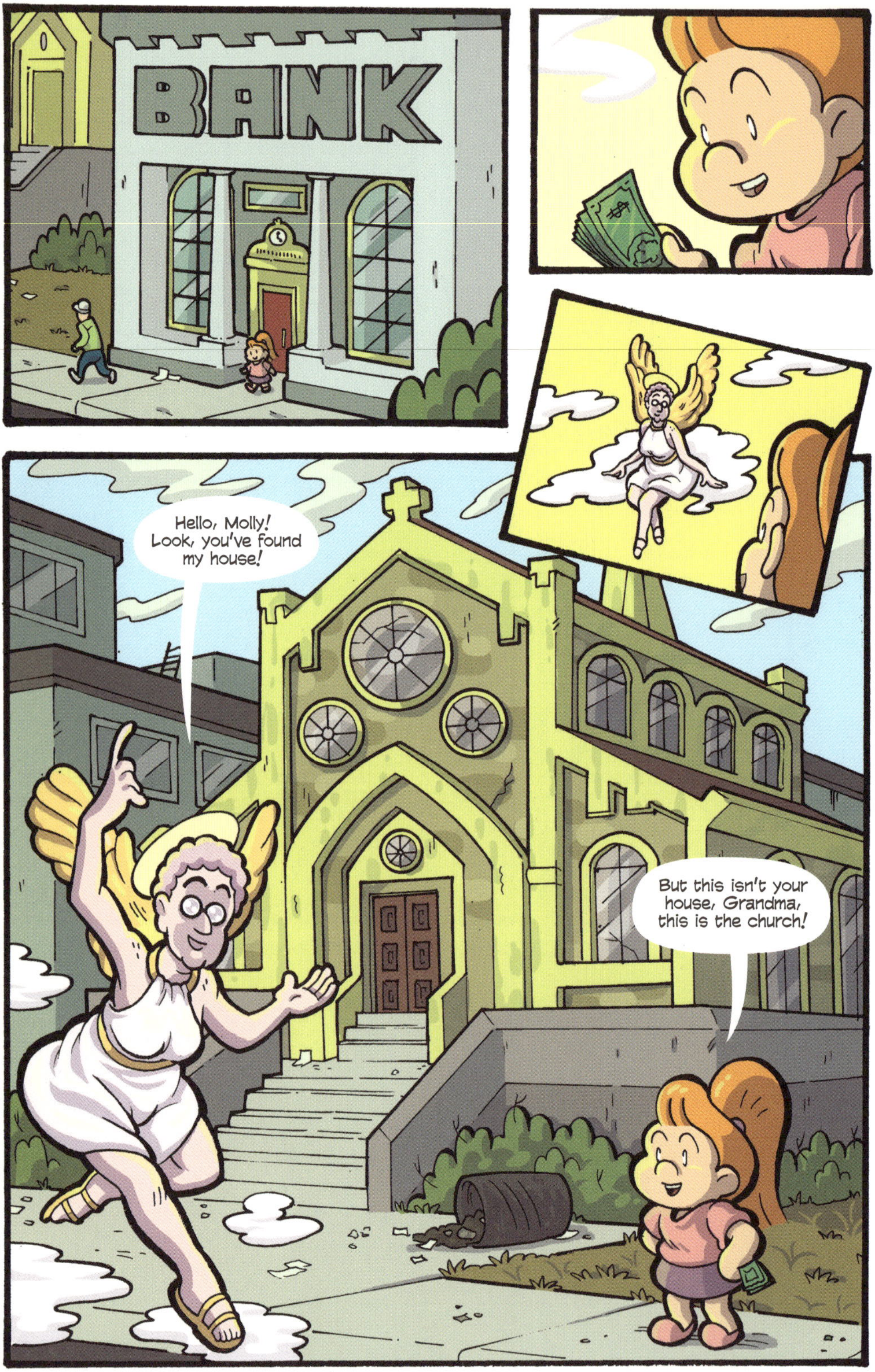
BANK
Hello, Molly! Look, you've found my house!
But this isn't your house, Grandma, this is the church!

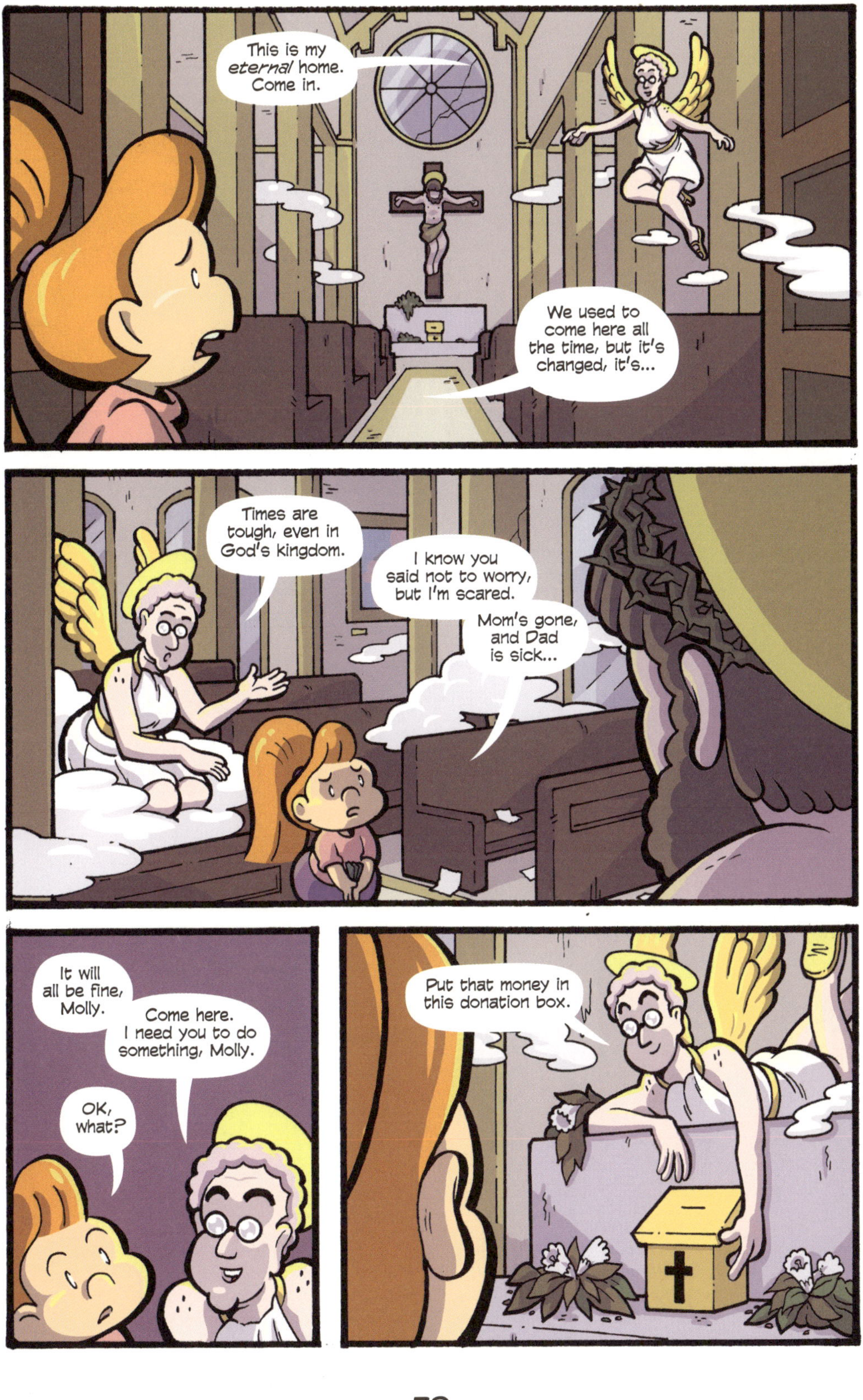

This is my *eternal* home. Come in.
We used to come here all the time, but it's changed, it's...
Times are tough, even in God's kingdom.
I know you said not to worry, but I'm scared.
Mom's gone, and Dad is sick...
It will all be fine, Molly.
Come here. I need you to do something, Molly.
OK, what?
Put that money in this donation box.

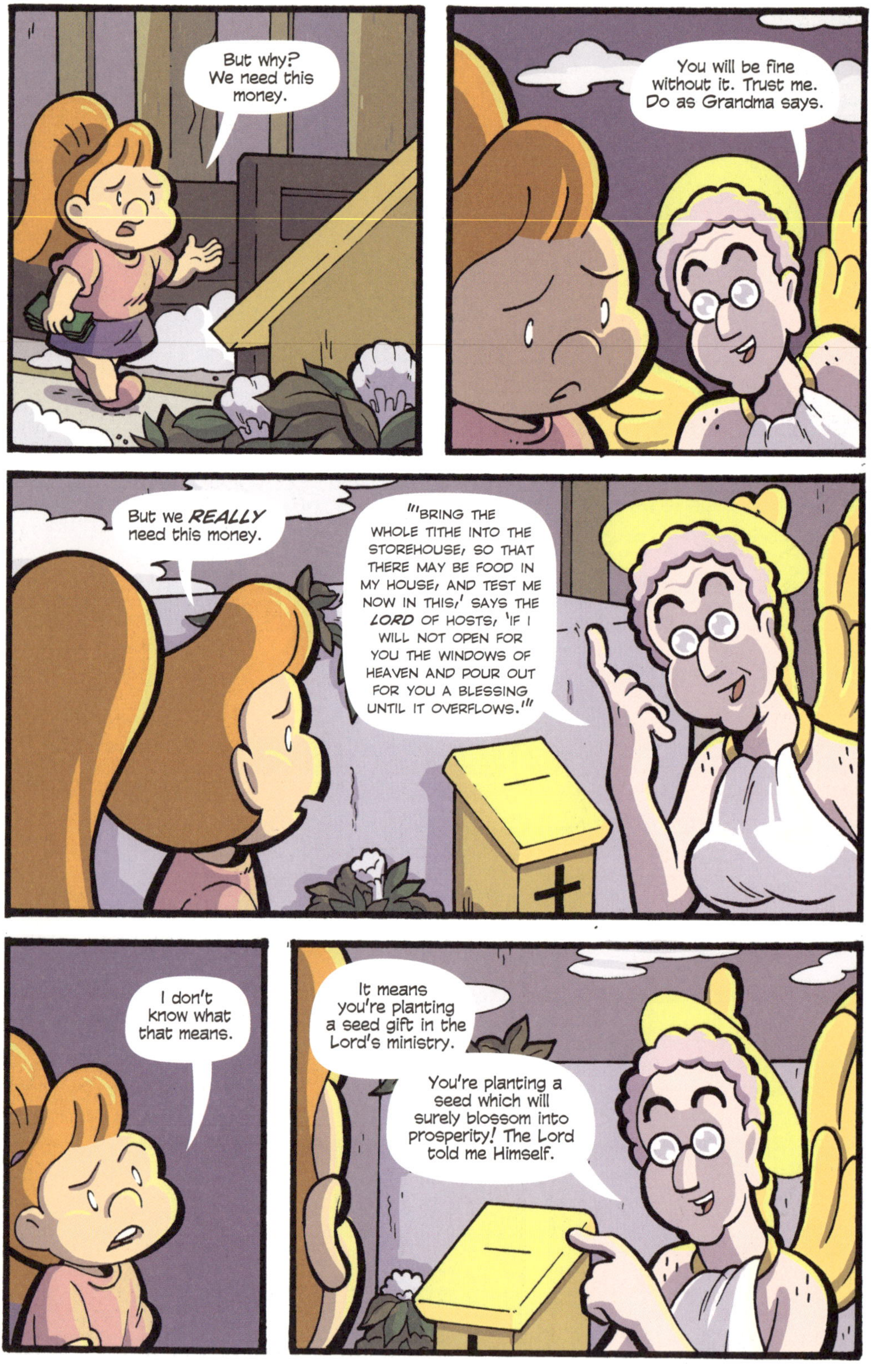
But why? We need this money.
You will be fine without it. Trust me. Do as Grandma says.
But we REALLY need this money.
"'BRING THE WHOLE TITHE INTO THE STOREHOUSE, SO THAT THERE MAY BE FOOD IN MY HOUSE, AND TEST ME NOW IN THIS,' SAYS THE LORD OF HOSTS, 'IF I WILL NOT OPEN FOR YOU THE WINDOWS OF HEAVEN AND POUR OUT FOR YOU A BLESSING UNTIL IT OVERFLOWS.'"
I don't know what that means.
It means you're planting a seed gift in the Lord's ministry.
You're planting a seed which will surely blossom into prosperity! The Lord told me Himself.

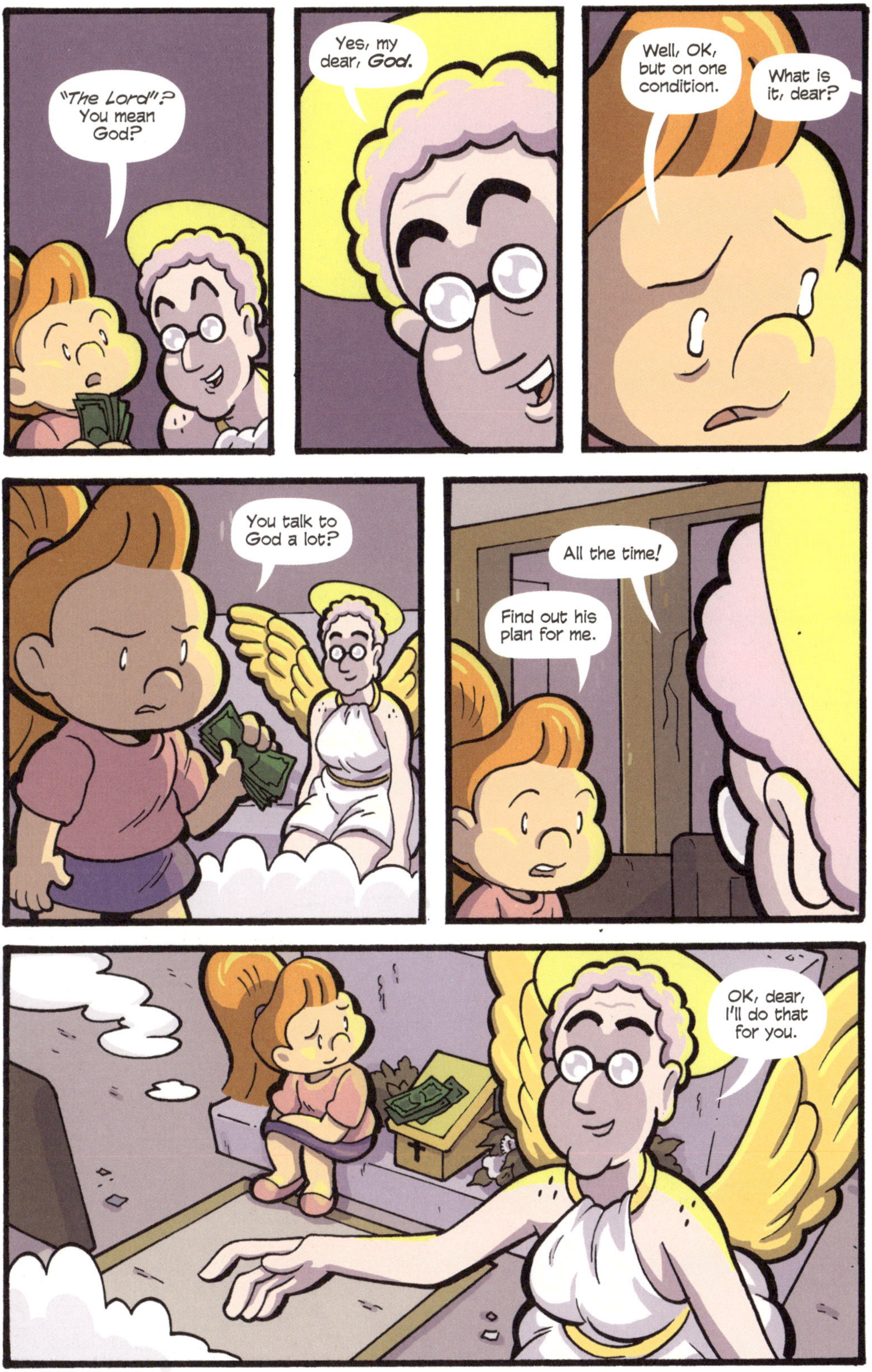
"The Lord"? You mean God?
Yes, my dear, God.
Well, OK, but on one condition.
What is it, dear?
You talk to God a lot?
All the time!
Find out his plan for me.
OK, dear, I'll do that for you.

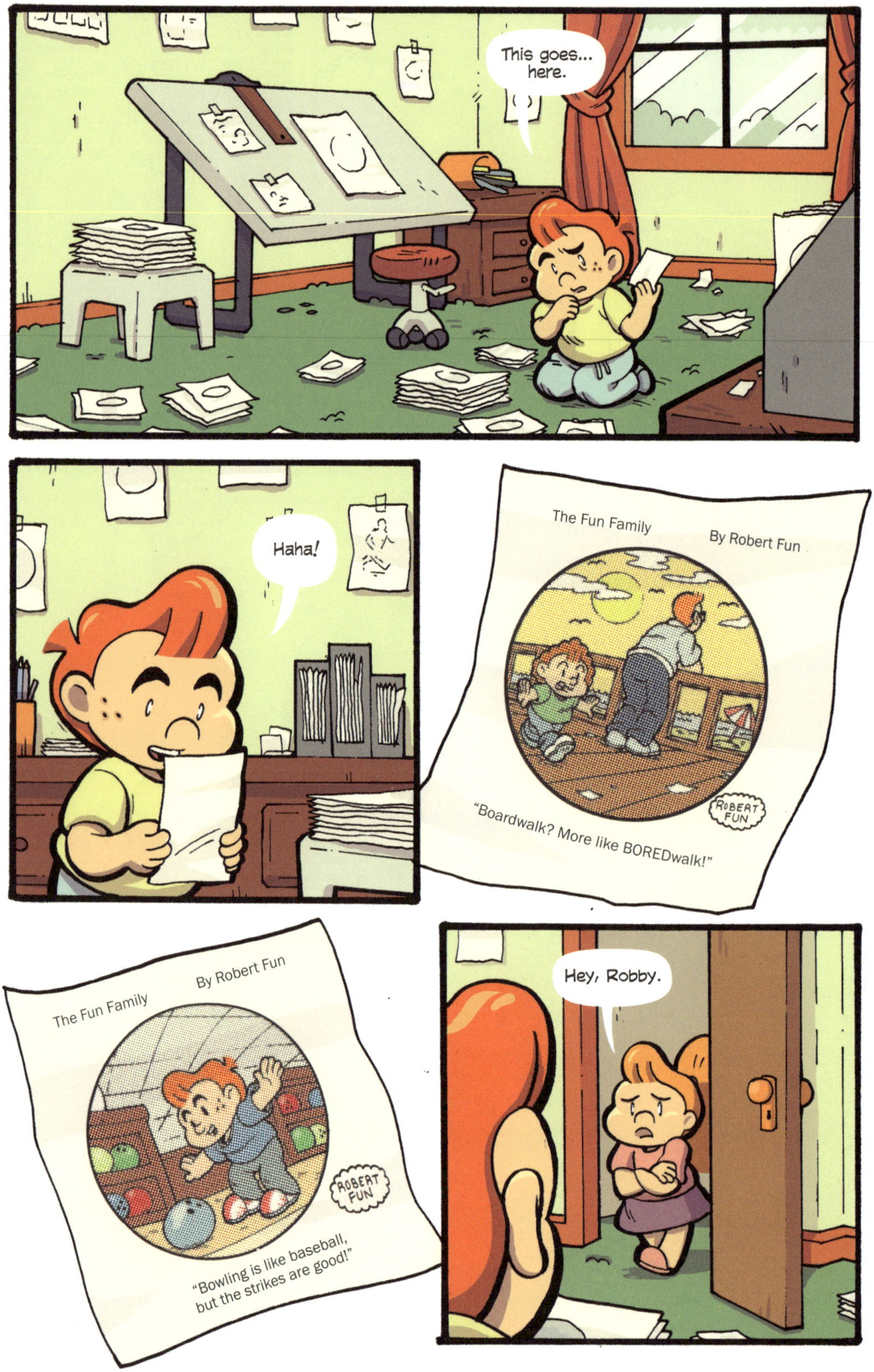
This goes... here.
Haha!
The Fun Family
By Robert Fun
ROBERT FUN
"Boardwalk? More like BOREDwalk!"
The Fun Family
By Robert Fun
ROBERT FUN
"Bowling is like baseball, but the strikes are good!"
Hey, Robby.

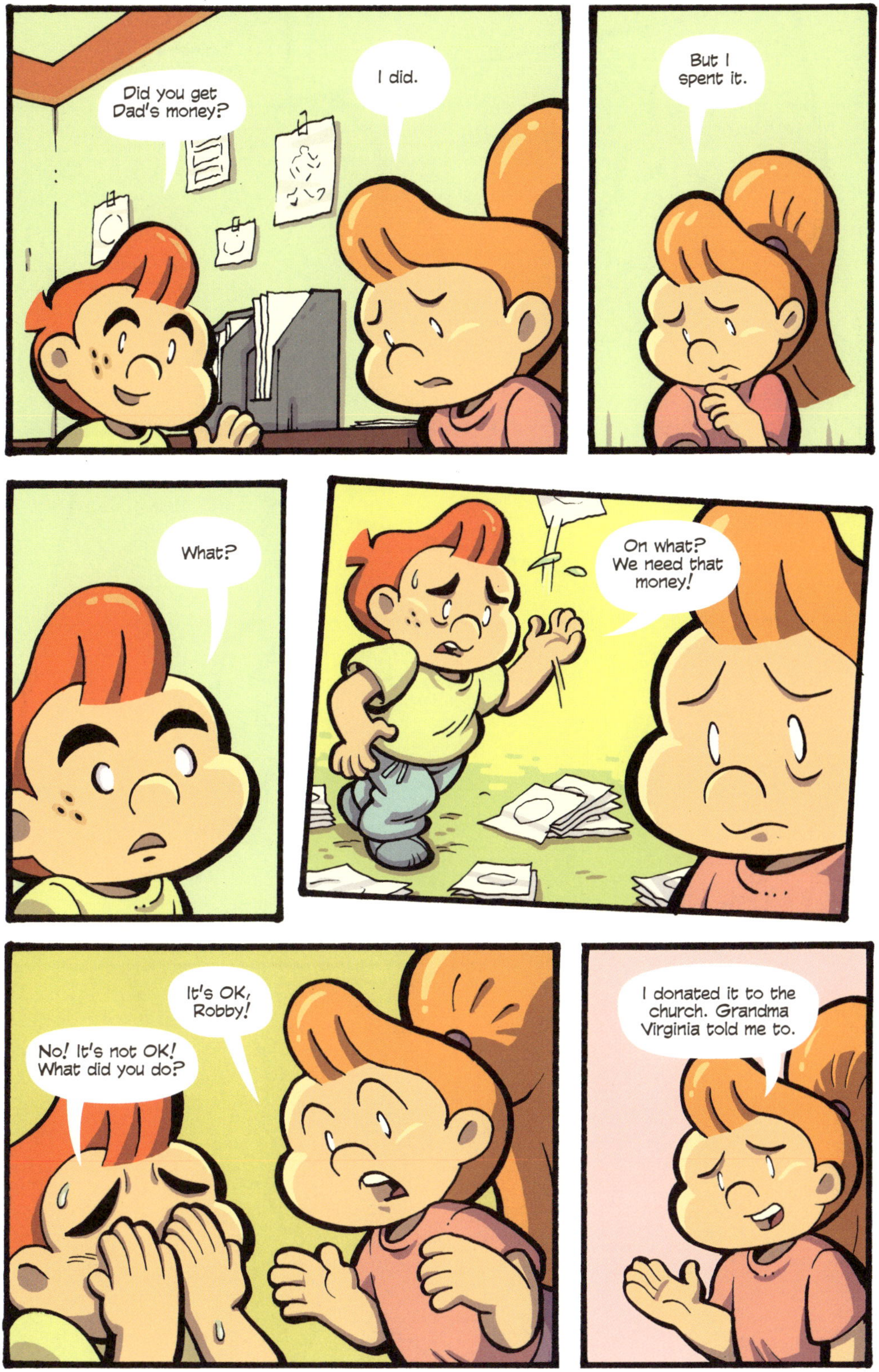
Did you get Dad's money?
I did.
But I spent it.
What?
On what? We need that money!
No! It's not OK! What did you do?
It's OK, Robby!
I donated it to the church. Grandma Virginia told me to.

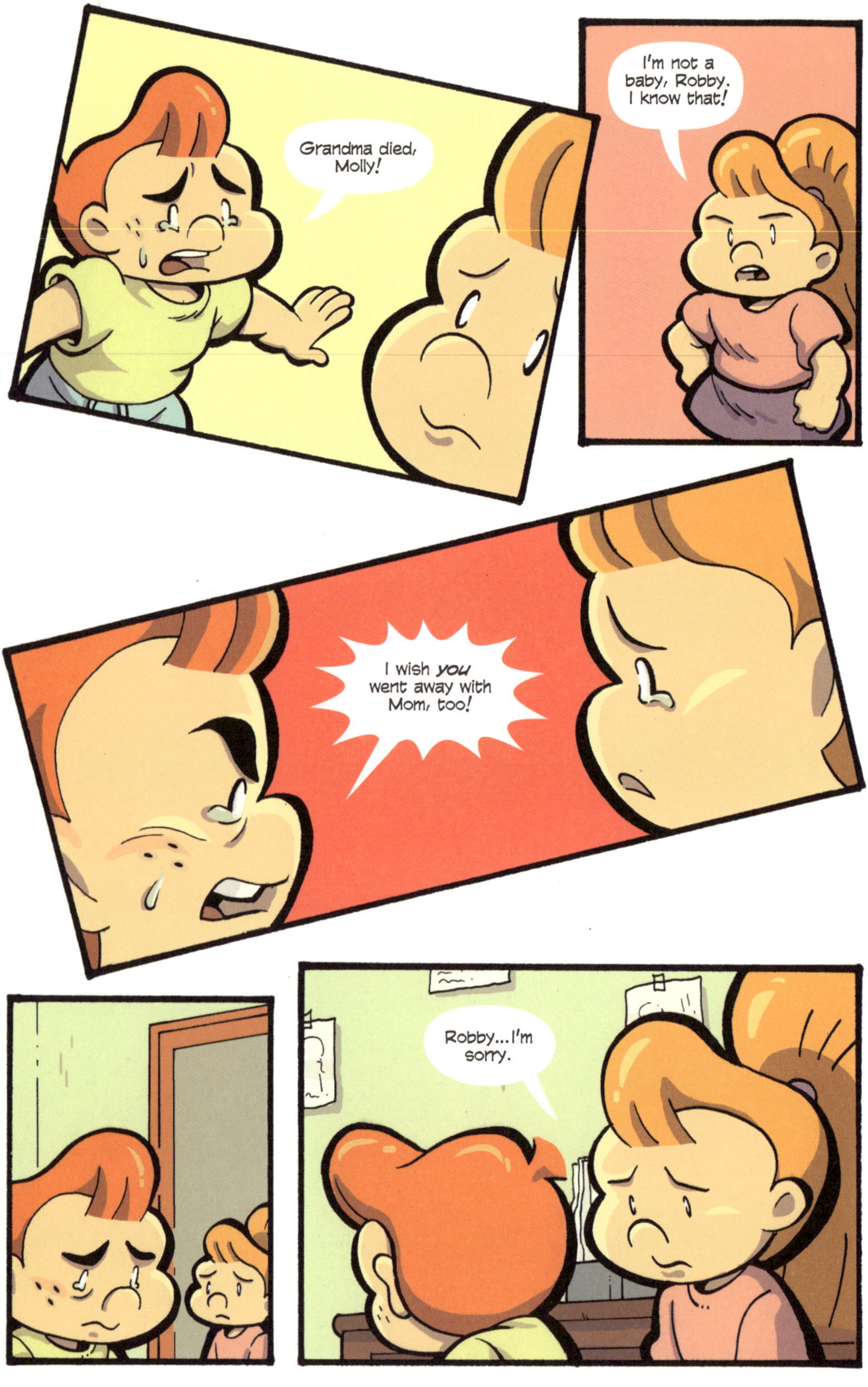
Grandma died, Molly!
I'm not a baby, Robby. I know that!
I wish *you* went away with Mom, too!
Robby...I'm sorry.

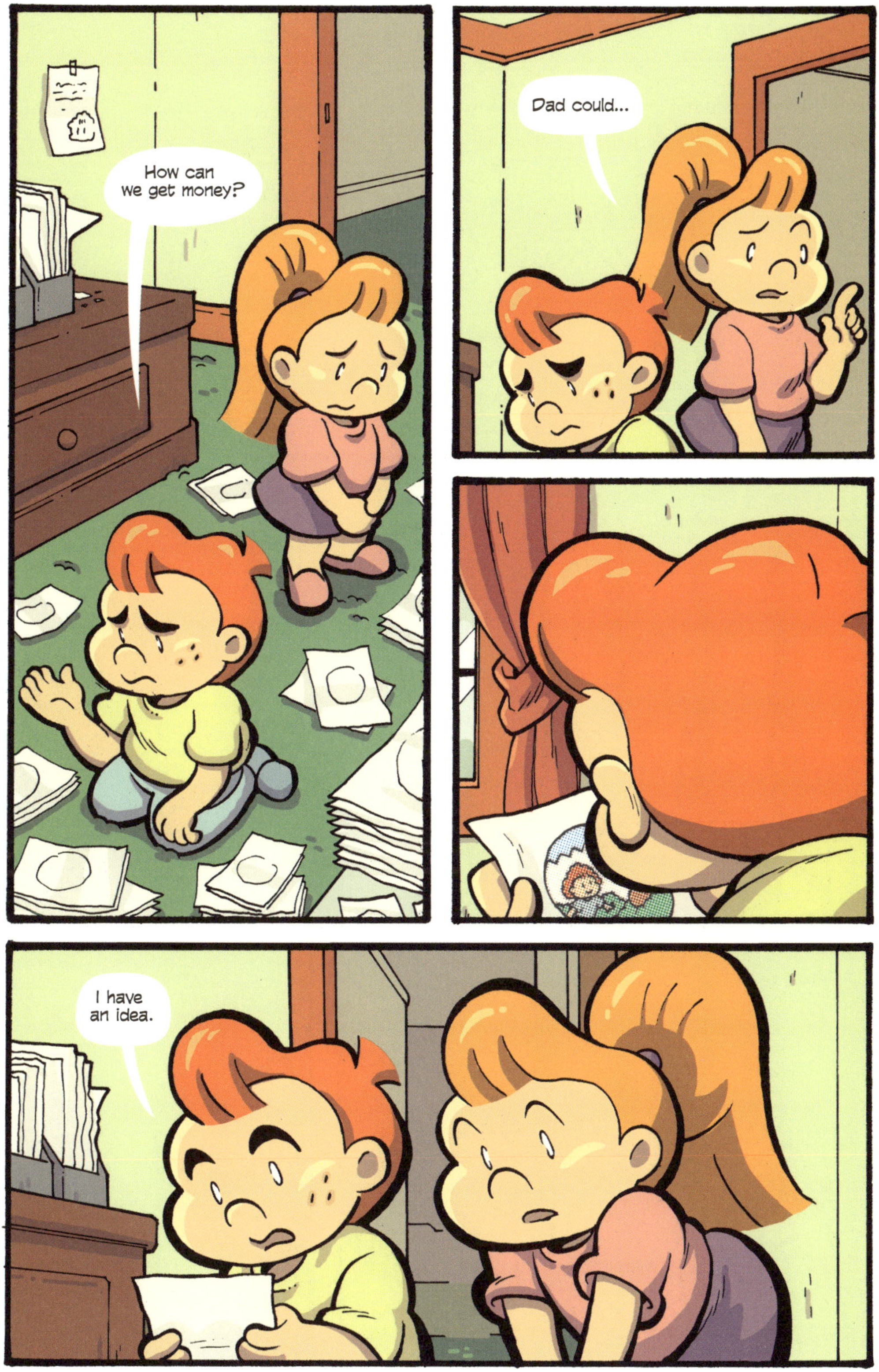
How can we get money?
Dad could...
I have an idea.

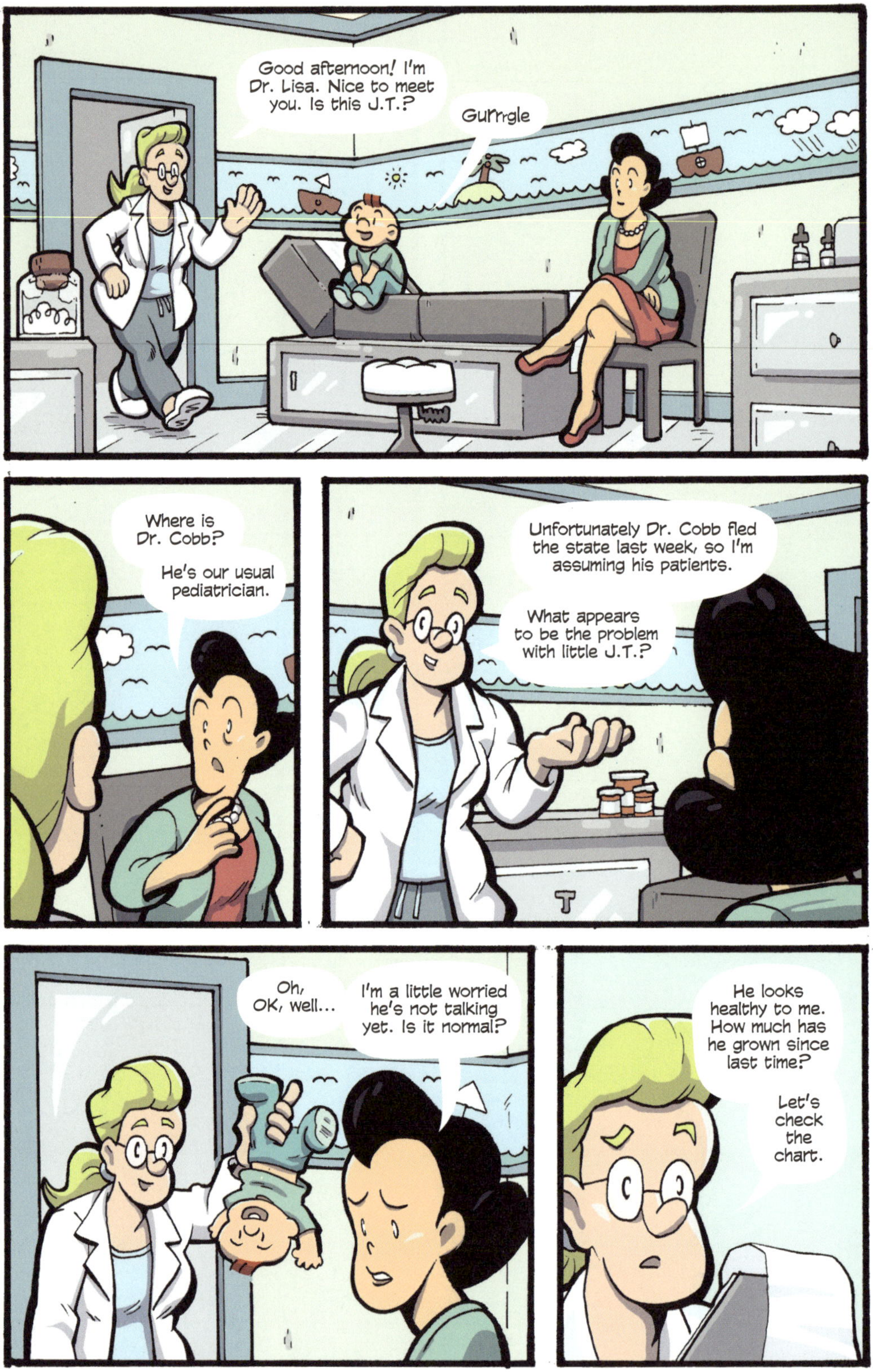
Good afternoon! I'm Dr. Lisa. Nice to meet you. Is this J.T.?
Gurrrgle
Where is Dr. Cobb?
He's our usual pediatrician.
Unfortunately Dr. Cobb fled the state last week, so I'm assuming his patients.
What appears to be the problem with little J.T.?
Oh, OK, well...
I'm a little worried he's not talking yet. Is it normal?
He looks healthy to me. How much has he grown since last time?
Let's check the chart.

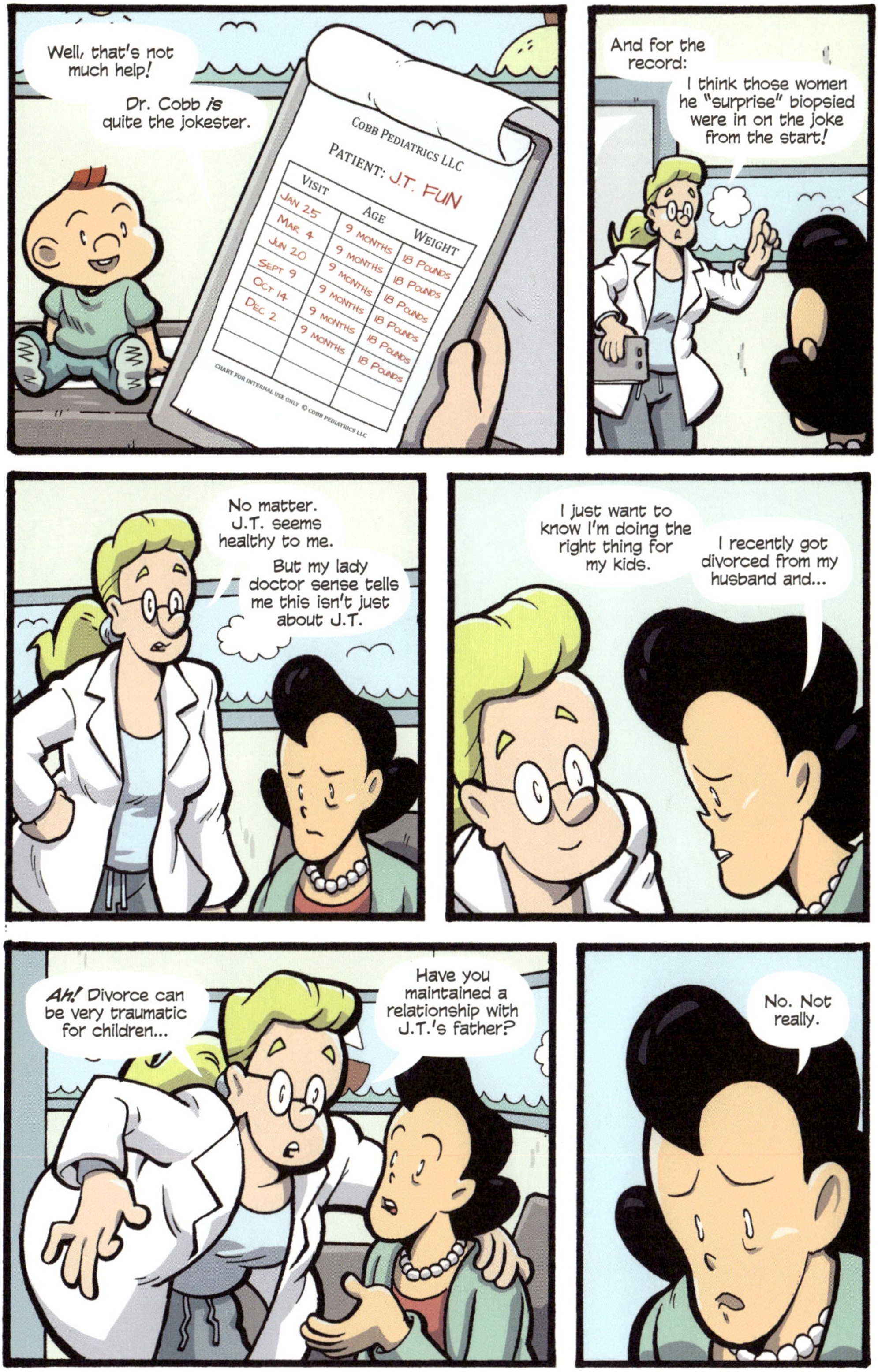
Well, that's not much help!
Dr. Cobb *is* quite the jokester.
Cobb Pediatrics LLC
Patient: J.T. Fun
Visit
Age
Weight
Jan 25
9 Months
18 Pounds
Mar 4
9 Months
18 Pounds
Jun 20
9 Months
18 Pounds
Sept 9
9 Months
18 Pounds
Oct 14
9 Months
18 Pounds
Dec 2
9 Months
18 Pounds
Chart for internal use only © Cobb Pediatrics LLC
And for the record:
I think those women he "surprise" biopsied were in on the joke from the start!
No matter. J.T. seems healthy to me.
But my lady doctor sense tells me this isn't just about J.T.
I just want to know I'm doing the right thing for my kids.
I recently got divorced from my husband and...
Ah! Divorce can be very traumatic for children...
Have you maintained a relationship with J.T.'s father?
No. Not really.

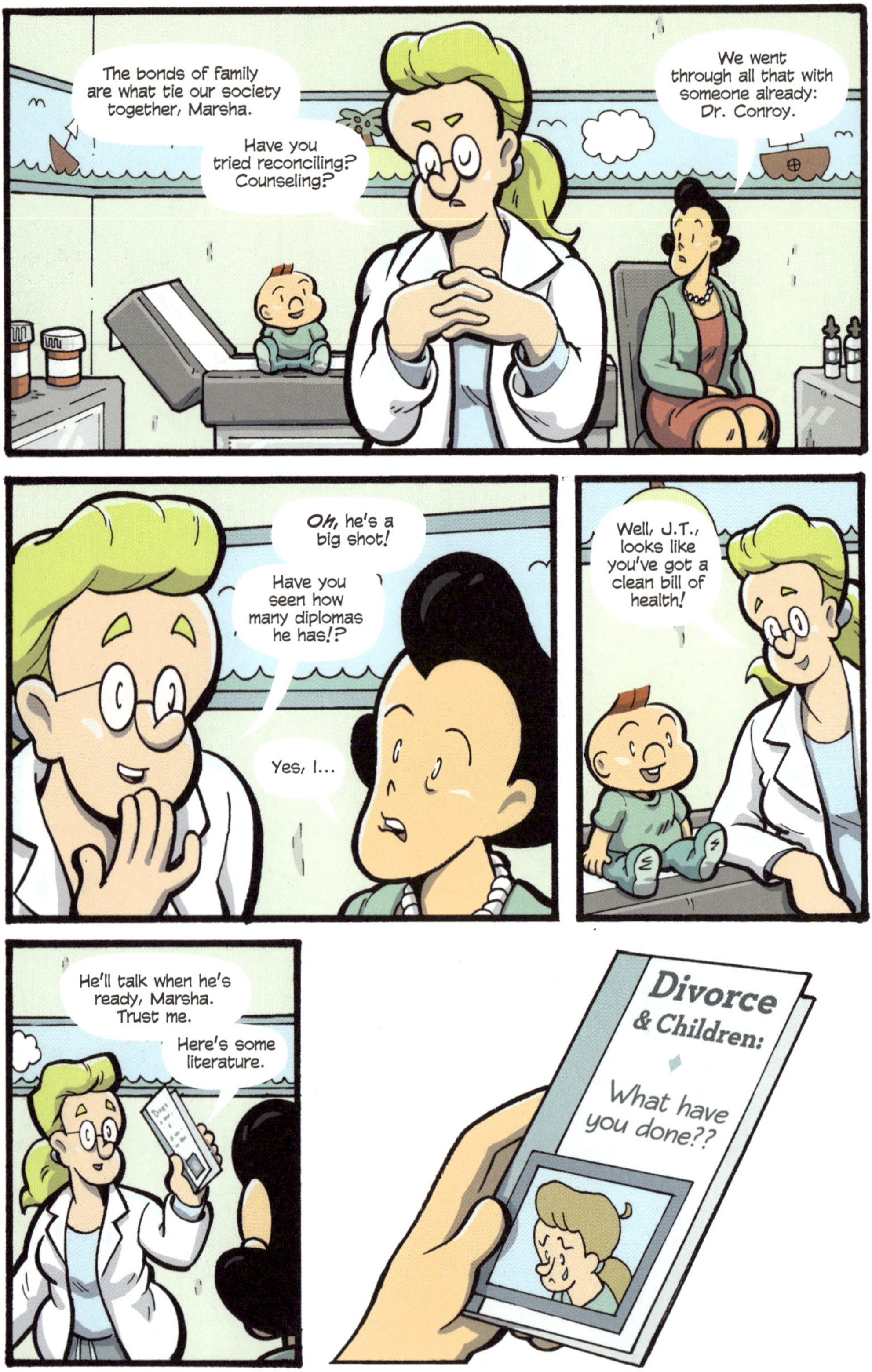
The bonds of family are what tie our society together, Marsha.
Have you tried reconciling? Counseling?
We went through all that with someone already: Dr. Conroy.
Oh, he's a big shot!
Have you seen how many diplomas he has!?
Yes, I...
Well, J.T., looks like you've got a clean bill of health!
He'll talk when he's ready, Marsha. Trust me.
Here's some literature.
Divorce & Children:
What have you done??

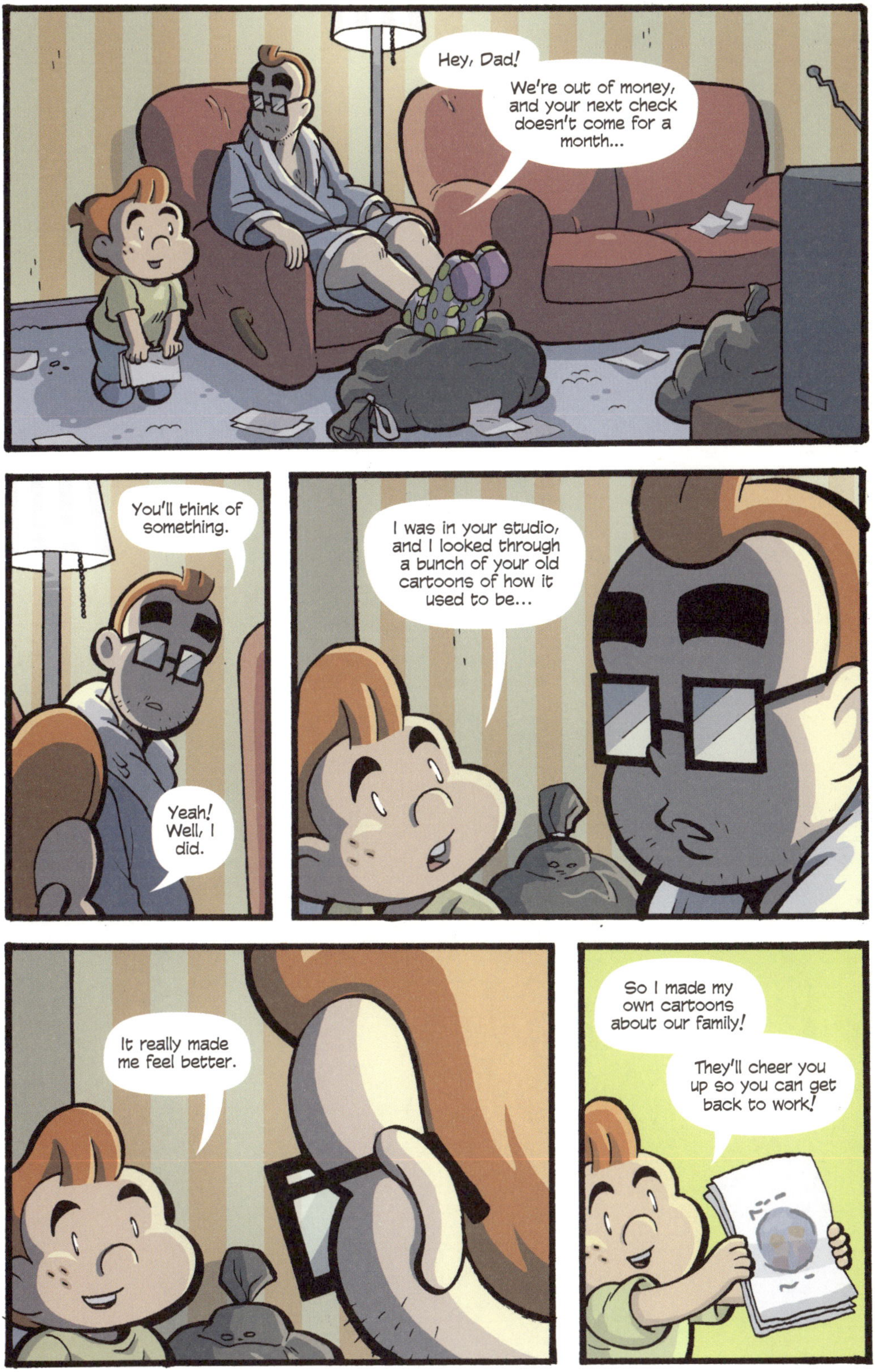

Hey, Dad!
We're out of money, and your next check doesn't come for a month...
You'll think of something.
Yeah! Well, I did.
I was in your studio, and I looked through a bunch of your old cartoons of how it used to be...
It really made me feel better.
So I made my own cartoons about our family!
They'll cheer you up so you can get back to work!

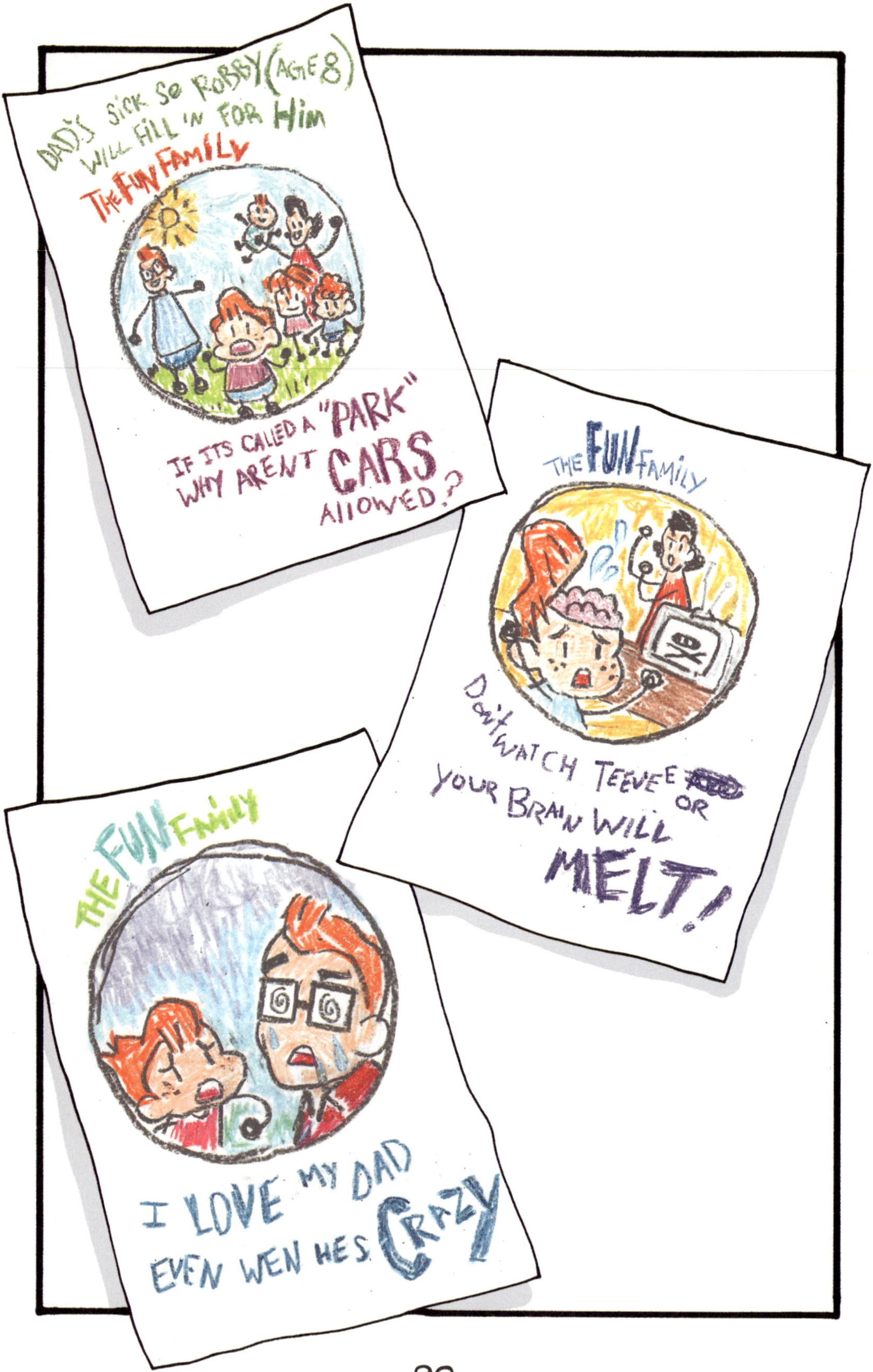
DAD'S SICK SO ROBBY (AGE 8) WILL FILL IN FOR HIM
THE FUN FAMILY
IF ITS CALLED A "PARK" WHY AREN'T CARS ALLOWED?
THE FUN FAMILY
Don't WATCH TEEVEE OR YOUR BRAIN WILL MELT!
THE FUN FAMILY
I LOVE MY DAD EVEN WEN HES CRAZY

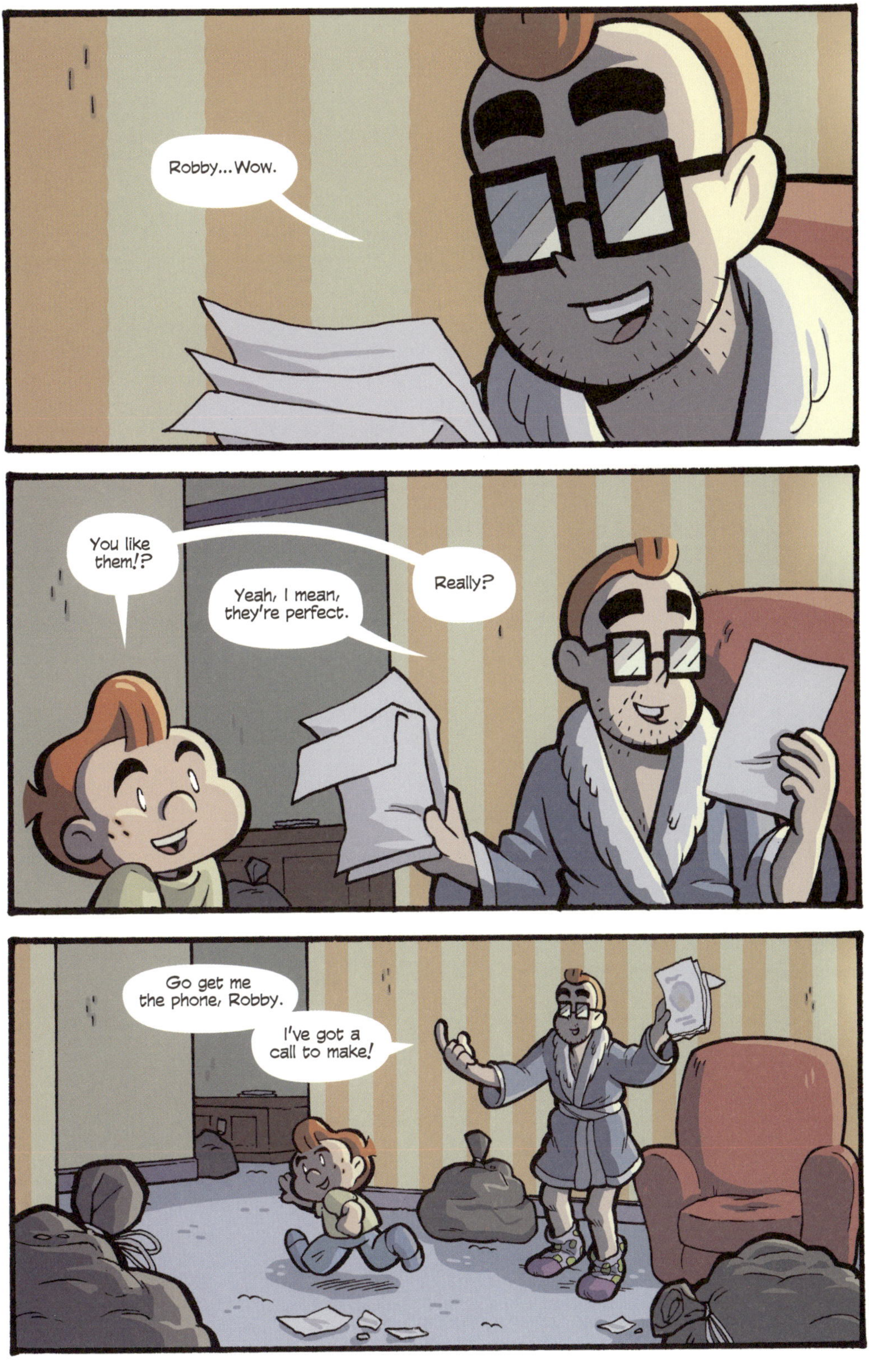
Robby... Wow.
You like them!?
Yeah, I mean, they're perfect.
Really?
Go get me the phone, Robby.
I've got a call to make!

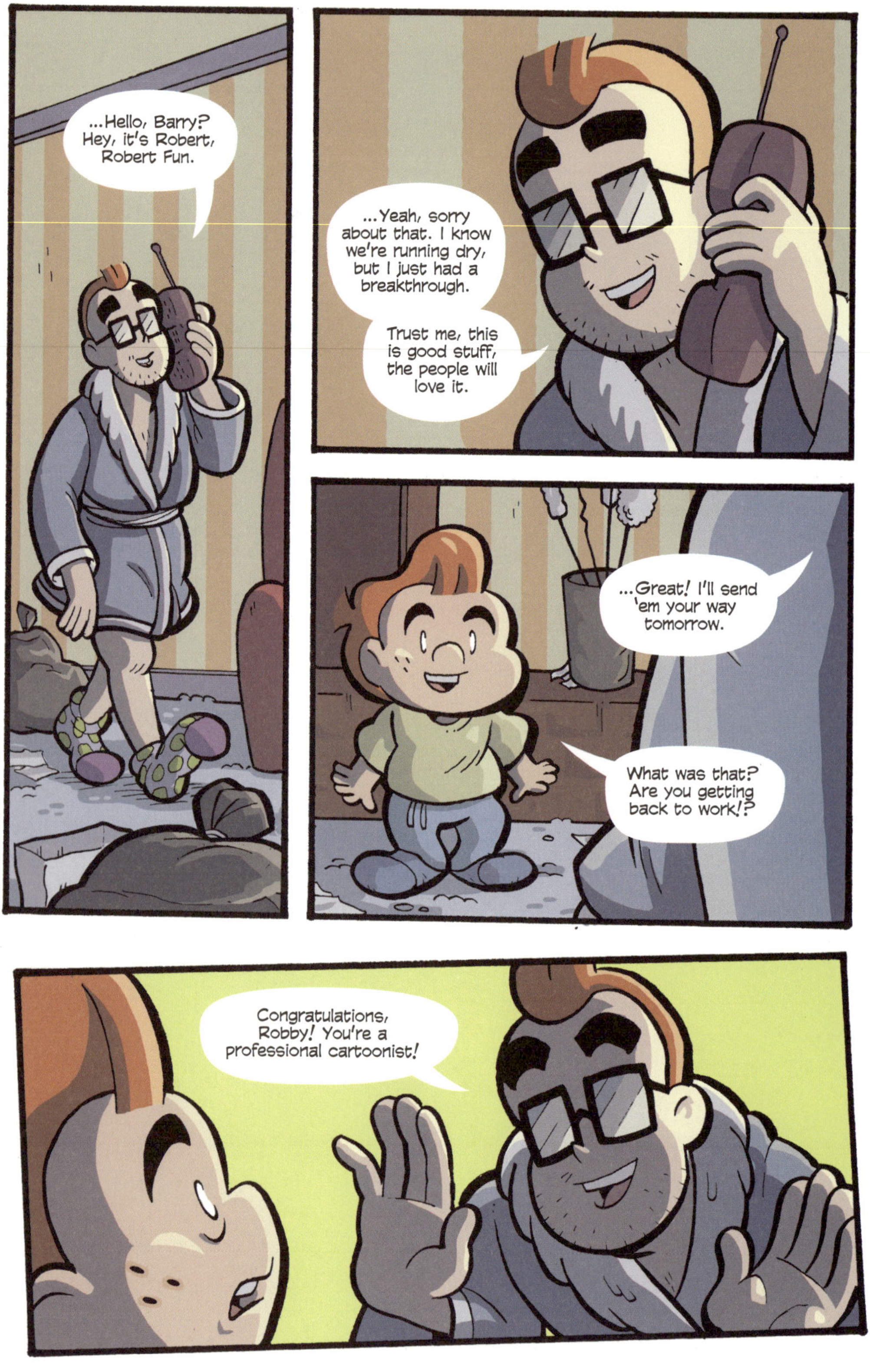
...Hello, Barry? Hey, it's Robert, Robert Fun.
...Yeah, sorry about that. I know we're running dry, but I just had a breakthrough.
Trust me, this is good stuff, the people will love it.
...Great! I'll send 'em your way tomorrow.
What was that? Are you getting back to work!?
Congratulations, Robby! You're a professional cartoonist!

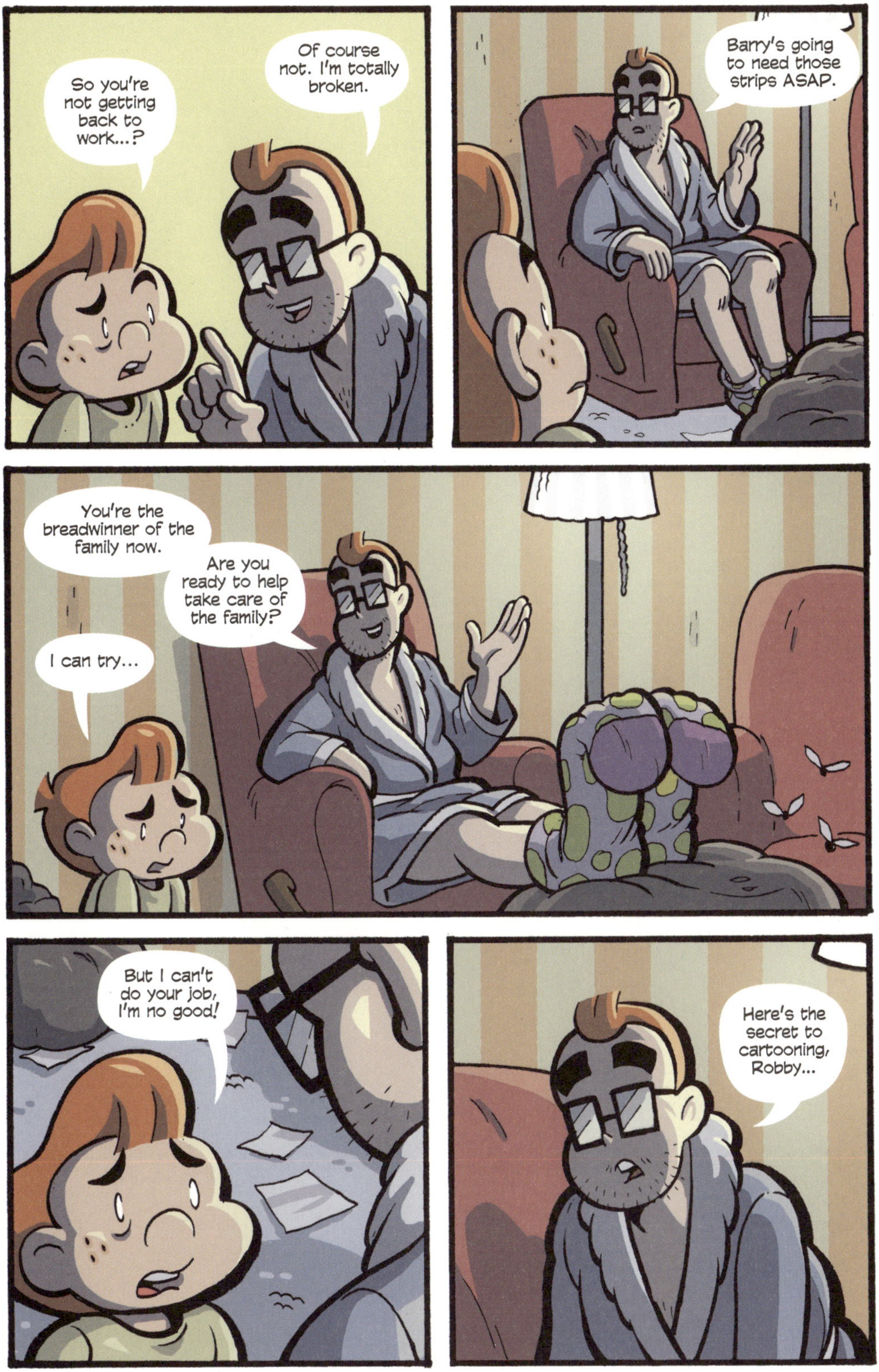
So you're not getting back to work...?
Of course not. I'm totally broken.
Barry's going to need those strips ASAP.
You're the breadwinner of the family now.
Are you ready to help take care of the family?
I can try...
But I can't do your job, I'm no good!
Here's the secret to cartooning, Robby...

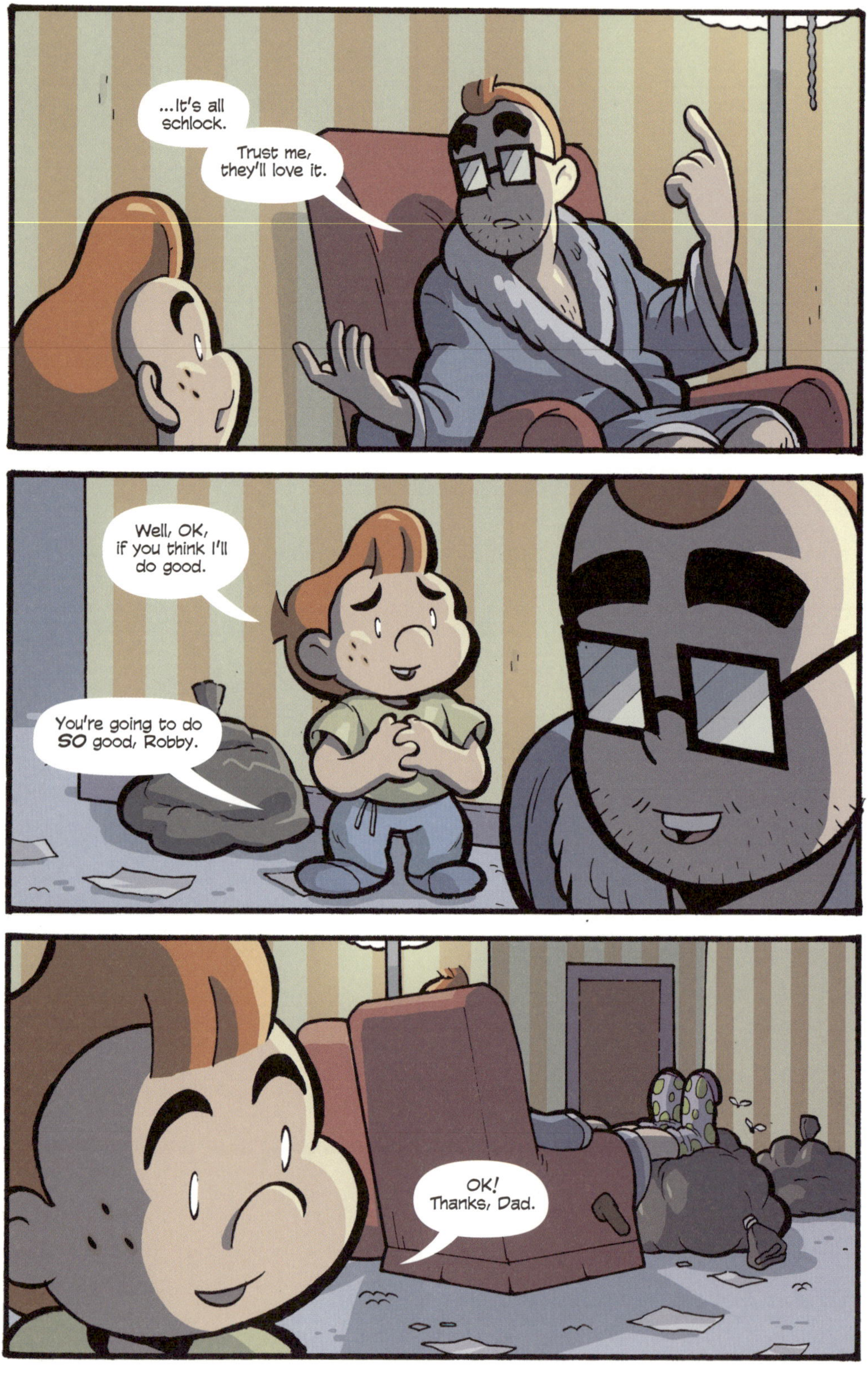
...It's all schlock.
Trust me, they'll love it.
Well, OK, if you think I'll do good.
You're going to do SO good, Robby.
OK! Thanks, Dad.

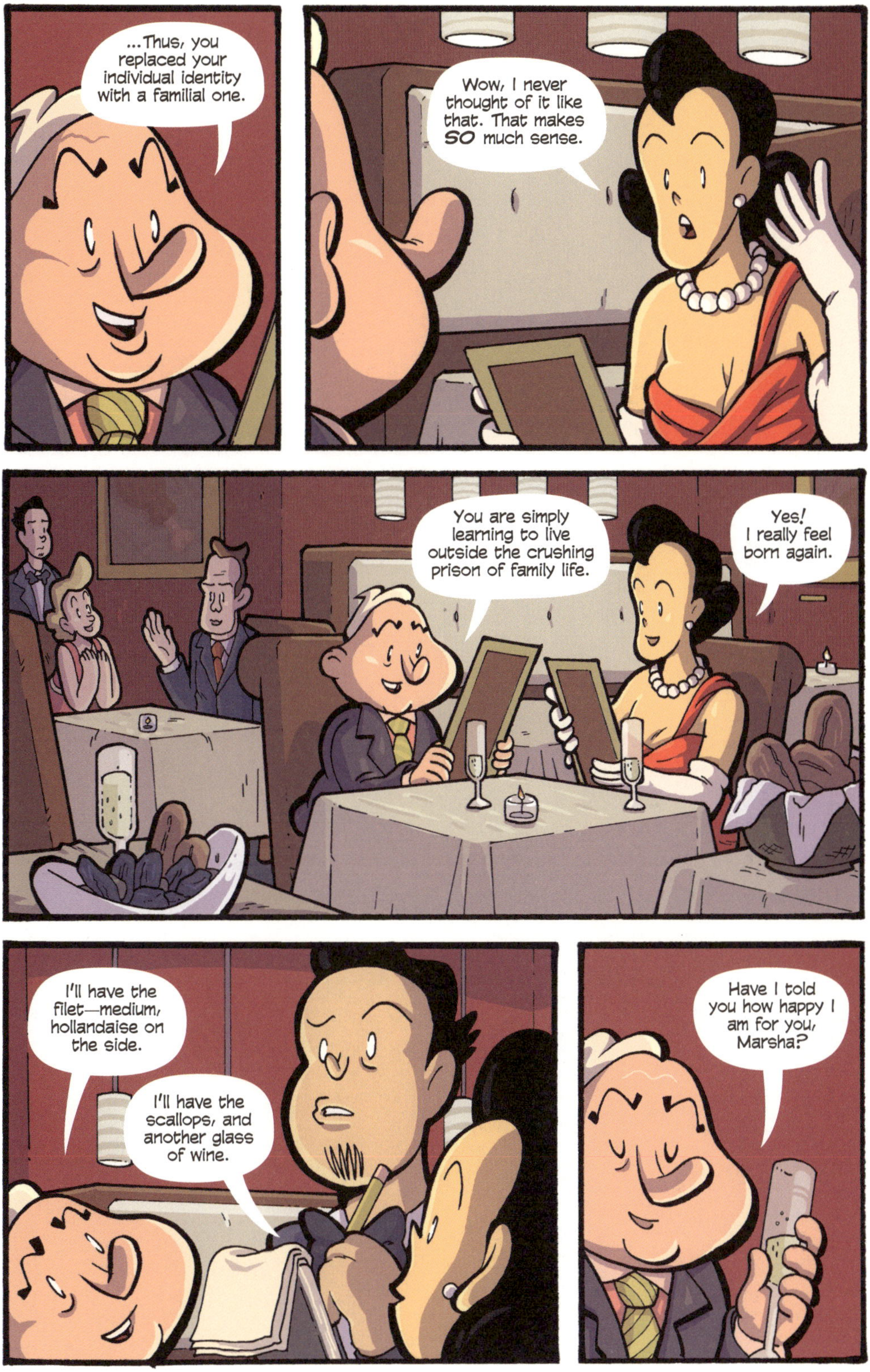
...Thus, you replaced your individual identity with a familial one.
Wow, I never thought of it like that. That makes SO much sense.
You are simply learning to live outside the crushing prison of family life.
Yes! I really feel born again.
I'll have the filet—medium, hollandaise on the side.
I'll have the scallops, and another glass of wine.
Have I told you how happy I am for you, Marsha?

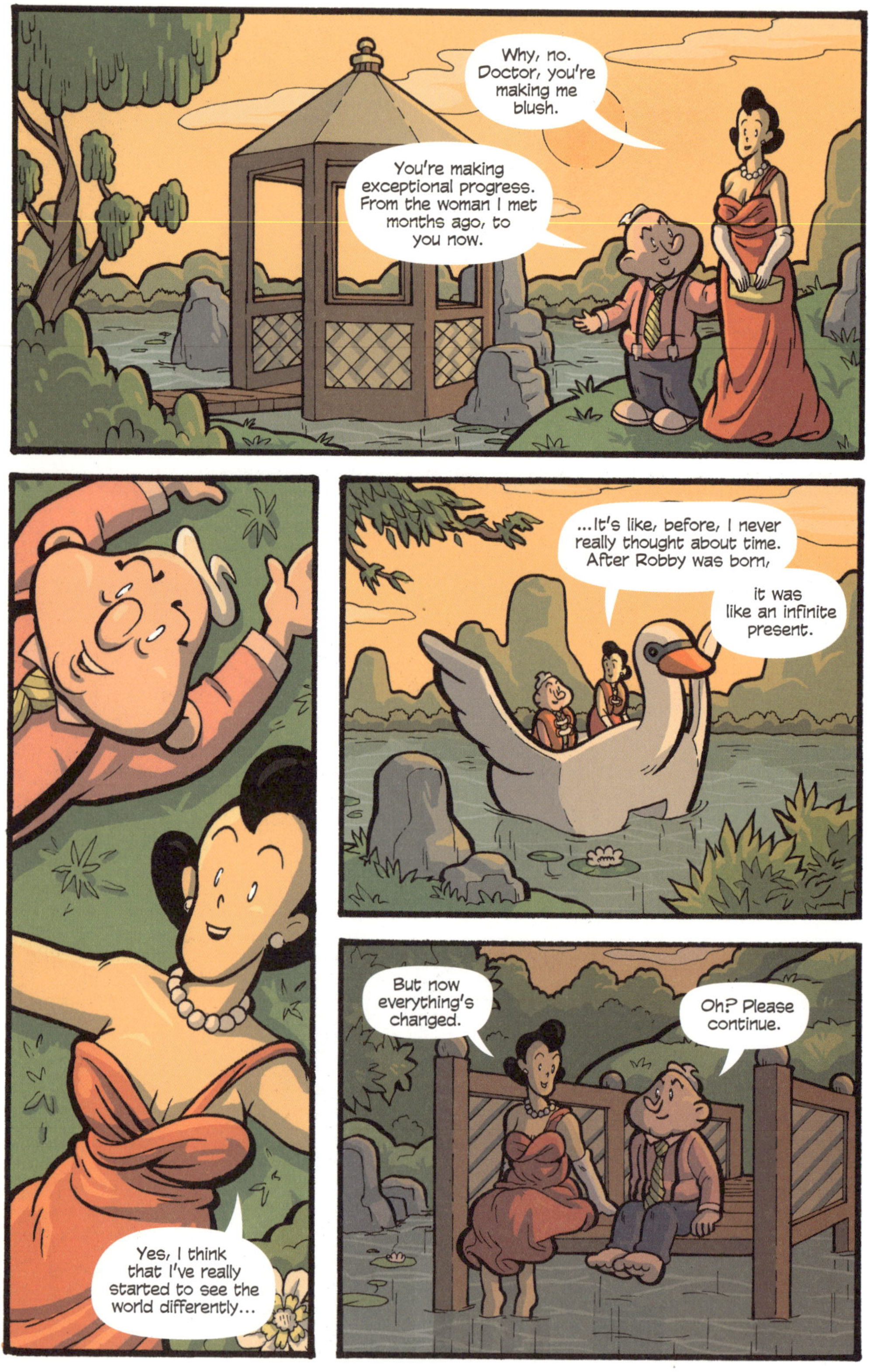

You're making exceptional progress. From the woman I met months ago, to you now.
Why, no. Doctor, you're making me blush.
Yes, I think that I've really started to see the world differently...
...It's like, before, I never really thought about time. After Robby was born,
it was like an infinite present.
But now everything's changed.
Oh? Please continue.

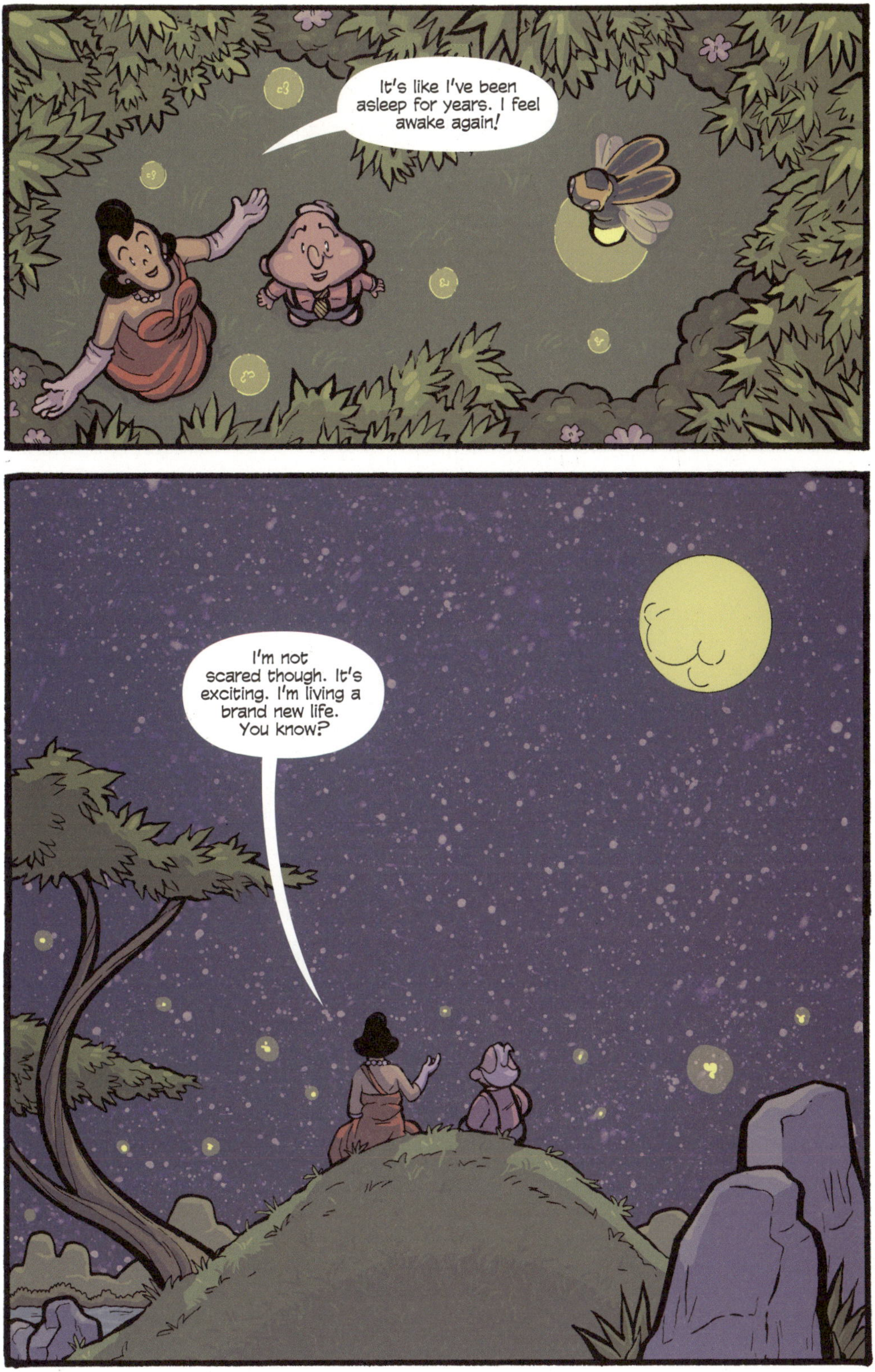
It's like I've been asleep for years. I feel awake again!
I'm not scared though. It's exciting. I'm living a brand new life. You know?

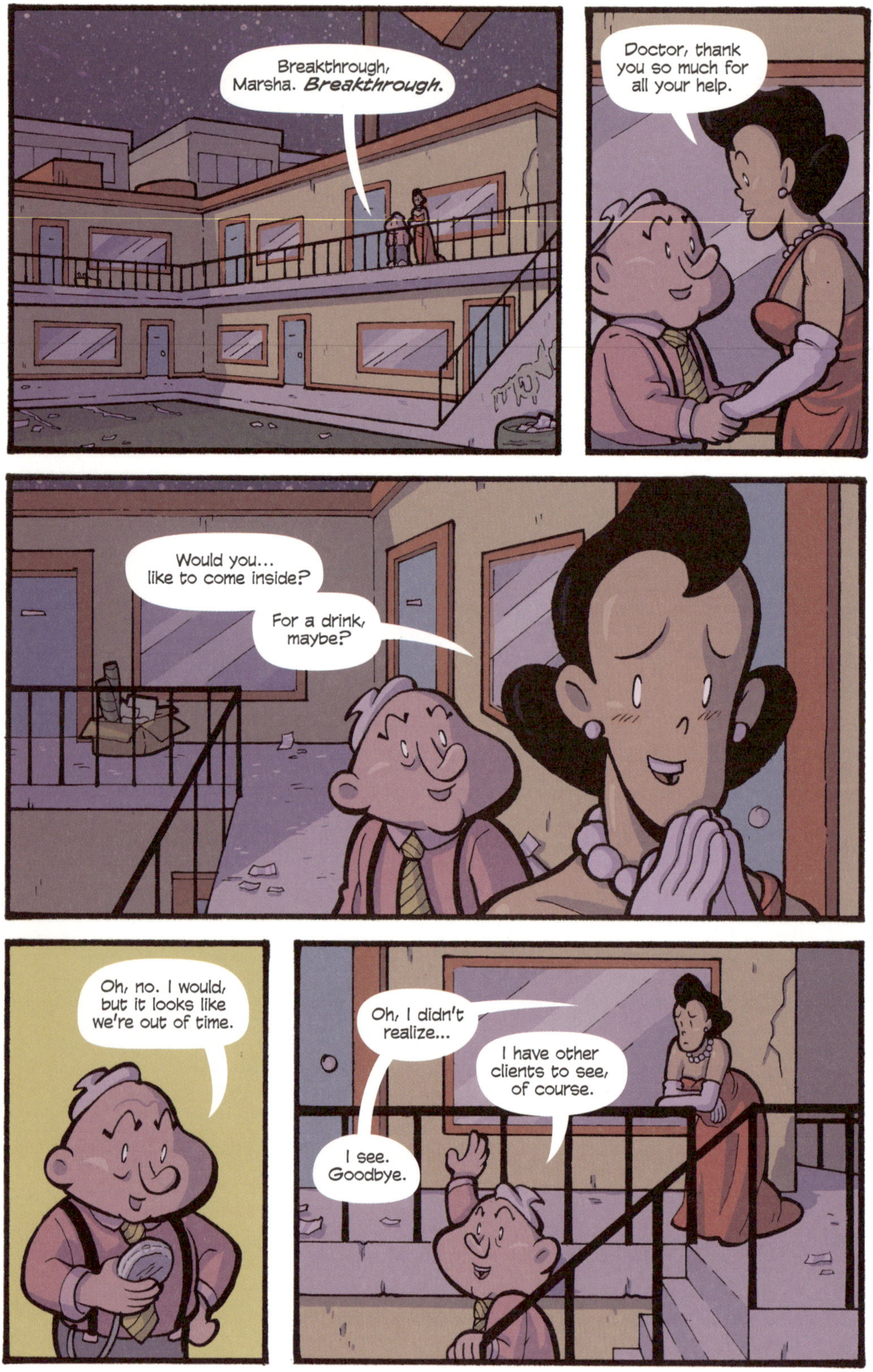
Breakthrough, Marsha. *Breakthrough.*
Doctor, thank you so much for all your help.
Would you... like to come inside?
For a drink, maybe?
Oh, no. I would, but it looks like we're out of time.
Oh, I didn't realize...
I have other clients to see, of course.
I see. Goodbye.

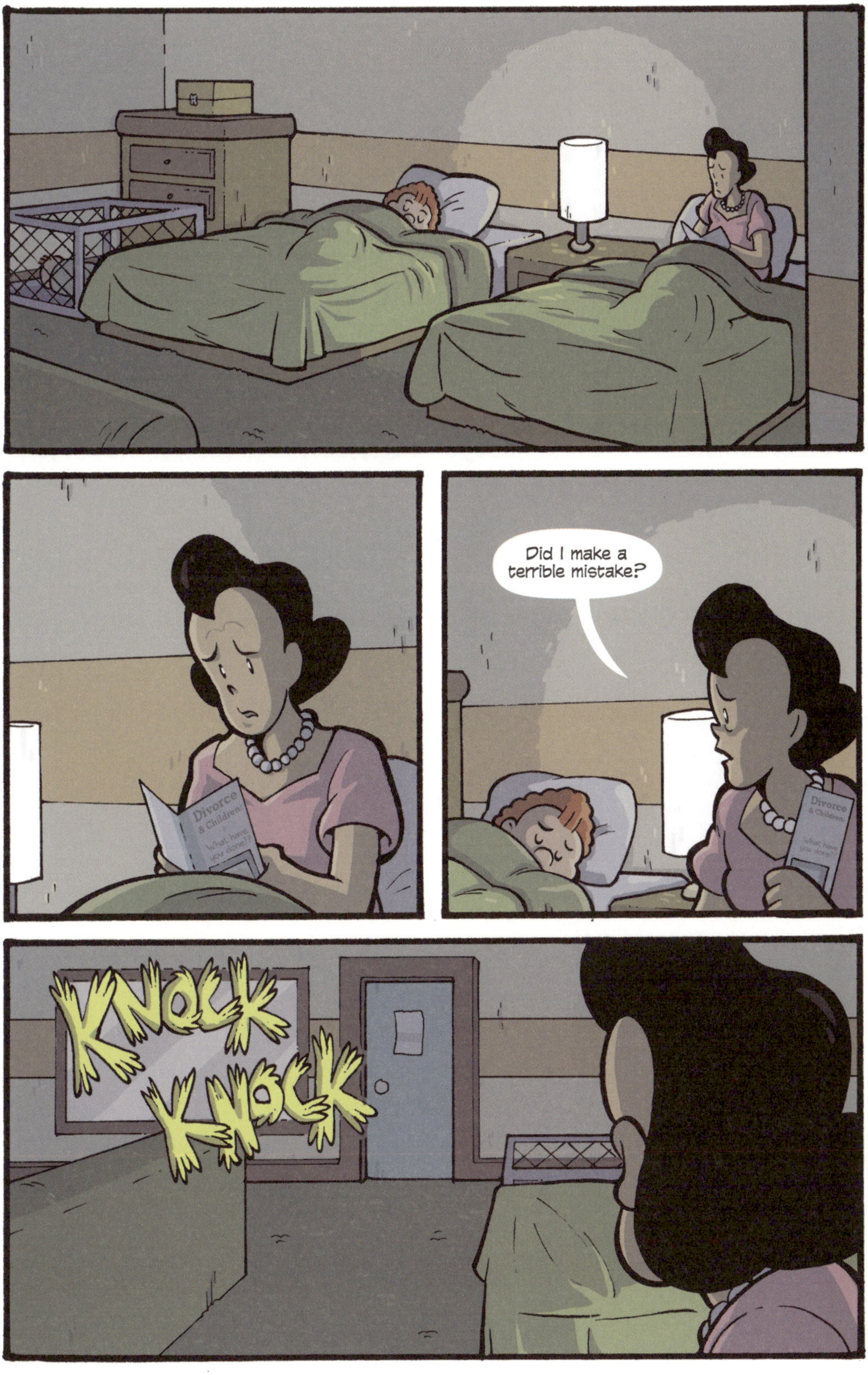
Divorce & Children: What have you done??
Did I make a terrible mistake?
KNOCK KNOCK

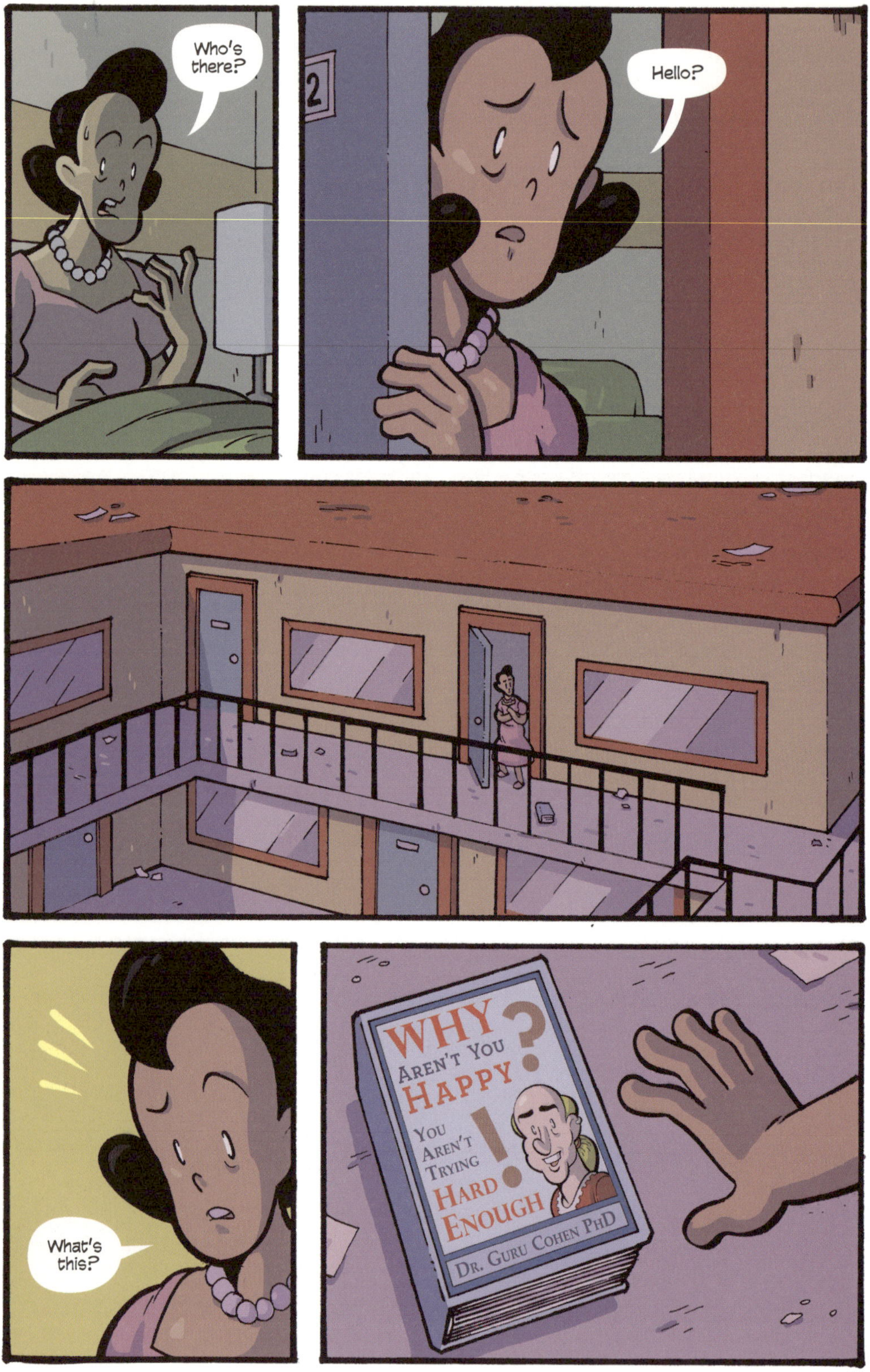
Who's there?
Hello?
What's this?
WHY AREN'T YOU HAPPY?
YOU AREN'T TRYING HARD ENOUGH!
DR. GURU COHEN PHD

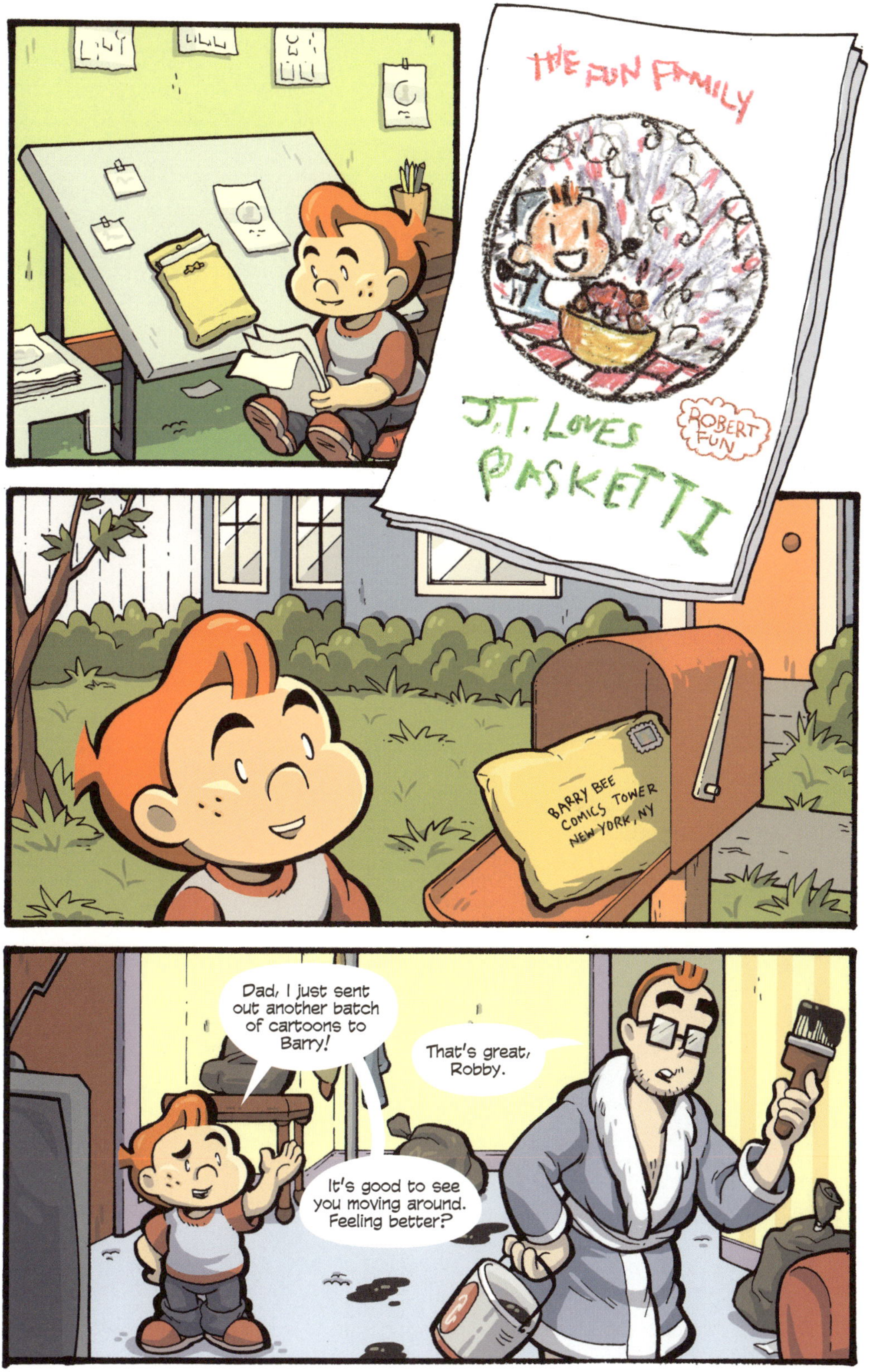
THE FUN FAMILY
J.T. LOVES PASKETTI
ROBERT FUN
BARRY BEE
COMICS TOWER
NEW YORK, NY
Dad, I just sent out another batch of cartoons to Barry!
That's great, Robby.
It's good to see you moving around. Feeling better?

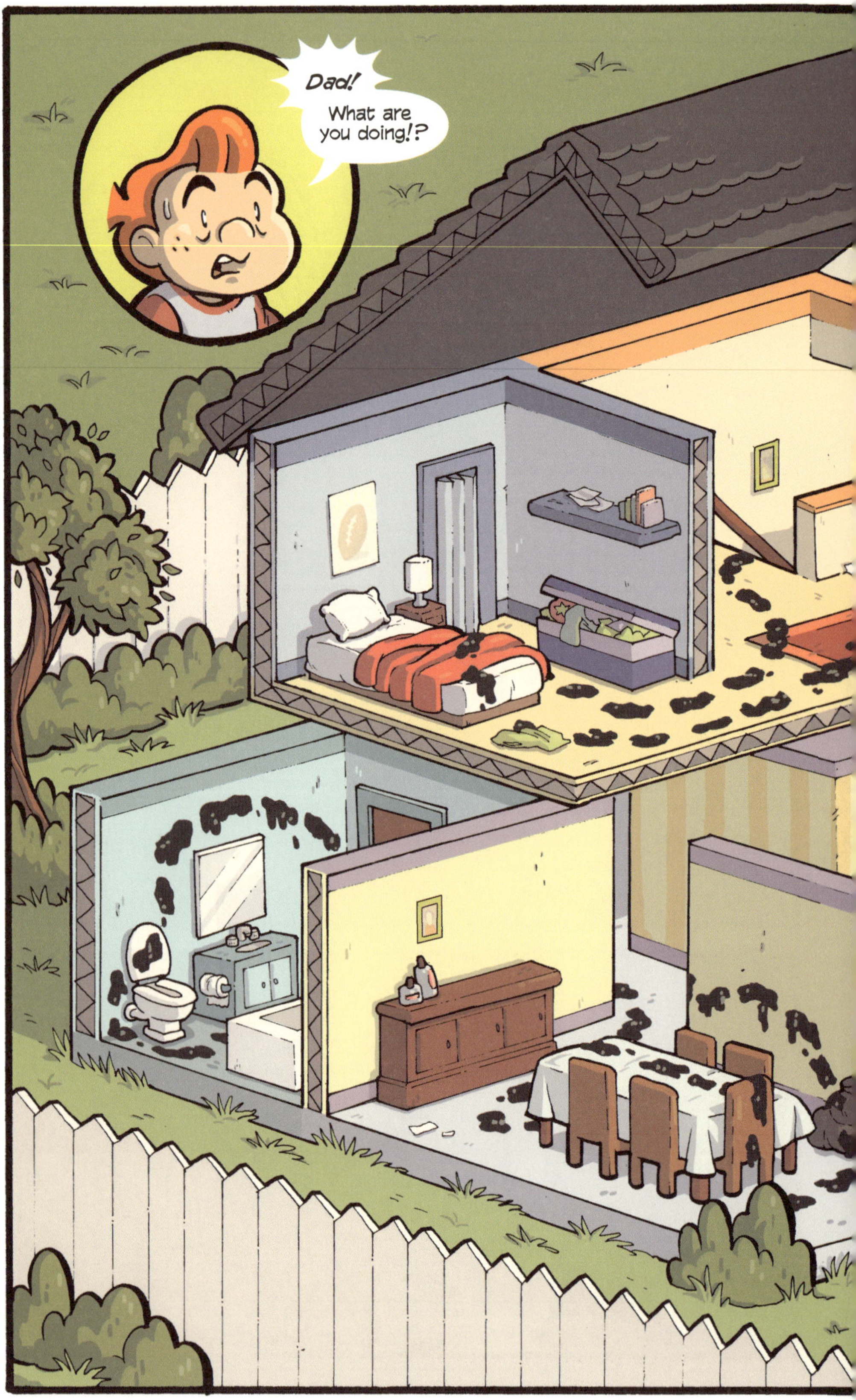
Dad! What are you doing!?

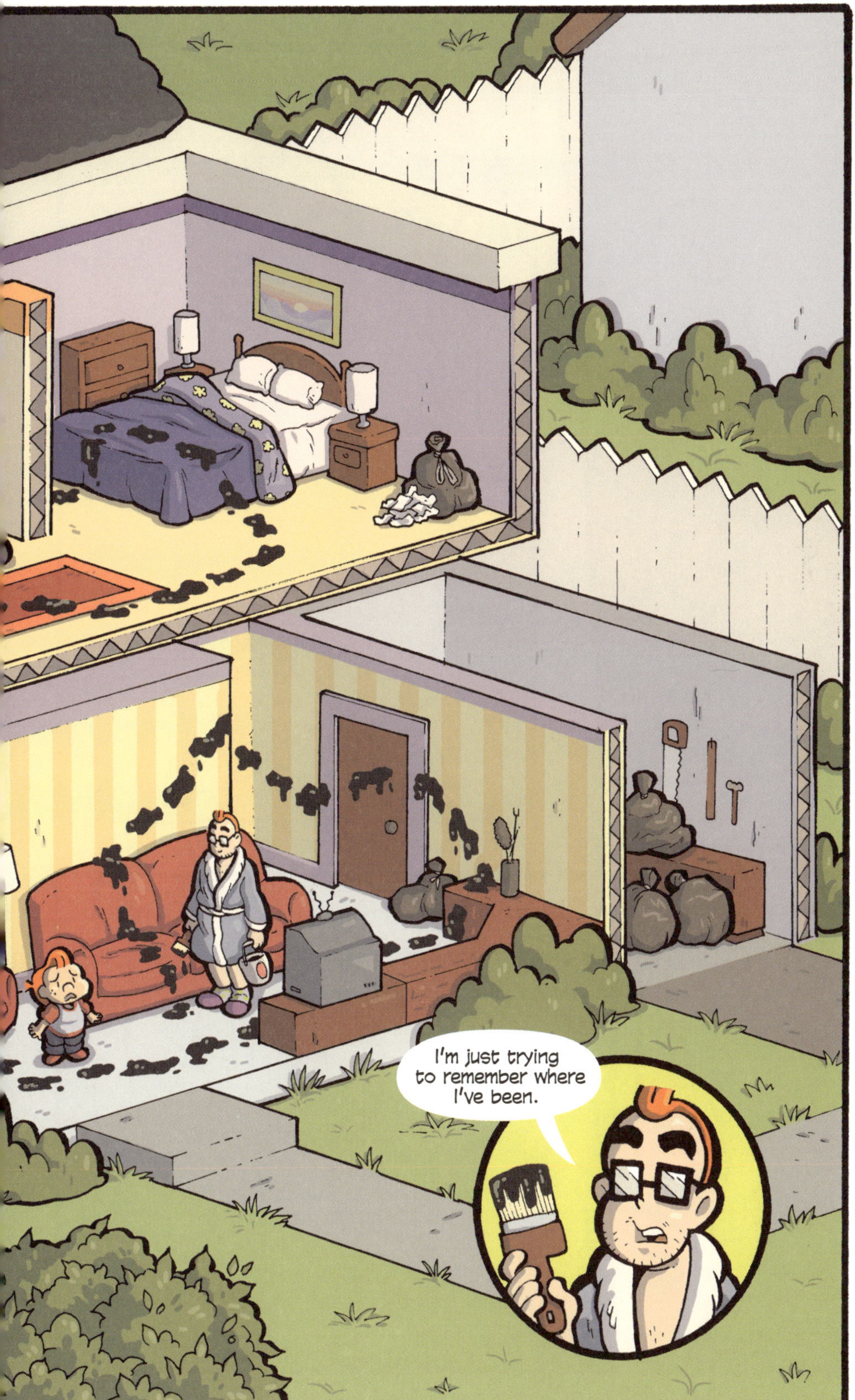
I'm just trying to remember where I've been.

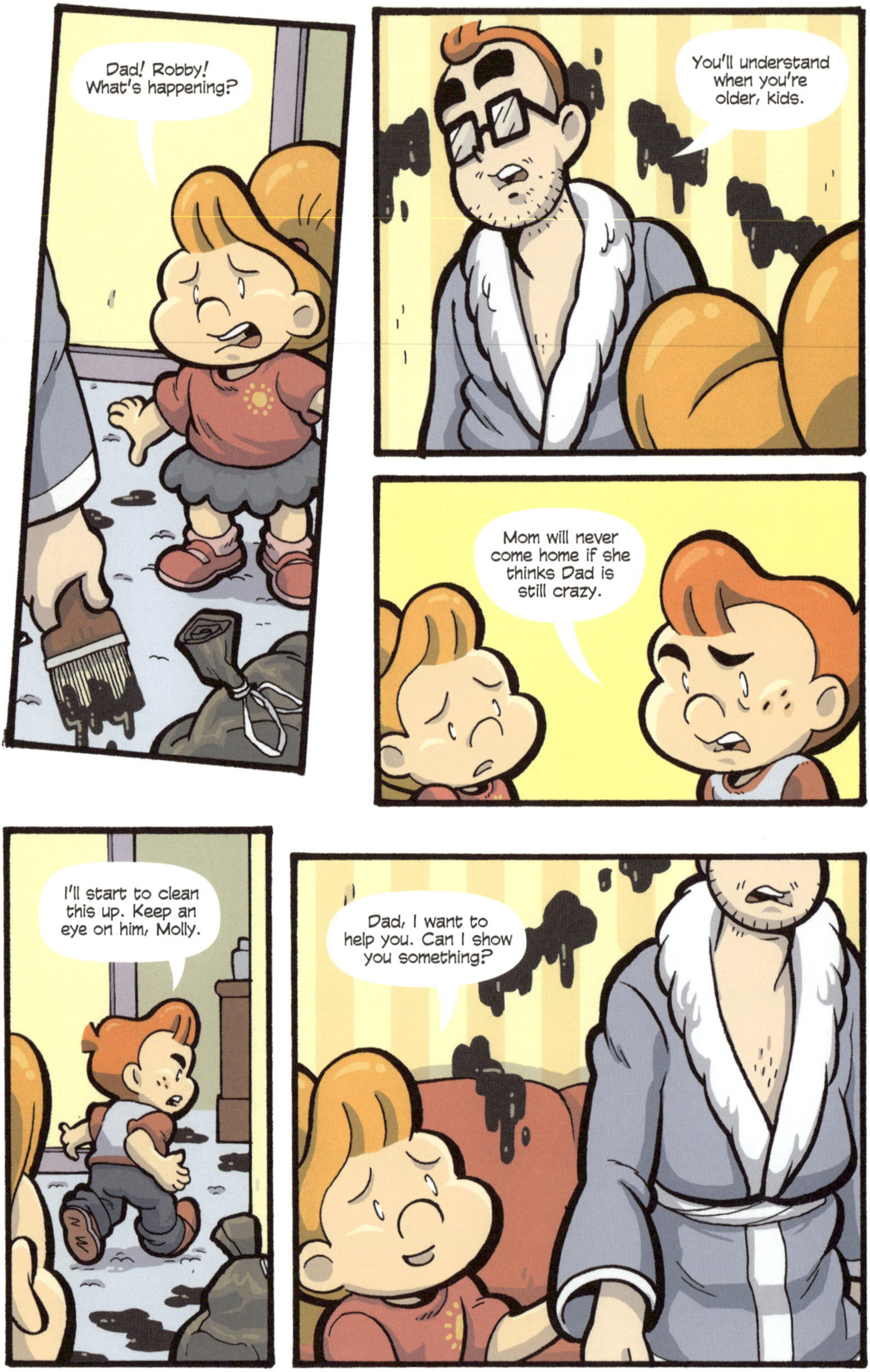
Dad! Robby! What's happening?
You'll understand when you're older, kids.
Mom will never come home if she thinks Dad is still crazy.
I'll start to clean this up. Keep an eye on him, Molly.
Dad, I want to help you. Can I show you something?

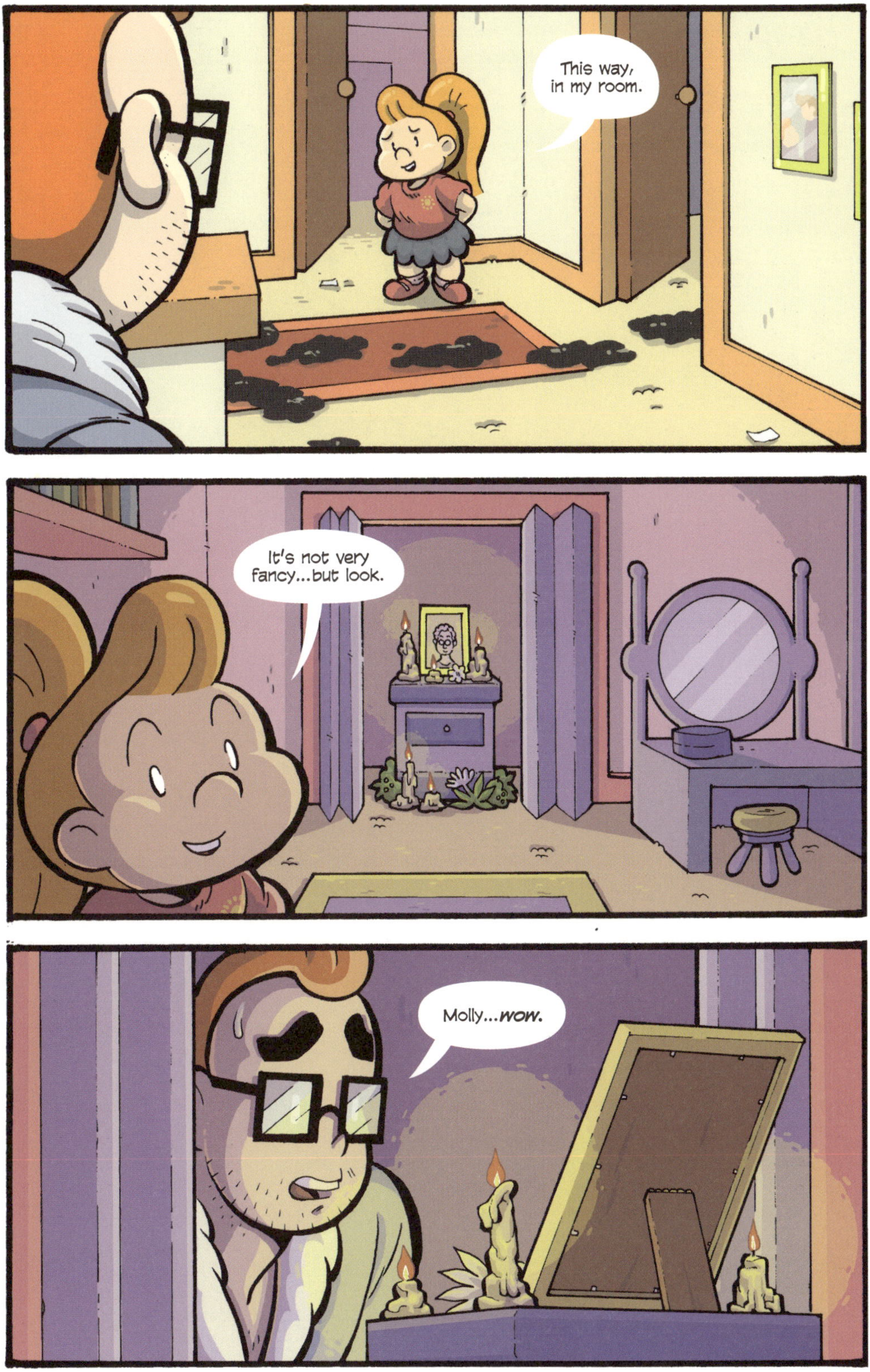
This way, in my room.
It's not very fancy...but look.
Molly...*wow*.

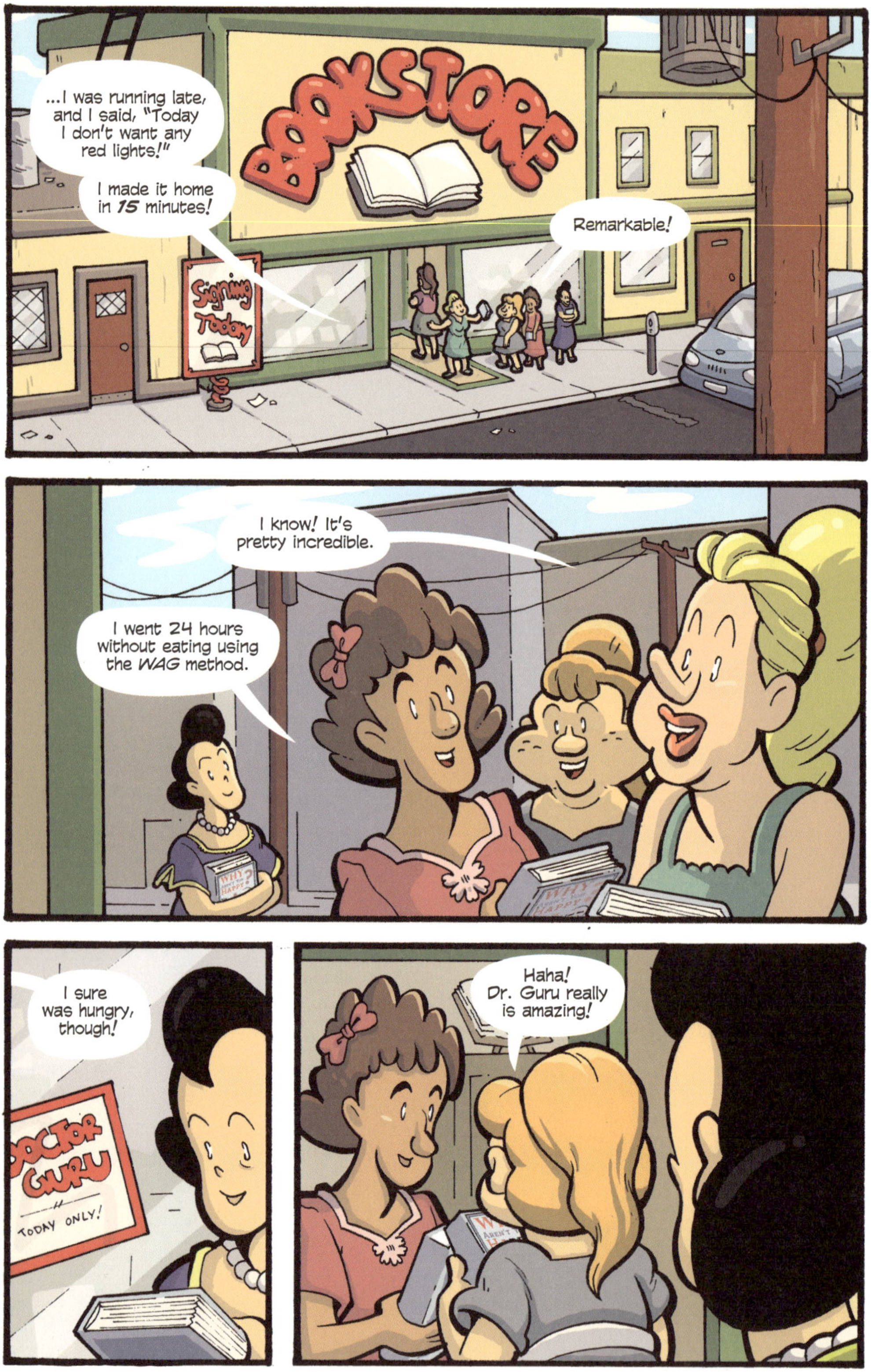
BOOKSTORE
...I was running late, and I said, "Today I don't want any red lights!"
I made it home in 15 minutes!
Remarkable!
Signing Today
I know! It's pretty incredible.
I went 24 hours without eating using the WAG method.
I sure was hungry, though!
DOCTOR GURU
TODAY ONLY!
Haha! Dr. Guru really is amazing!

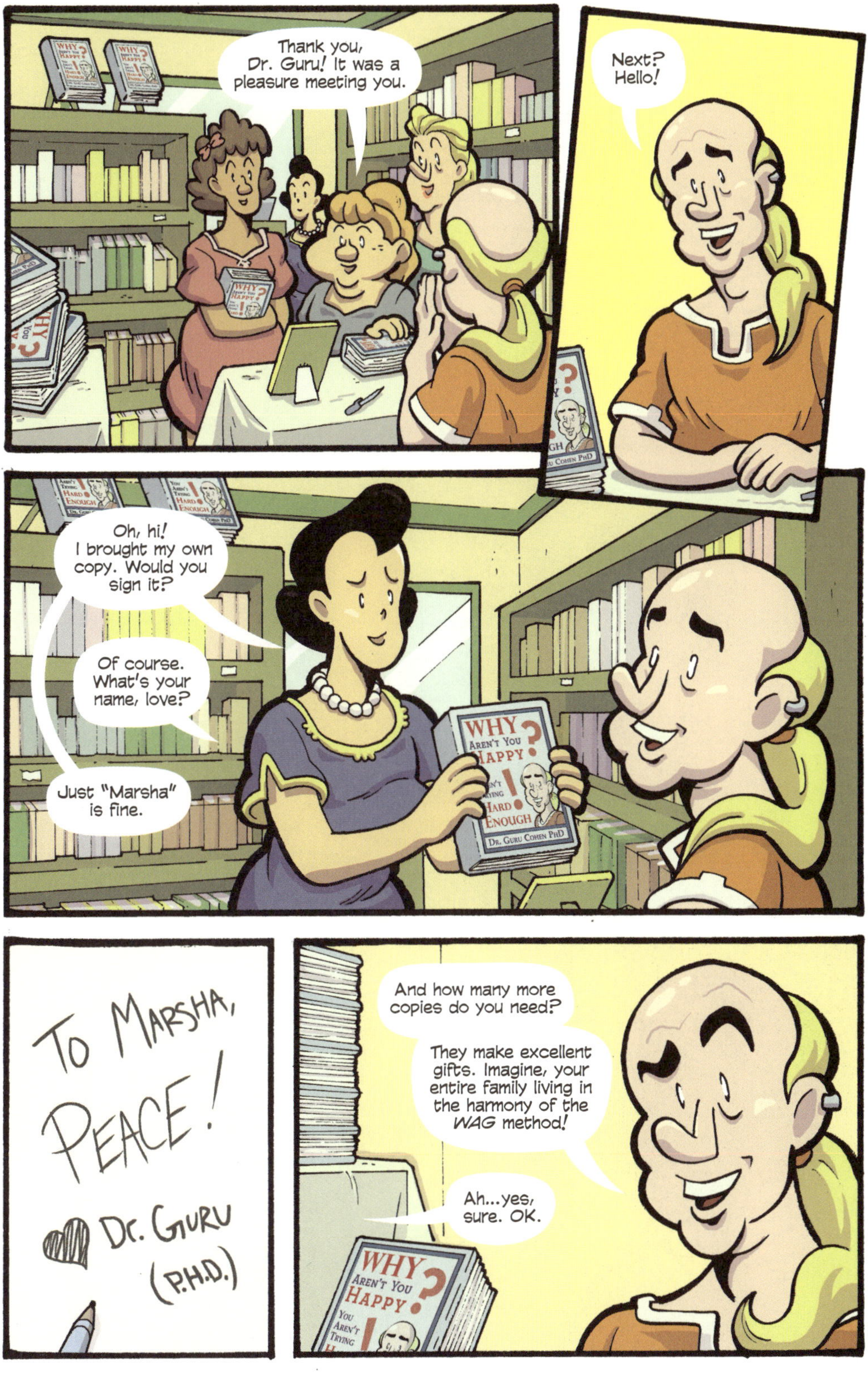

Thank you, Dr. Guru! It was a pleasure meeting you.
Next? Hello!
Oh, hi! I brought my own copy. Would you sign it?
Of course. What's your name, love?
Just "Marsha" is fine.
WHY AREN'T YOU HAPPY? DR. GURU COHEN PHD
TO MARSHA, PEACE! DR. GURU (P.H.D.)
And how many more copies do you need?
They make excellent gifts. Imagine, your entire family living in the harmony of the *WAG* method!
Ah...yes, sure. OK.

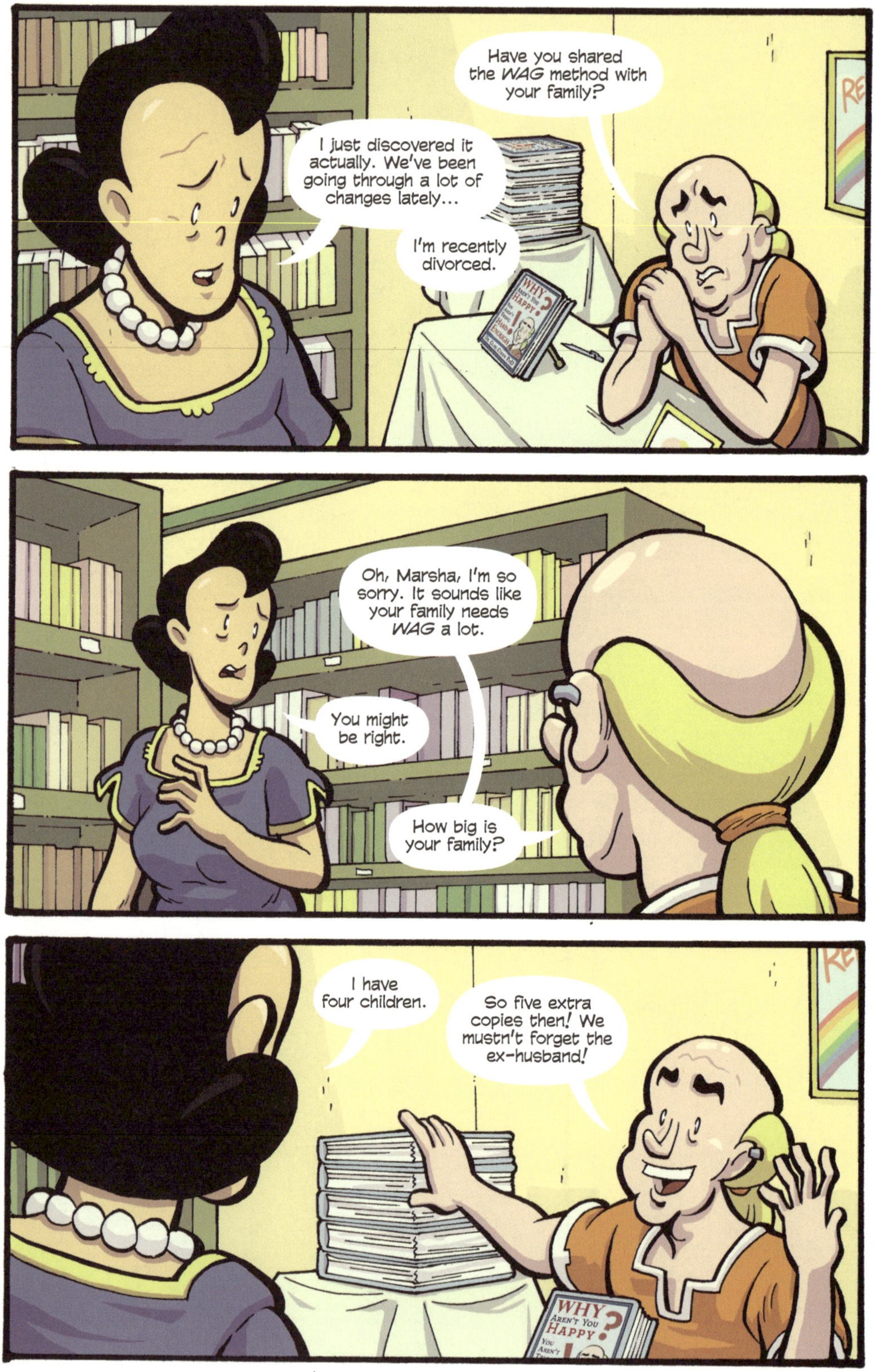
Have you shared the WAG method with your family?
I just discovered it actually. We've been going through a lot of changes lately...
I'm recently divorced.
WHY AREN'T YOU HAPPY?
Oh, Marsha, I'm so sorry. It sounds like your family needs WAG a lot.
You might be right.
How big is your family?
I have four children.
So five extra copies then! We mustn't forget the ex-husband!
WHY AREN'T YOU HAPPY?

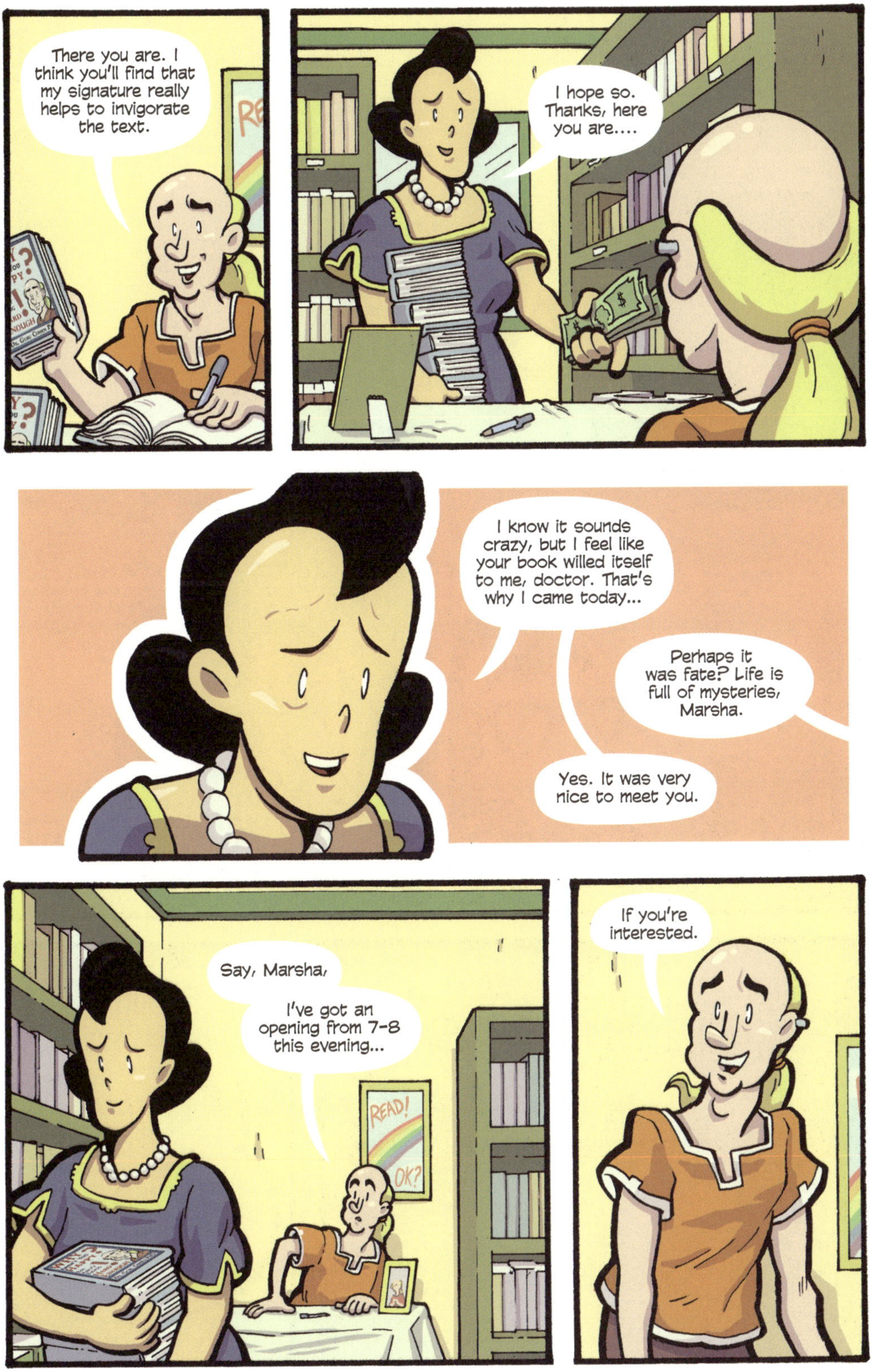
There you are. I think you'll find that my signature really helps to invigorate the text.
I hope so. Thanks, here you are....
I know it sounds crazy, but I feel like your book willed itself to me, doctor. That's why I came today...
Perhaps it was fate? Life is full of mysteries, Marsha.
Yes. It was very nice to meet you.
Say, Marsha,
I've got an opening from 7-8 this evening...
If you're interested.
READ!
OK?

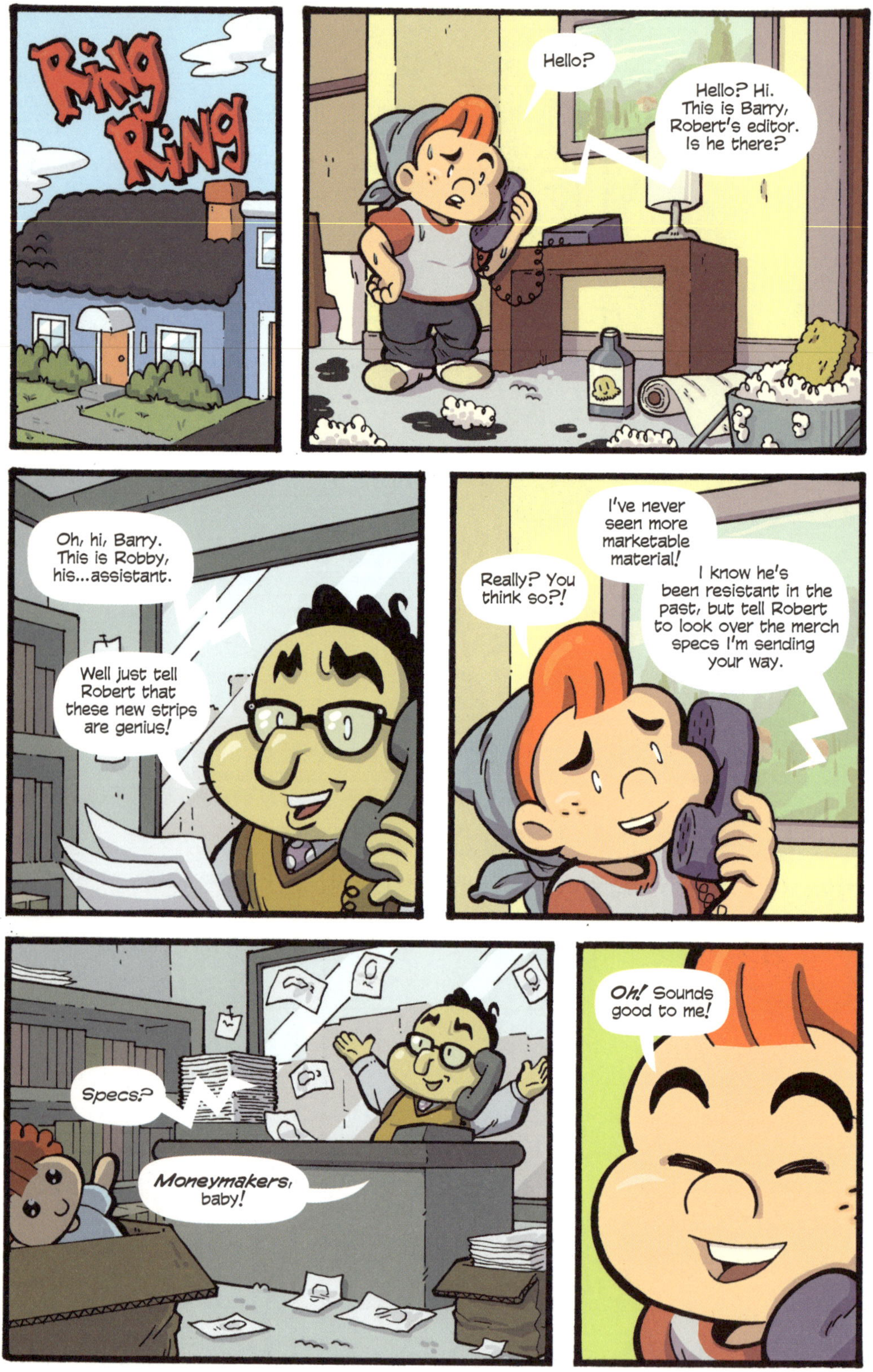
Ring Ring
Hello?
Hello? Hi. This is Barry, Robert's editor. Is he there?
Oh, hi, Barry. This is Robby, his...assistant.
Well just tell Robert that these new strips are genius!
I've never seen more marketable material!
Really? You think so?!
I know he's been resistant in the past, but tell Robert to look over the merch specs I'm sending your way.
Specs?
Moneymakers, baby!
Oh! Sounds good to me!

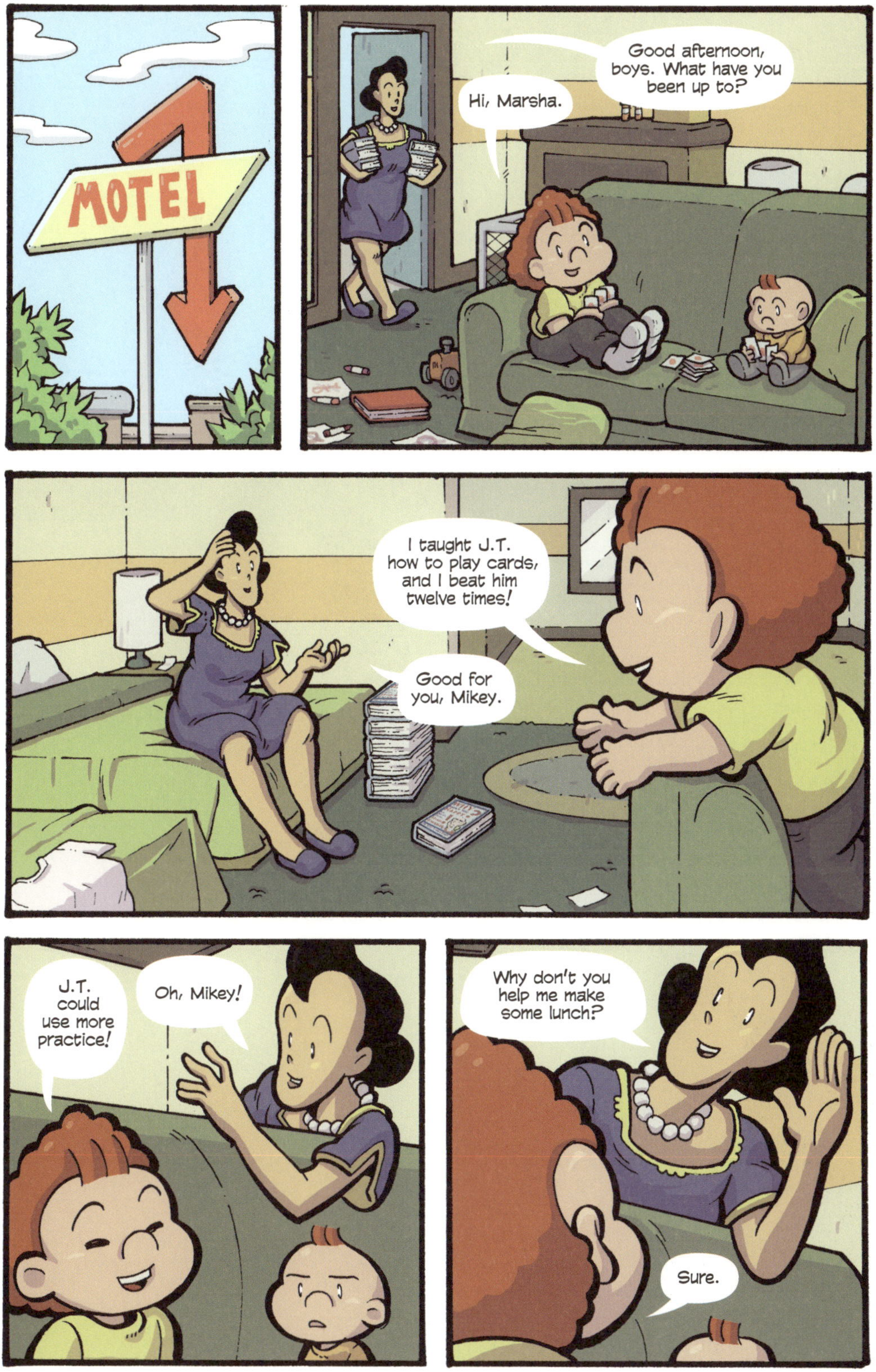
MOTEL
Good afternoon, boys. What have you been up to?
Hi, Marsha.
I taught J.T. how to play cards, and I beat him twelve times!
Good for you, Mikey.
J.T. could use more practice!
Oh, Mikey!
Why don't you help me make some lunch?
Sure.

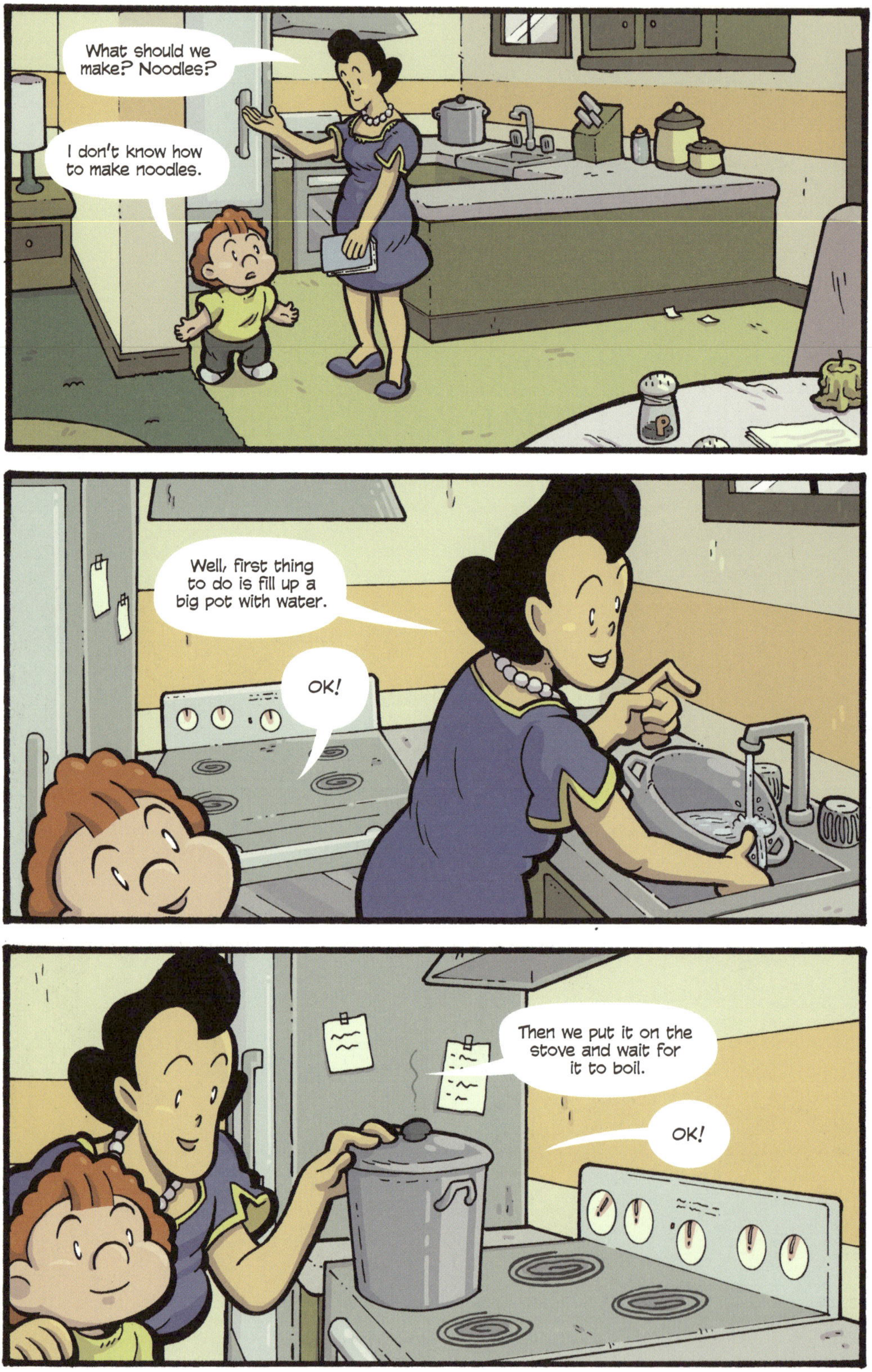
What should we make? Noodles?
I don't know how to make noodles.
Well, first thing to do is fill up a big pot with water.
OK!
Then we put it on the stove and wait for it to boil.
OK!

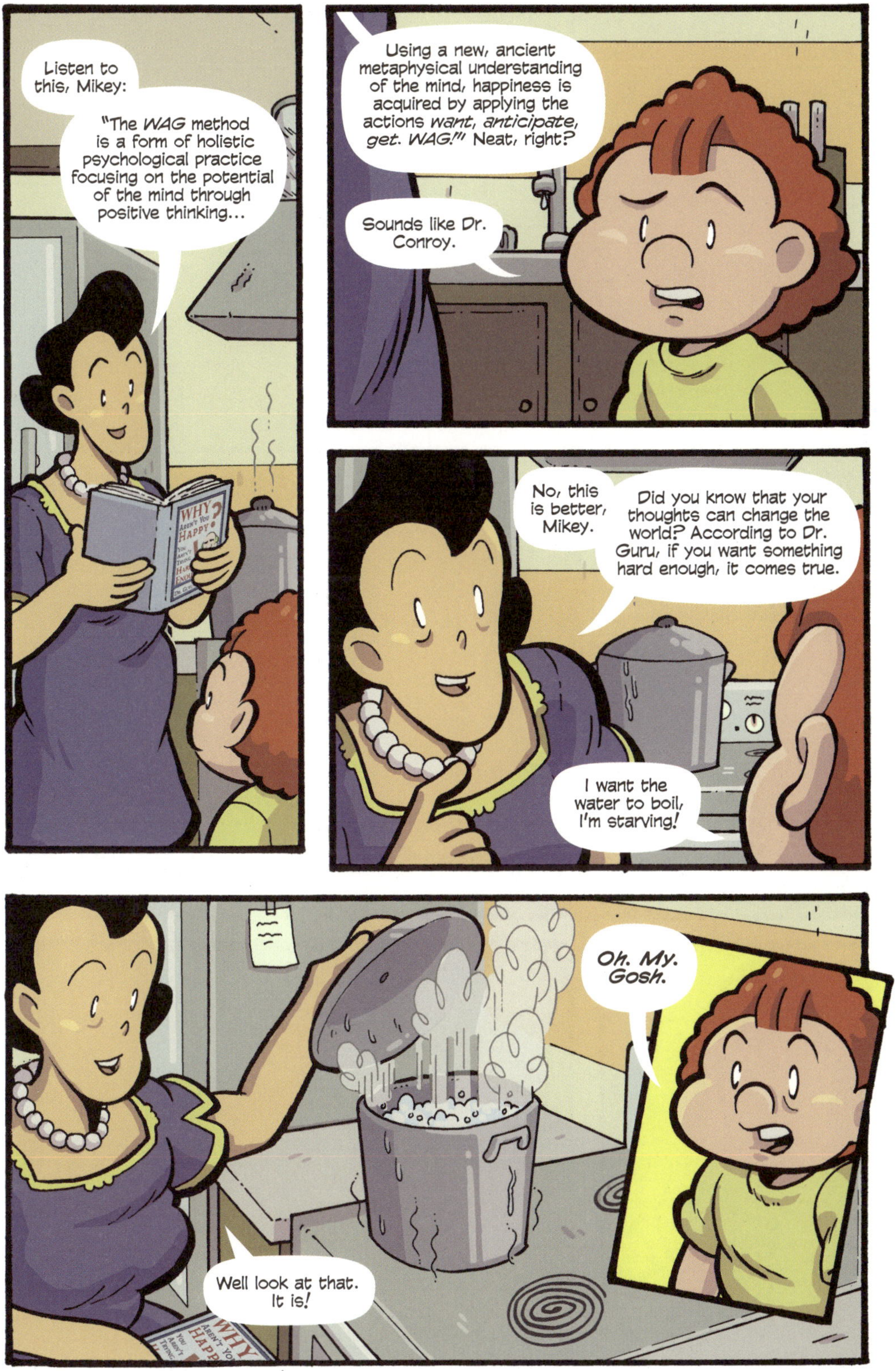
Listen to this, Mikey:
"The *WAG* method is a form of holistic psychological practice focusing on the potential of the mind through positive thinking...
Using a new, ancient metaphysical understanding of the mind, happiness is acquired by applying the actions *want, anticipate, get. WAG!*" Neat, right?
Sounds like Dr. Conroy.
No, this is better, Mikey.
Did you know that your thoughts can change the world? According to Dr. Guru, if you want something hard enough, it comes true.
I want the water to boil, I'm starving!
Oh. My. Gosh.
Well look at that. It is!

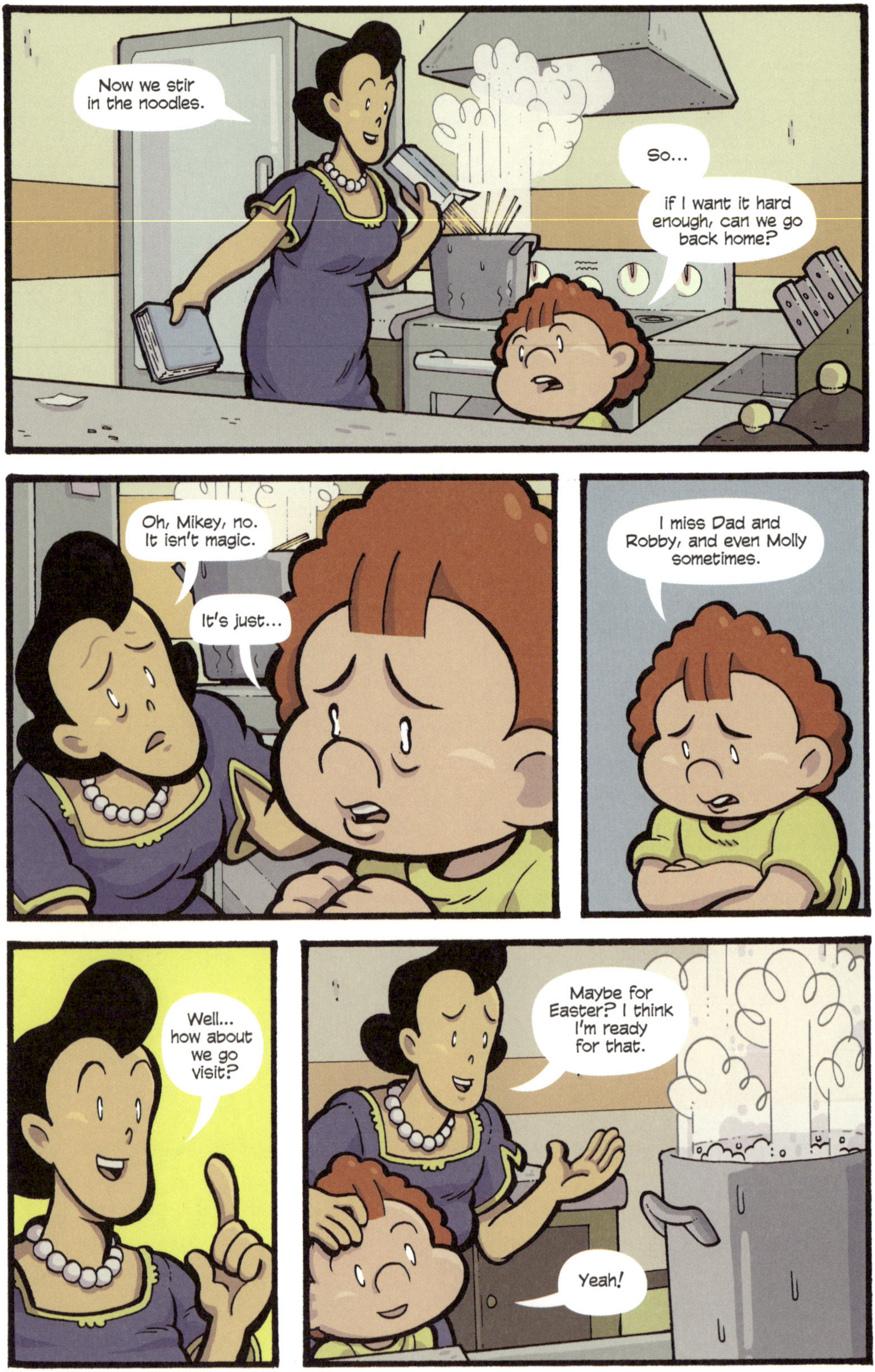
Now we stir in the noodles.
So...
if I want it hard enough, can we go back home?
Oh, Mikey, no. It isn't magic.
It's just...
I miss Dad and Robby, and even Molly sometimes.
Well... how about we go visit?
Maybe for Easter? I think I'm ready for that.
Yeah!

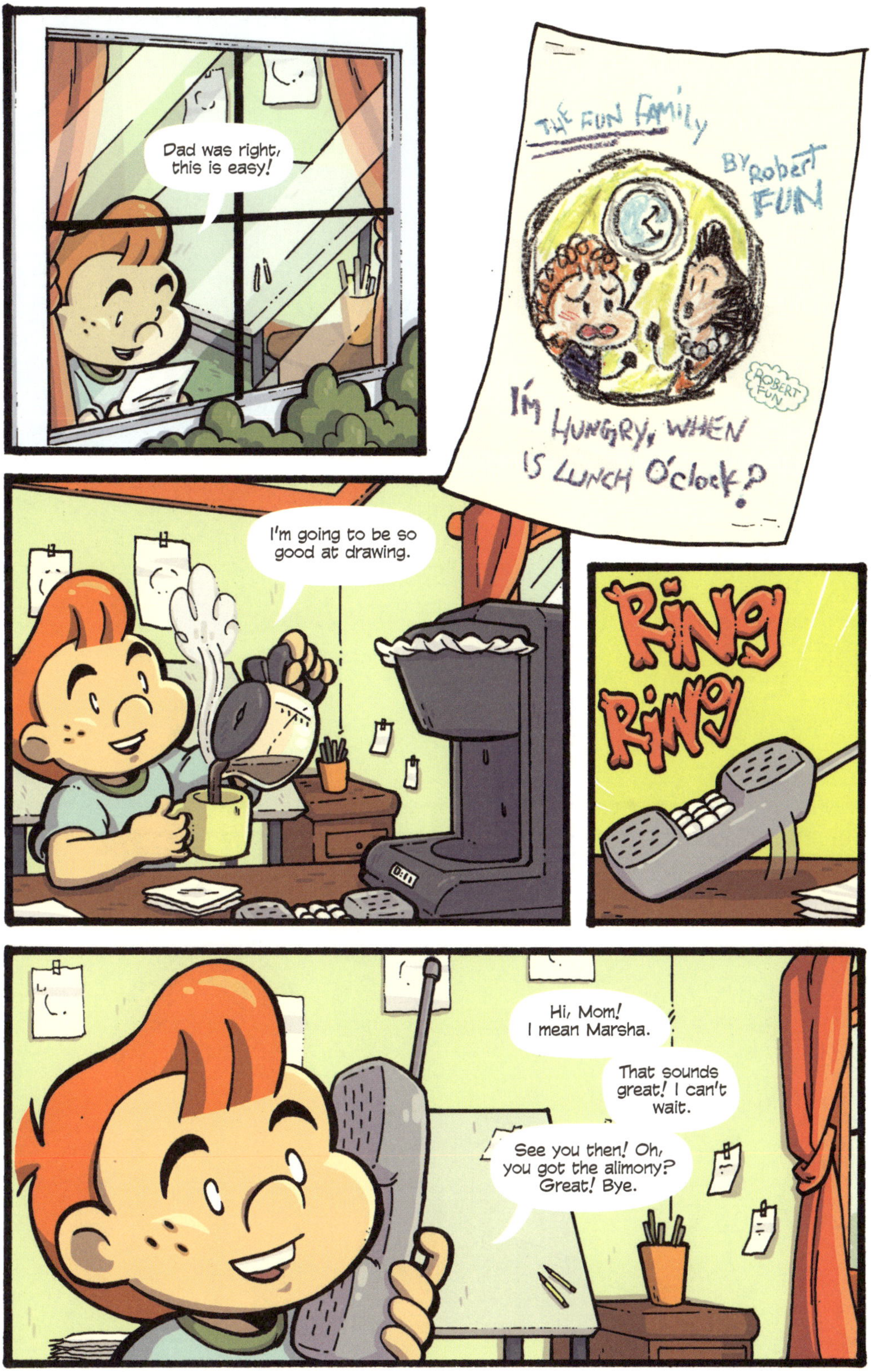
Dad was right, this is easy!
THE FUN FAMILY
BY Robert FUN
ROBERT FUN
I'M HUNGRY, WHEN IS LUNCH O'clock?
I'm going to be so good at drawing.
Ring Ring
Hi, Mom! I mean Marsha.
That sounds great! I can't wait.
See you then! Oh, you got the alimony? Great! Bye.

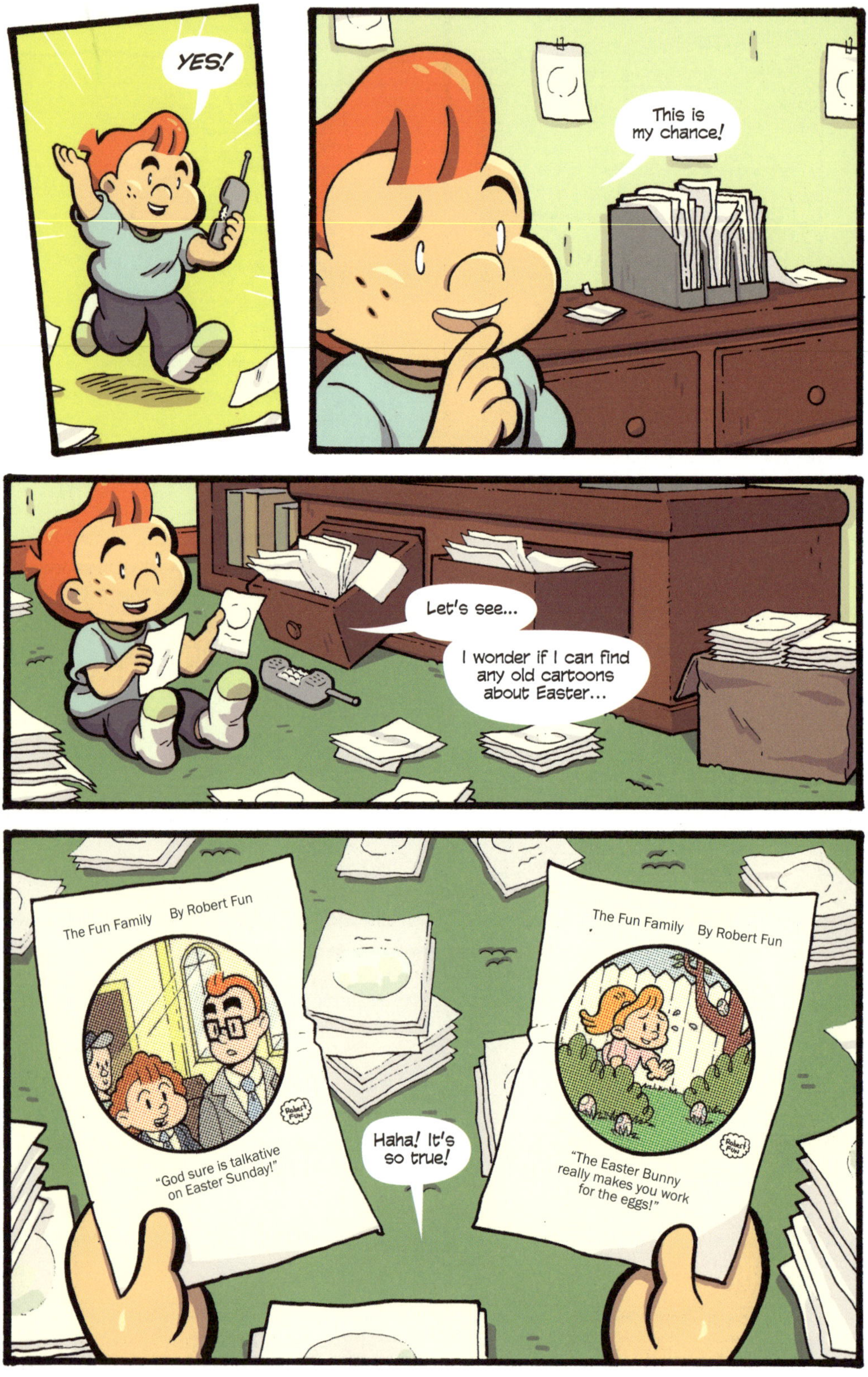
YES!
This is my chance!
Let's see...
I wonder if I can find any old cartoons about Easter...
The Fun Family By Robert Fun
"God sure is talkative on Easter Sunday!"
Haha! It's so true!
The Fun Family By Robert Fun
"The Easter Bunny really makes you work for the eggs!"

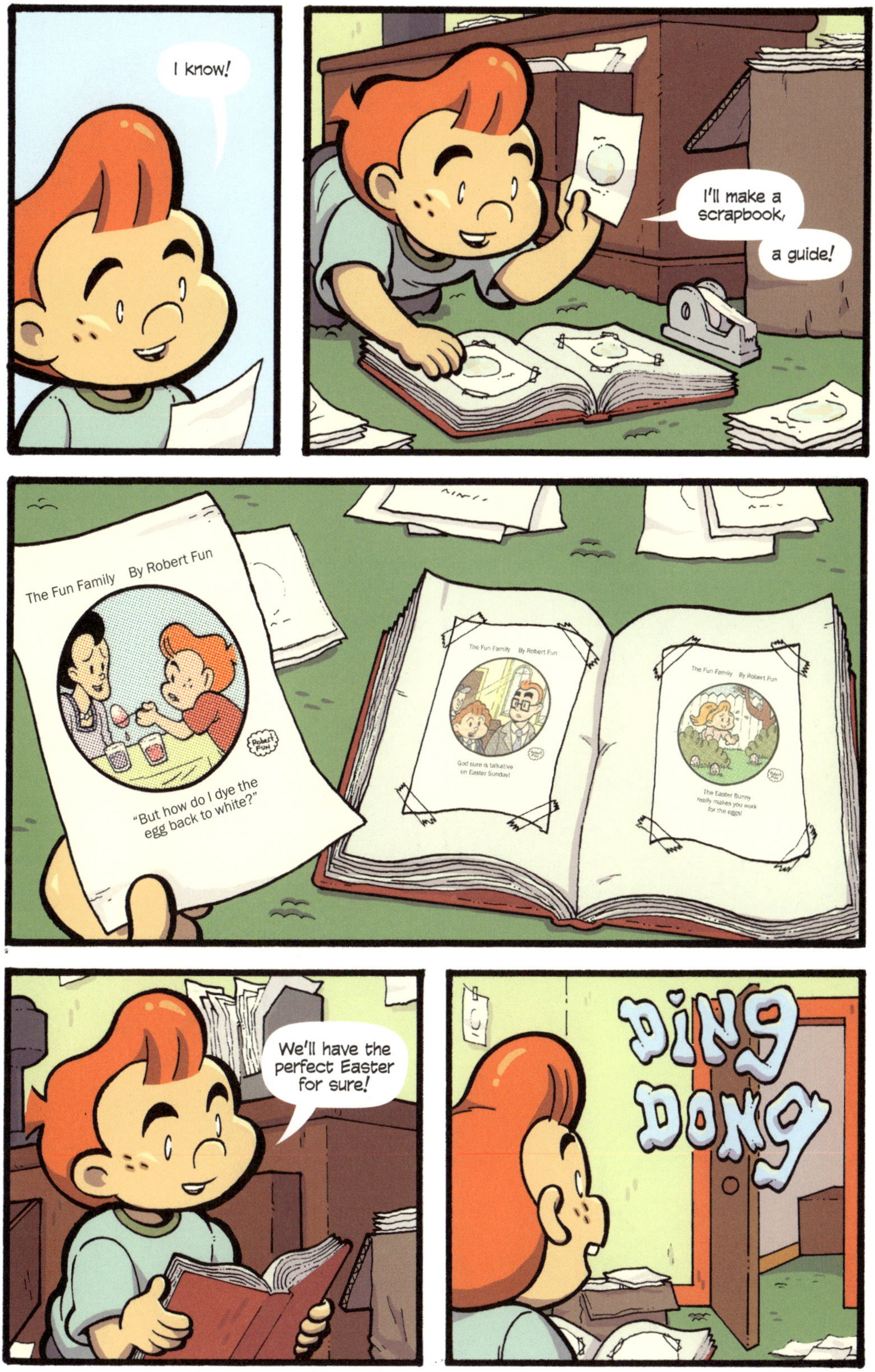
I know!
I'll make a scrapbook,
a guide!
The Fun Family By Robert Fun
Robert Fun
"But how do I dye the egg back to white?"
The Fun Family By Robert Fun
God sure is talkative on Easter Sunday!
The Fun Family By Robert Fun
The Easter Bunny really makes you work for the eggs!
We'll have the perfect Easter for sure!
DING DONG

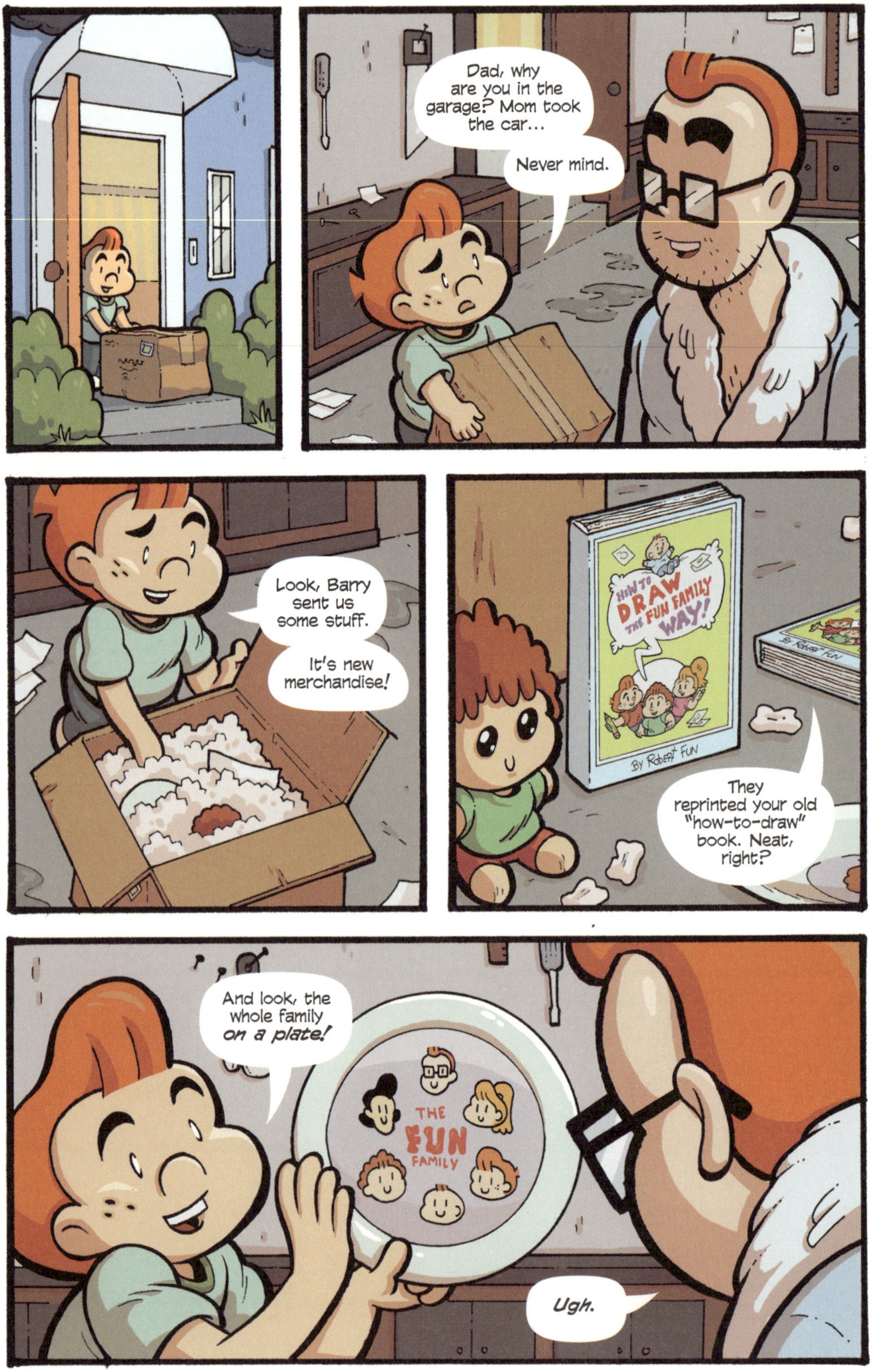
Dad, why are you in the garage? Mom took the car...
Never mind.
Look, Barry sent us some stuff.
It's new merchandise!
HOW TO DRAW THE FUN FAMILY WAY!
BY ROBERT FUN
They reprinted your old "how-to-draw" book. Neat, right?
And look, the whole family *on a plate!*
THE FUN FAMILY
Ugh.

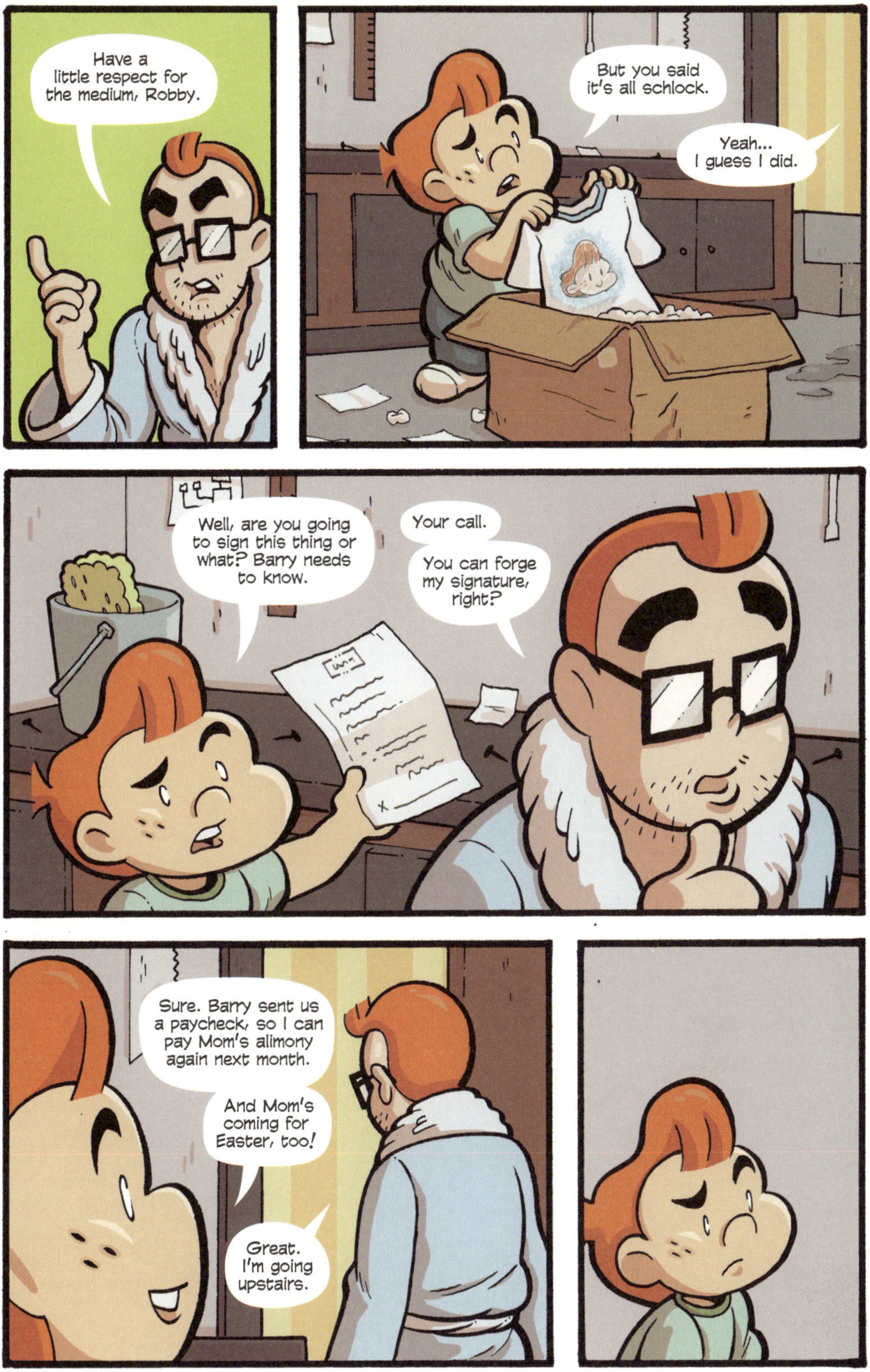
Have a little respect for the medium, Robby.
But you said it's all schlock.
Yeah... I guess I did.
Well, are you going to sign this thing or what? Barry needs to know.
Your call.
You can forge my signature, right?
Sure. Barry sent us a paycheck, so I can pay Mom's alimony again next month.
And Mom's coming for Easter, too!
Great. I'm going upstairs.

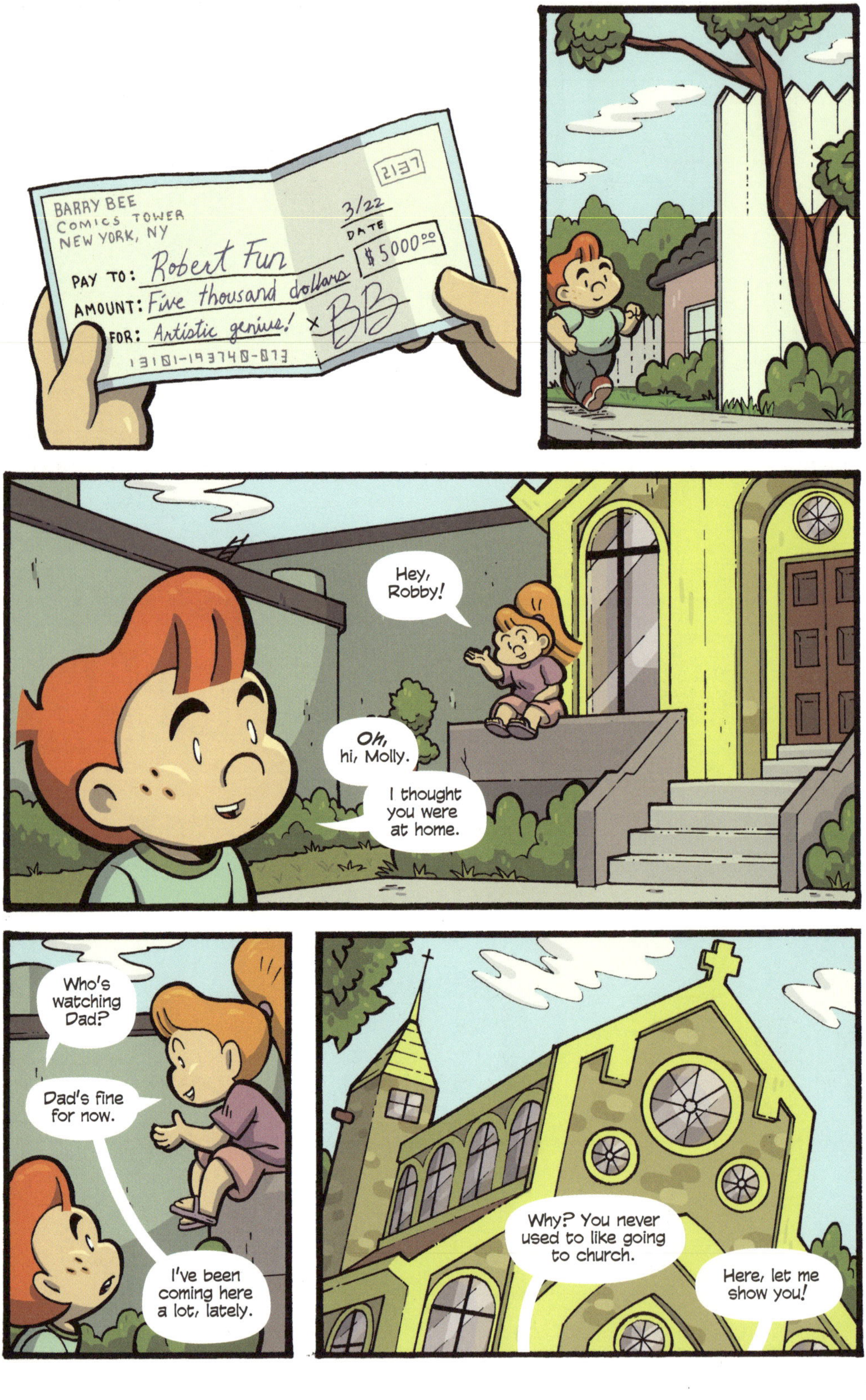
BARRY BEE
COMICS TOWER
NEW YORK, NY
2137
3/22
DATE
PAY TO: Robert Fun
$5000.00
AMOUNT: Five thousand dollars
FOR: Artistic genius!
x BB
Hey, Robby!
Oh, hi, Molly.
I thought you were at home.
Who's watching Dad?
Dad's fine for now.
I've been coming here a lot, lately.
Why? You never used to like going to church.
Here, let me show you!

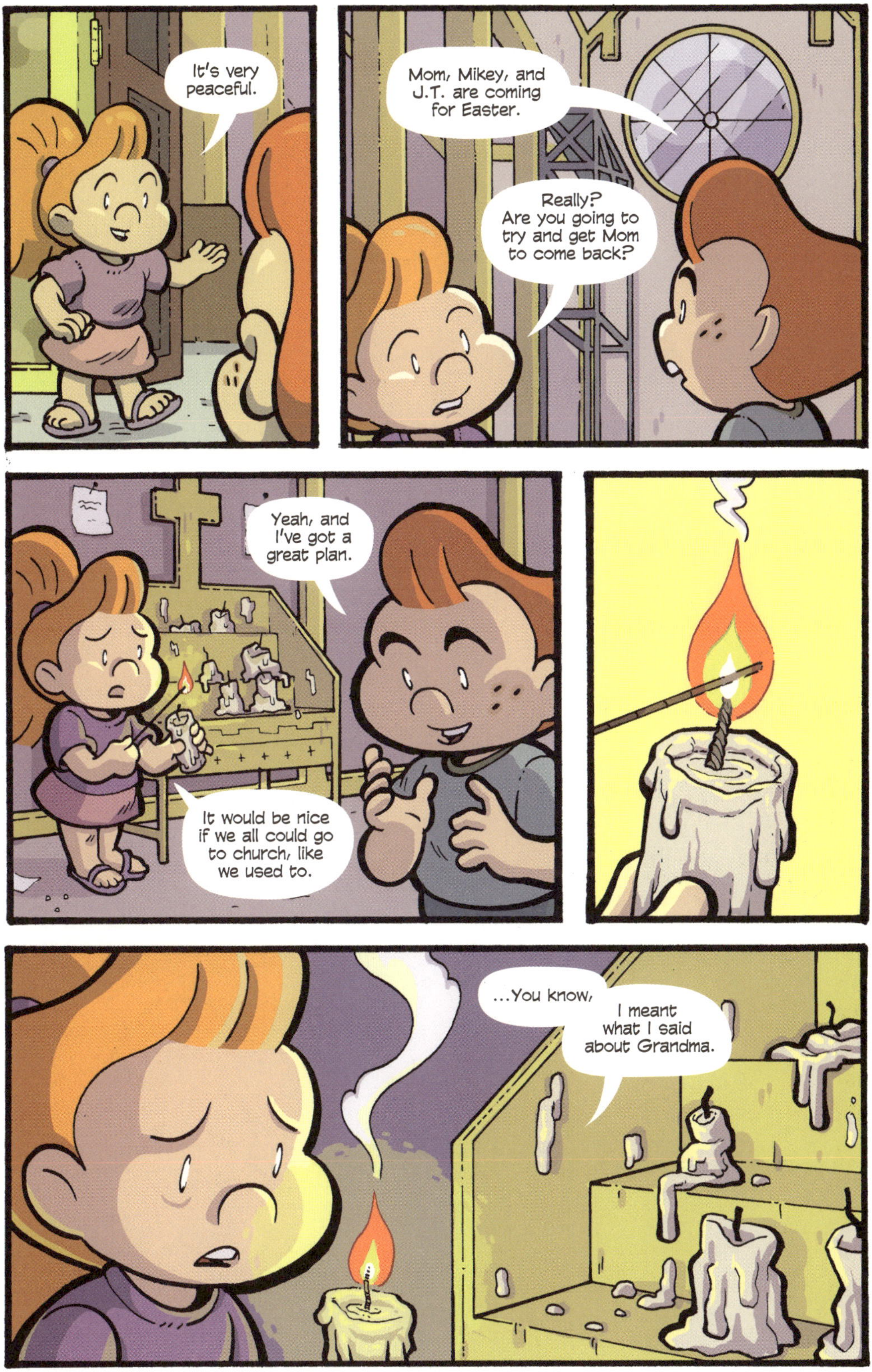
It's very peaceful.
Mom, Mikey, and J.T. are coming for Easter.
Really? Are you going to try and get Mom to come back?
Yeah, and I've got a great plan.
It would be nice if we all could go to church, like we used to.
...You know,
I meant what I said about Grandma.

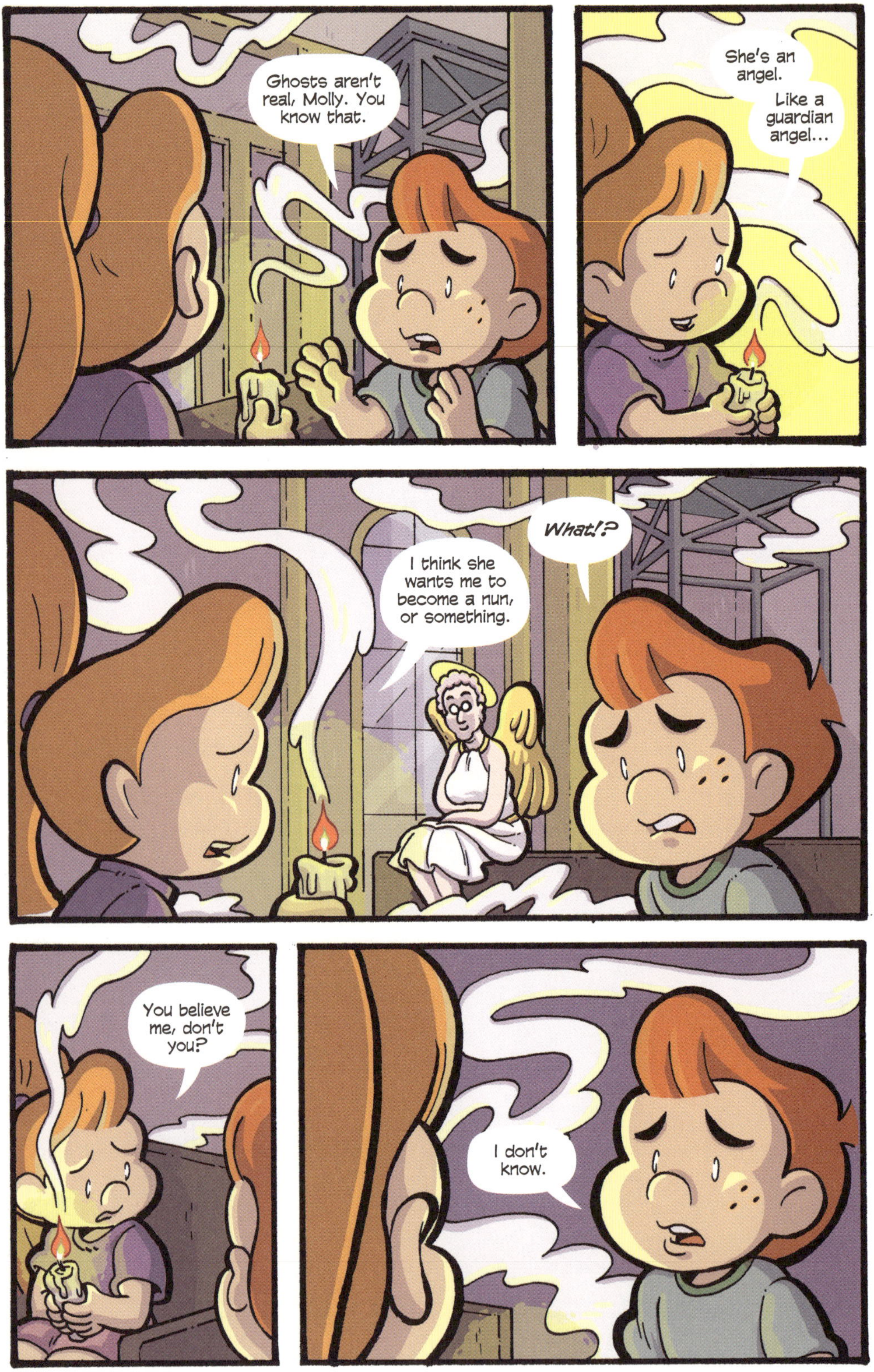
Ghosts aren't real, Molly. You know that.
She's an angel.
Like a guardian angel...
I think she wants me to become a nun, or something.
What!?
You believe me, don't you?
I don't know.

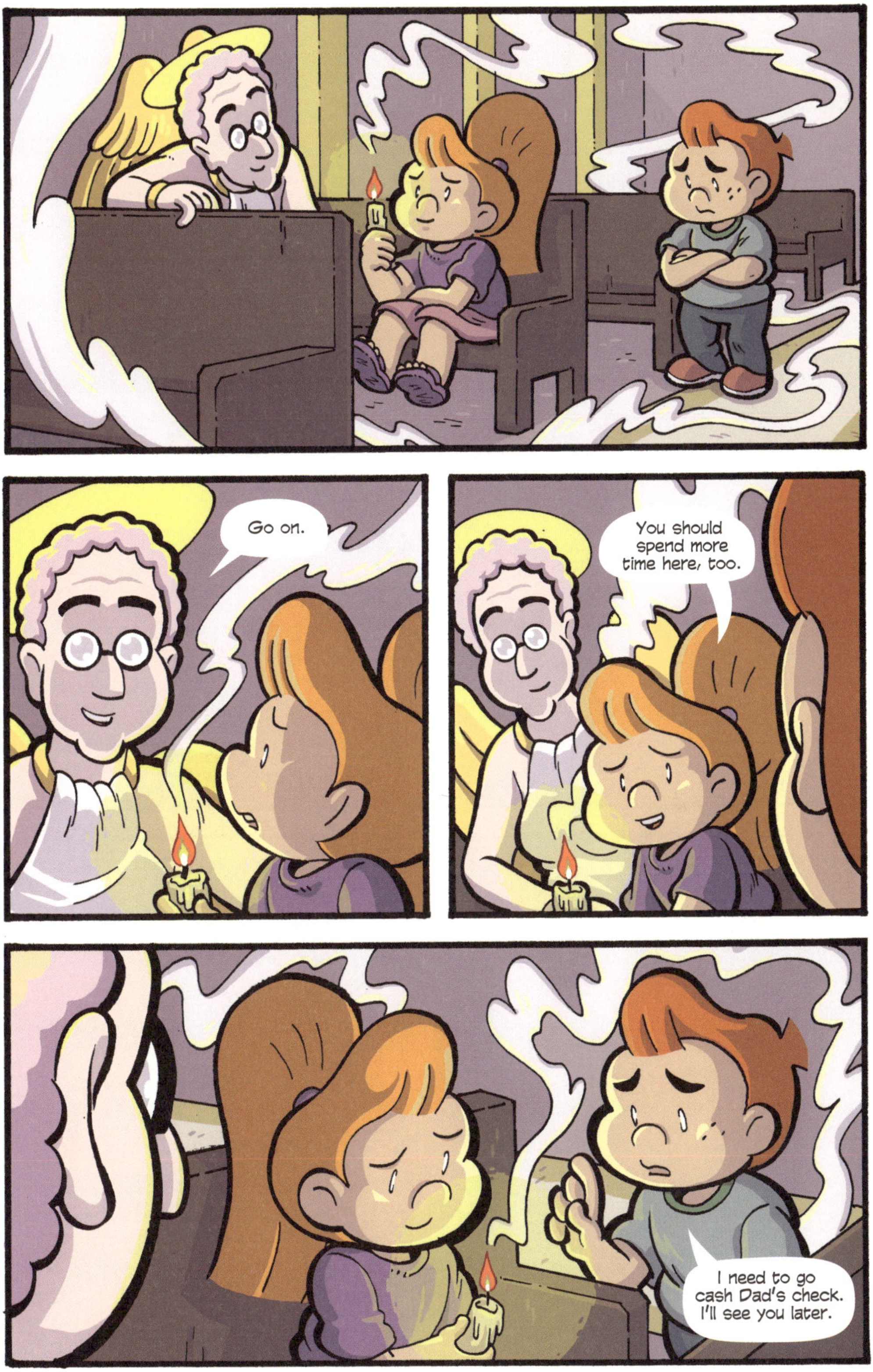
Go on.
You should spend more time here, too.
I need to go cash Dad's check. I'll see you later.

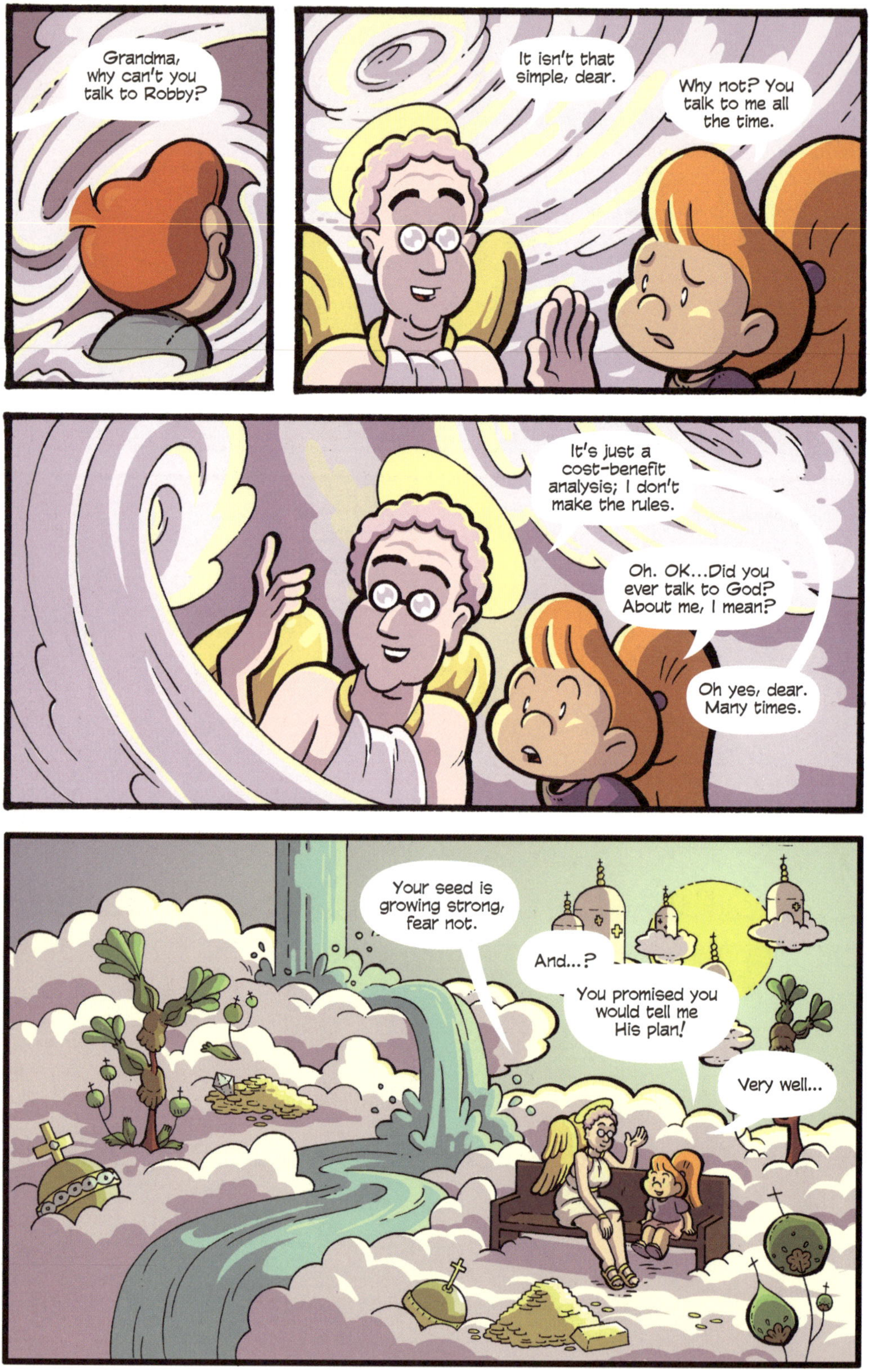
Grandma, why can't you talk to Robby?
It isn't that simple, dear.
Why not? You talk to me all the time.
It's just a cost-benefit analysis; I don't make the rules.
Oh. OK...Did you ever talk to God? About me, I mean?
Oh yes, dear. Many times.
Your seed is growing strong, fear not.
And...?
You promised you would tell me His plan!
Very well...

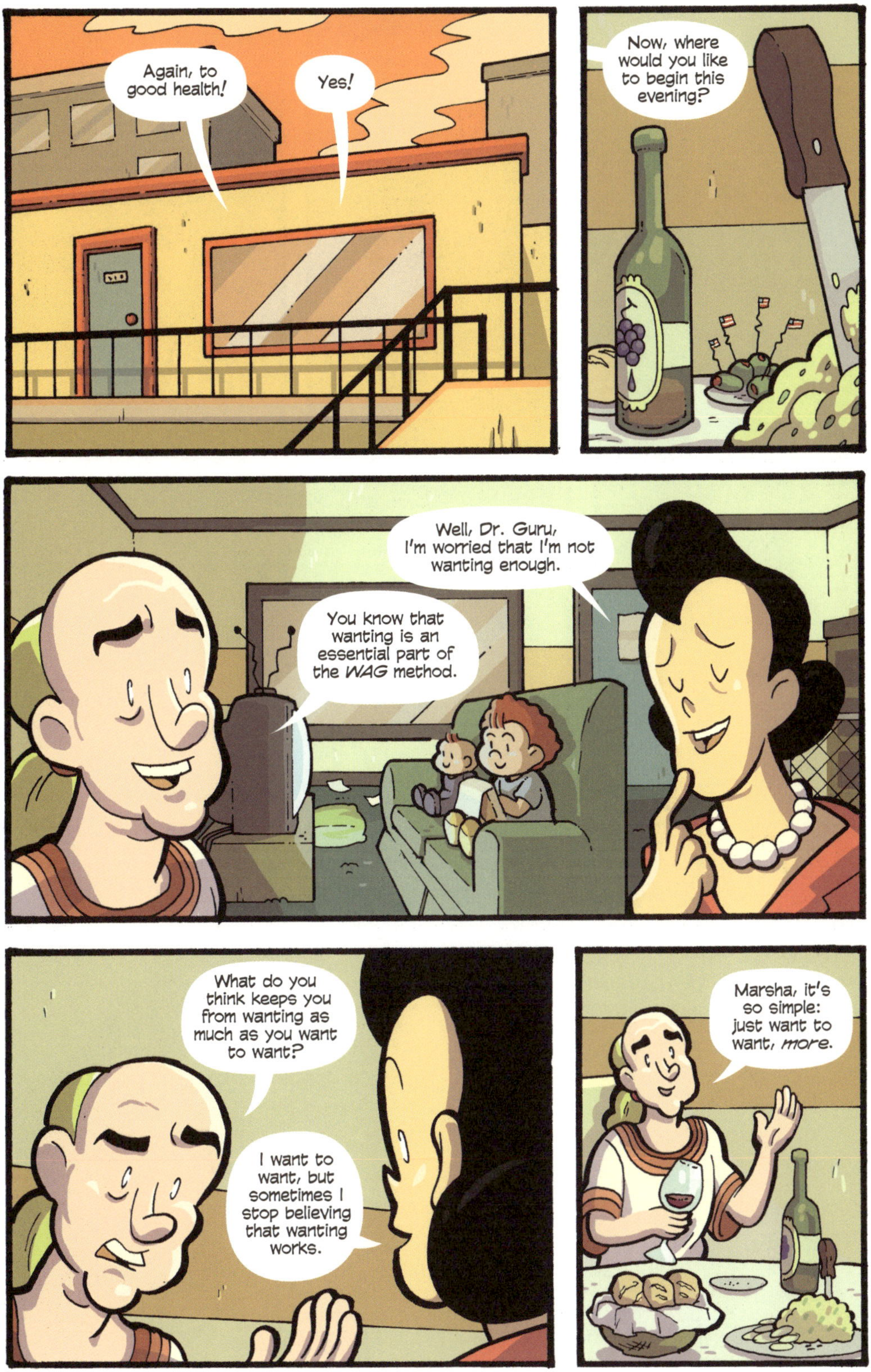
Again, to good health!
Yes!
Now, where would you like to begin this evening?
Well, Dr. Guru, I'm worried that I'm not wanting enough.
You know that wanting is an essential part of the *WAG* method.
What do you think keeps you from wanting as much as you want to want?
I want to want, but sometimes I stop believing that wanting works.
Marsha, it's so simple: just want to want, *more*.

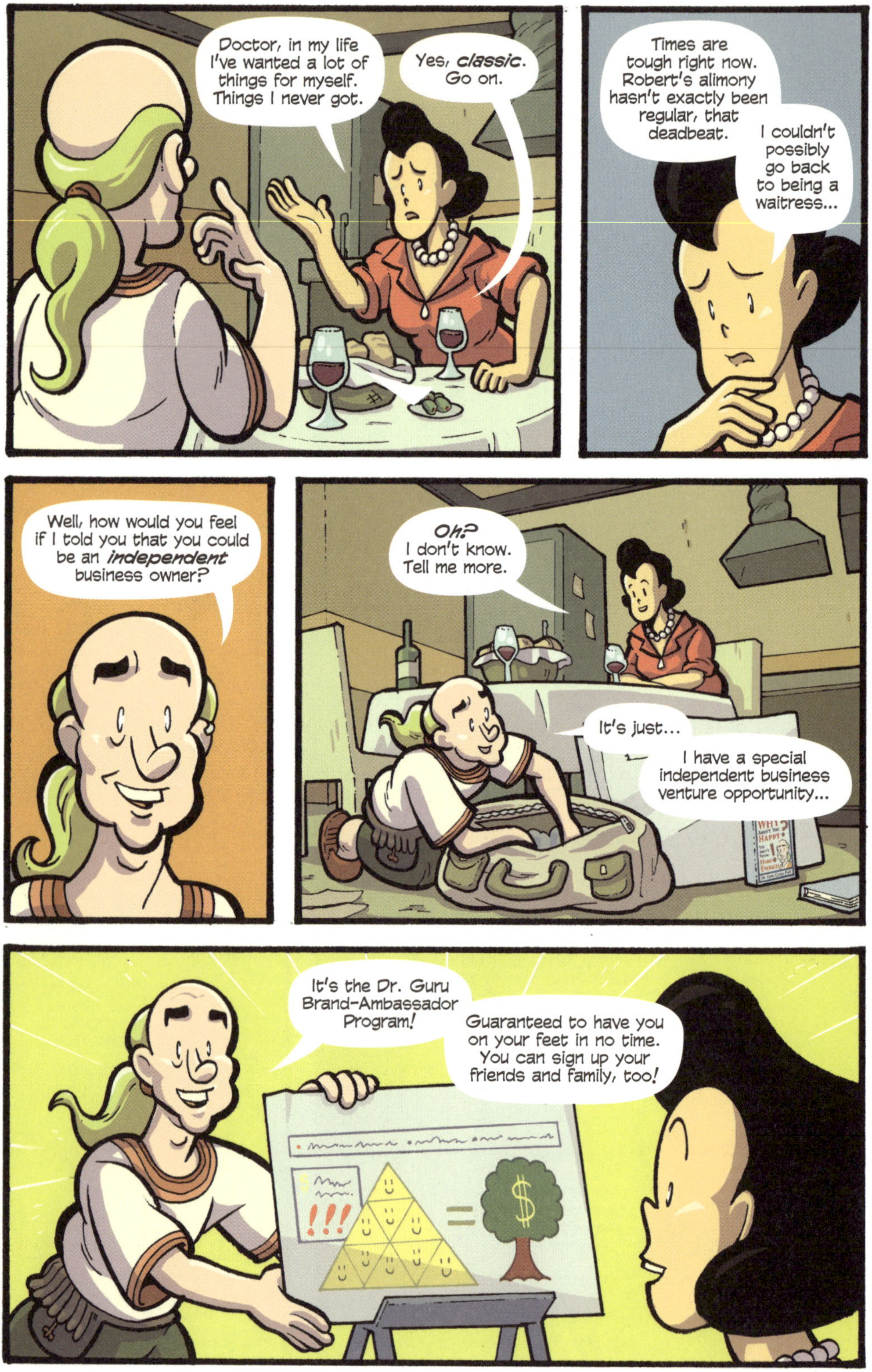

Doctor, in my life I've wanted a lot of things for myself. Things I never got.
Yes, *classic*. Go on.
Times are tough right now. Robert's alimony hasn't exactly been regular, that deadbeat.
I couldn't possibly go back to being a waitress...
Well, how would you feel if I told you that you could be an *independent* business owner?
Oh? I don't know. Tell me more.
It's just...
I have a special independent business venture opportunity...
It's the Dr. Guru Brand-Ambassador Program!
Guaranteed to have you on your feet in no time. You can sign up your friends and family, too!

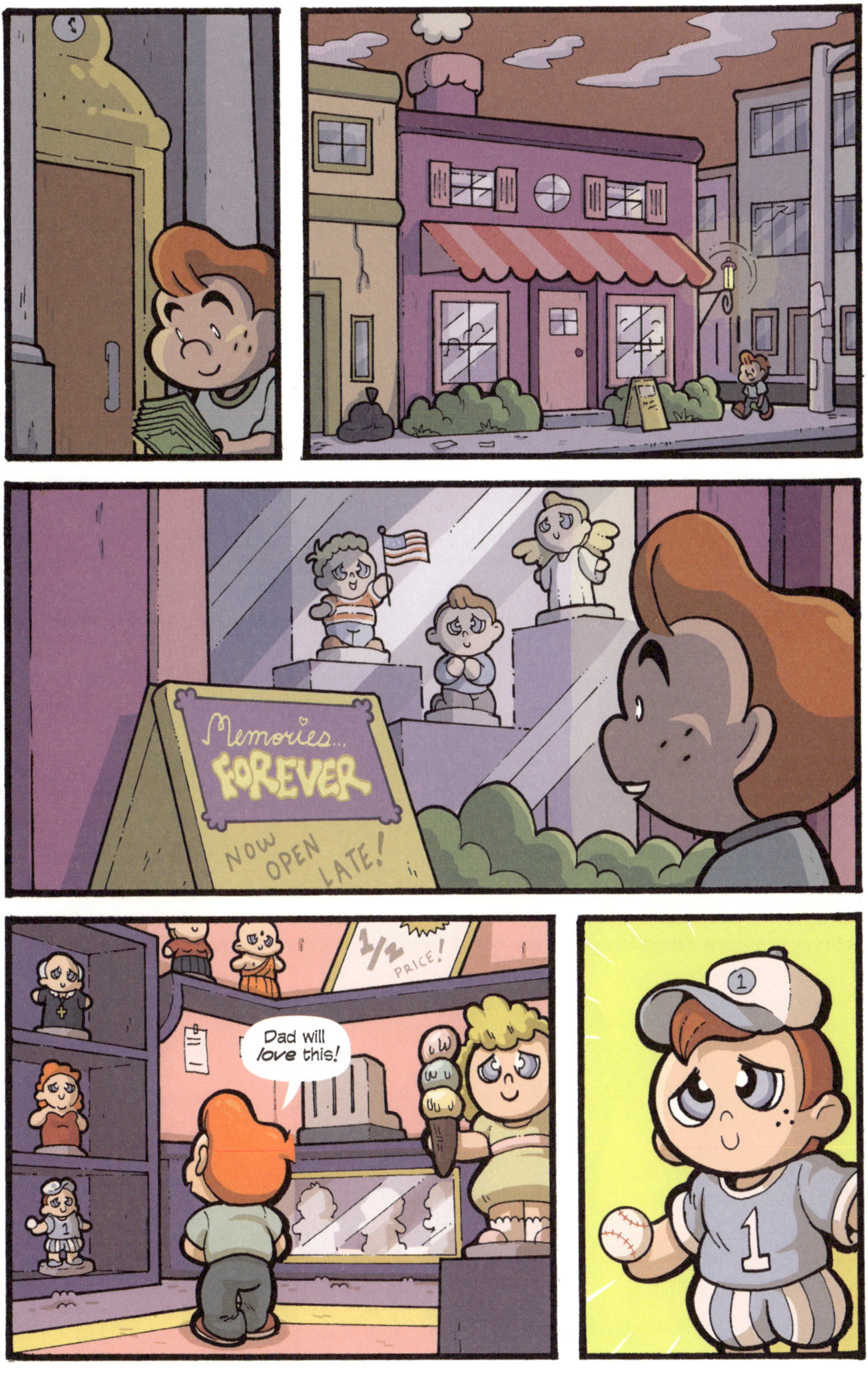
Memories...
FOREVER
NOW OPEN LATE!
1/2 PRICE!
Dad will *love* this!
1

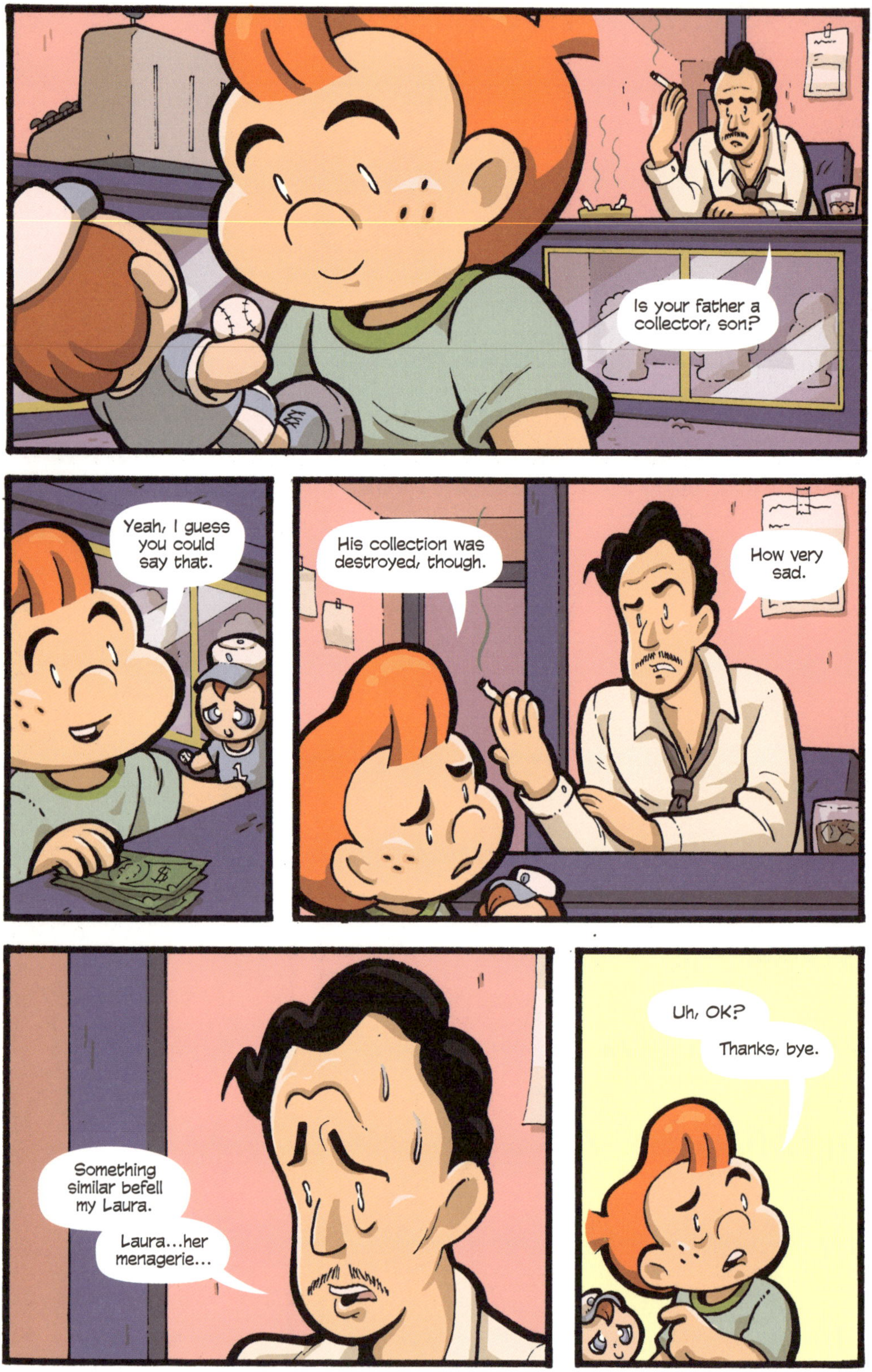
Is your father a collector, son?
Yeah, I guess you could say that.
His collection was destroyed, though.
How very sad.
Something similar befell my Laura.
Laura...her menagerie...
Uh, OK?
Thanks, bye.

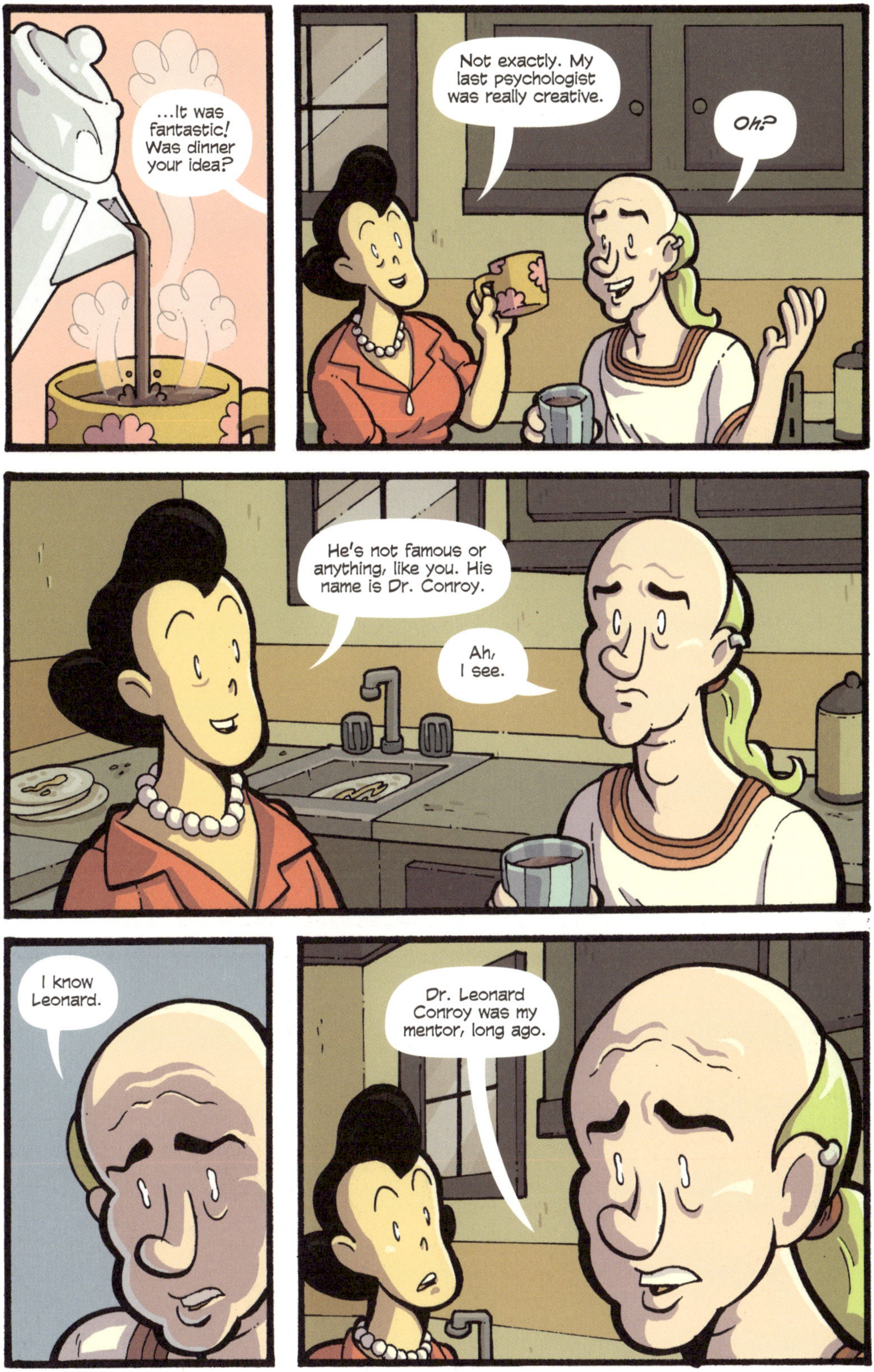
...It was fantastic! Was dinner your idea?
Not exactly. My last psychologist was really creative.
Oh?
He's not famous or anything, like you. His name is Dr. Conroy.
Ah, I see.
I know Leonard.
Dr. Leonard Conroy was my mentor, long ago.

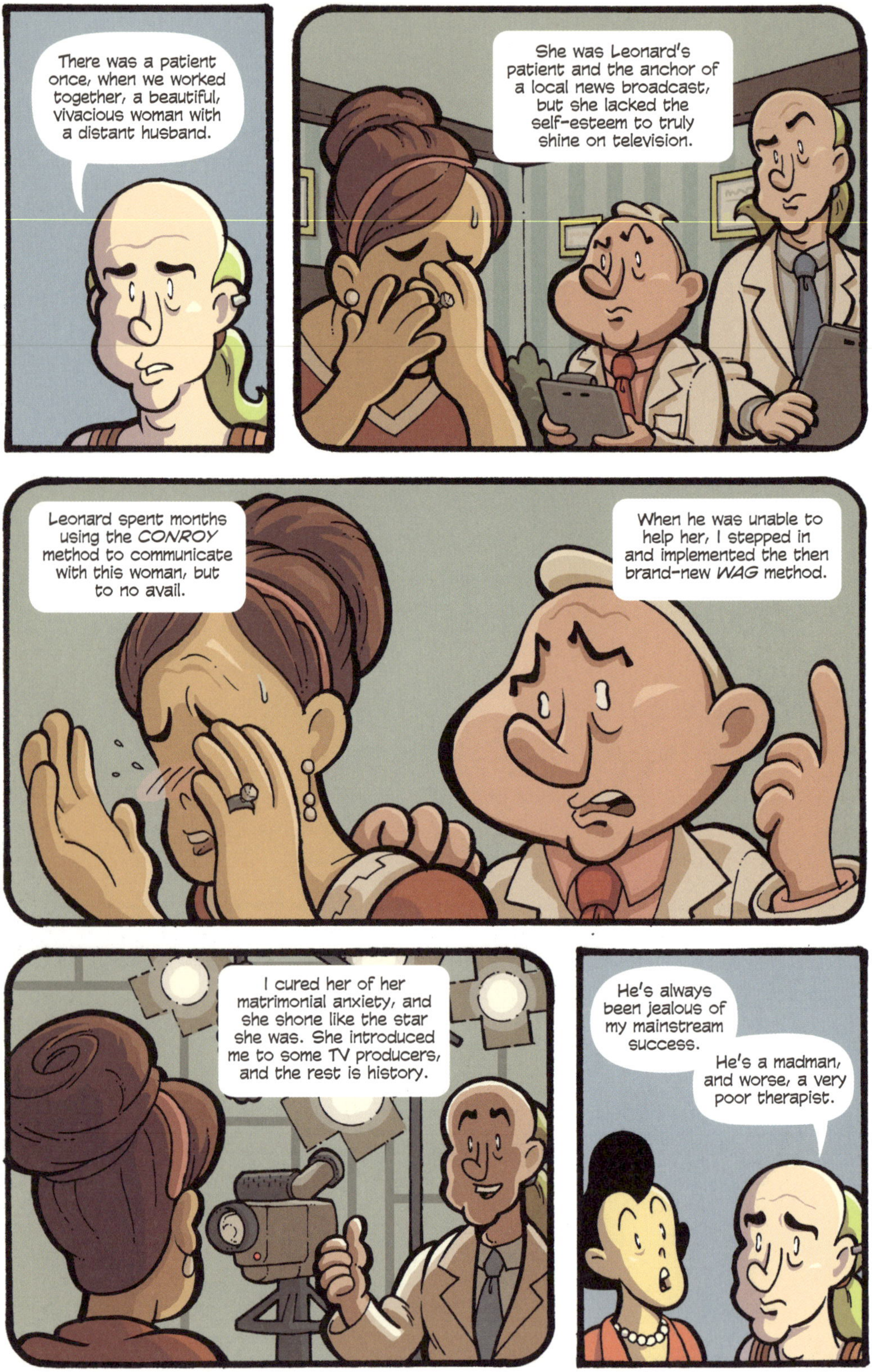
There was a patient once, when we worked together, a beautiful, vivacious woman with a distant husband.
She was Leonard's patient and the anchor of a local news broadcast, but she lacked the self-esteem to truly shine on television.
Leonard spent months using the *CONROY* method to communicate with this woman, but to no avail.
When he was unable to help her, I stepped in and implemented the then brand-new *WAG* method.
I cured her of her matrimonial anxiety, and she shone like the star she was. She introduced me to some TV producers, and the rest is history.
He's always been jealous of my mainstream success.
He's a madman, and worse, a very poor therapist.

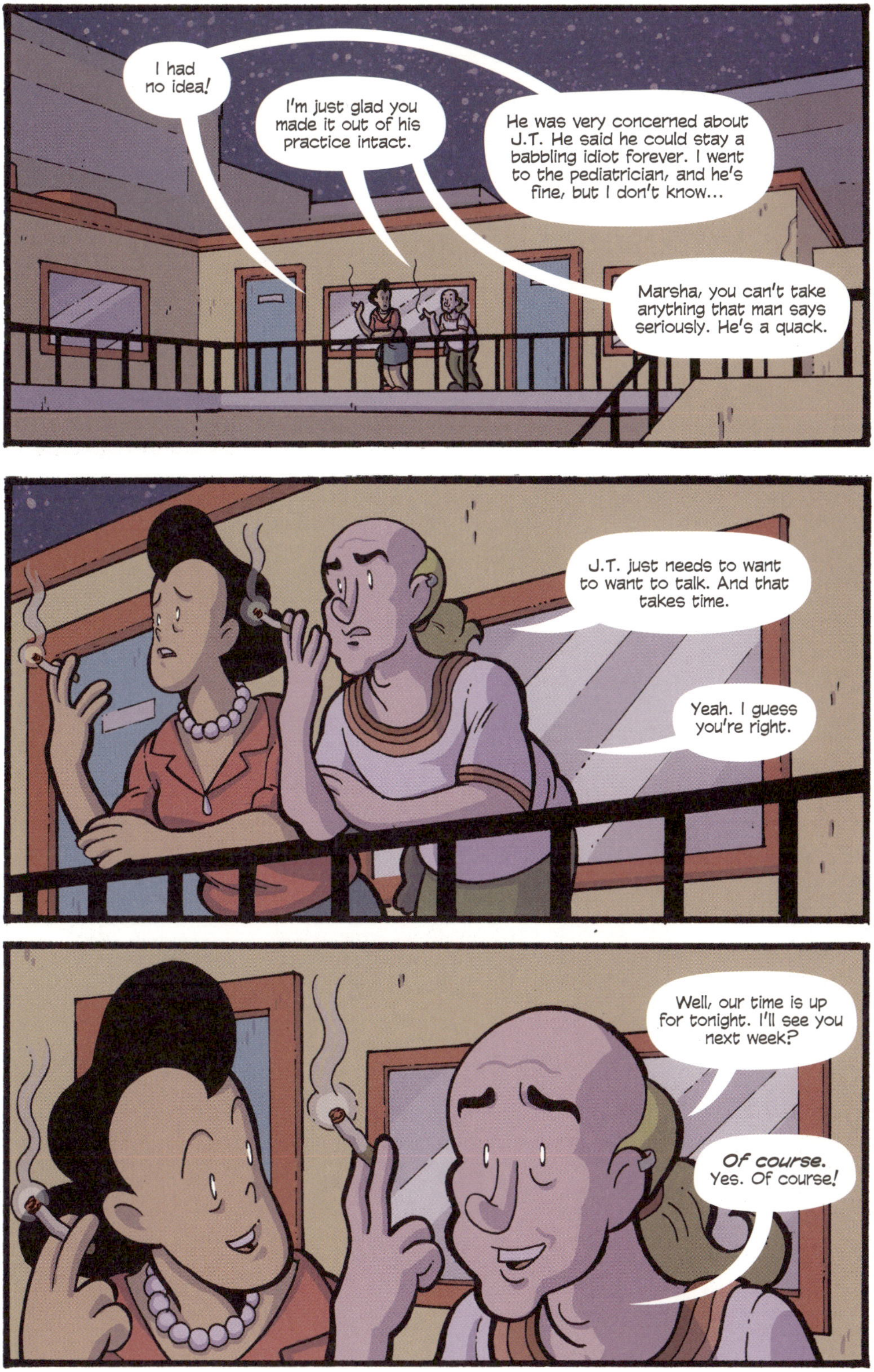
I had no idea!
I'm just glad you made it out of his practice intact.
He was very concerned about J.T. He said he could stay a babbling idiot forever. I went to the pediatrician, and he's fine, but I don't know...
Marsha, you can't take anything that man says seriously. He's a quack.
J.T. just needs to want to want to talk. And that takes time.
Yeah. I guess you're right.
Well, our time is up for tonight. I'll see you next week?
Of course. Yes. Of course!

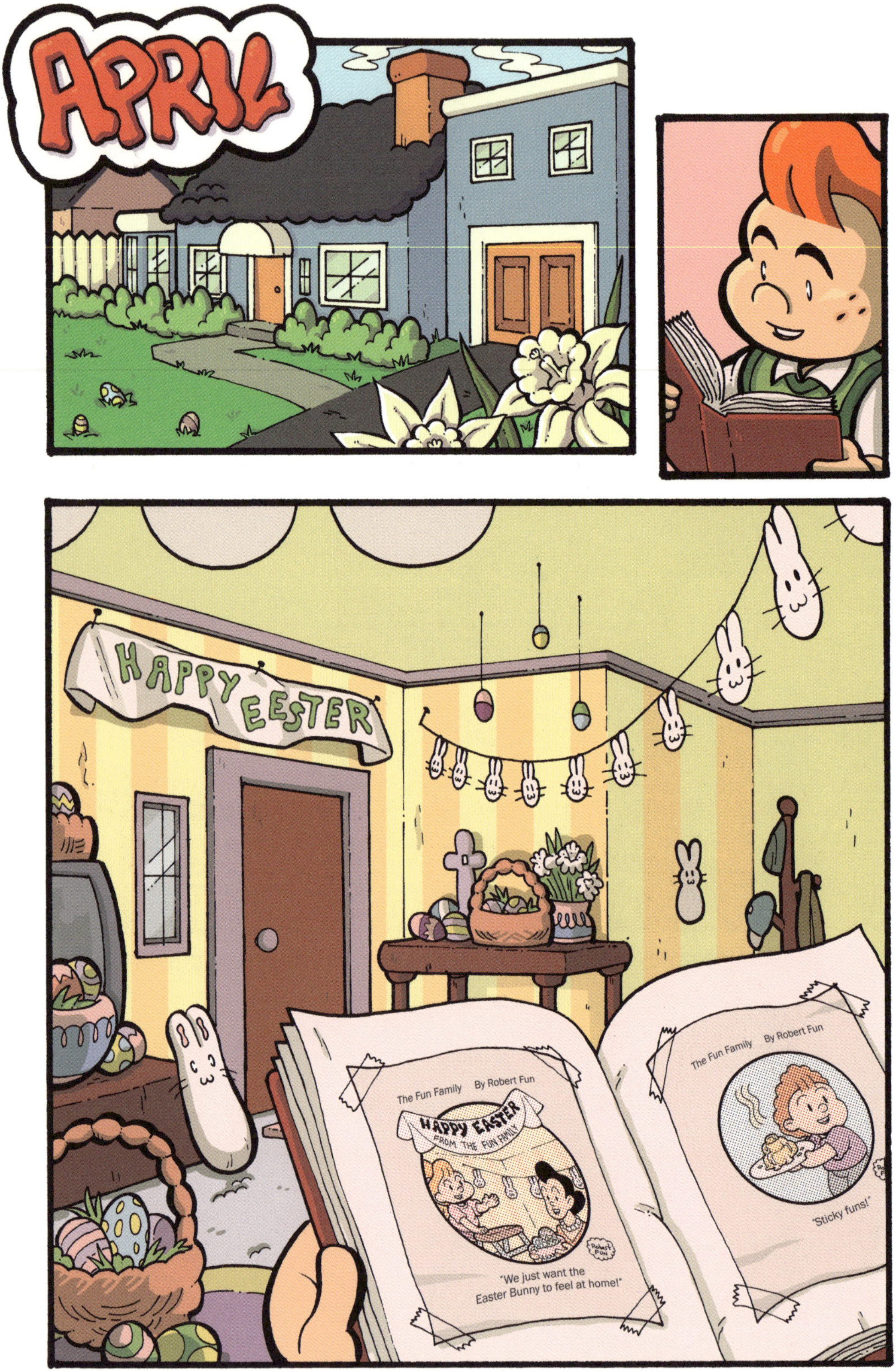
APRIL
HAPPY EESTER
The Fun Family By Robert Fun
HAPPY EASTER FROM THE FUN FAMILY
"We just want the Easter Bunny to feel at home!"
The Fun Family By Robert Fun
"Sticky funs!"

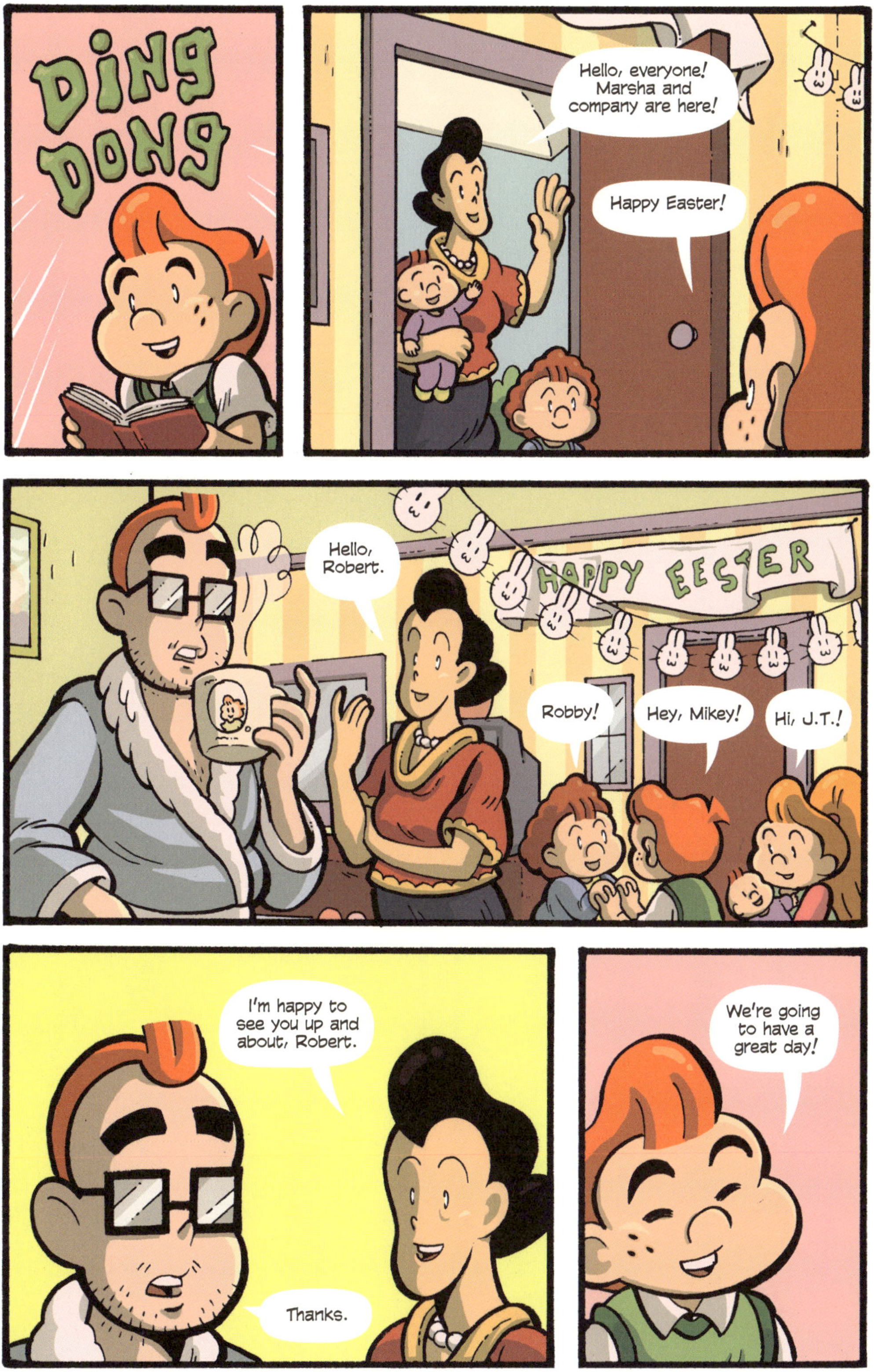
DING DONG
Hello, everyone! Marsha and company are here!
Happy Easter!
Hello, Robert.
HAPPY EASTER
Robby!
Hey, Mikey!
Hi, J.T.!
I'm happy to see you up and about, Robert.
Thanks.
We're going to have a great day!

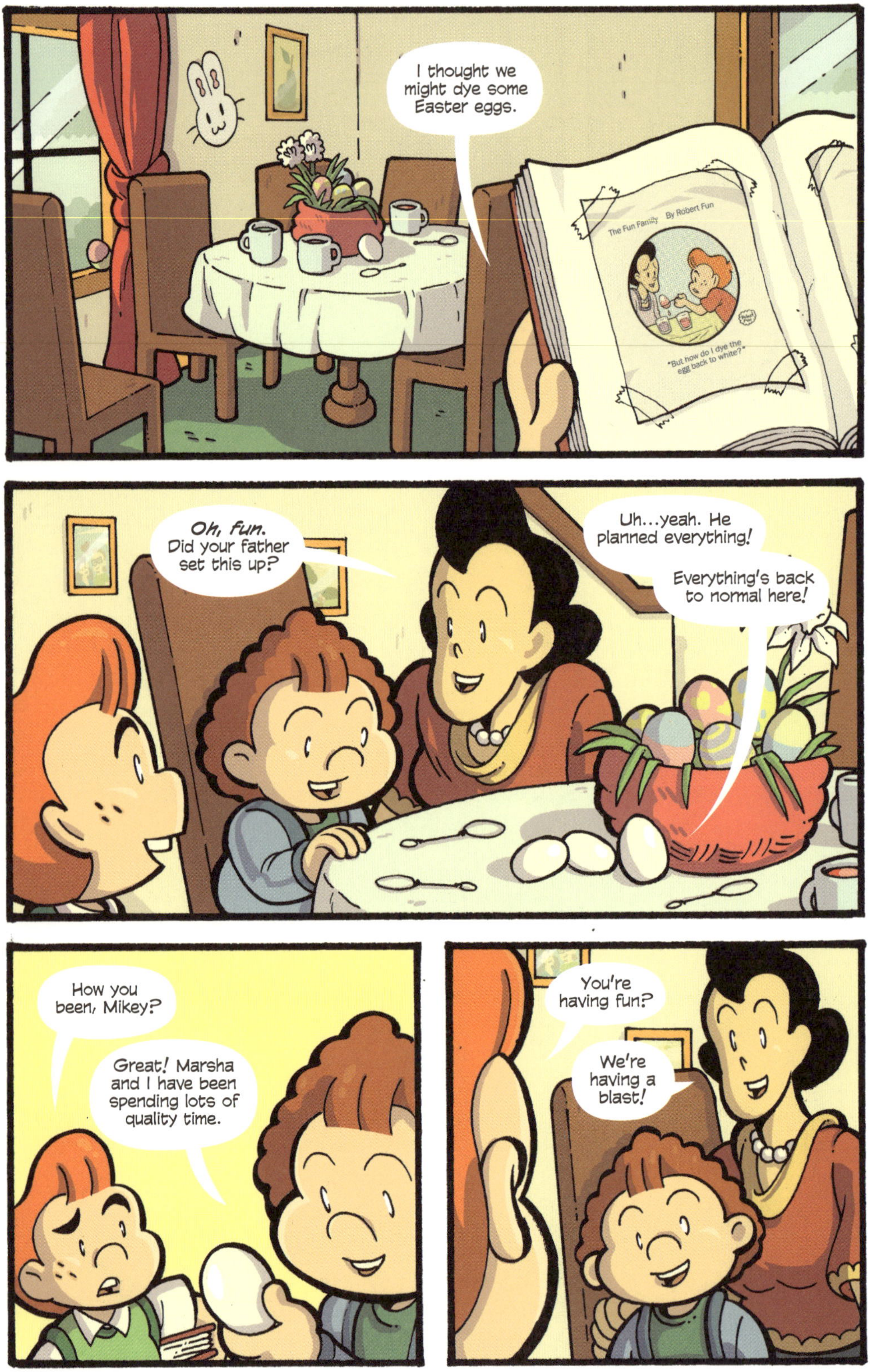
I thought we might dye some Easter eggs.
The Fun Family By Robert Fun
"But how do I dye the egg back to white?"
Oh, fun. Did your father set this up?
Uh...yeah. He planned everything!
Everything's back to normal here!
How you been, Mikey?
Great! Marsha and I have been spending lots of quality time.
You're having fun?
We're having a blast!

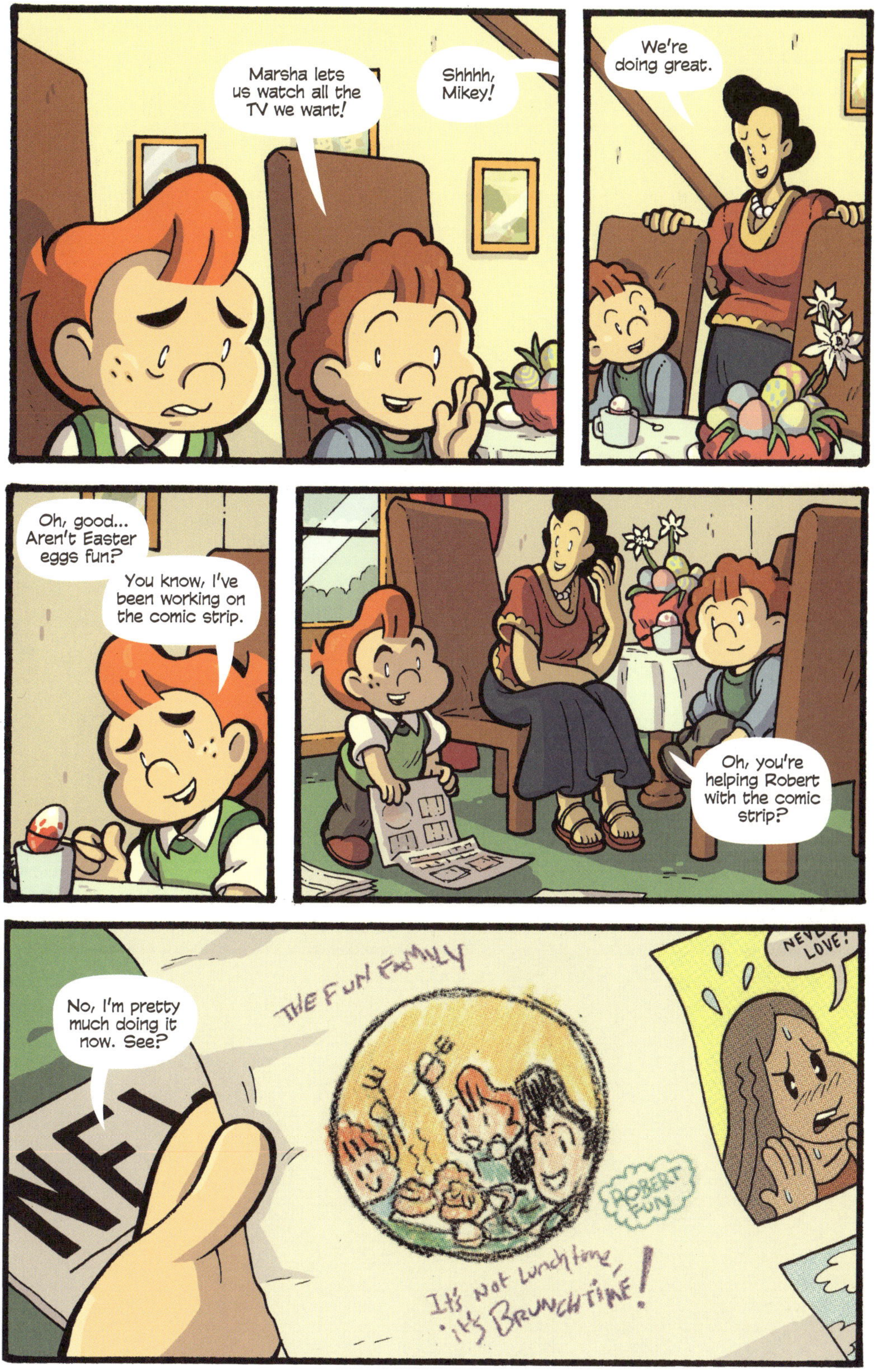

Marsha lets us watch all the TV we want!
Shhhh, Mikey!
We're doing great.
Oh, good... Aren't Easter eggs fun?
You know, I've been working on the comic strip.
Oh, you're helping Robert with the comic strip?
No, I'm pretty much doing it now. See?
THE FUN FAMILY
ROBERT FUN
It's not lunchtime, it's BRUNCHTIME!

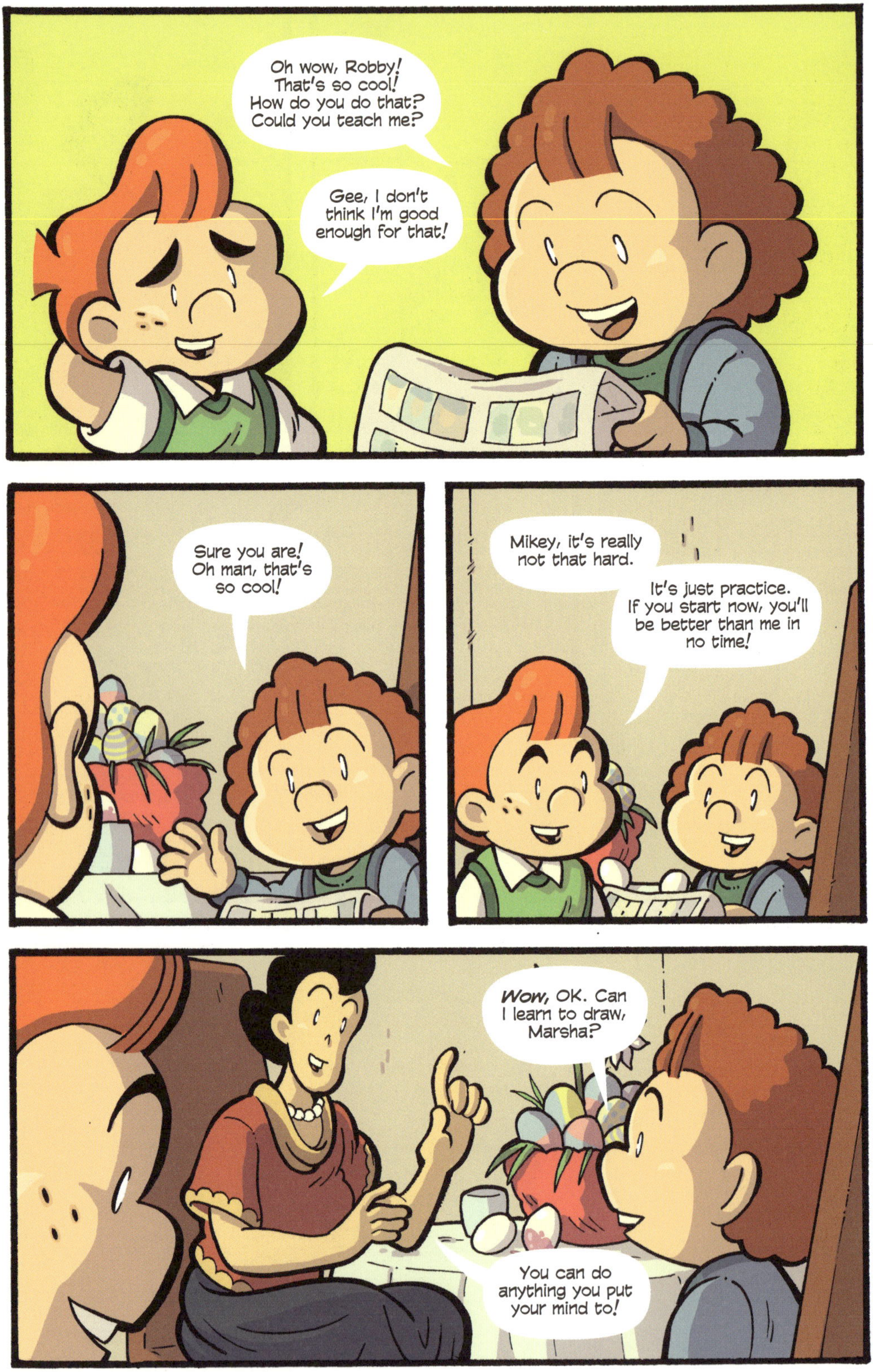
Oh wow, Robby! That's so cool! How do you do that? Could you teach me?
Gee, I don't think I'm good enough for that!
Sure you are! Oh man, that's so cool!
Mikey, it's really not that hard.
It's just practice. If you start now, you'll be better than me in no time!
Wow, OK. Can I learn to draw, Marsha?
You can do anything you put your mind to!

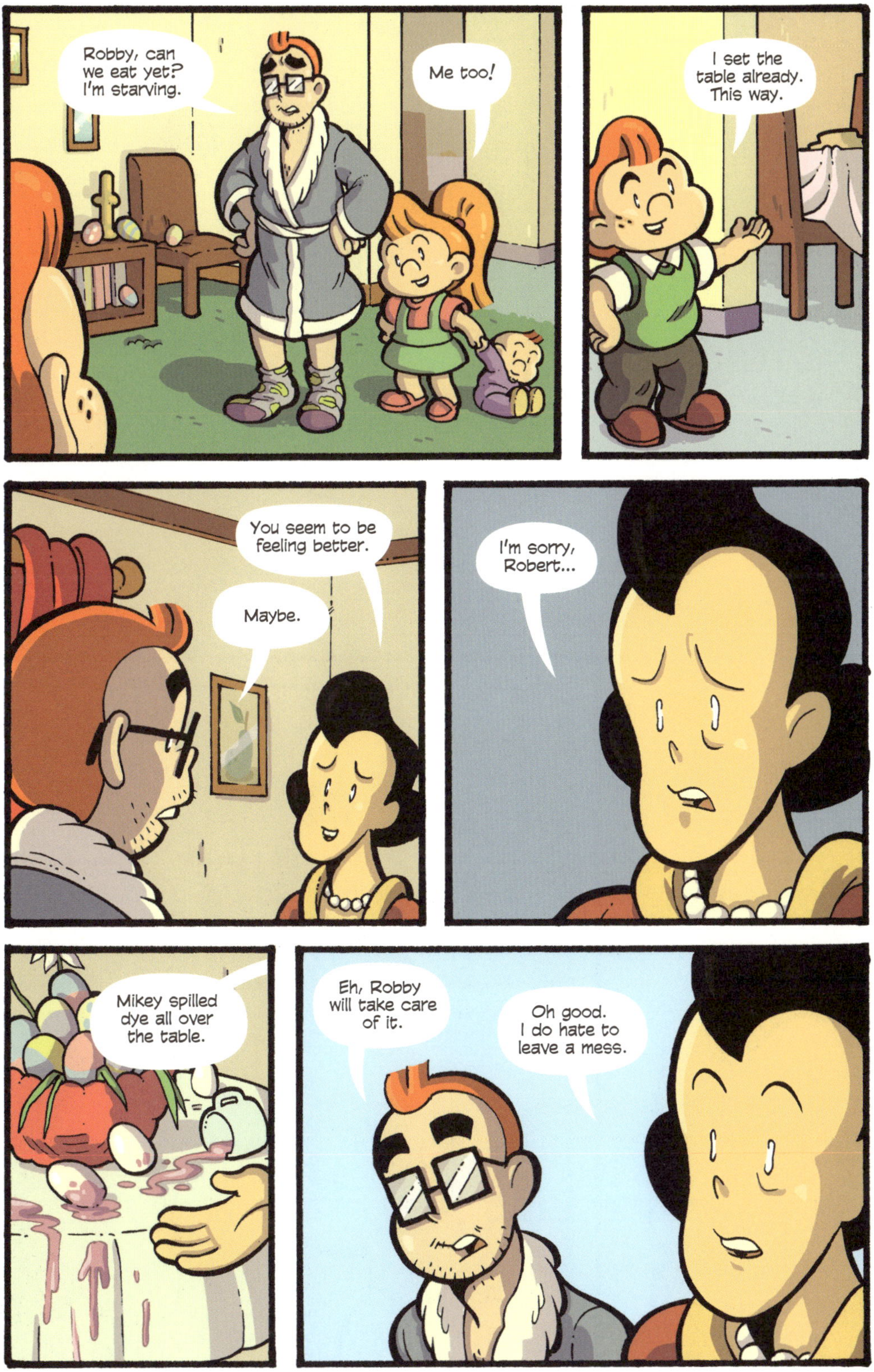
Robby, can we eat yet? I'm starving.
Me too!
I set the table already. This way.
You seem to be feeling better.
Maybe.
I'm sorry, Robert...
Mikey spilled dye all over the table.
Eh, Robby will take care of it.
Oh good. I do hate to leave a mess.

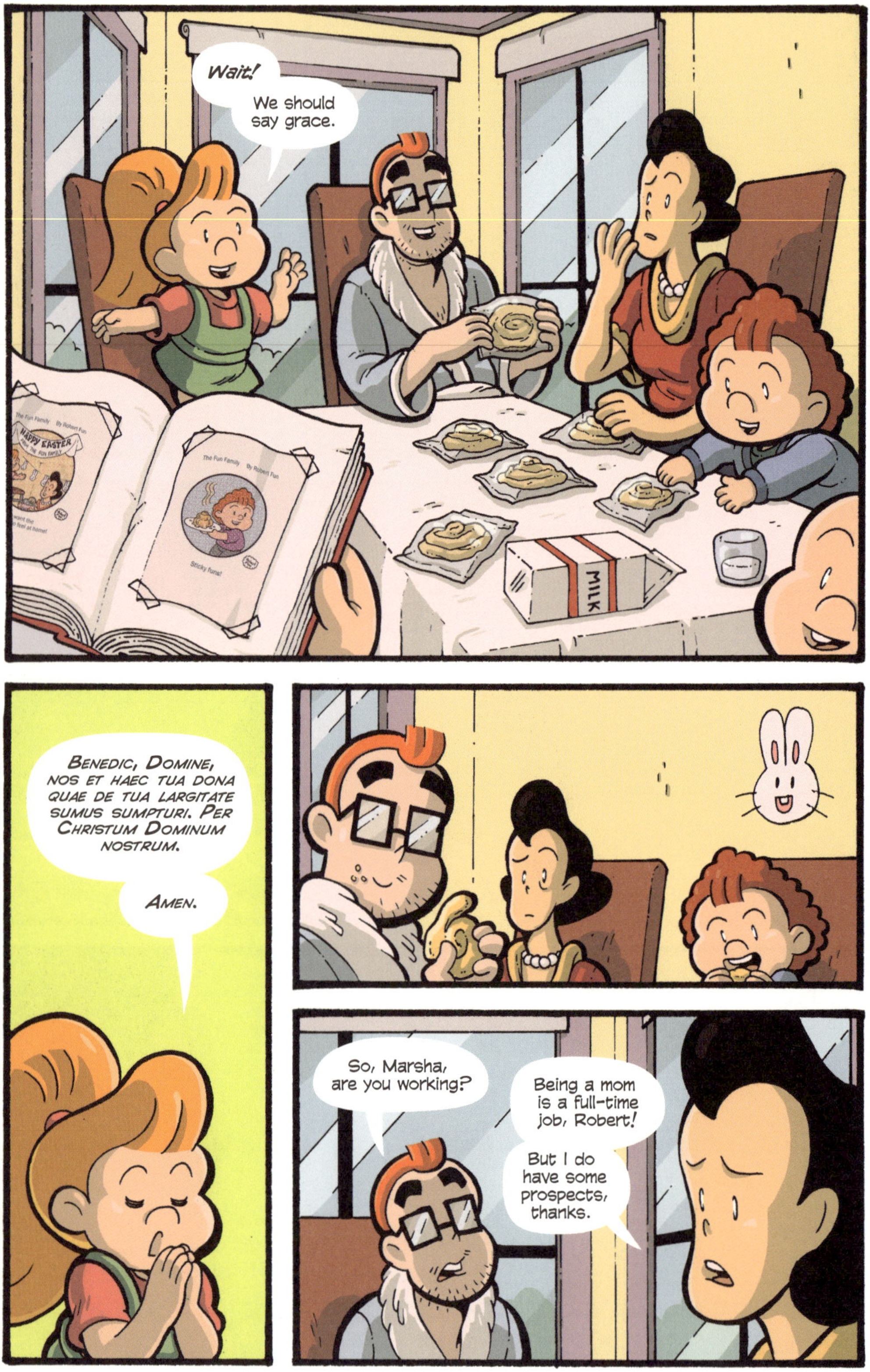
Wait!
We should say grace.
MILK
Benedic, Domine, nos et haec tua dona quae de tua largitate sumus sumpturi. Per Christum Dominum nostrum.
Amen.
So, Marsha, are you working?
Being a mom is a full-time job, Robert!
But I do have some prospects, thanks.

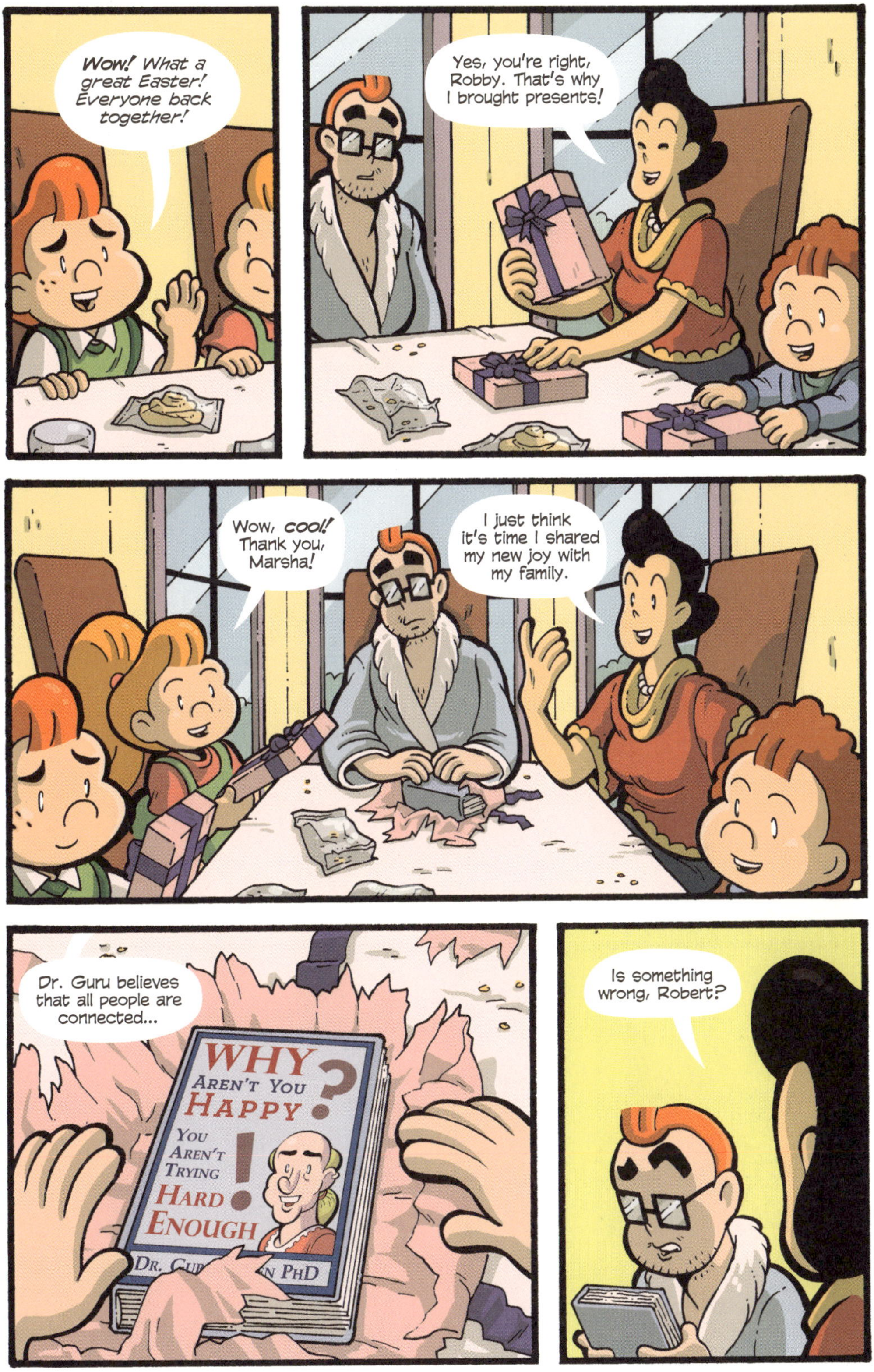
Wow! What a great Easter! Everyone back together!
Yes, you're right, Robby. That's why I brought presents!
Wow, cool! Thank you, Marsha!
I just think it's time I shared my new joy with my family.
Dr. Guru believes that all people are connected...
WHY AREN'T YOU HAPPY? YOU AREN'T TRYING HARD ENOUGH!
Is something wrong, Robert?

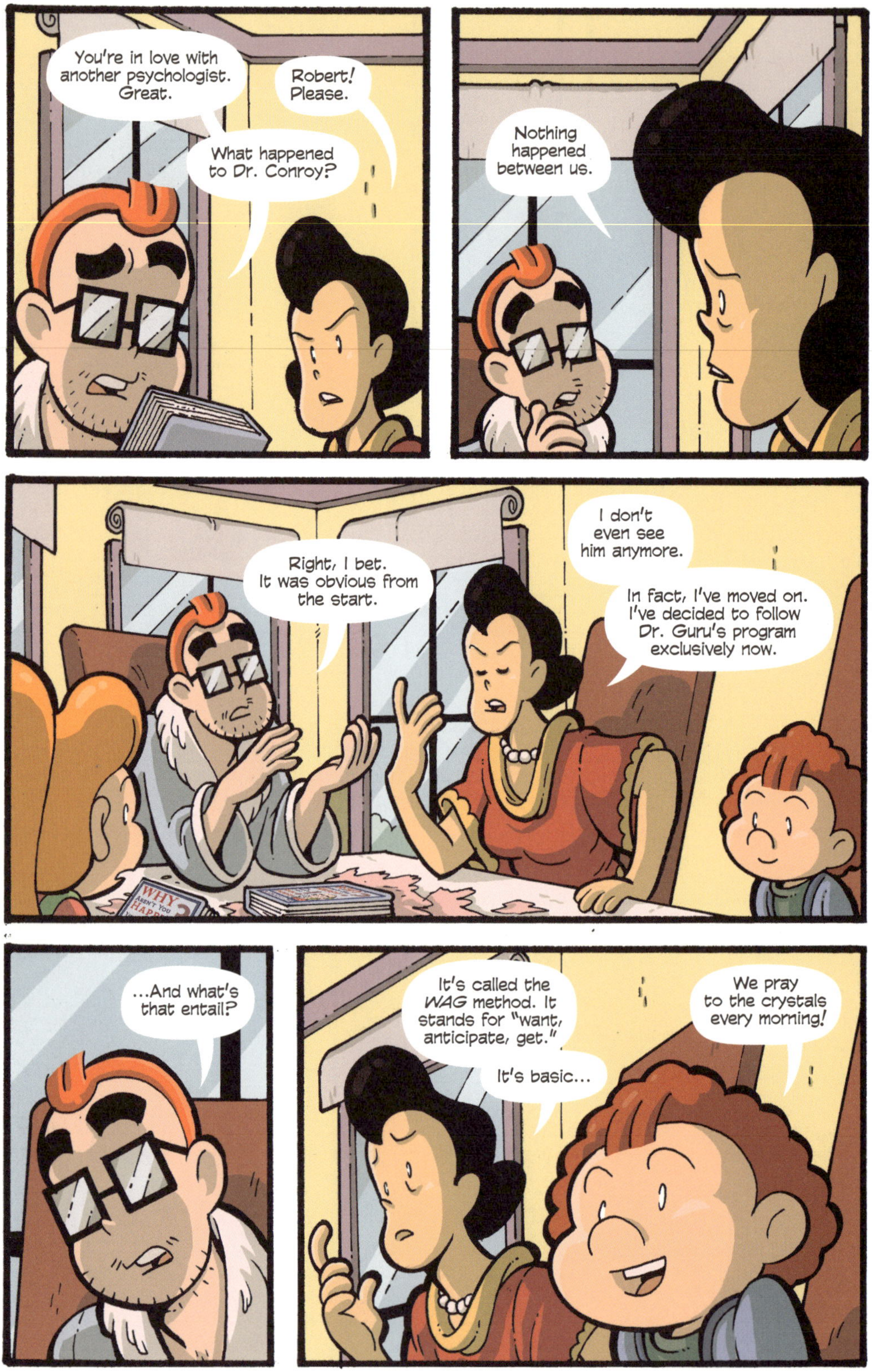
You're in love with another psychologist. Great.
What happened to Dr. Conroy?
Robert! Please.
Nothing happened between us.
Right, I bet. It was obvious from the start.
I don't even see him anymore.
In fact, I've moved on. I've decided to follow Dr. Guru's program exclusively now.
WHY AREN'T YOU HAPP
...And what's that entail?
It's called the *WAG* method. It stands for "want, anticipate, get."
It's basic...
We pray to the crystals every morning!

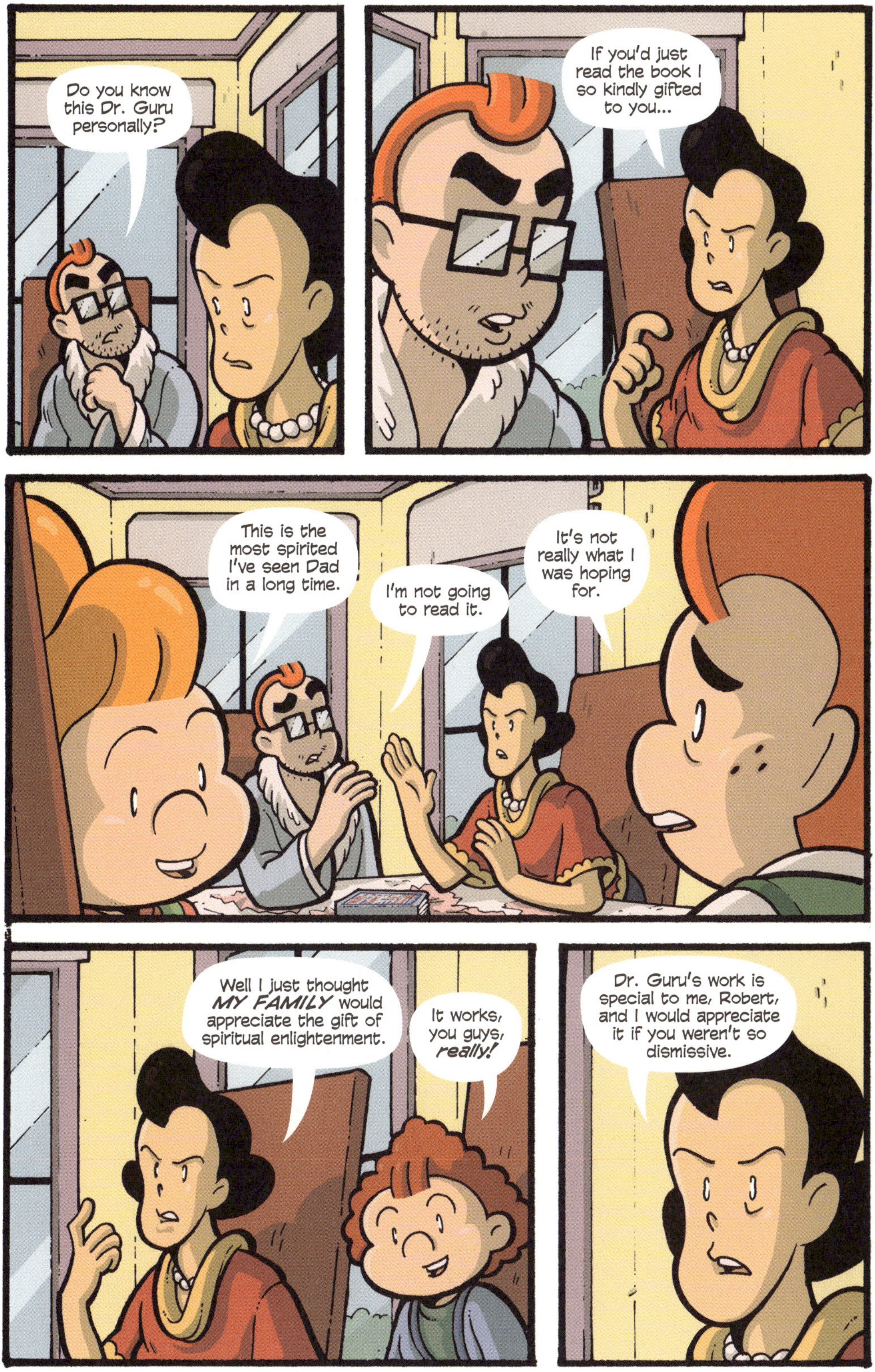
Do you know this Dr. Guru personally?
If you'd just read the book I so kindly gifted to you...
This is the most spirited I've seen Dad in a long time.
I'm not going to read it.
It's not really what I was hoping for.
Well I just thought MY FAMILY would appreciate the gift of spiritual enlightenment.
It works, you guys, really!
Dr. Guru's work is special to me, Robert, and I would appreciate it if you weren't so dismissive.

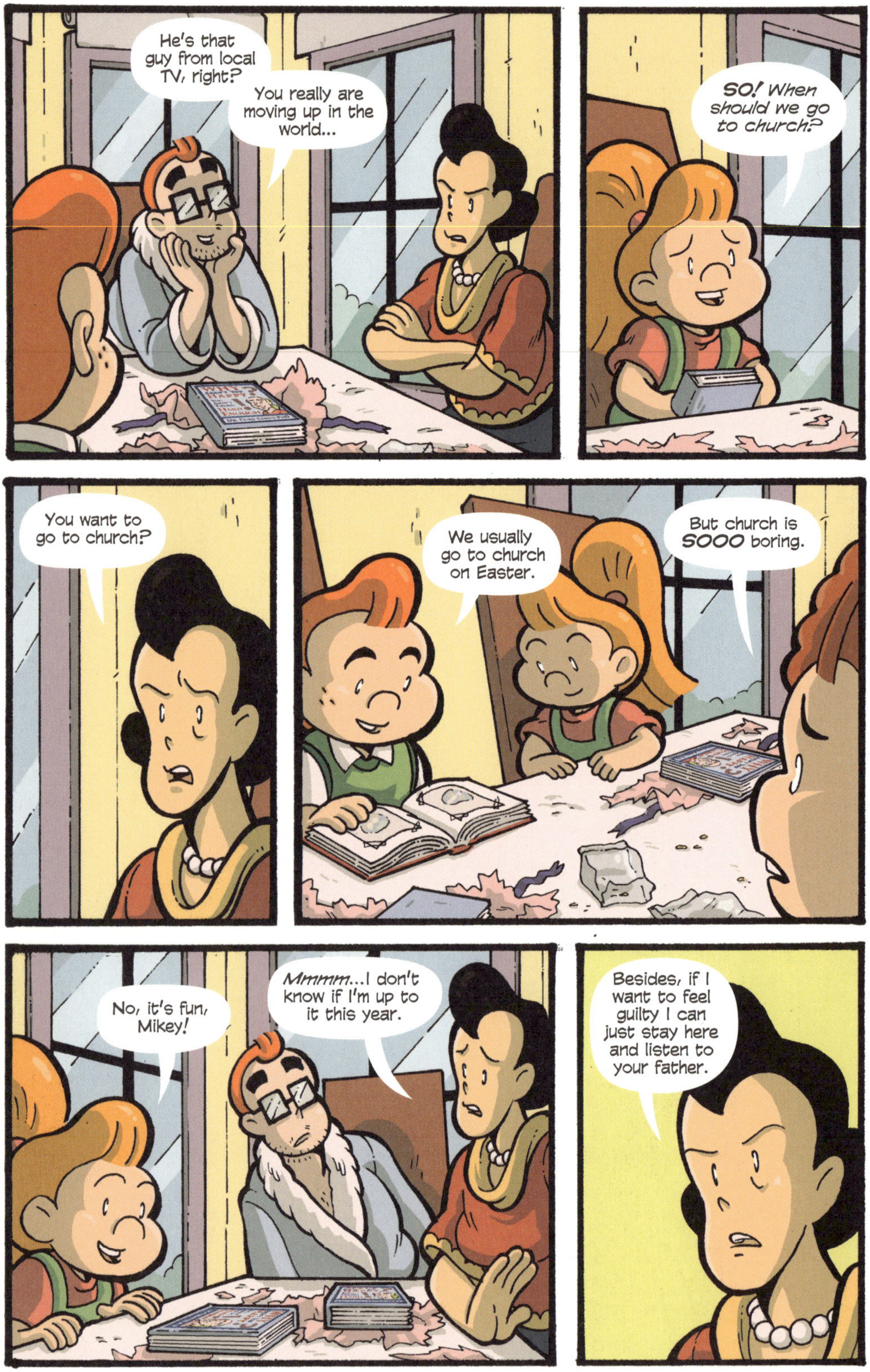
He's that guy from local TV, right?
You really are moving up in the world...
SO! When should we go to church?
You want to go to church?
We usually go to church on Easter.
But church is SOOO boring.
No, it's fun, Mikey!
Mmmm...I don't know if I'm up to it this year.
Besides, if I want to feel guilty I can just stay here and listen to your father.

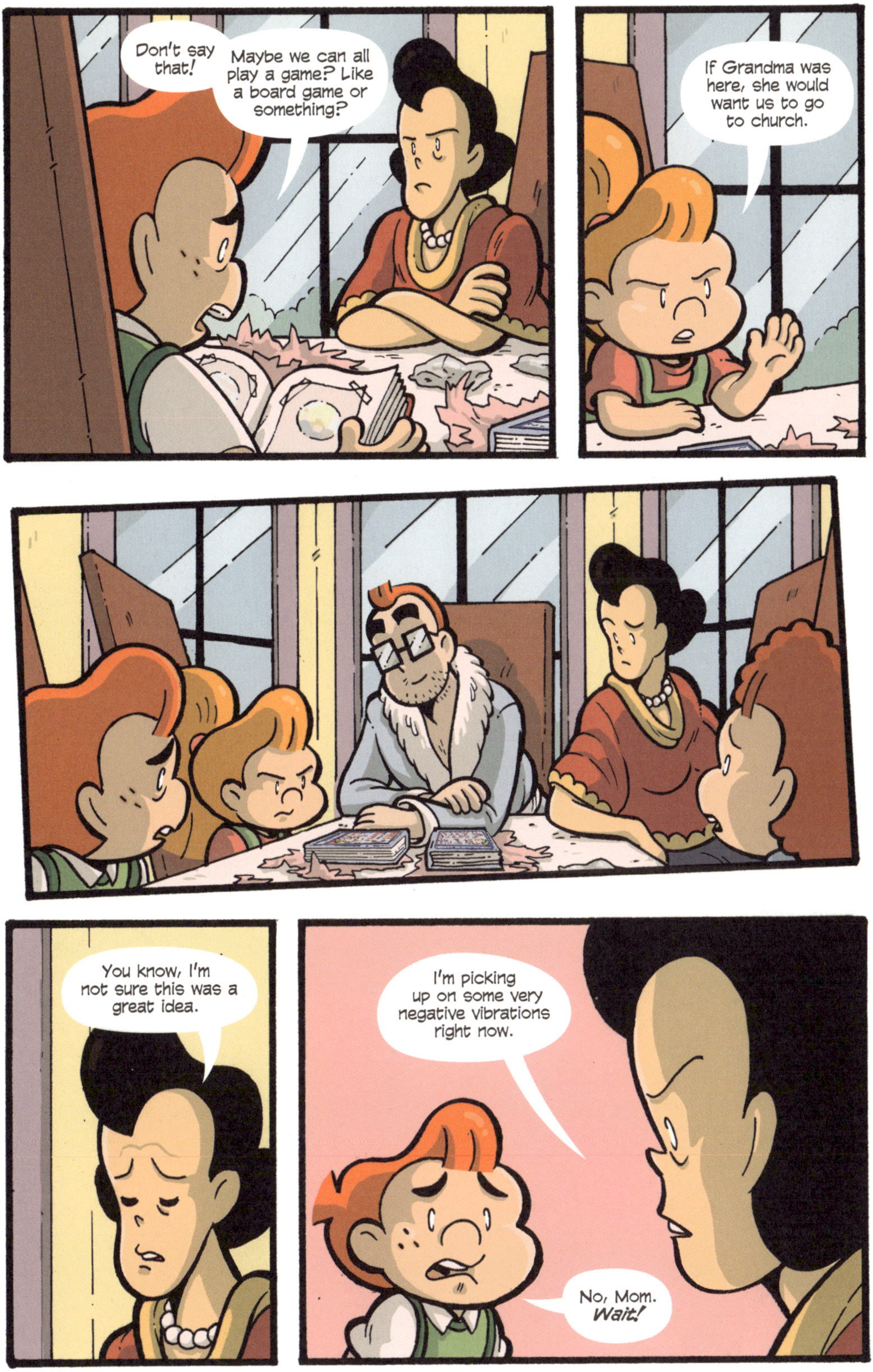
Don't say that!
Maybe we can all play a game? Like a board game or something?
If Grandma was here, she would want us to go to church.
You know, I'm not sure this was a great idea.
I'm picking up on some very negative vibrations right now.
No, Mom. *Wait!*

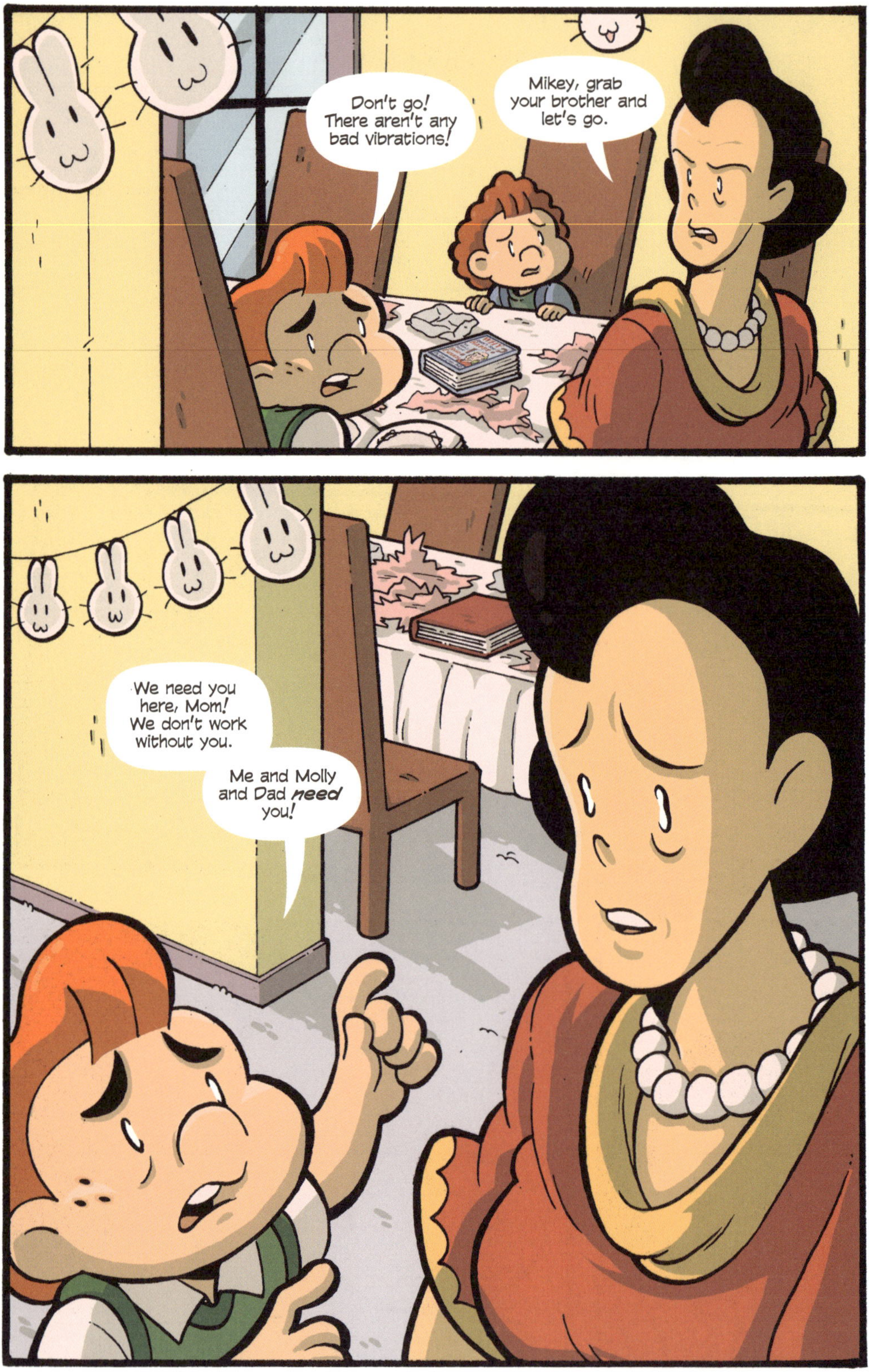
Mikey, grab your brother and let's go.
Don't go! There aren't any bad vibrations!
We need you here, Mom! We don't work without you.
Me and Molly and Dad *need* you!

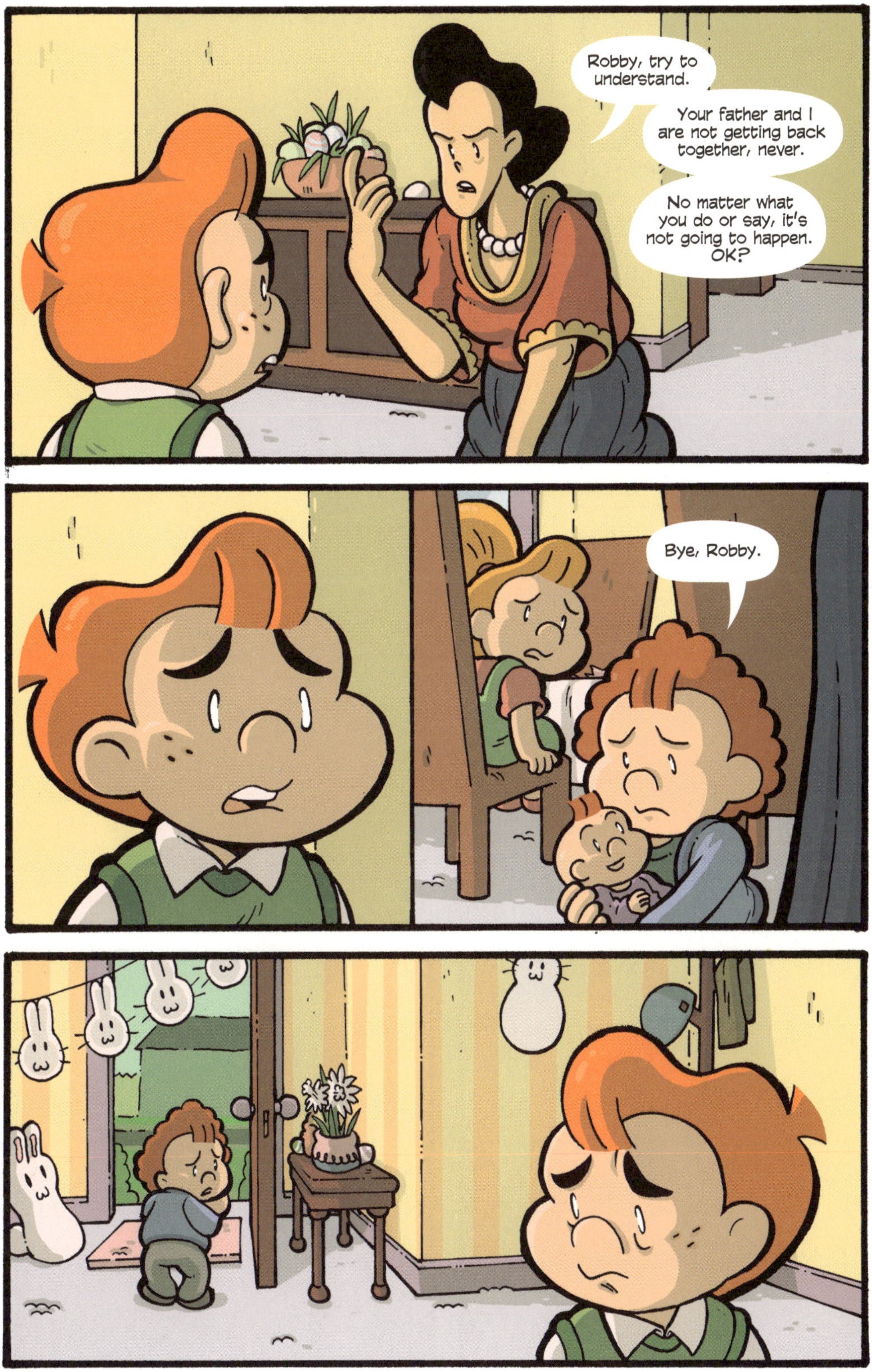
Robby, try to understand.
Your father and I are not getting back together, never.
No matter what you do or say, it's not going to happen. OK?
Bye, Robby.

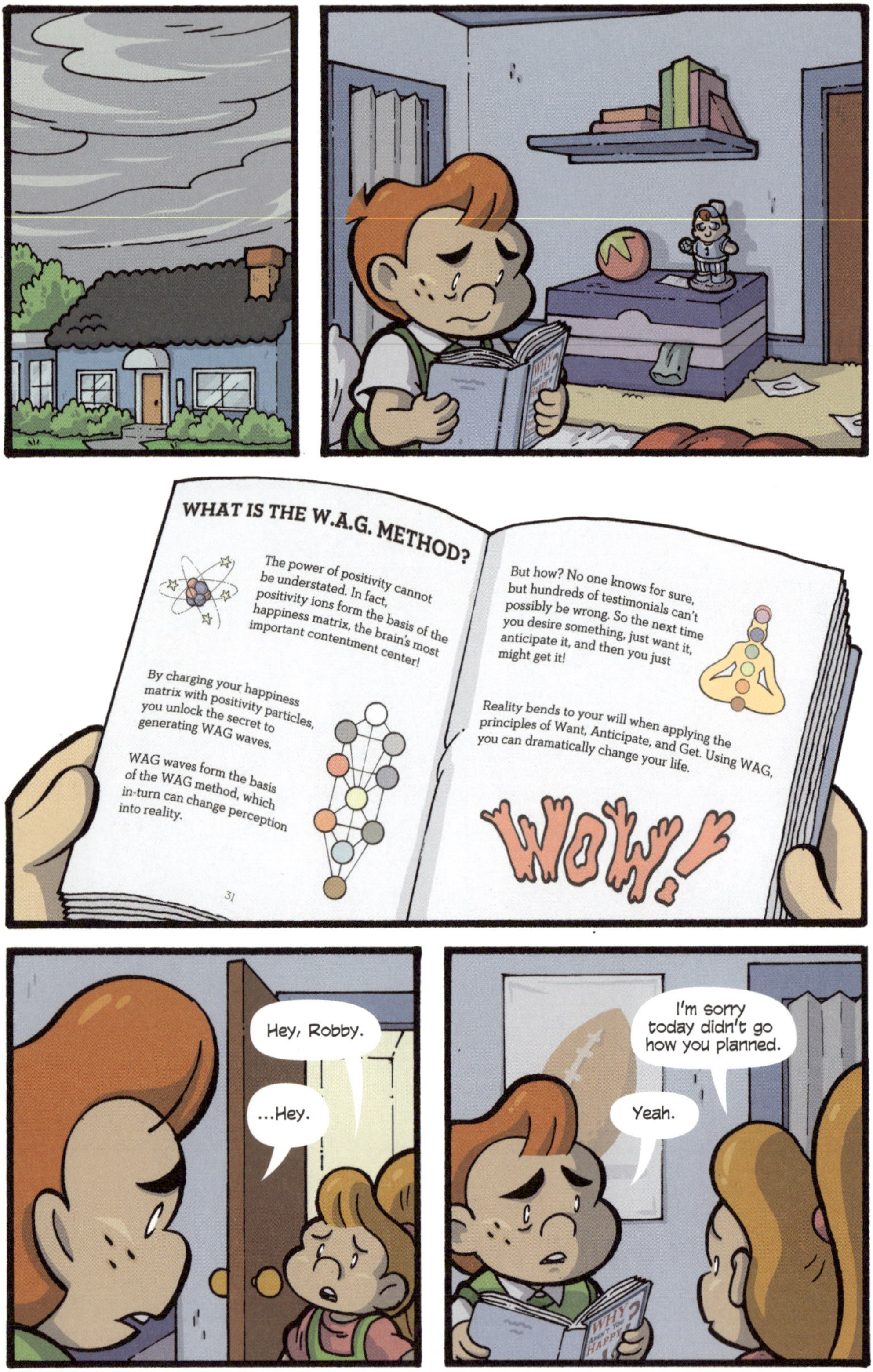
WHAT IS THE W.A.G. METHOD?
The power of positivity cannot be understated. In fact, positivity ions form the basis of the happiness matrix, the brain's most important contentment center!
By charging your happiness matrix with positivity particles, you unlock the secret to generating WAG waves.
WAG waves form the basis of the WAG method, which in-turn can change perception into reality.
31
But how? No one knows for sure, but hundreds of testimonials can't possibly be wrong. So the next time you desire something, just want it, anticipate it, and then you just might get it!
Reality bends to your will when applying the principles of Want, Anticipate, and Get. Using WAG, you can dramatically change your life.
WOW!
Hey, Robby.
...Hey.
I'm sorry today didn't go how you planned.
Yeah.

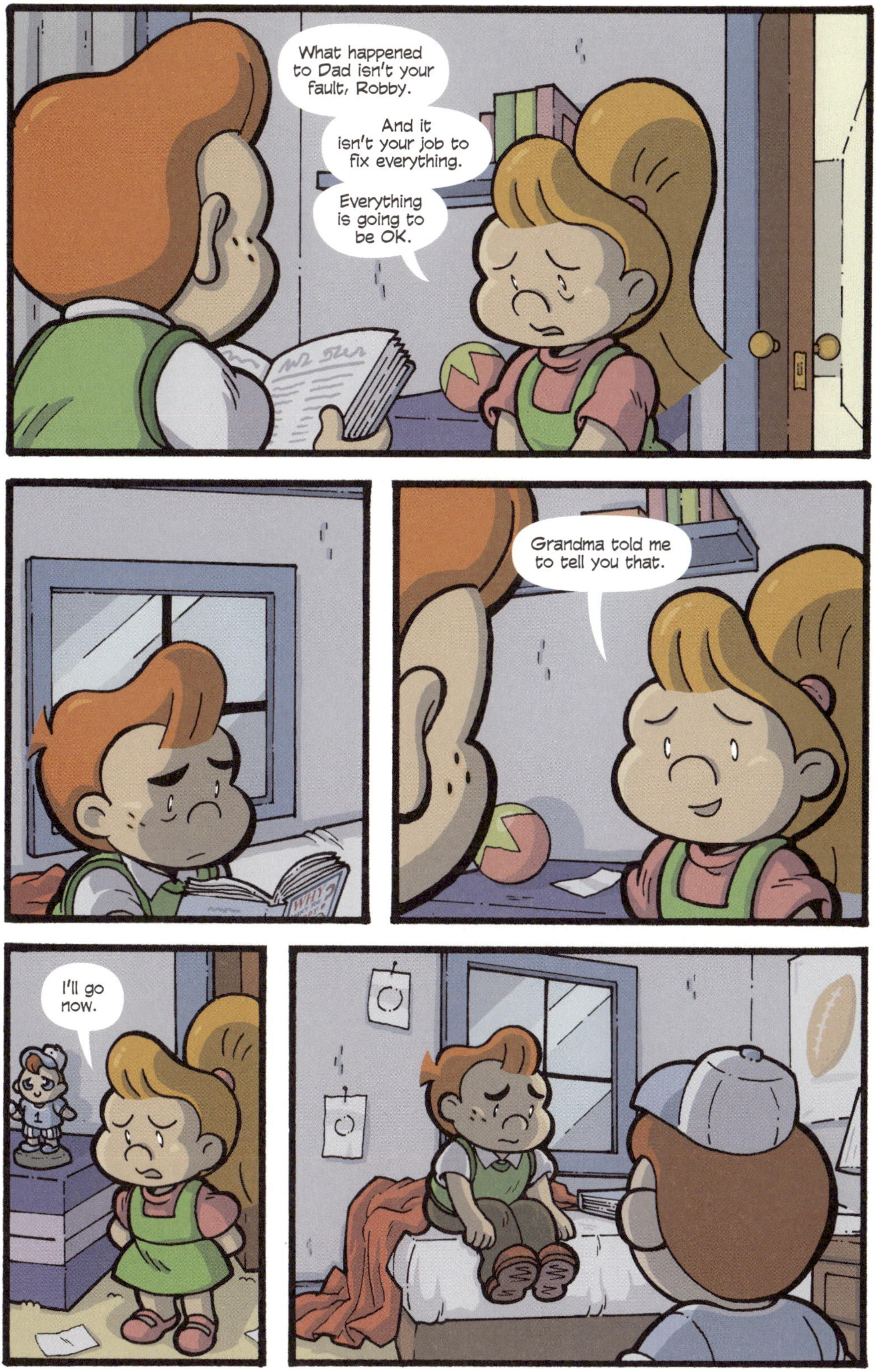
What happened to Dad isn't your fault, Robby.
And it isn't your job to fix everything.
Everything is going to be OK.
Grandma told me to tell you that.
I'll go now.

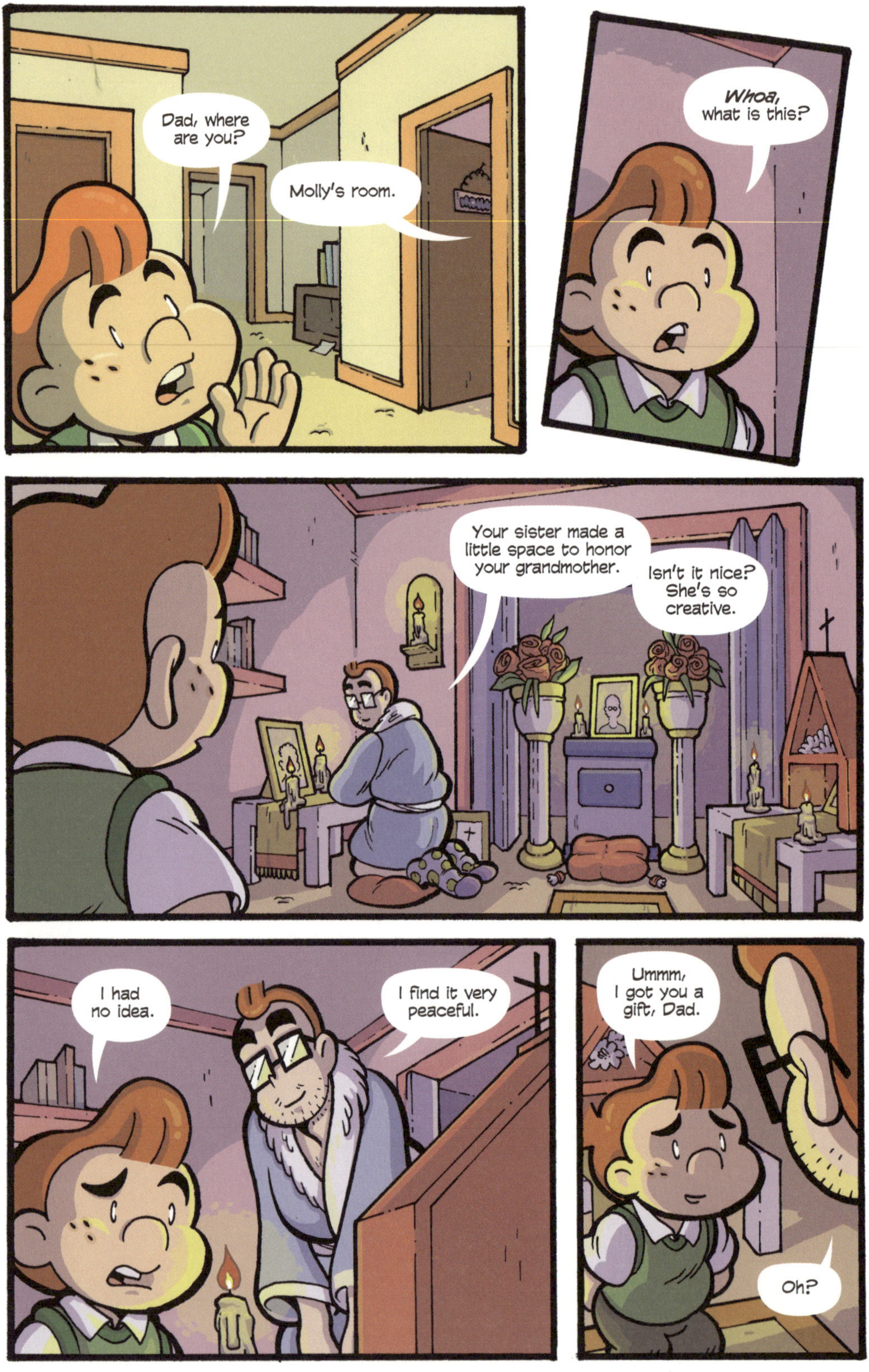
Dad, where are you?
Molly's room.
Whoa, what is this?
Your sister made a little space to honor your grandmother.
Isn't it nice? She's so creative.
I had no idea.
I find it very peaceful.
Ummm, I got you a gift, Dad.
Oh?

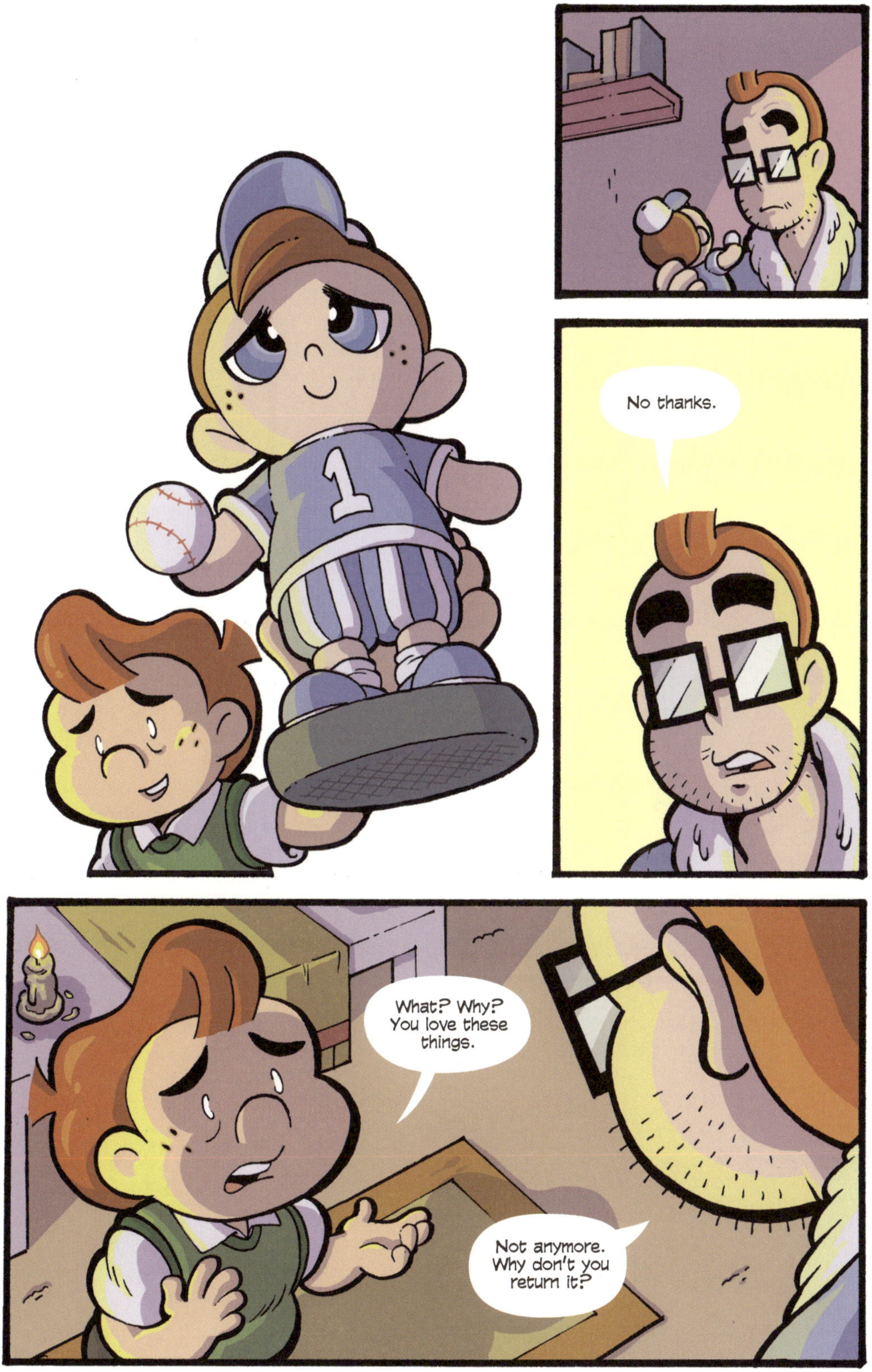
No thanks.
What? Why? You love these things.
Not anymore. Why don't you return it?

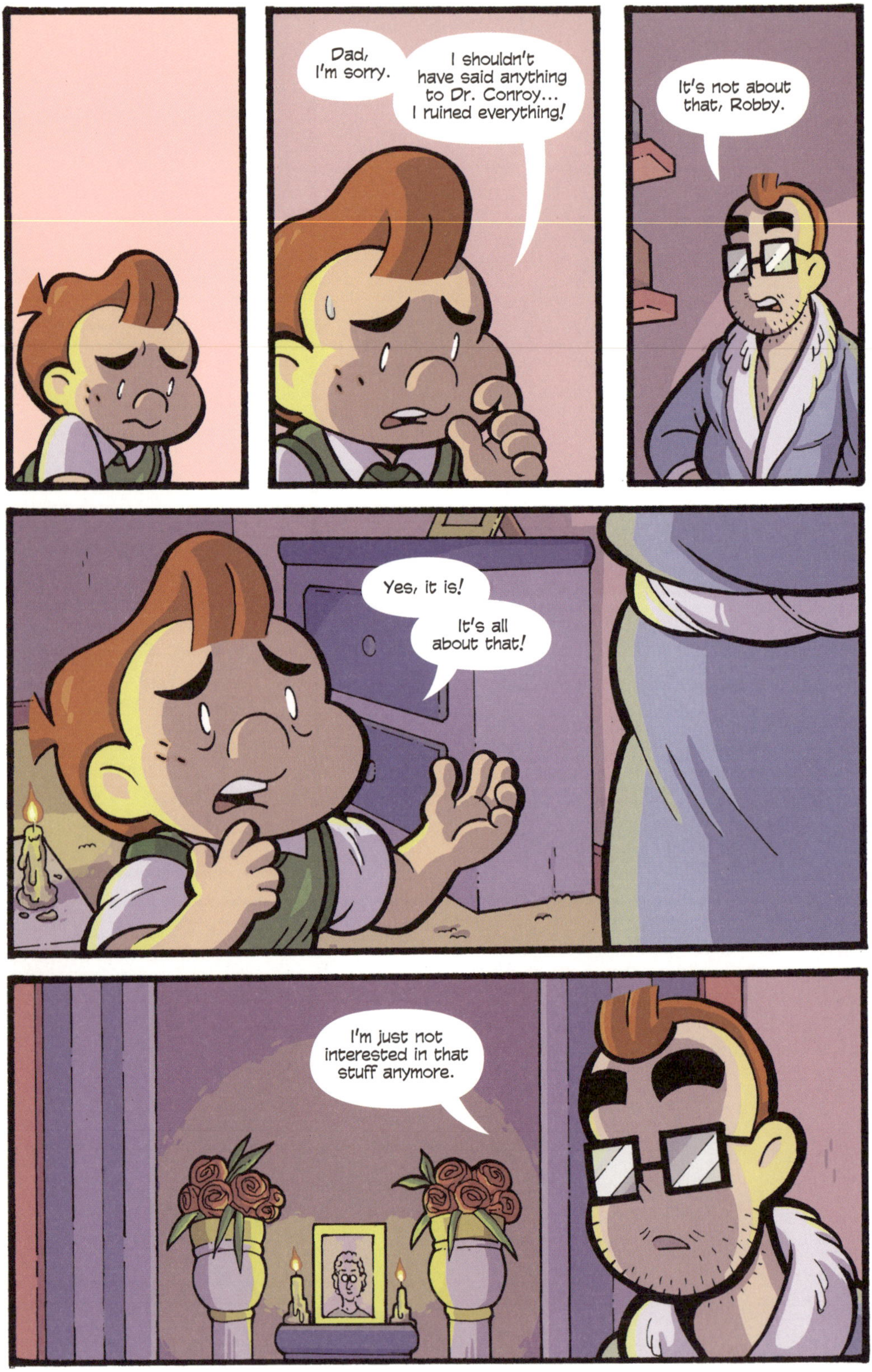
Dad, I'm sorry.
I shouldn't have said anything to Dr. Conroy... I ruined everything!
It's not about that, Robby.
Yes, it is!
It's all about that!
I'm just not interested in that stuff anymore.

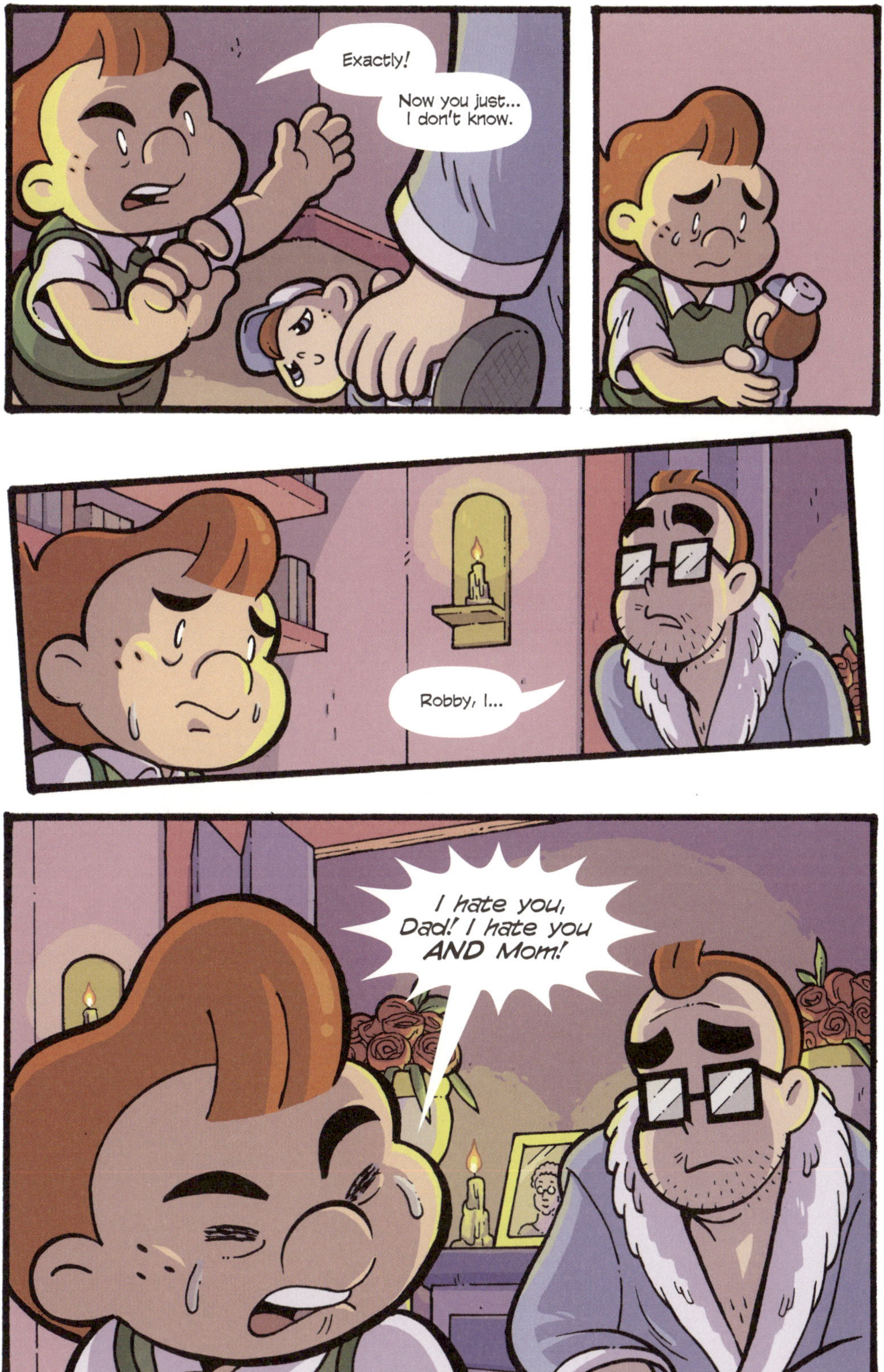
Exactly!
Now you just... I don't know.
Robby, I...
I hate you, Dad! I hate you AND Mom!

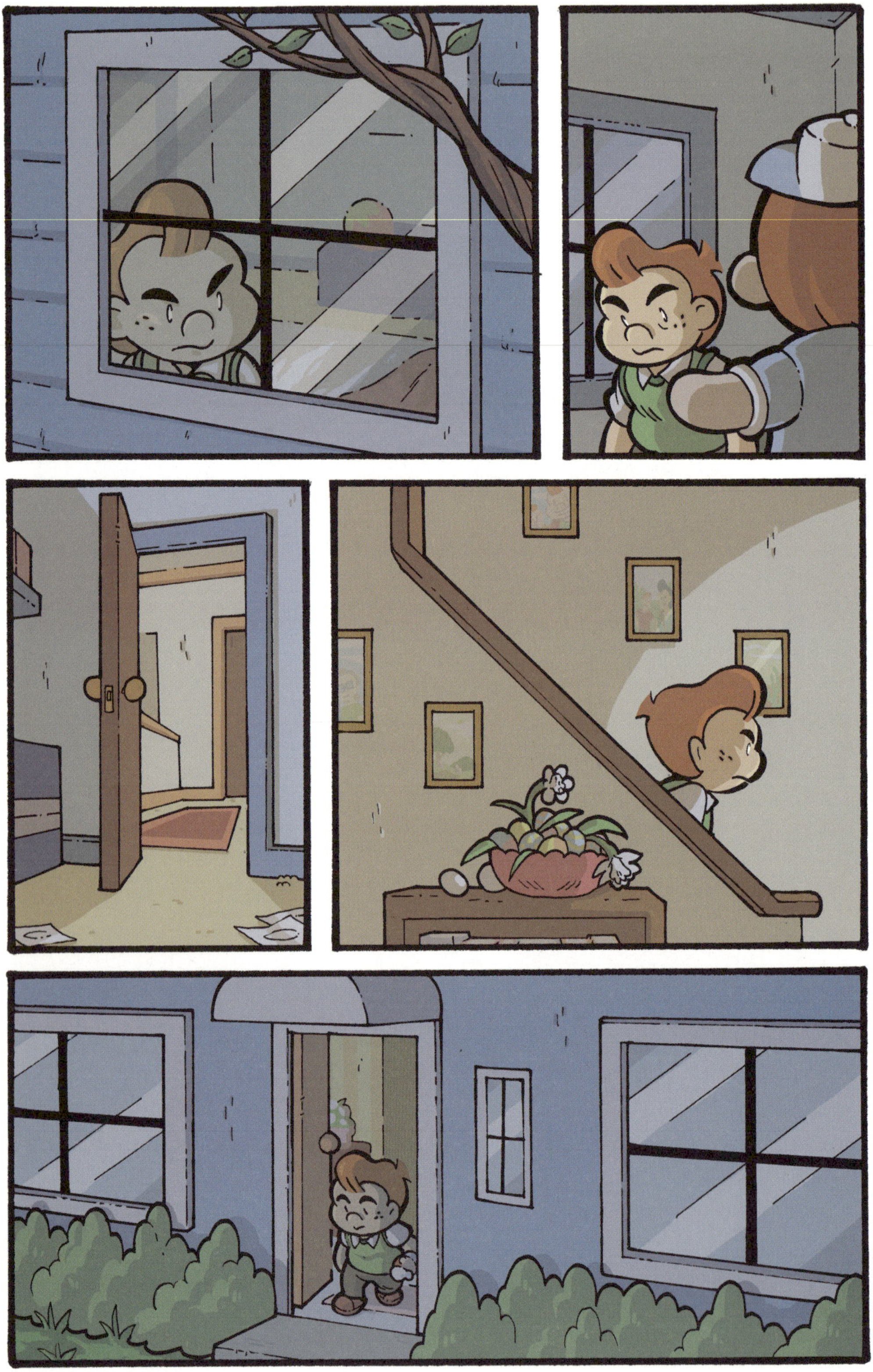

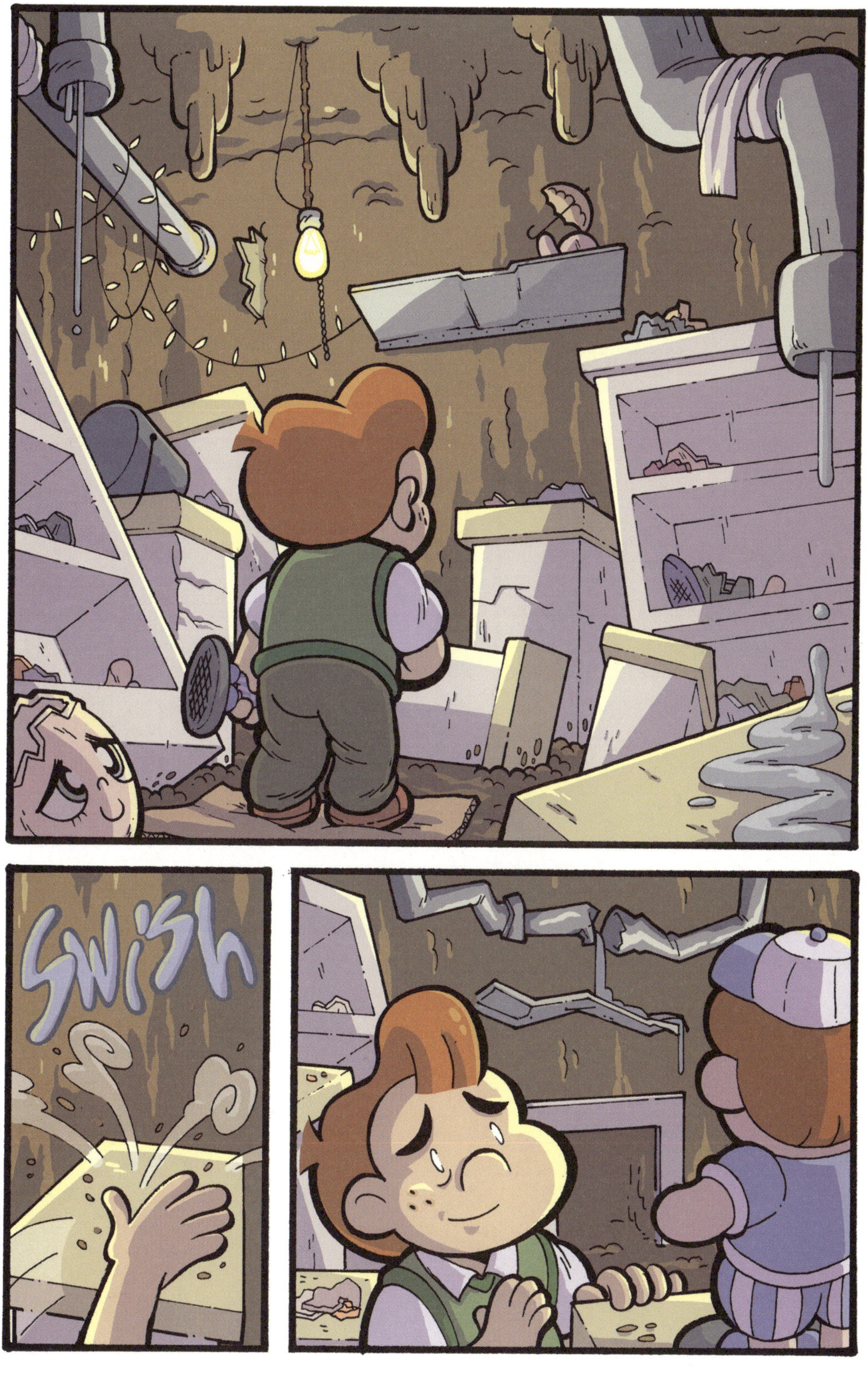
SWISH

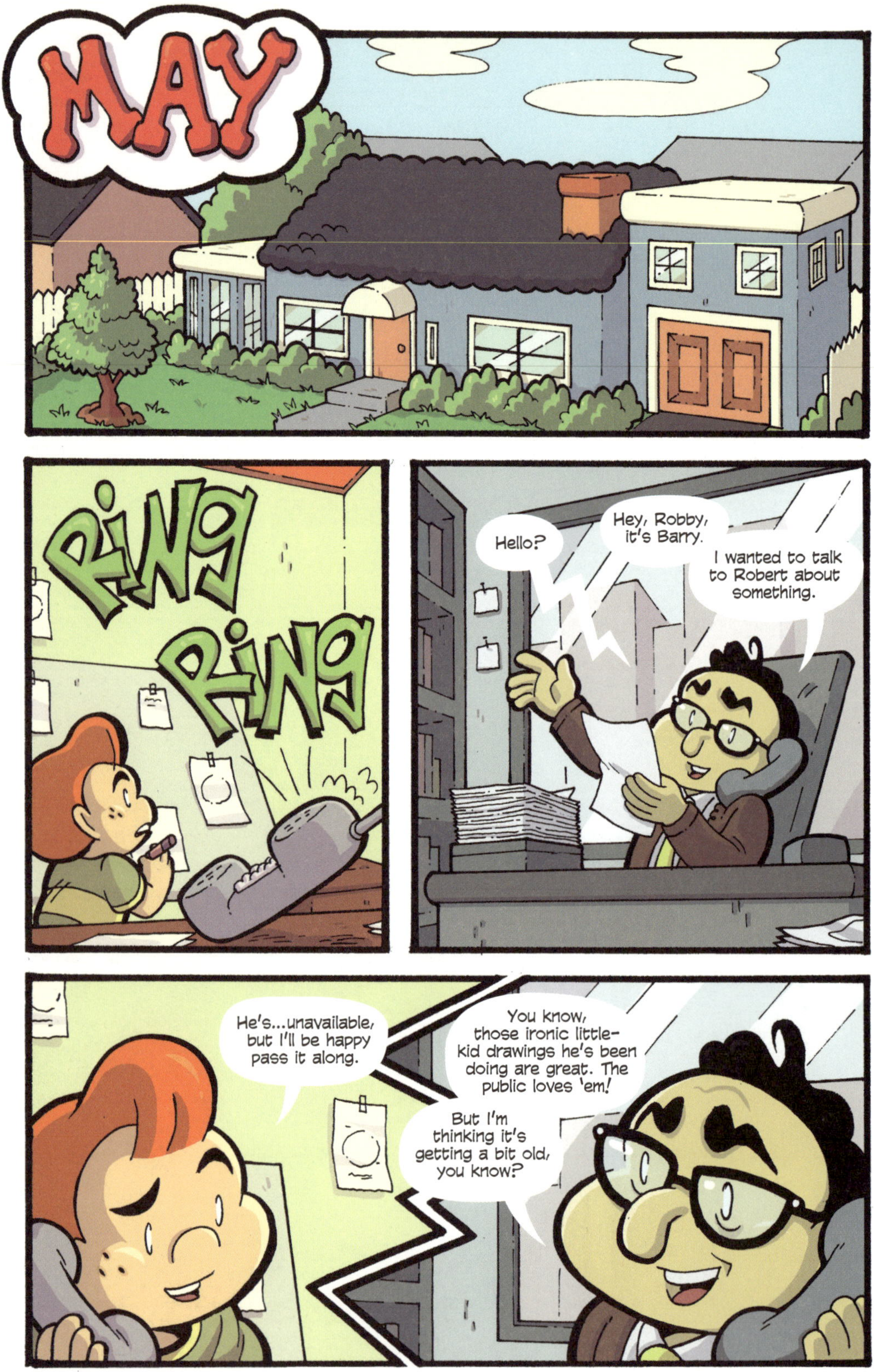
MAY
RING RING
Hello?
Hey, Robby, it's Barry.
I wanted to talk to Robert about something.
He's...unavailable, but I'll be happy pass it along.
You know, those ironic little-kid drawings he's been doing are great. The public loves 'em!
But I'm thinking it's getting a bit old, you know?

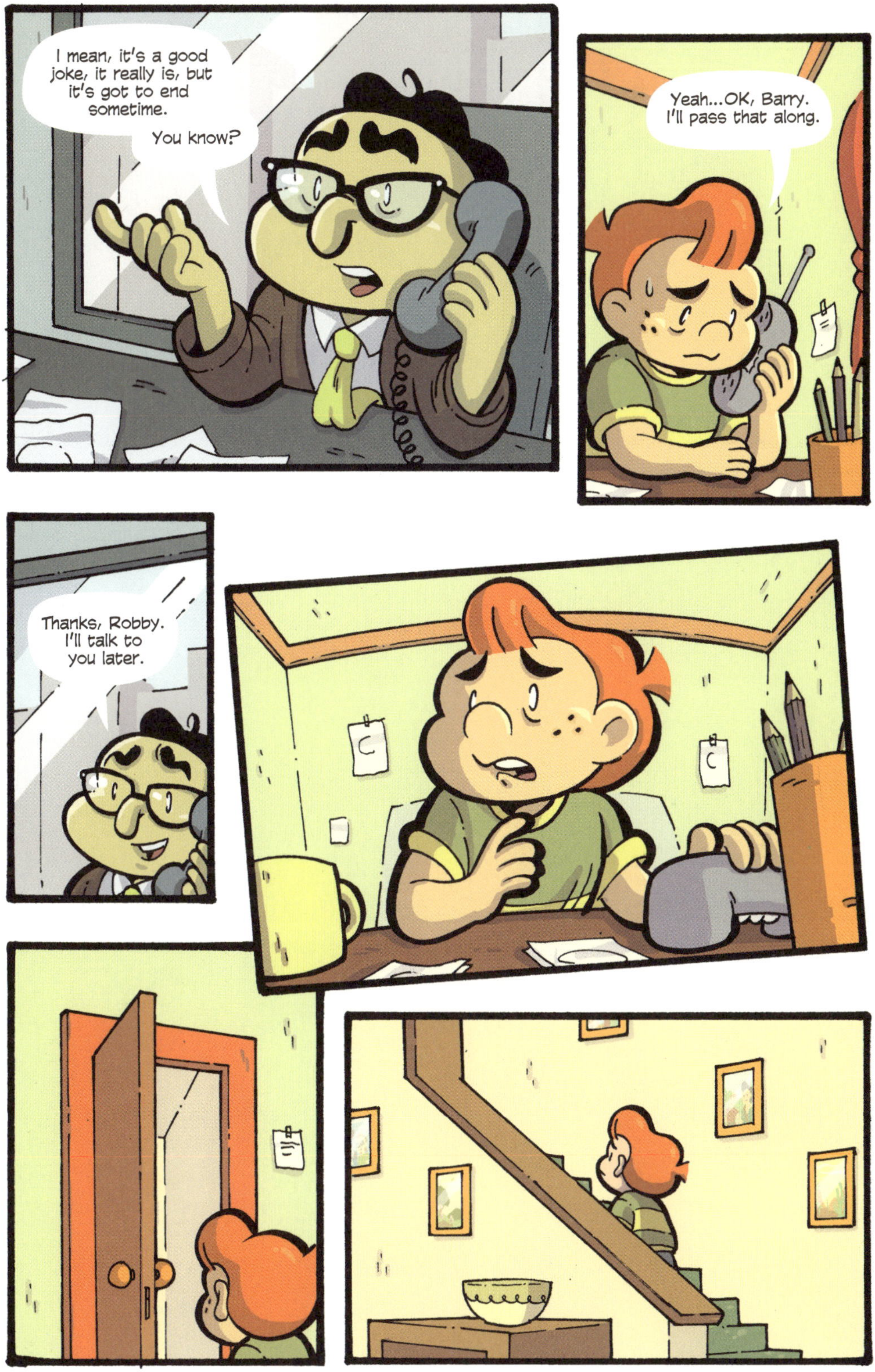
I mean, it's a good joke, it really is, but it's got to end sometime.
You know?
Yeah...OK, Barry. I'll pass that along.
Thanks, Robby. I'll talk to you later.

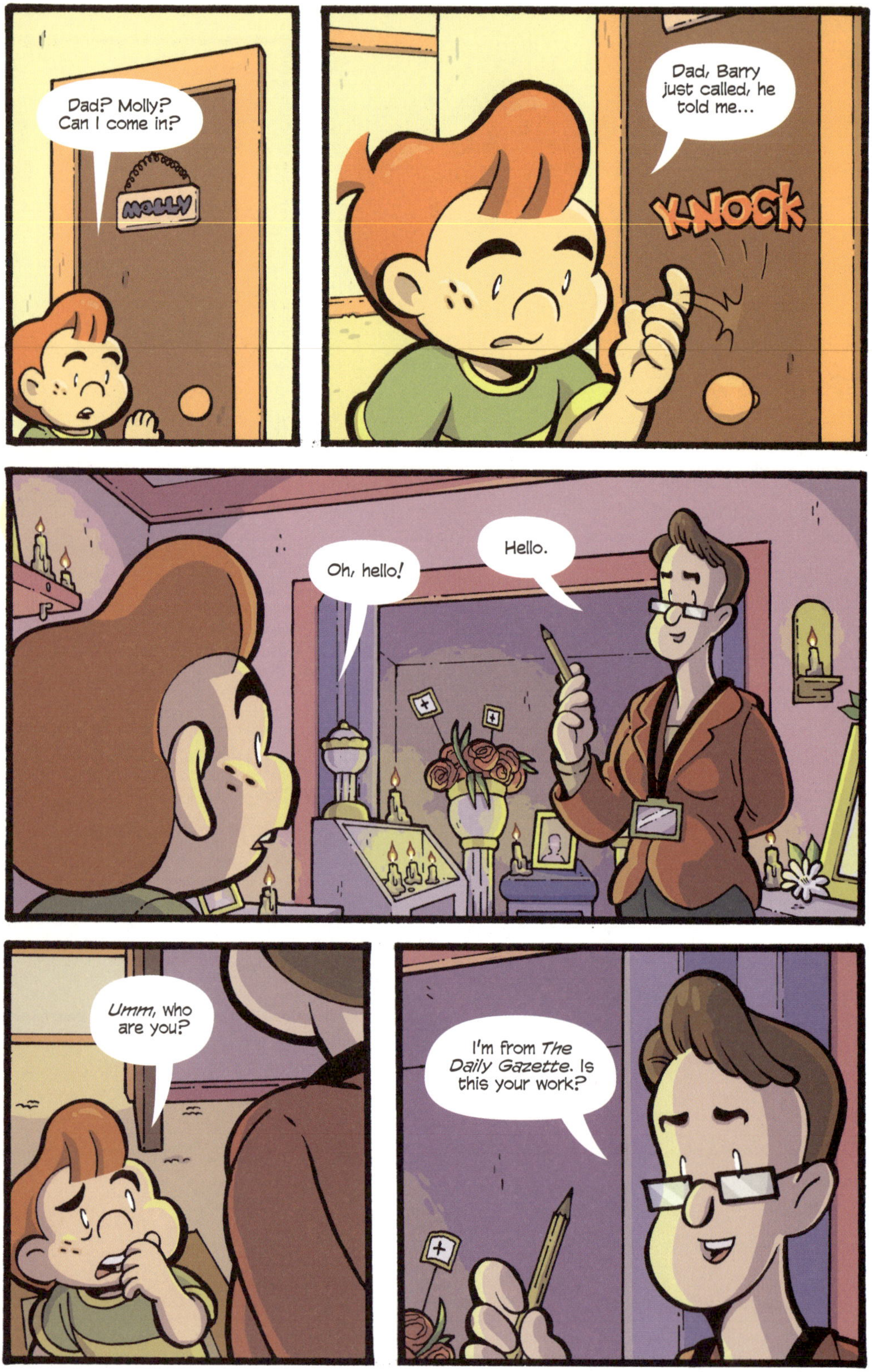
Dad? Molly? Can I come in?
MOLLY
Dad, Barry just called, he told me...
KNOCK
Oh, hello!
Hello.
Umm, who are you?
I'm from *The Daily Gazette*. Is this your work?

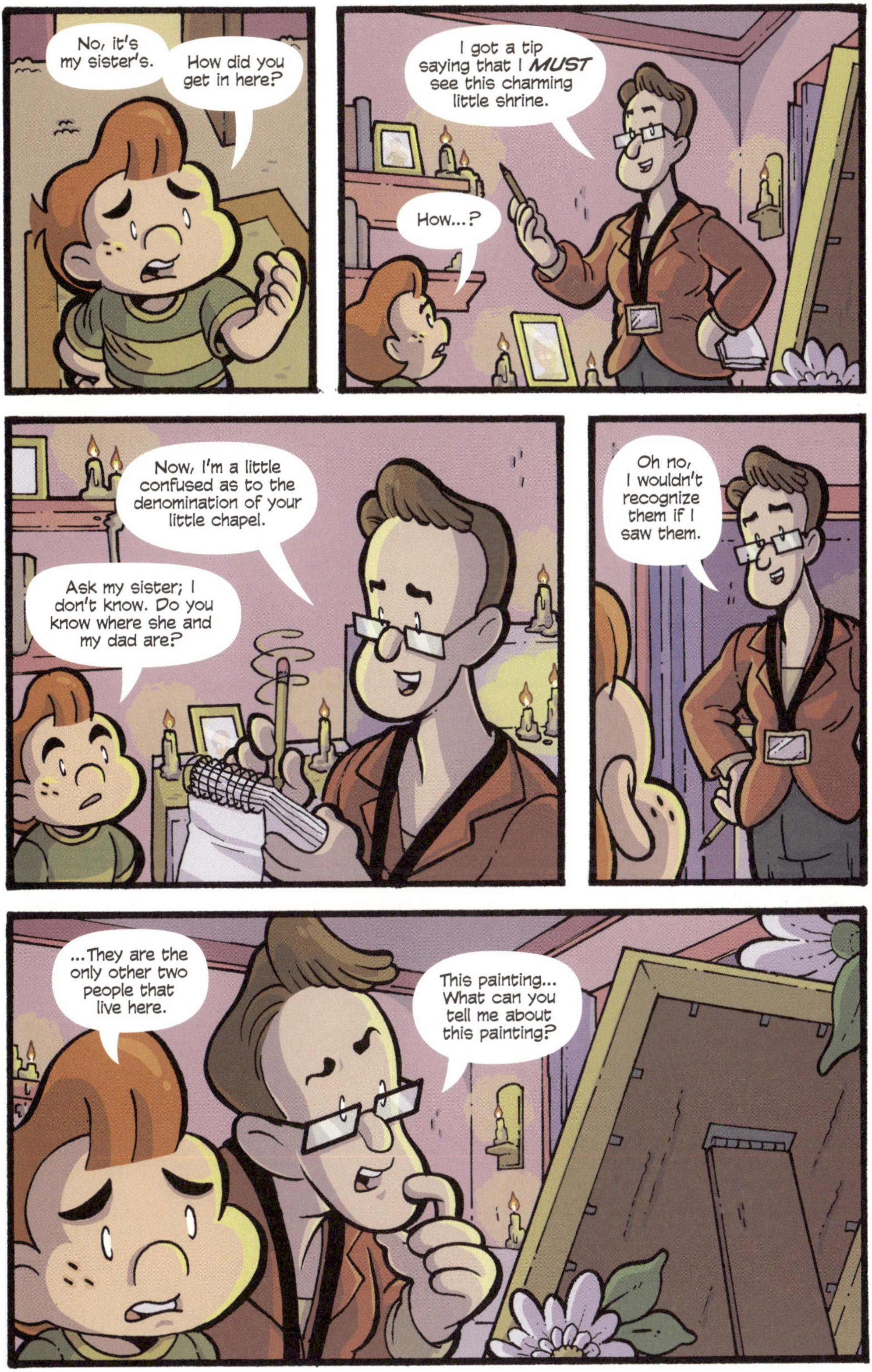
No, it's my sister's.
How did you get in here?
I got a tip saying that I MUST see this charming little shrine.
How...?
Now, I'm a little confused as to the denomination of your little chapel.
Ask my sister; I don't know. Do you know where she and my dad are?
Oh no, I wouldn't recognize them if I saw them.
...They are the only other two people that live here.
This painting... What can you tell me about this painting?

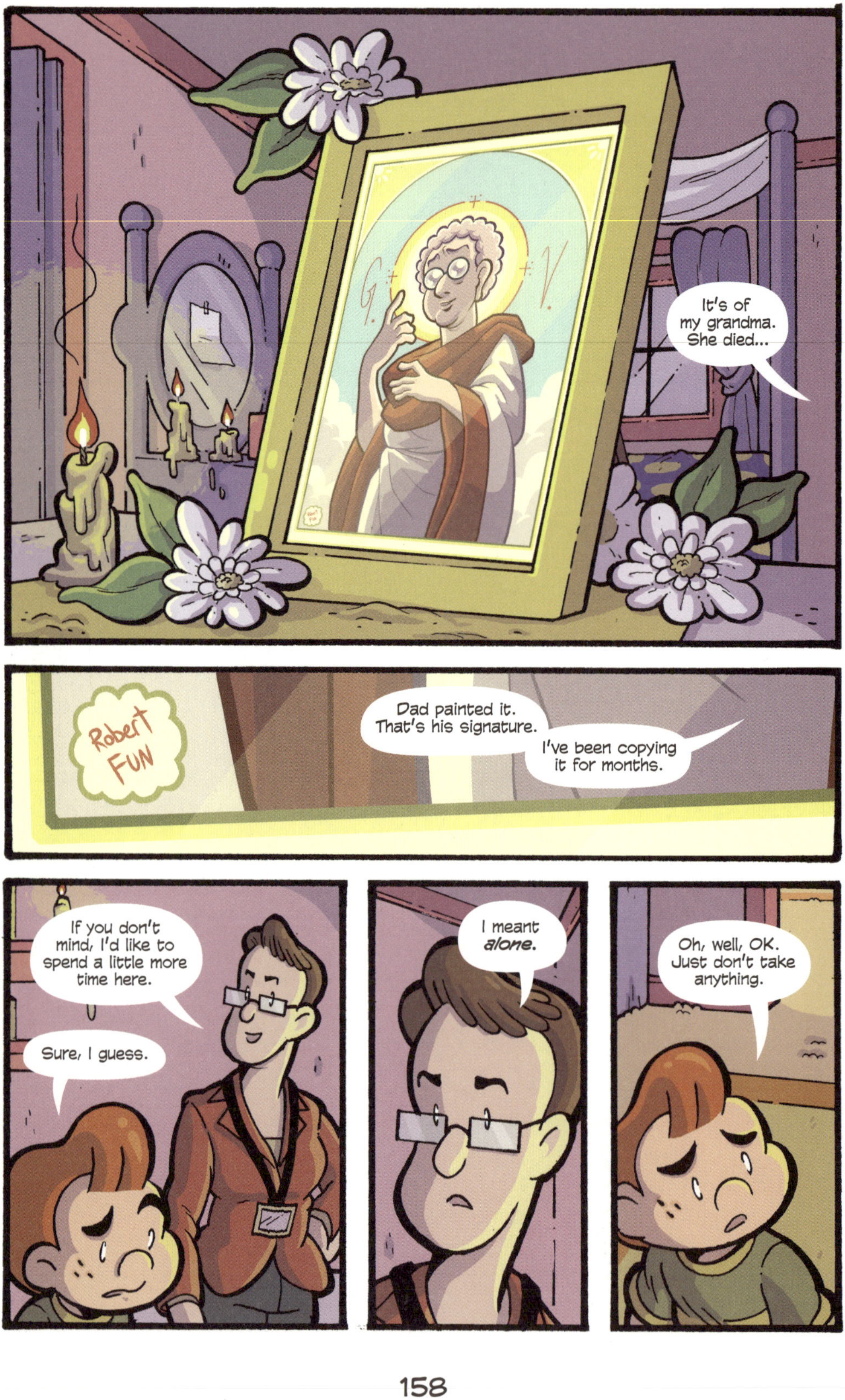

It's of my grandma. She died...
Robert FUN
Dad painted it. That's his signature.
I've been copying it for months.
If you don't mind, I'd like to spend a little more time here.
Sure, I guess.
I meant *alone.*
Oh, well, OK. Just don't take anything.

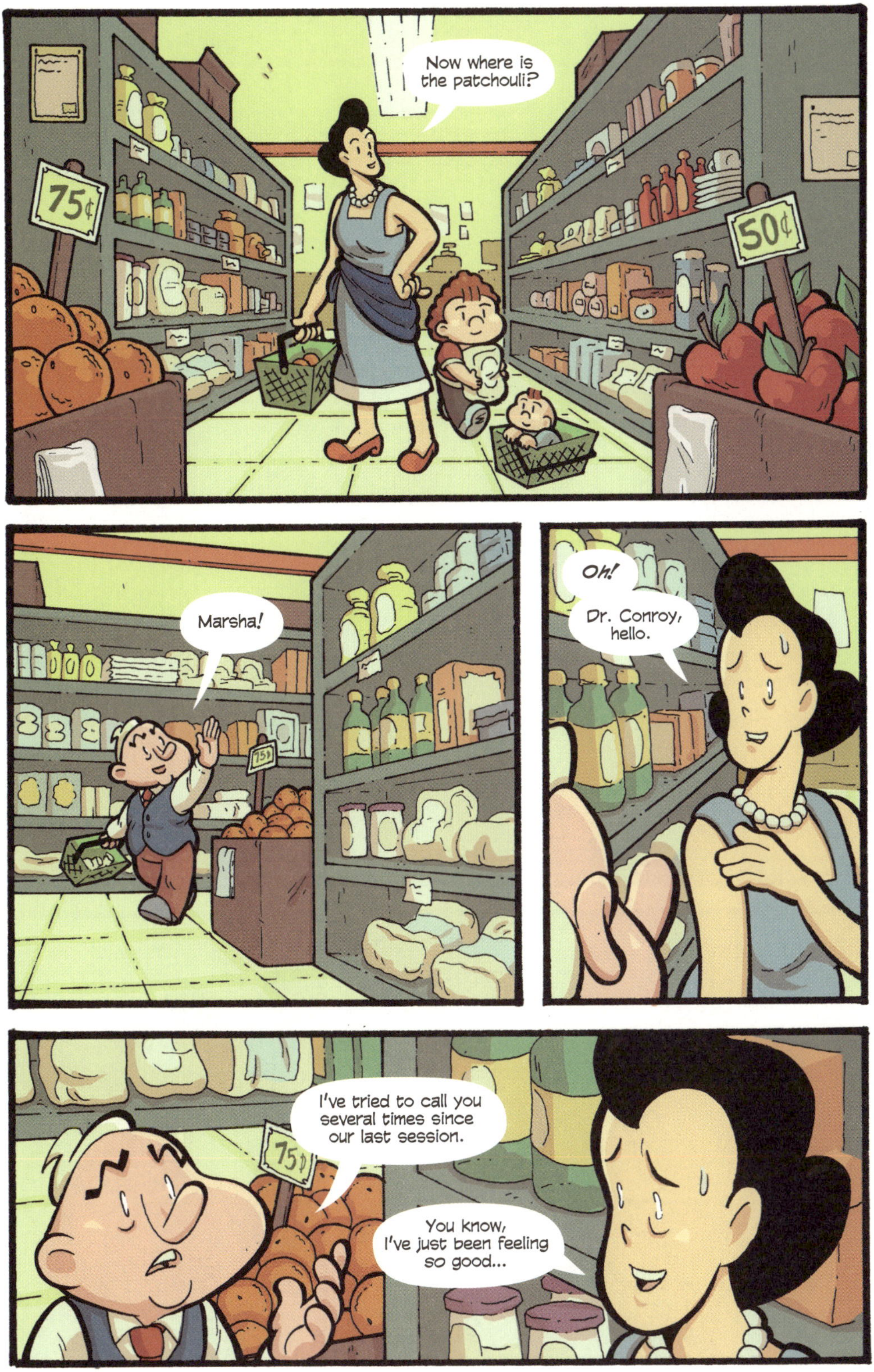
Now where is the patchouli?
75¢
50¢
Marsha!
75¢
Oh!
Dr. Conroy, hello.
I've tried to call you several times since our last session.
75¢
You know, I've just been feeling so good...

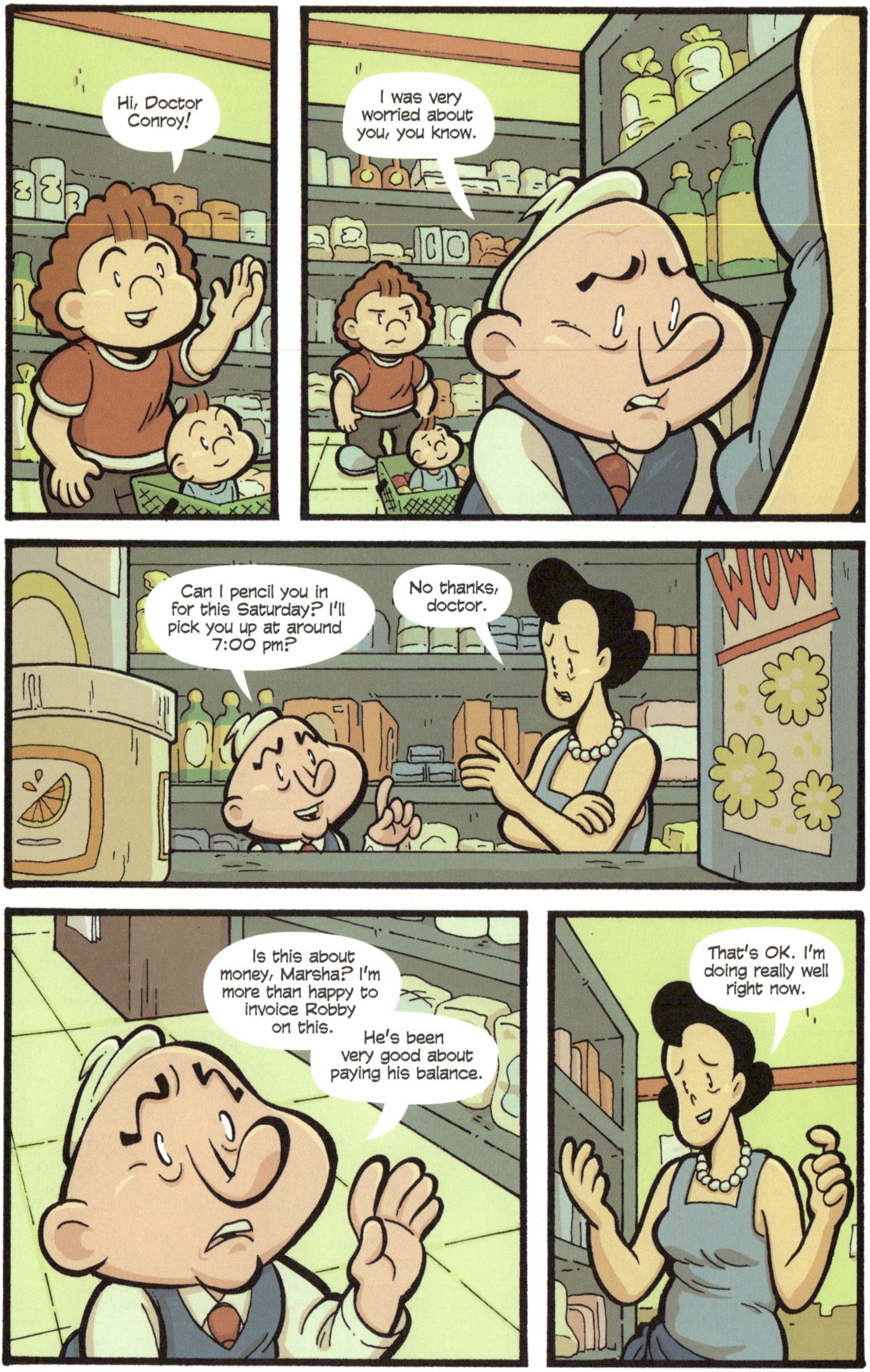
Hi, Doctor Conroy!
I was very worried about you, you know.
Can I pencil you in for this Saturday? I'll pick you up at around 7:00 pm?
No thanks, doctor.
WOW
Is this about money, Marsha? I'm more than happy to invoice Robby on this.
He's been very good about paying his balance.
That's OK. I'm doing really well right now.

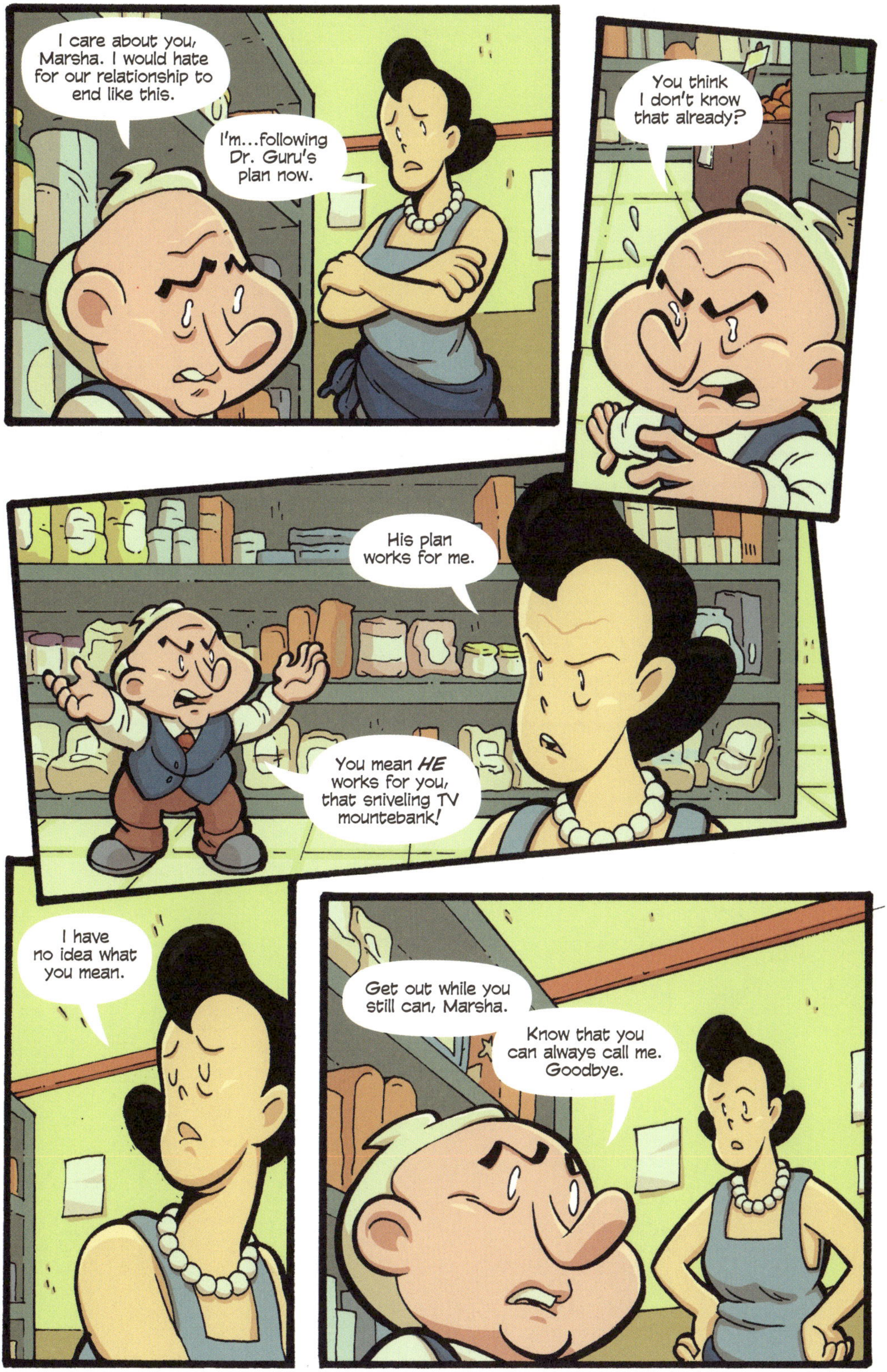
I care about you, Marsha. I would hate for our relationship to end like this.
I'm...following Dr. Guru's plan now.
You think I don't know that already?
His plan works for me.
You mean HE works for you, that sniveling TV mountebank!
I have no idea what you mean.
Get out while you still can, Marsha.
Know that you can always call me. Goodbye.

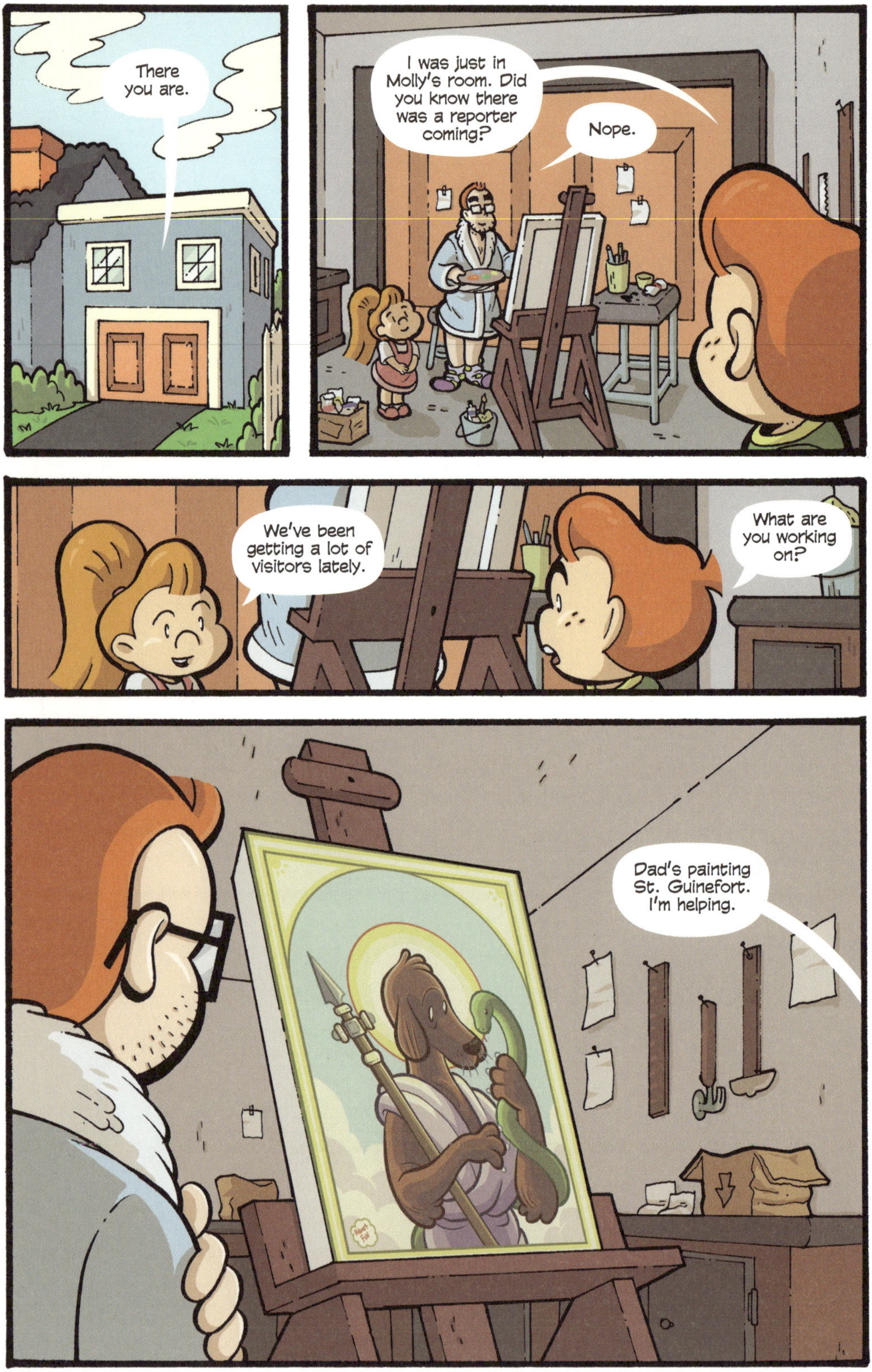
There you are.
I was just in Molly's room. Did you know there was a reporter coming?
Nope.
We've been getting a lot of visitors lately.
What are you working on?
Dad's painting St. Guinefort. I'm helping.

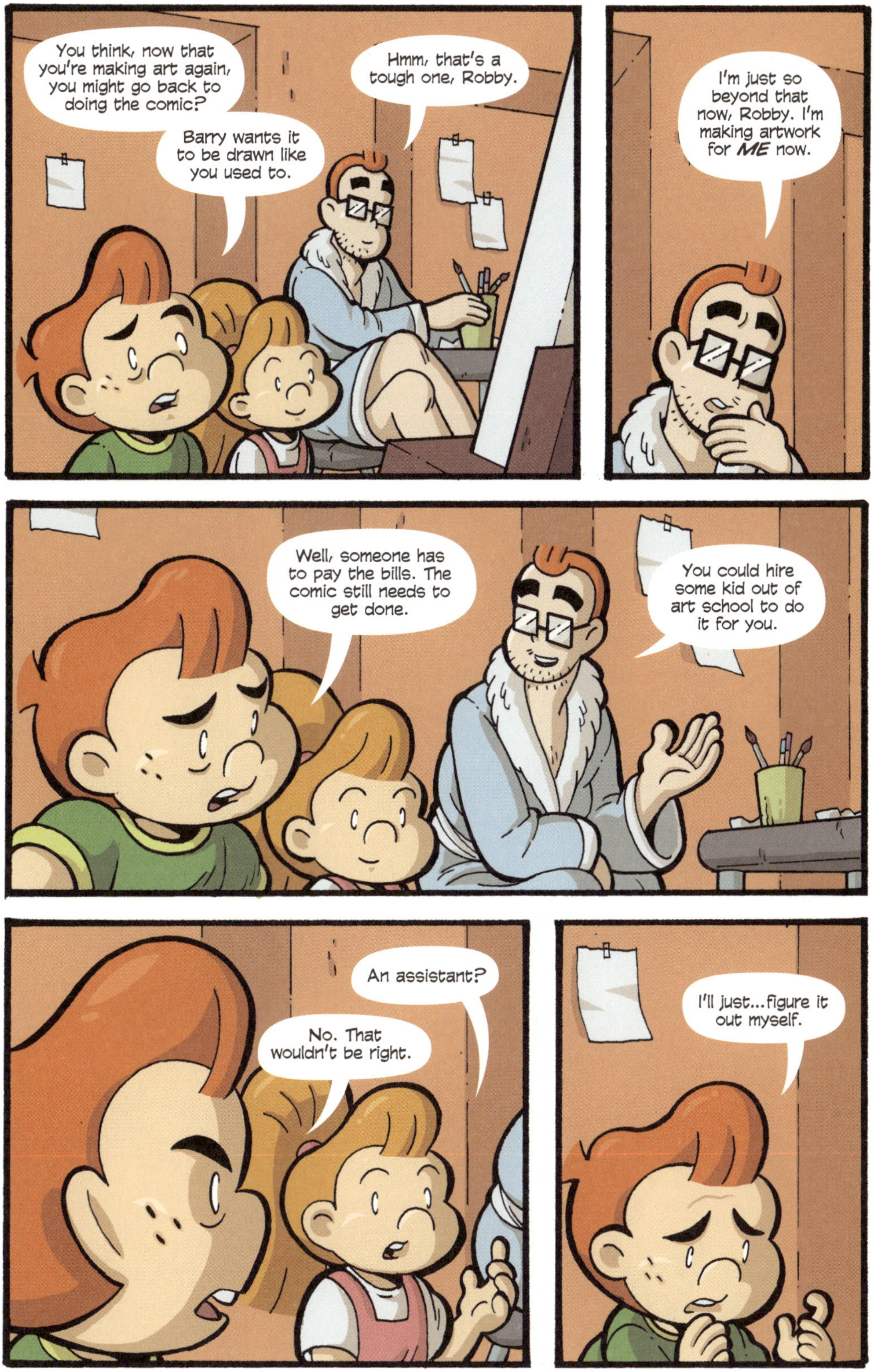
You think, now that you're making art again, you might go back to doing the comic?
Barry wants it to be drawn like you used to.
Hmm, that's a tough one, Robby.
I'm just so beyond that now, Robby. I'm making artwork for *ME* now.
Well, someone has to pay the bills. The comic still needs to get done.
You could hire some kid out of art school to do it for you.
An assistant?
No. That wouldn't be right.
I'll just...figure it out myself.

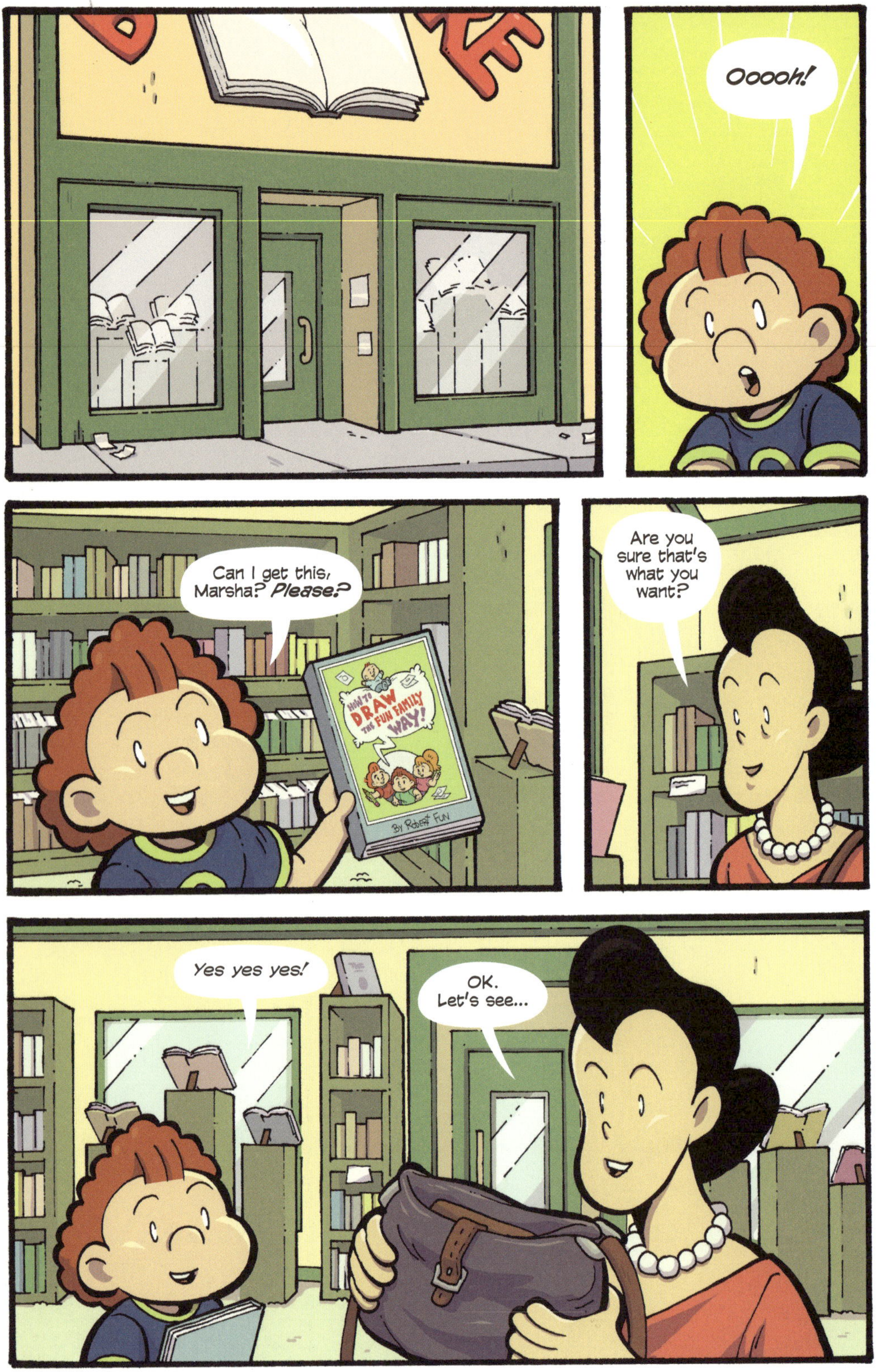
Ooooh!
Can I get this, Marsha? *Please?*
HOW TO DRAW THE FUN FAMILY WAY!
BY Robert FUN
Are you sure that's what you want?
Yes yes yes!
OK. Let's see...

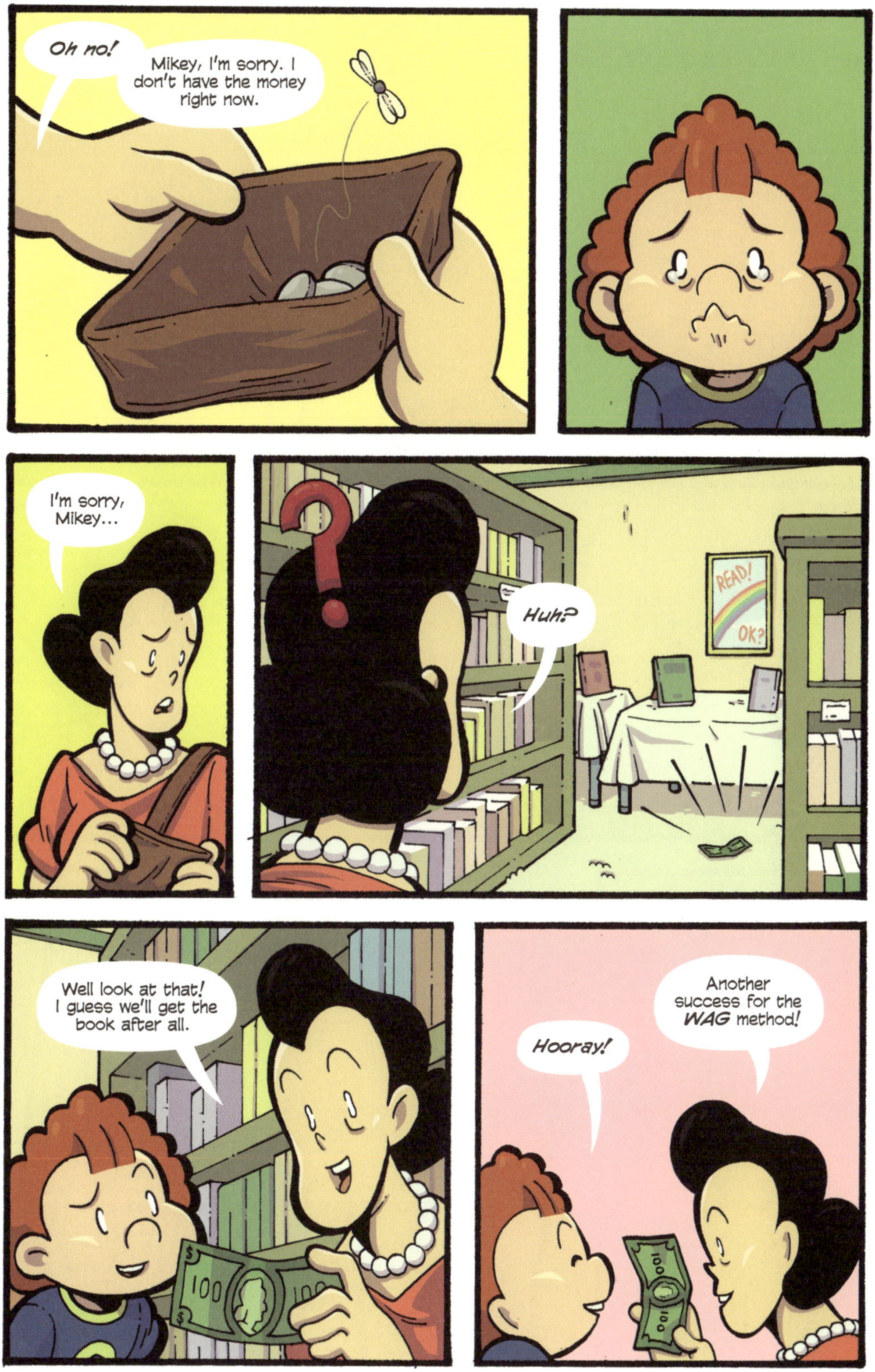
Oh no!
Mikey, I'm sorry. I don't have the money right now.
I'm sorry, Mikey...
Huh?
READ! OK?
Well look at that! I guess we'll get the book after all.
Hooray!
Another success for the WAG method!

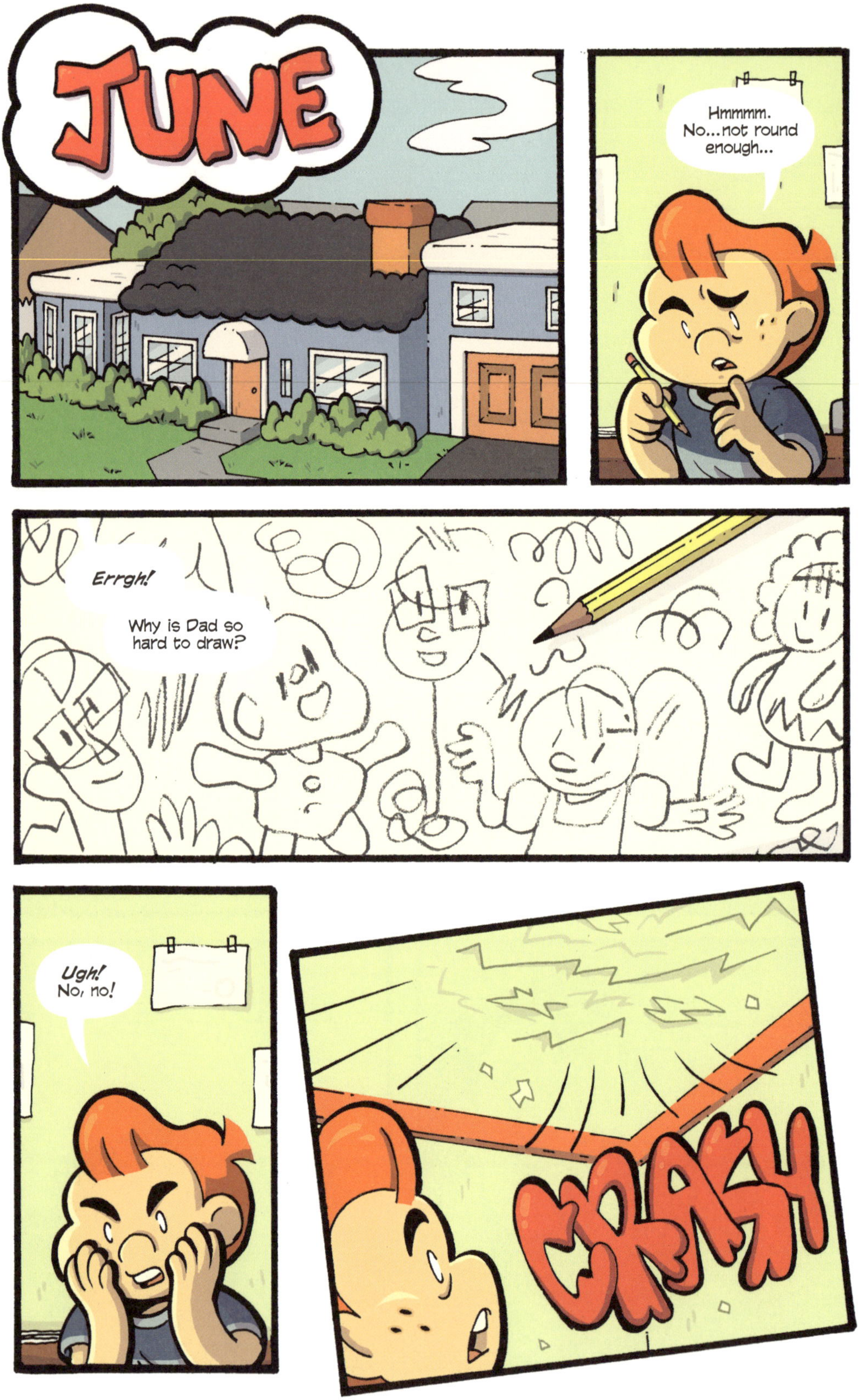
JUNE
Hmmmm. No...not round enough...
Errgh!
Why is Dad so hard to draw?
Ugh! No, no!
CRASH

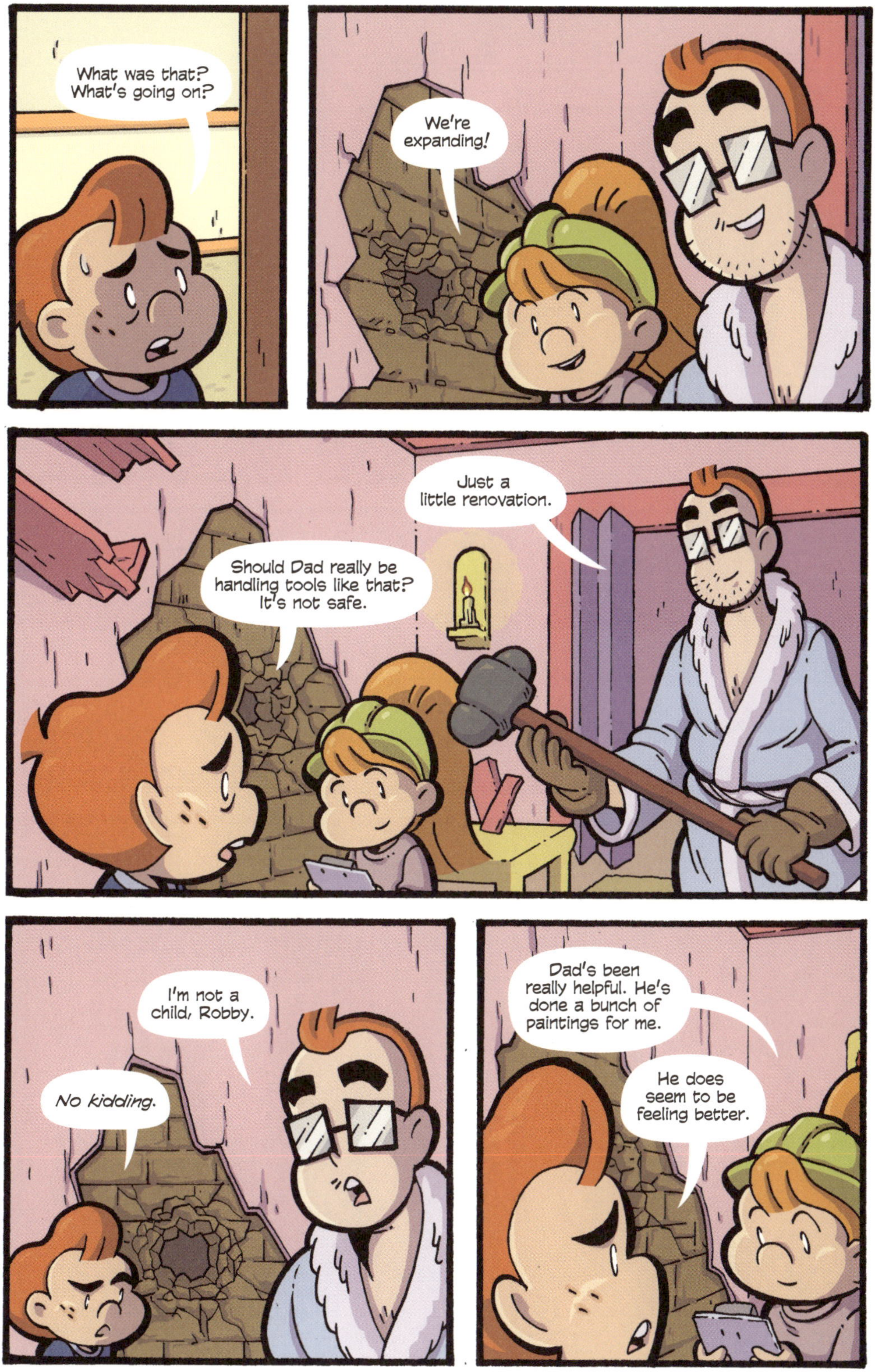
What was that? What's going on?
We're expanding!
Just a little renovation.
Should Dad really be handling tools like that? It's not safe.
I'm not a child, Robby.
No kidding.
Dad's been really helpful. He's done a bunch of paintings for me.
He does seem to be feeling better.

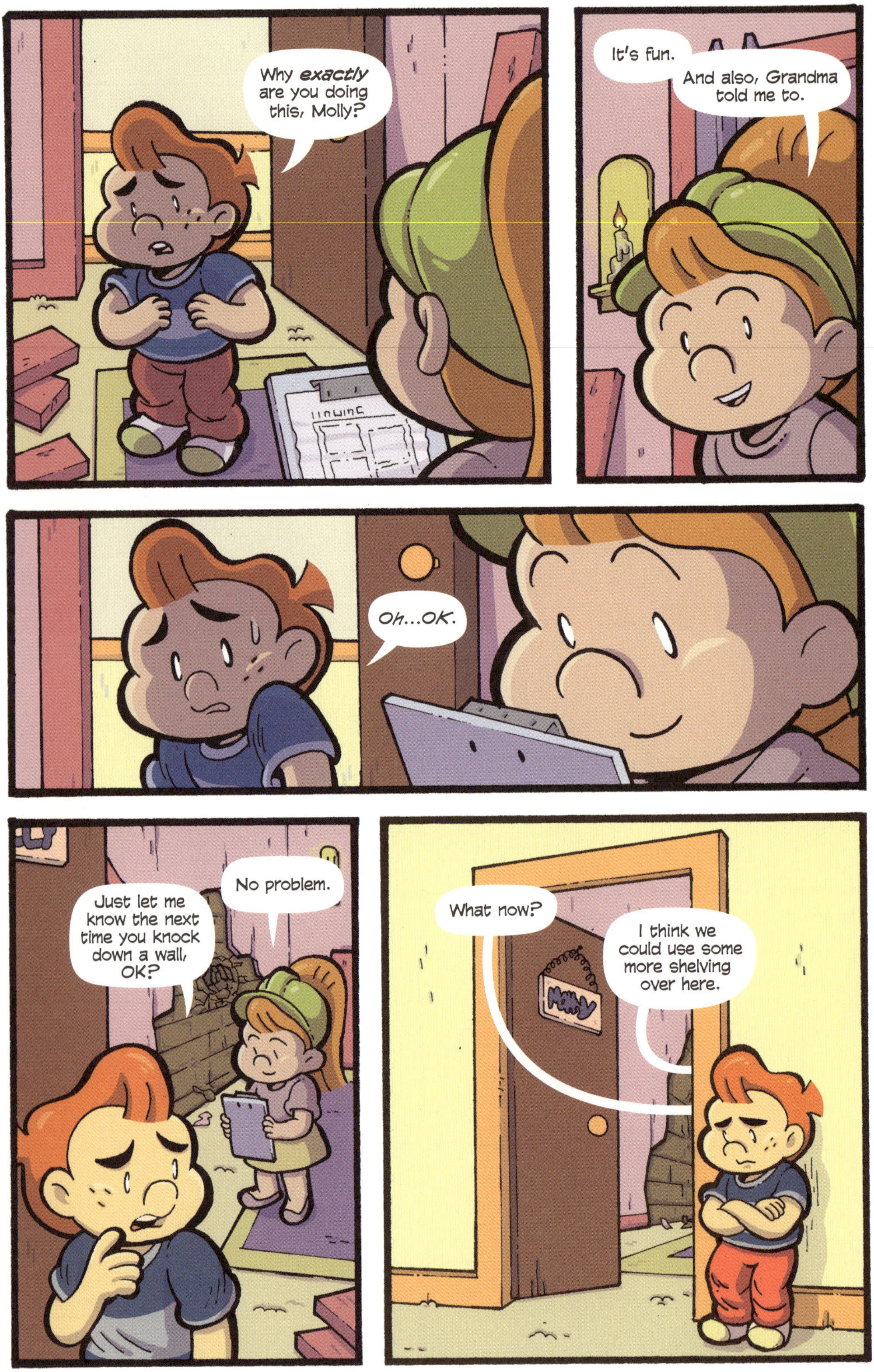
Why *exactly* are you doing this, Molly?
It's fun.
And also, Grandma told me to.
Oh...OK.
No problem.
Just let me know the next time you knock down a wall, OK?
What now?
I think we could use some more shelving over here.

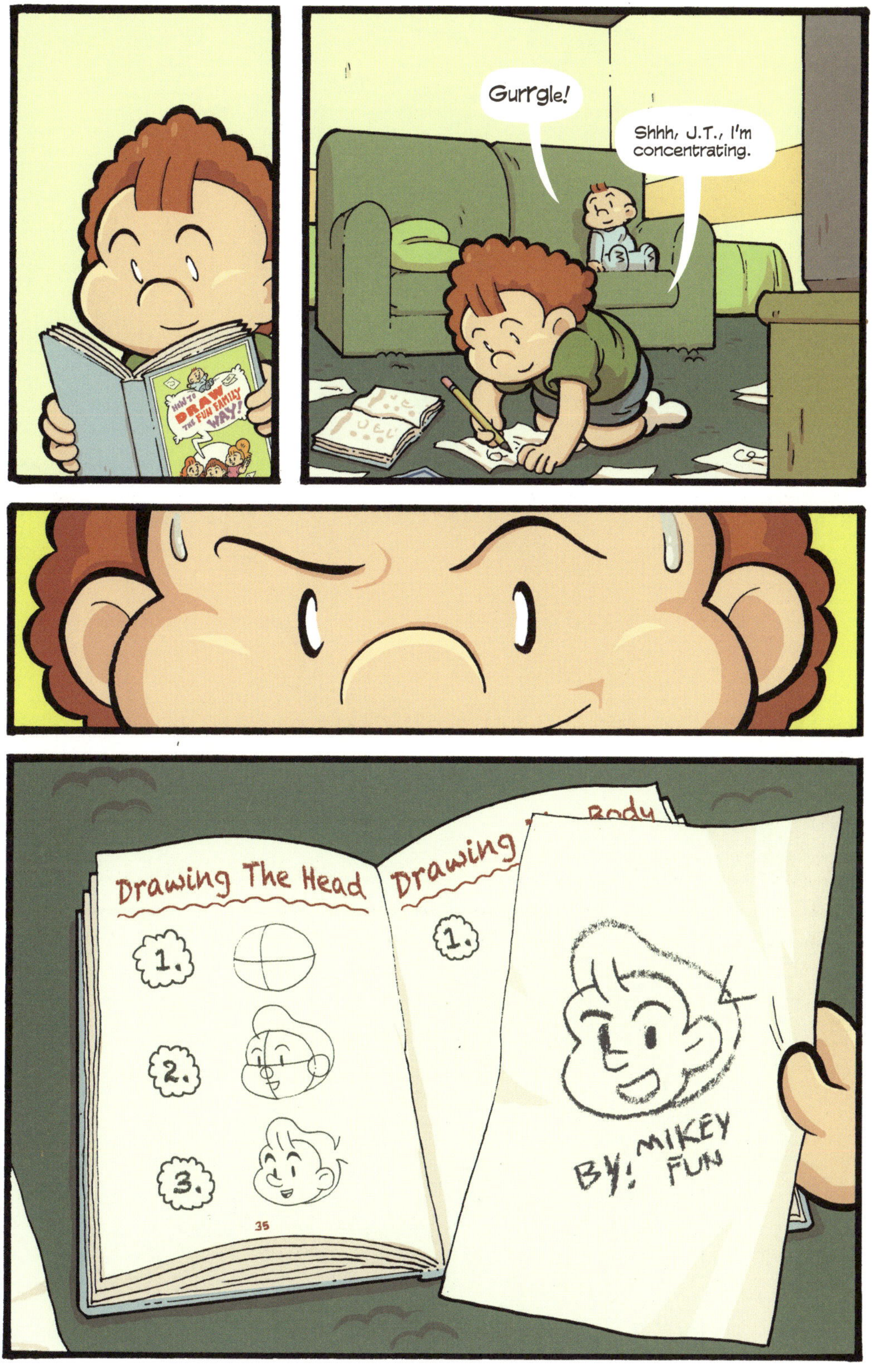
HOW TO DRAW THE FUN FAMILY WAY!
Gurrgle!
Shhh, J.T., I'm concentrating.
Drawing The Head
1.
2.
3.
35
Drawing
1.
BY: MIKEY FUN

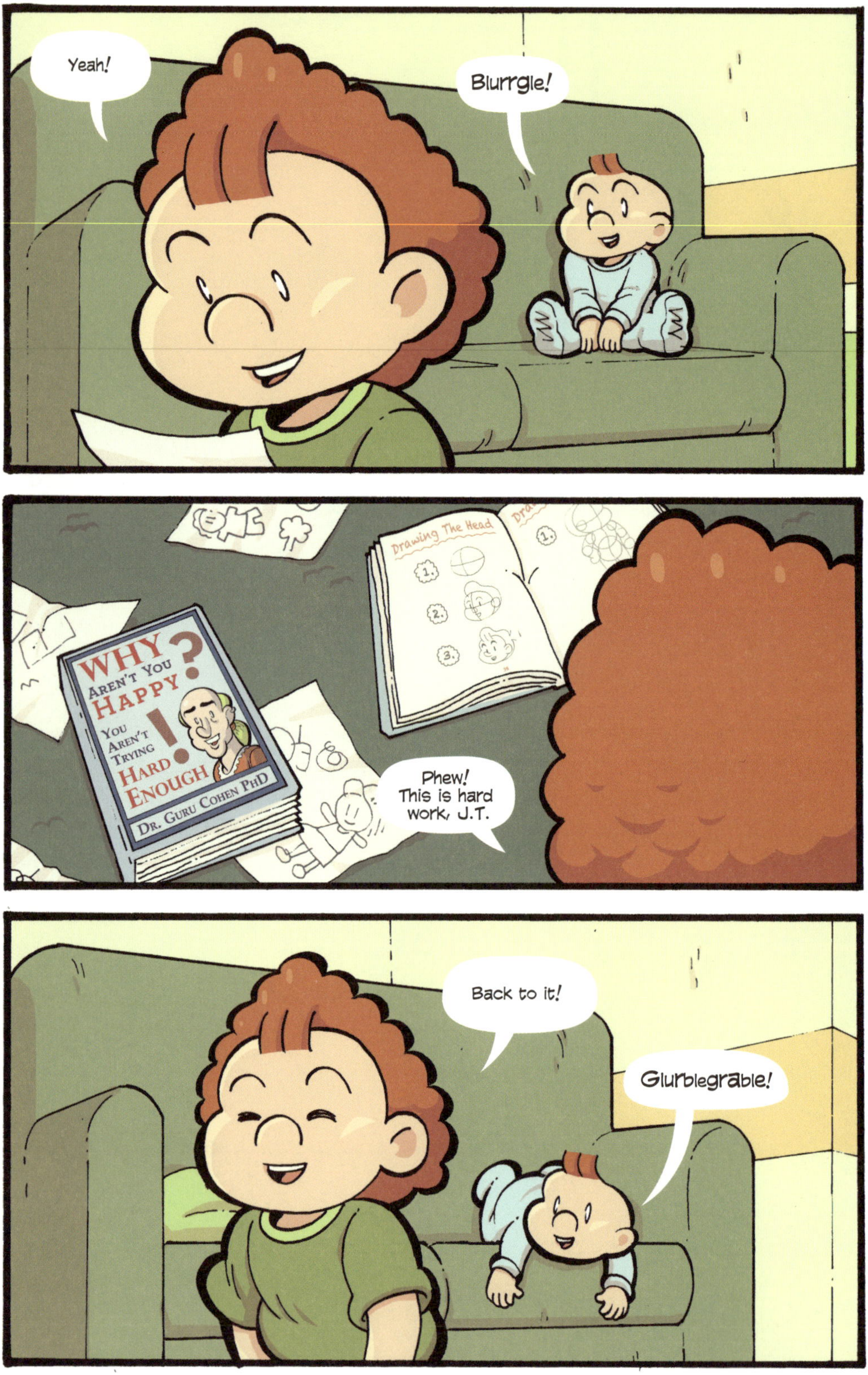
Yeah!
Blurrgle!
WHY AREN'T YOU HAPPY?! YOU AREN'T TRYING HARD ENOUGH
DR. GURU COHEN PhD
Drawing The Head
Phew! This is hard work, J.T.
Back to it!
Glurblegrable!

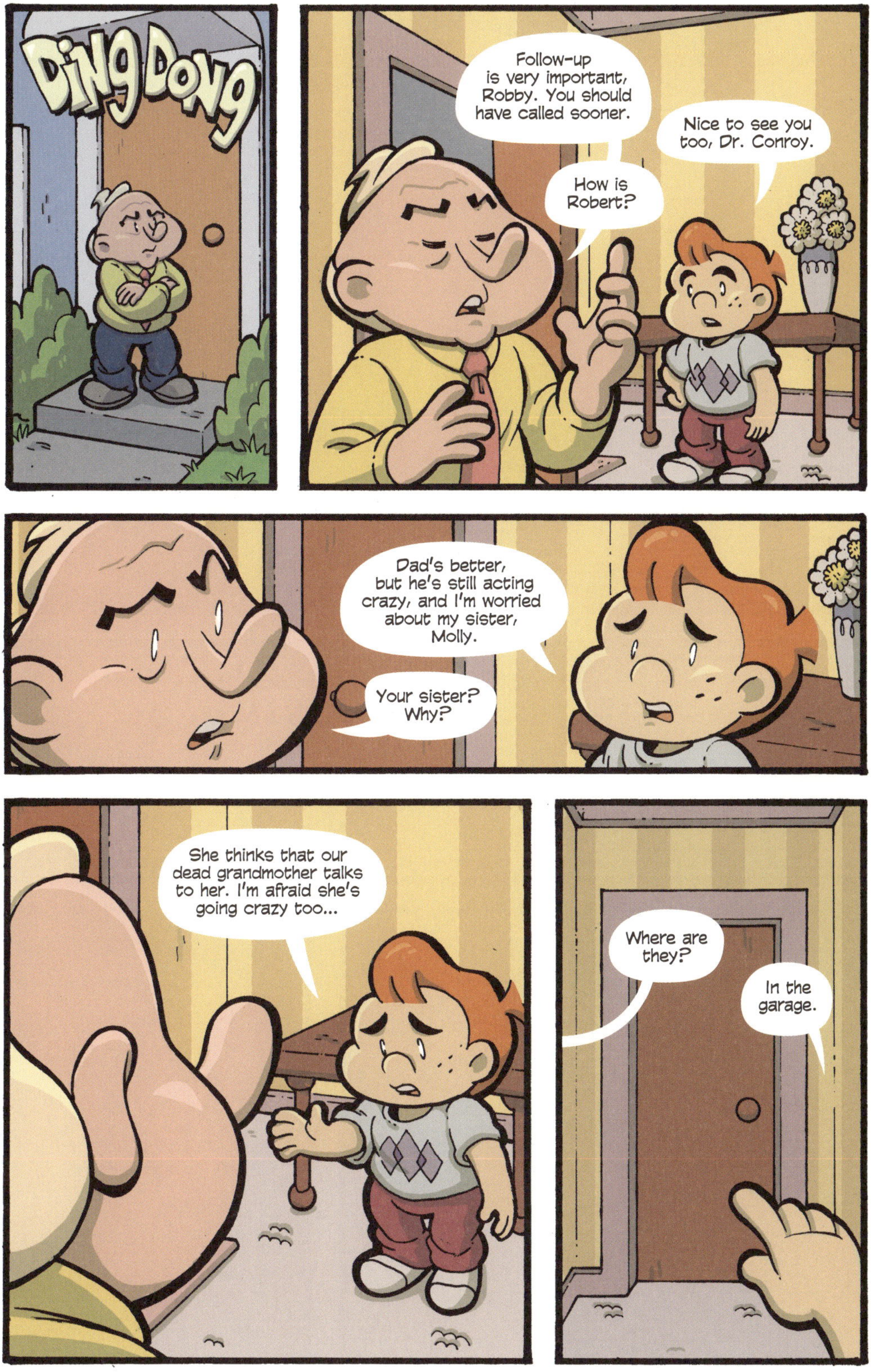
DING DONG
Follow-up is very important, Robby. You should have called sooner.
How is Robert?
Nice to see you too, Dr. Conroy.
Dad's better, but he's still acting crazy, and I'm worried about my sister, Molly.
Your sister? Why?
She thinks that our dead grandmother talks to her. I'm afraid she's going crazy too...
Where are they?
In the garage.

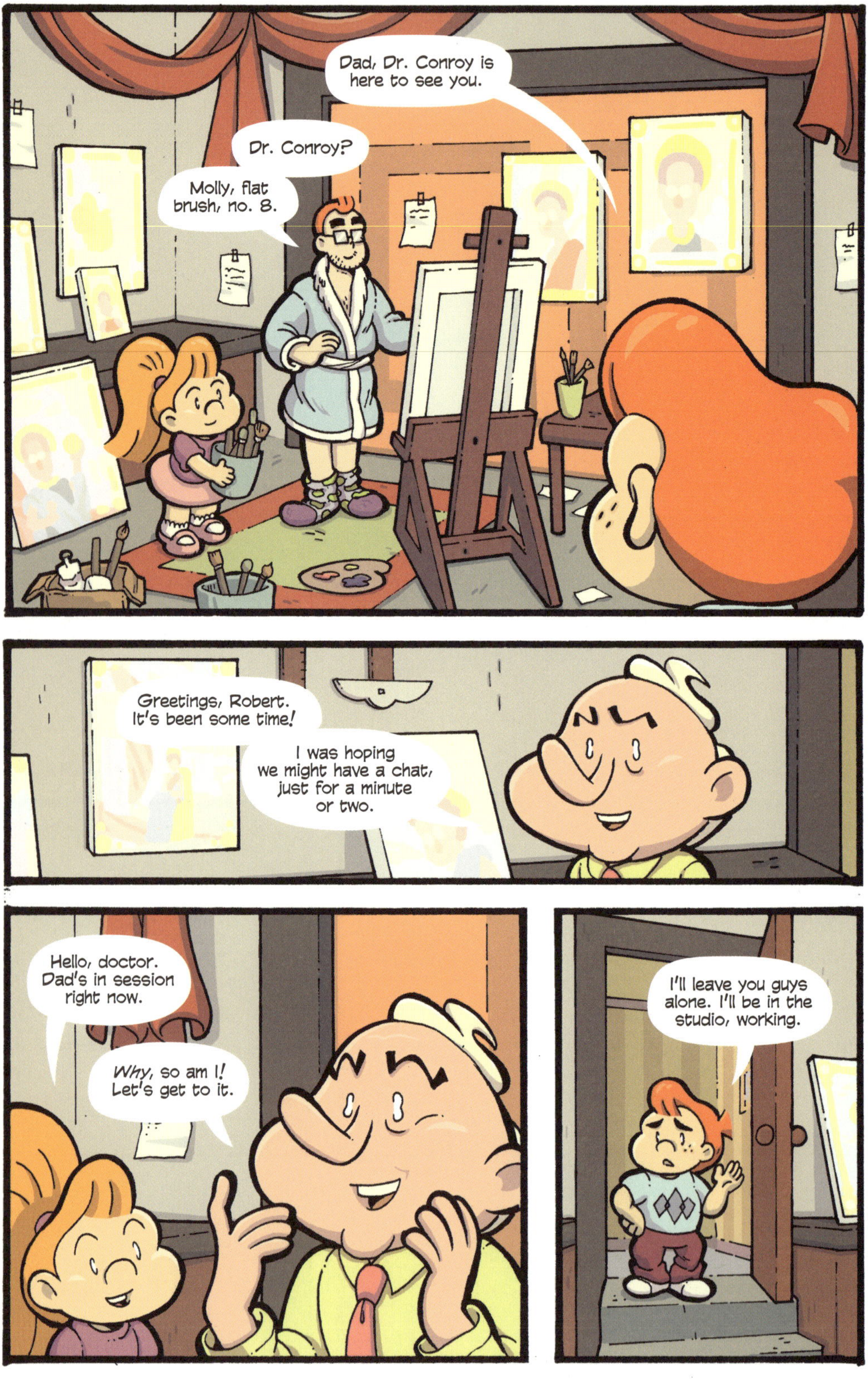
Dad, Dr. Conroy is here to see you.
Dr. Conroy?
Molly, flat brush, no. 8.
Greetings, Robert. It's been some time!
I was hoping we might have a chat, just for a minute or two.
Hello, doctor. Dad's in session right now.
Why, so am I! Let's get to it.
I'll leave you guys alone. I'll be in the studio, working.

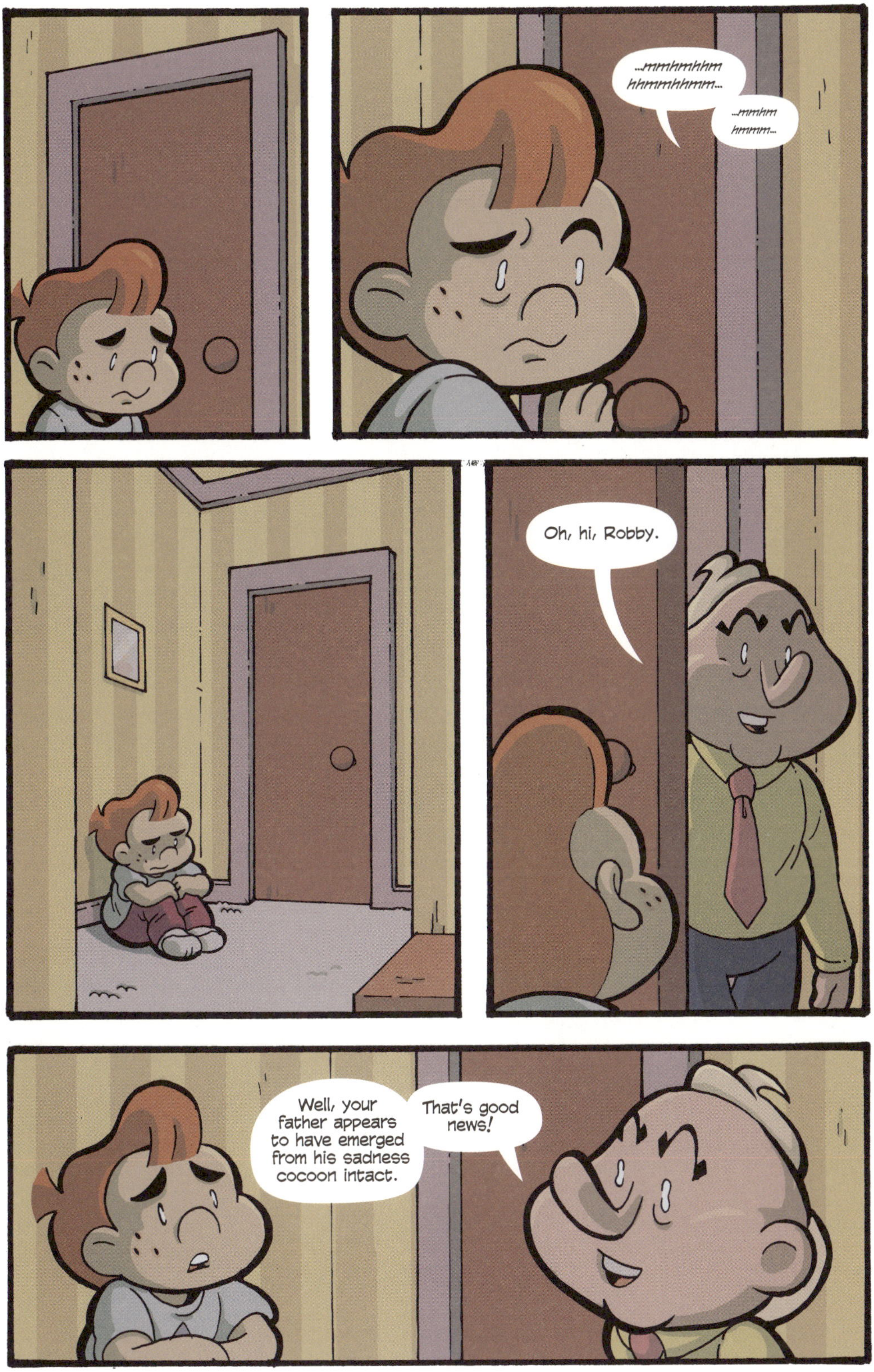
...mmhmhhm hhmmhhmm...
...mmhm hmmm...
Oh, hi, Robby.
Well, your father appears to have emerged from his sadness cocoon intact.
That's good news!

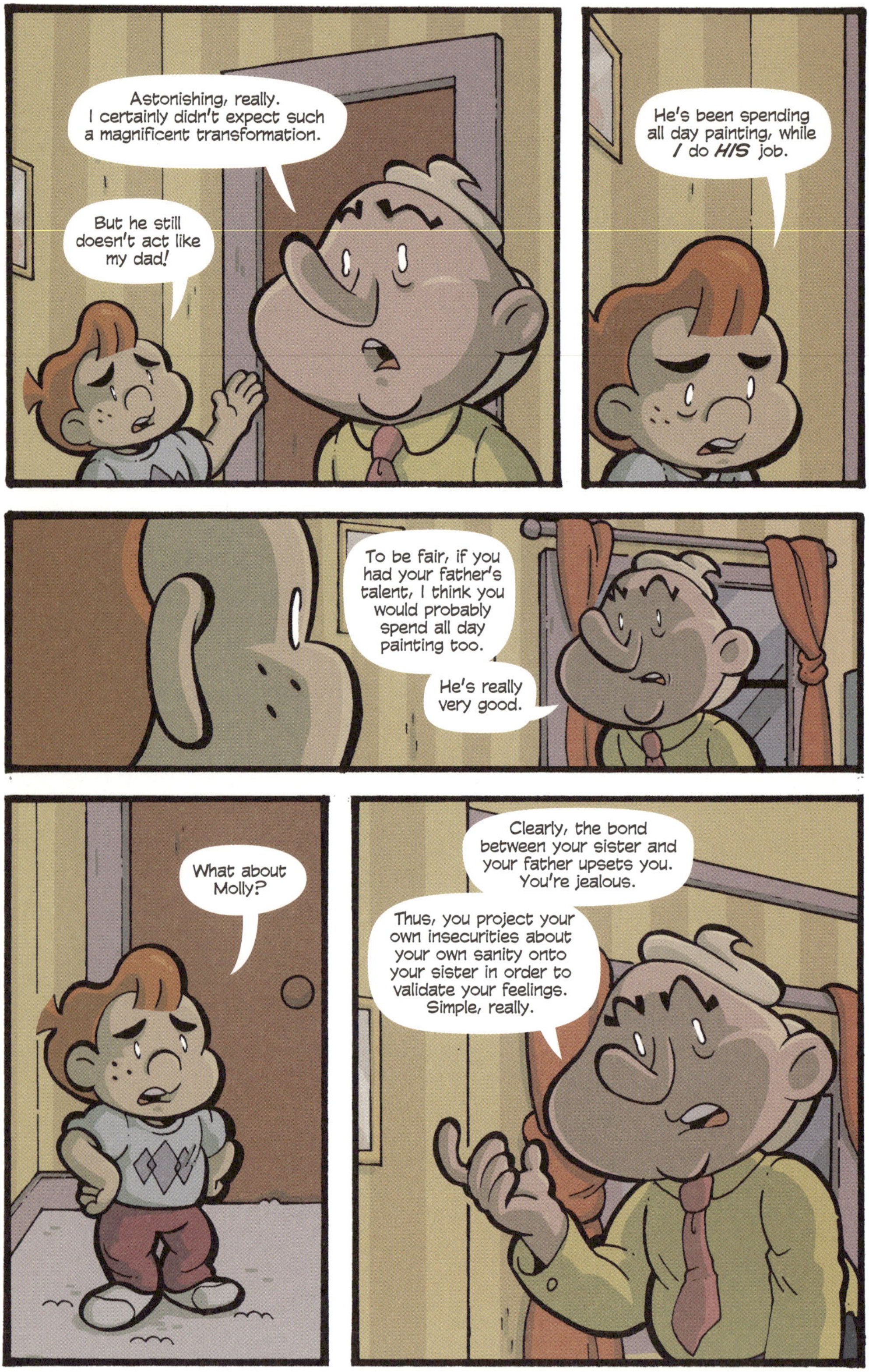
Astonishing, really. I certainly didn't expect such a magnificent transformation.
But he still doesn't act like my dad!
He's been spending all day painting, while *I* do *HIS* job.
To be fair, if you had your father's talent, I think you would probably spend all day painting too.
He's really very good.
What about Molly?
Clearly, the bond between your sister and your father upsets you. You're jealous.
Thus, you project your own insecurities about your own sanity onto your sister in order to validate your feelings. Simple, really.

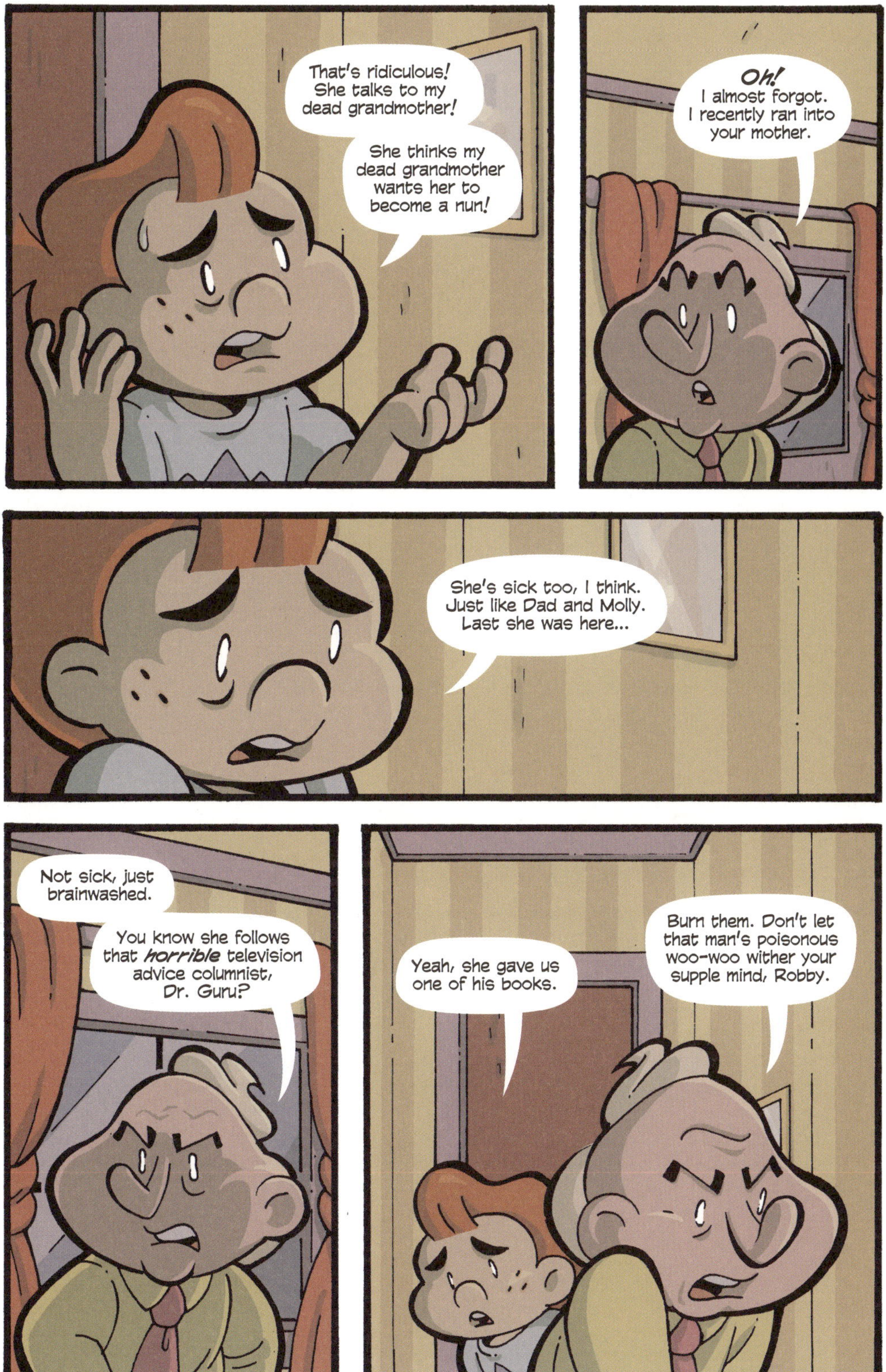
That's ridiculous! She talks to my dead grandmother!
She thinks my dead grandmother wants her to become a nun!
Oh! I almost forgot. I recently ran into your mother.
She's sick too, I think. Just like Dad and Molly. Last she was here...
Not sick, just brainwashed.
You know she follows that *horrible* television advice columnist, Dr. Guru?
Yeah, she gave us one of his books.
Burn them. Don't let that man's poisonous woo-woo wither your supple mind, Robby.

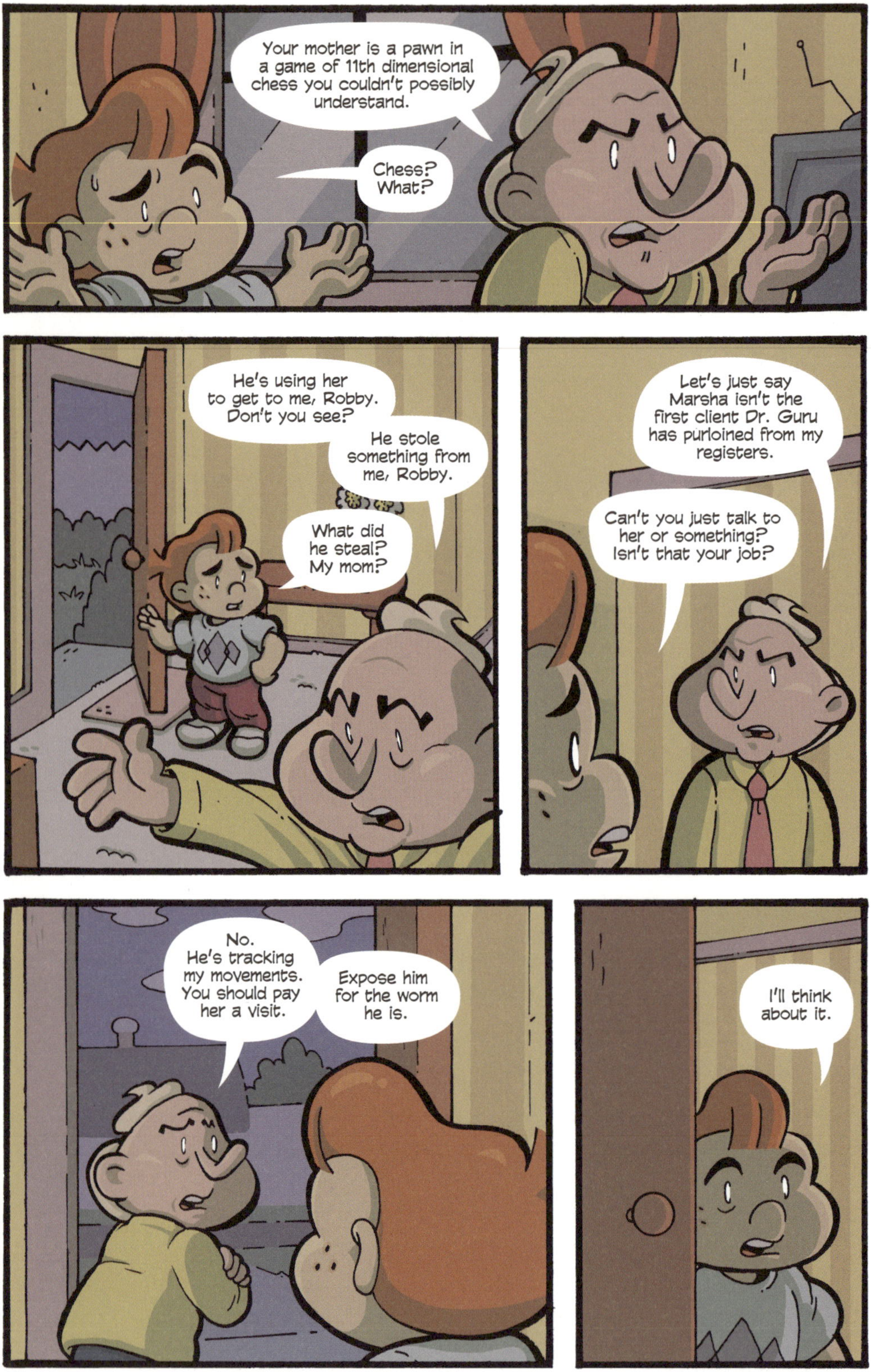
Your mother is a pawn in a game of 11th dimensional chess you couldn't possibly understand.
Chess? What?
He's using her to get to me, Robby. Don't you see?
He stole something from me, Robby.
What did he steal? My mom?
Let's just say Marsha isn't the first client Dr. Guru has purloined from my registers.
Can't you just talk to her or something? Isn't that your job?
No. He's tracking my movements. You should pay her a visit.
Expose him for the worm he is.
I'll think about it.

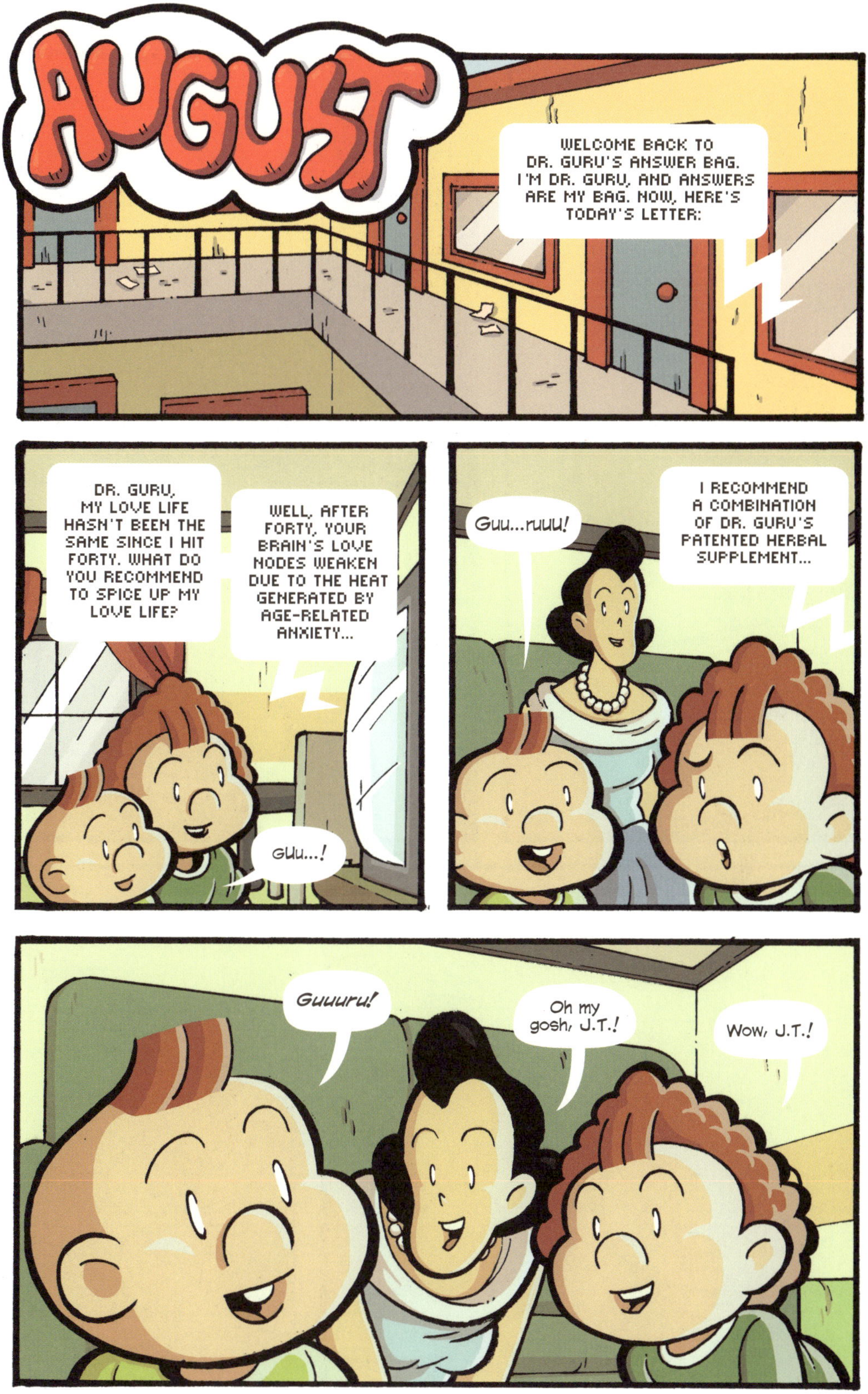
AUGUST
WELCOME BACK TO DR. GURU'S ANSWER BAG. I'M DR. GURU, AND ANSWERS ARE MY BAG. NOW, HERE'S TODAY'S LETTER:
DR. GURU, MY LOVE LIFE HASN'T BEEN THE SAME SINCE I HIT FORTY. WHAT DO YOU RECOMMEND TO SPICE UP MY LOVE LIFE?
WELL, AFTER FORTY, YOUR BRAIN'S LOVE NODES WEAKEN DUE TO THE HEAT GENERATED BY AGE-RELATED ANXIETY...
Guu...!
Guu...ruuu!
I RECOMMEND A COMBINATION OF DR. GURU'S PATENTED HERBAL SUPPLEMENT...
Guuuru!
Oh my gosh, J.T.!
Wow, J.T.!

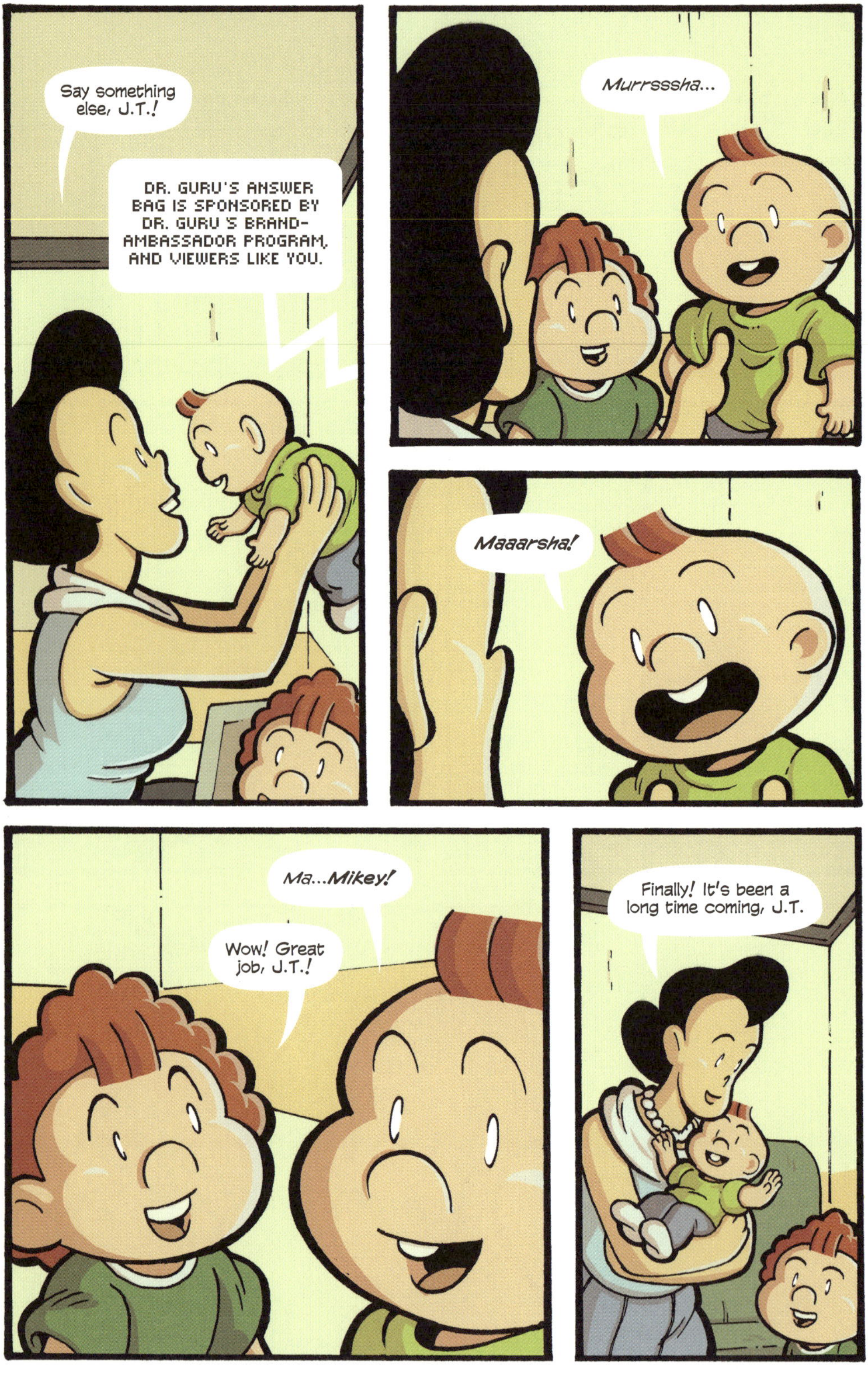
Say something else, J.T.!
DR. GURU'S ANSWER BAG IS SPONSORED BY DR. GURU'S BRAND-AMBASSADOR PROGRAM, AND VIEWERS LIKE YOU.
Murrsssha...
Maaarsha!
Ma...Mikey!
Wow! Great job, J.T.!
Finally! It's been a long time coming, J.T.

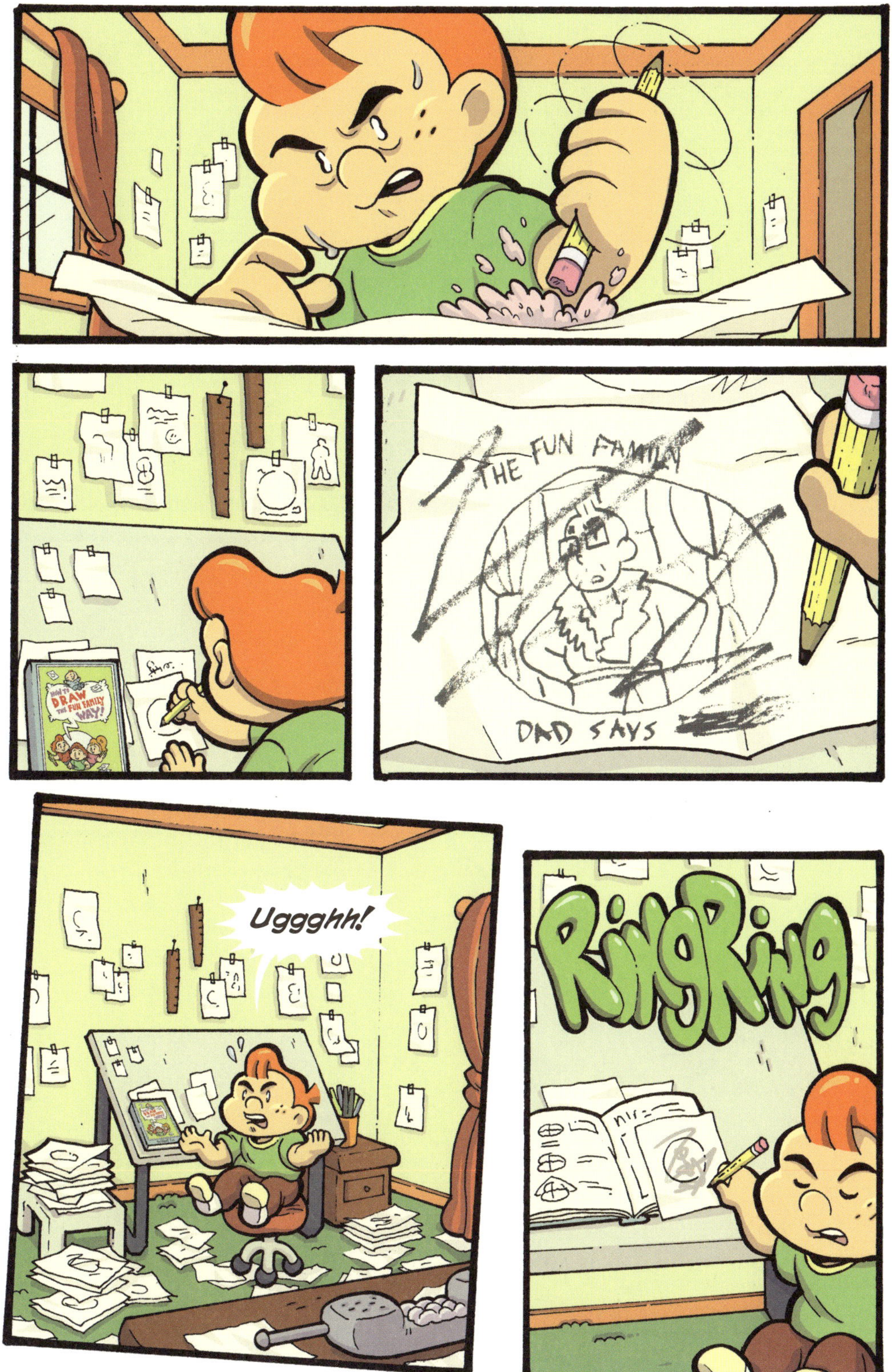
HOW TO DRAW THE FUN FAMILY WAY!
THE FUN FAMILY
DAD SAYS
Uggghh!
RingRing

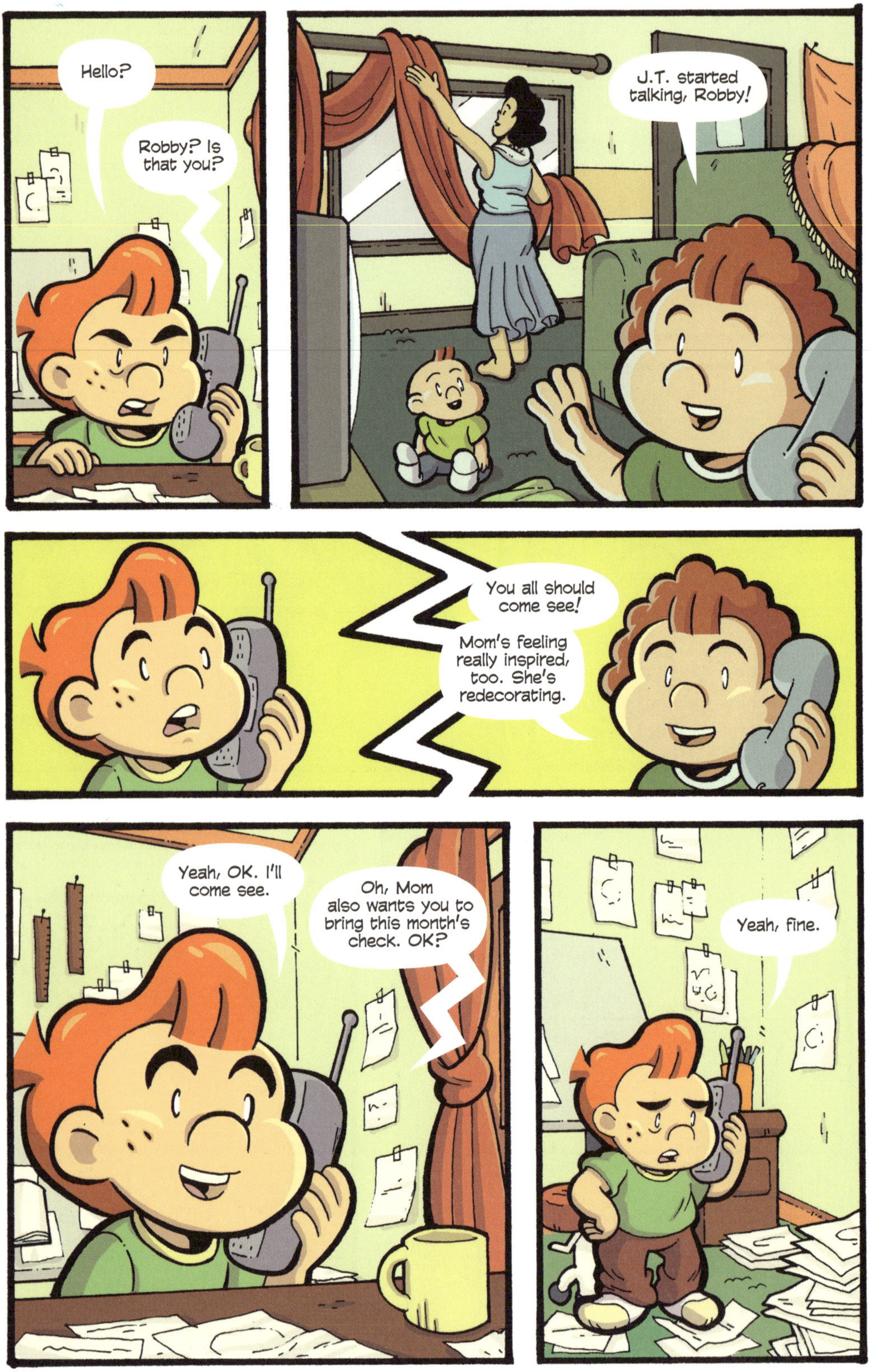
Hello?
Robby? Is that you?
J.T. started talking, Robby!
You all should come see!
Mom's feeling really inspired, too. She's redecorating.
Yeah, OK. I'll come see.
Oh, Mom also wants you to bring this month's check. OK?
Yeah, fine.

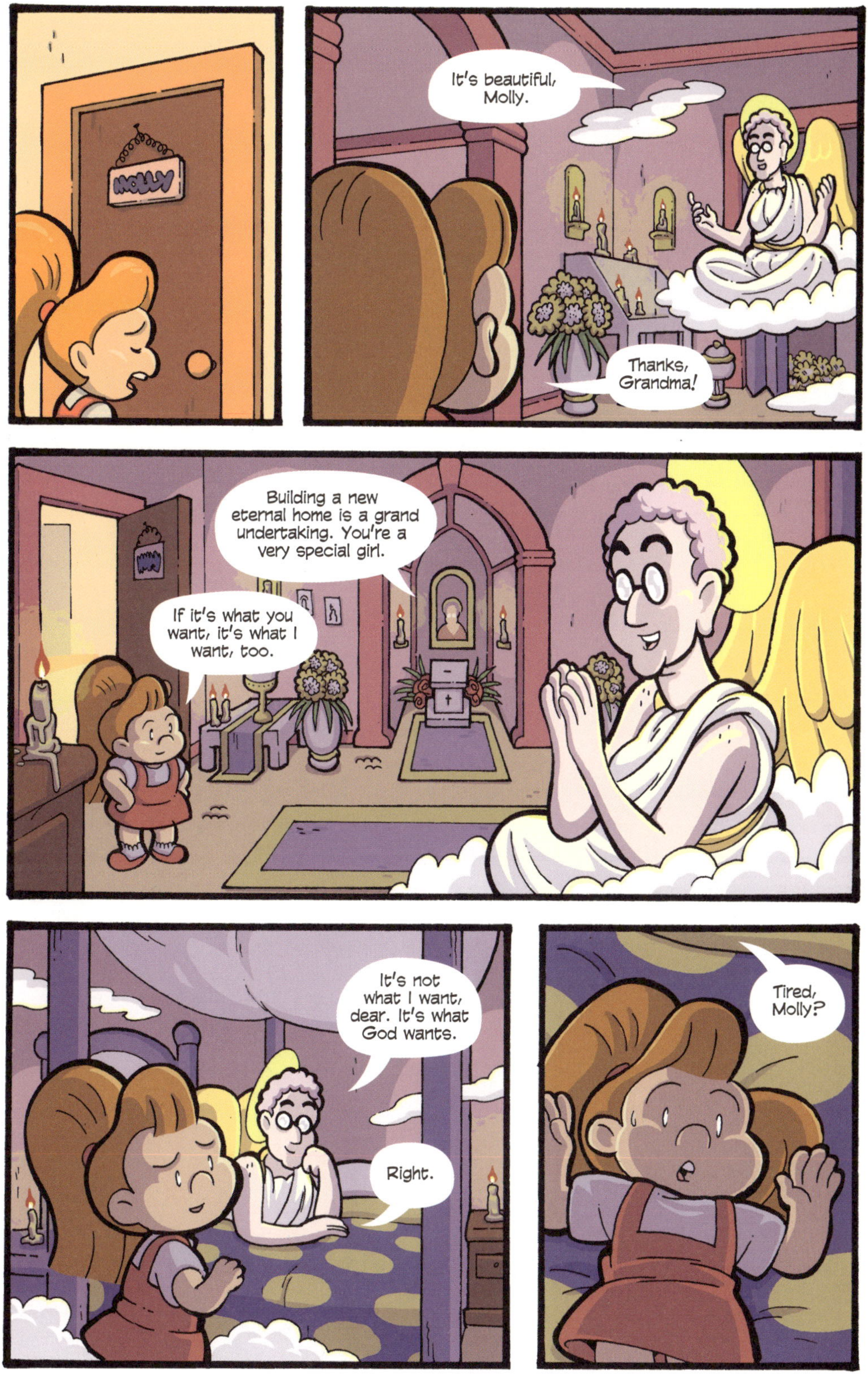
MOLLY
It's beautiful, Molly.
Thanks, Grandma!
Building a new eternal home is a grand undertaking. You're a very special girl.
If it's what you want, it's what I want, too.
It's not what I want, dear. It's what God wants.
Right.
Tired, Molly?

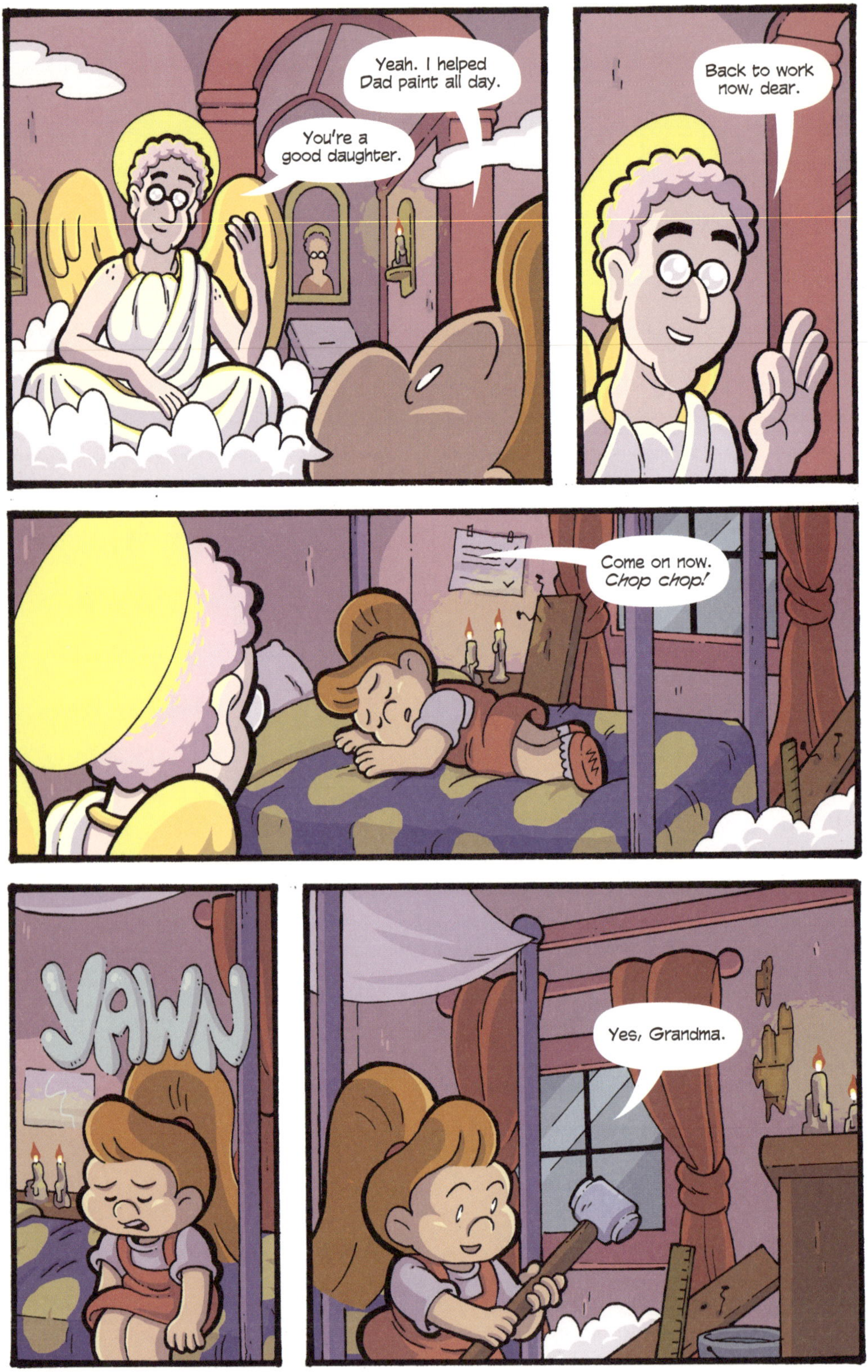
Yeah. I helped Dad paint all day.
You're a good daughter.
Back to work now, dear.
Come on now. *Chop chop!*
YAWN
Yes, Grandma.

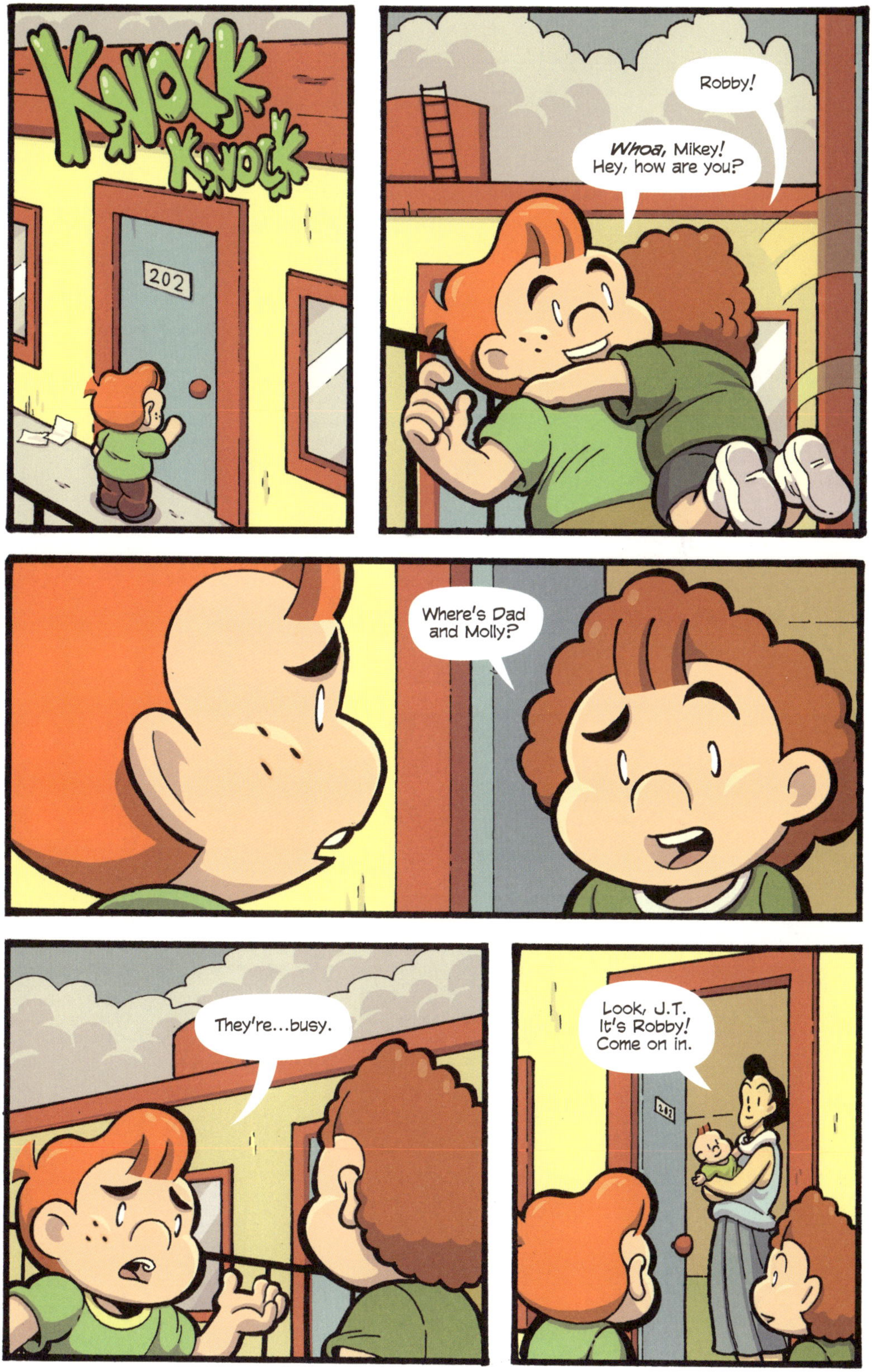
KNOCK KNOCK
202
Robby!
Whoa, Mikey! Hey, how are you?
Where's Dad and Molly?
They're...busy.
Look, J.T. It's Robby! Come on in.

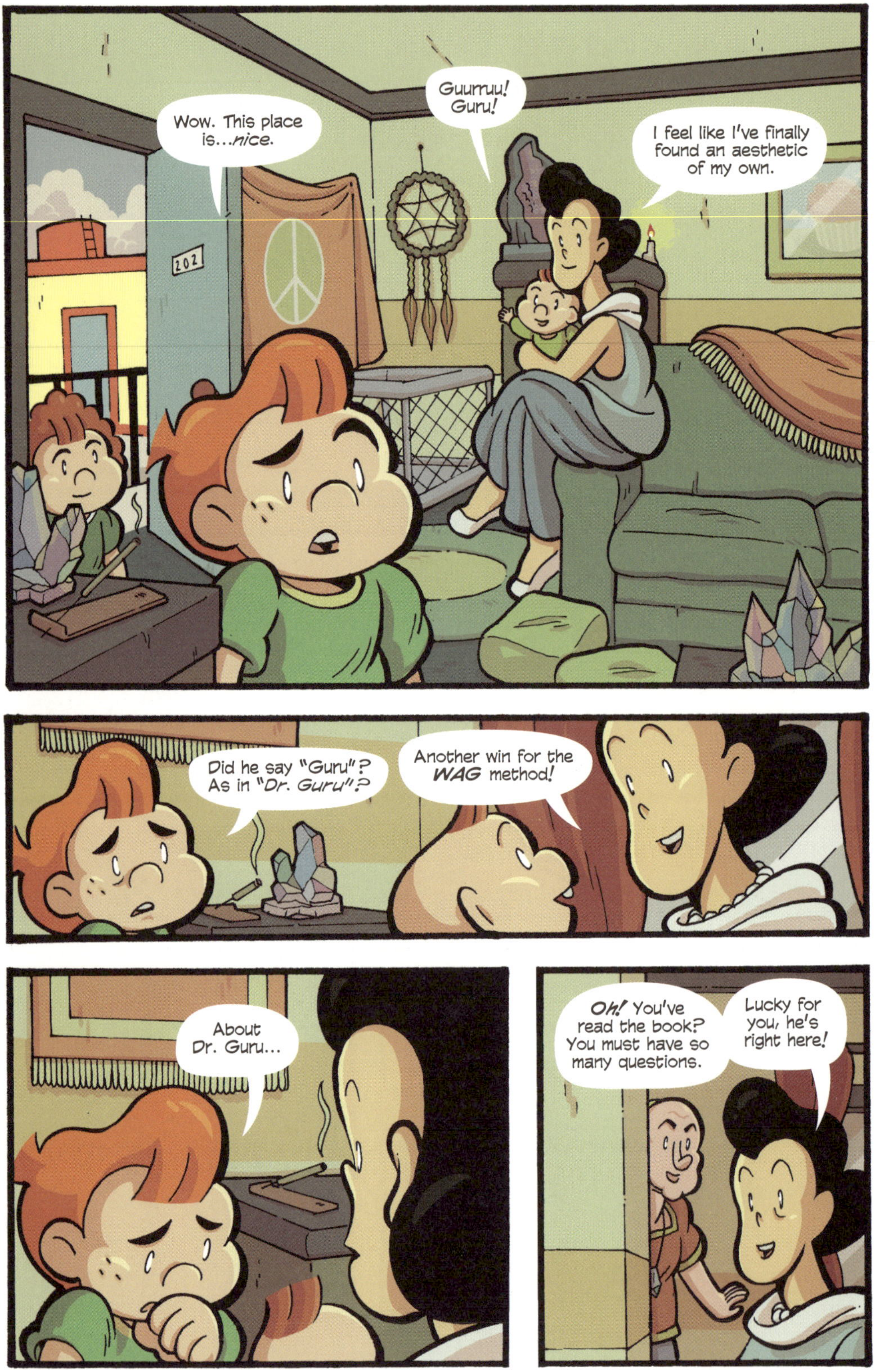
Wow. This place is...*nice*.
Guurruu! Guru!
I feel like I've finally found an aesthetic of my own.
Did he say "Guru"? As in "Dr. Guru"?
Another win for the *WAG* method!
About Dr. Guru...
Oh! You've read the book? You must have so many questions.
Lucky for you, he's right here!

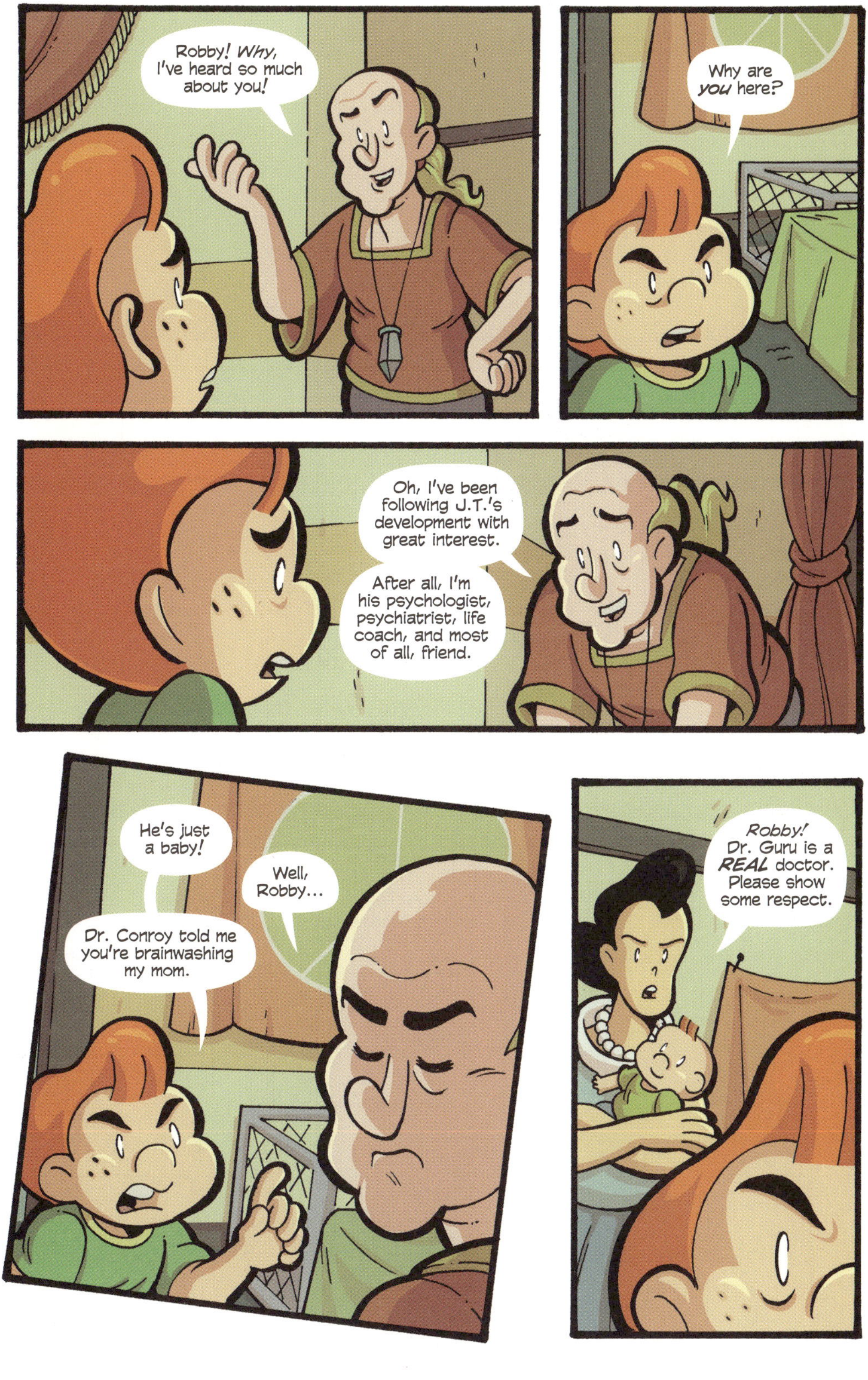
Robby! *Why,* I've heard so much about you!
Why are *you* here?
Oh, I've been following J.T.'s development with great interest.
After all, I'm his psychologist, psychiatrist, life coach, and most of all, friend.
He's just a baby!
Dr. Conroy told me you're brainwashing my mom.
Well, Robby...
Robby! Dr. Guru is a ***REAL*** doctor. Please show some respect.

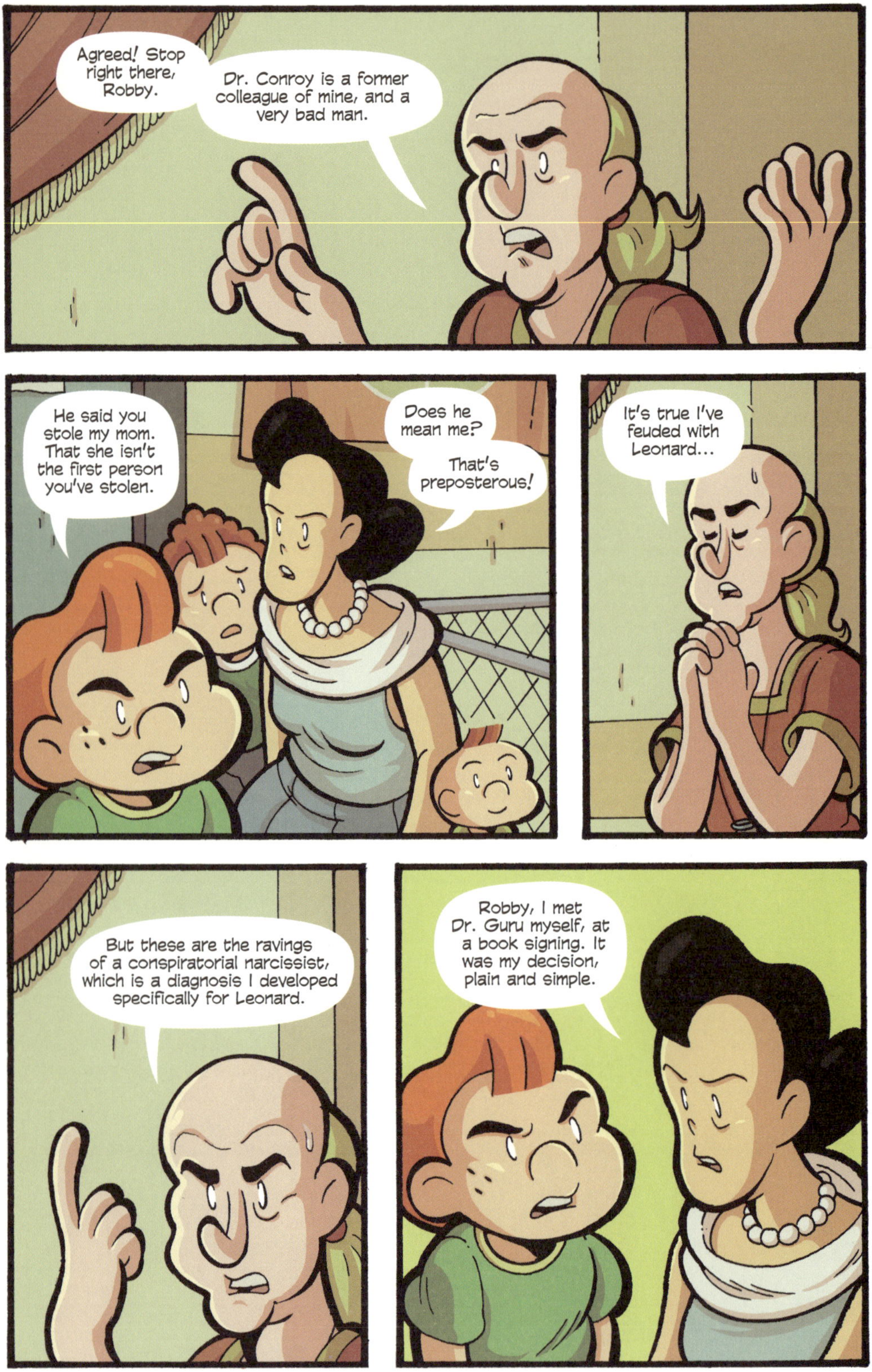
Agreed! Stop right there, Robby.
Dr. Conroy is a former colleague of mine, and a very bad man.
He said you stole my mom. That she isn't the first person you've stolen.
Does he mean me?
That's preposterous!
It's true I've feuded with Leonard...
But these are the ravings of a conspiratorial narcissist, which is a diagnosis I developed specifically for Leonard.
Robby, I met Dr. Guru myself, at a book signing. It was my decision, plain and simple.

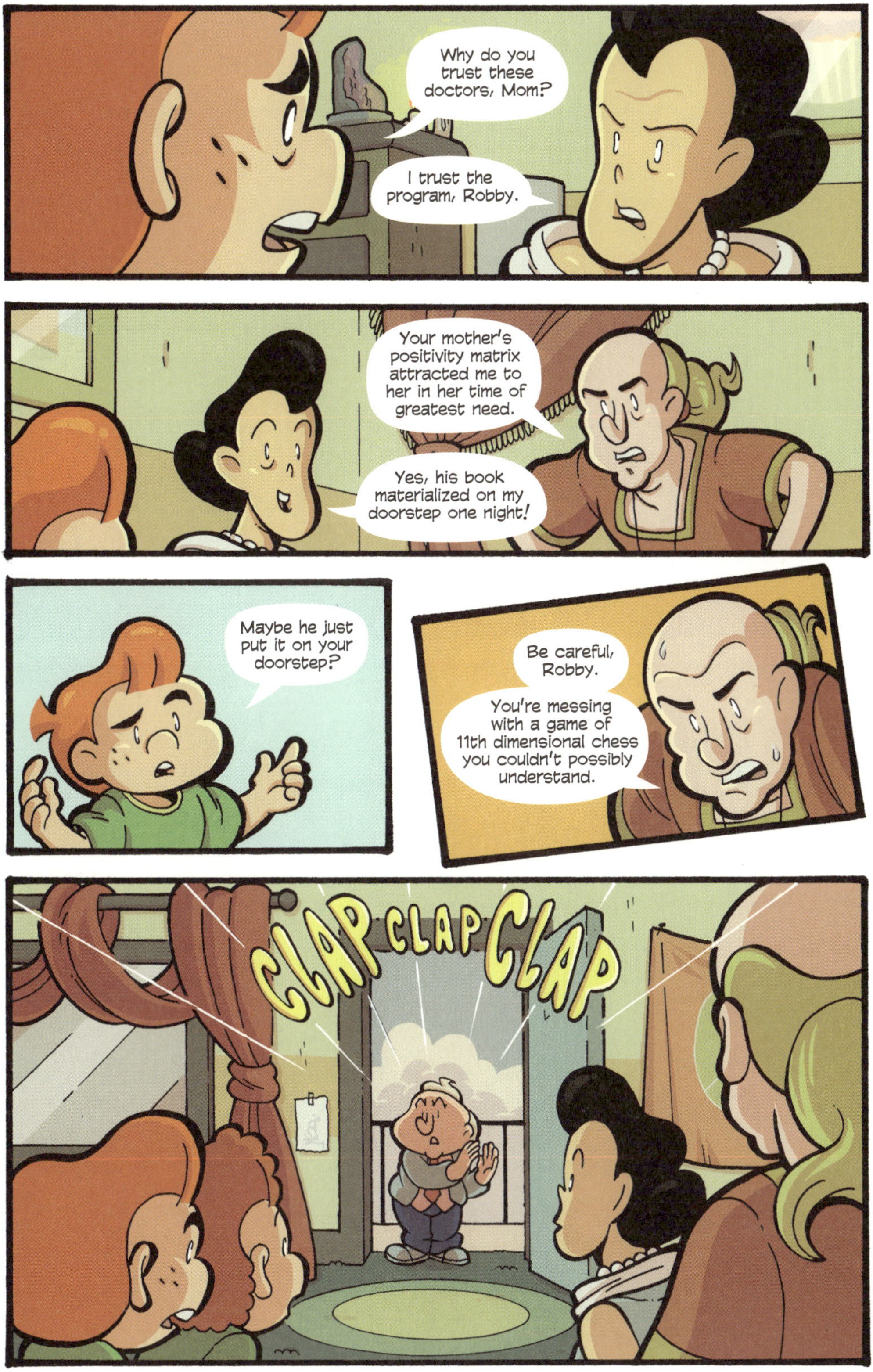
Why do you trust these doctors, Mom?
I trust the program, Robby.
Your mother's positivity matrix attracted me to her in her time of greatest need.
Yes, his book materialized on my doorstep one night!
Maybe he just put it on your doorstep?
Be careful, Robby.
You're messing with a game of 11th dimensional chess you couldn't possibly understand.
CLAP CLAP CLAP

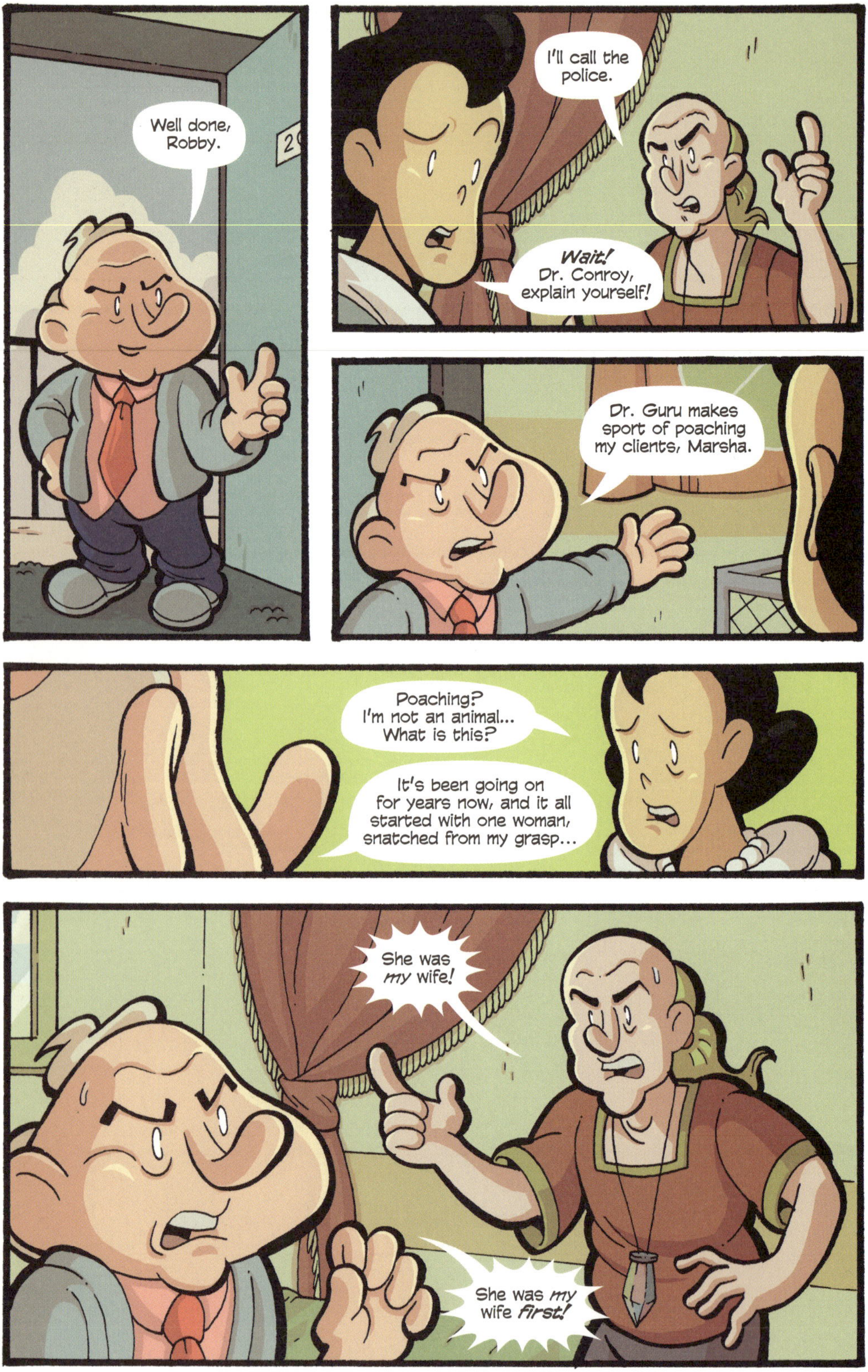
Well done, Robby.
I'll call the police.
Wait! Dr. Conroy, explain yourself!
Dr. Guru makes sport of poaching my clients, Marsha.
Poaching? I'm not an animal... What is this?
It's been going on for years now, and it all started with one woman, snatched from my grasp...
She was my wife!
She was my wife first!

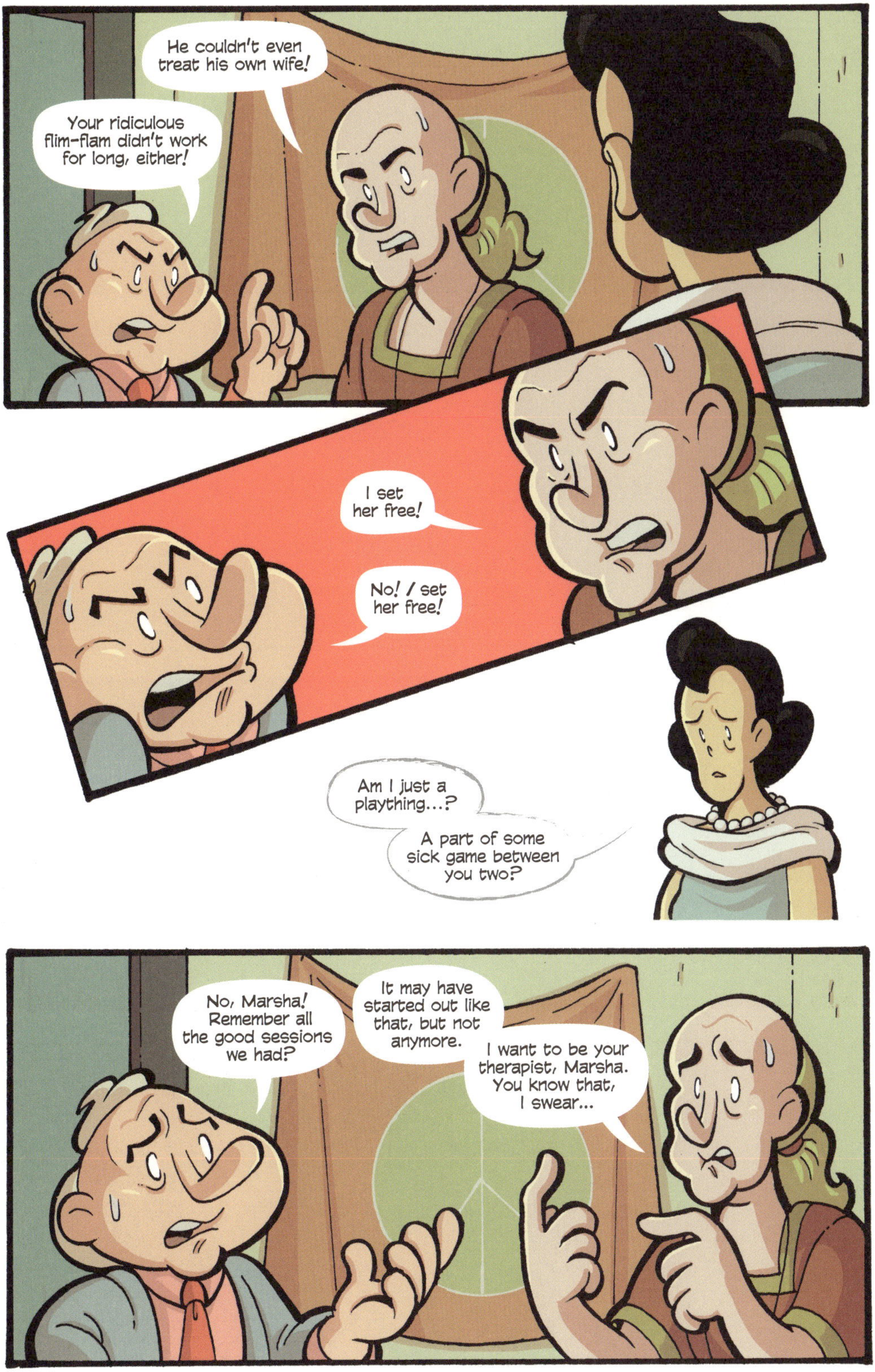
He couldn't even treat his own wife!
Your ridiculous flim-flam didn't work for long, either!
I set her free!
No! I set her free!
Am I just a plaything...?
A part of some sick game between you two?
No, Marsha! Remember all the good sessions we had?
It may have started out like that, but not anymore.
I want to be your therapist, Marsha. You know that, I swear...

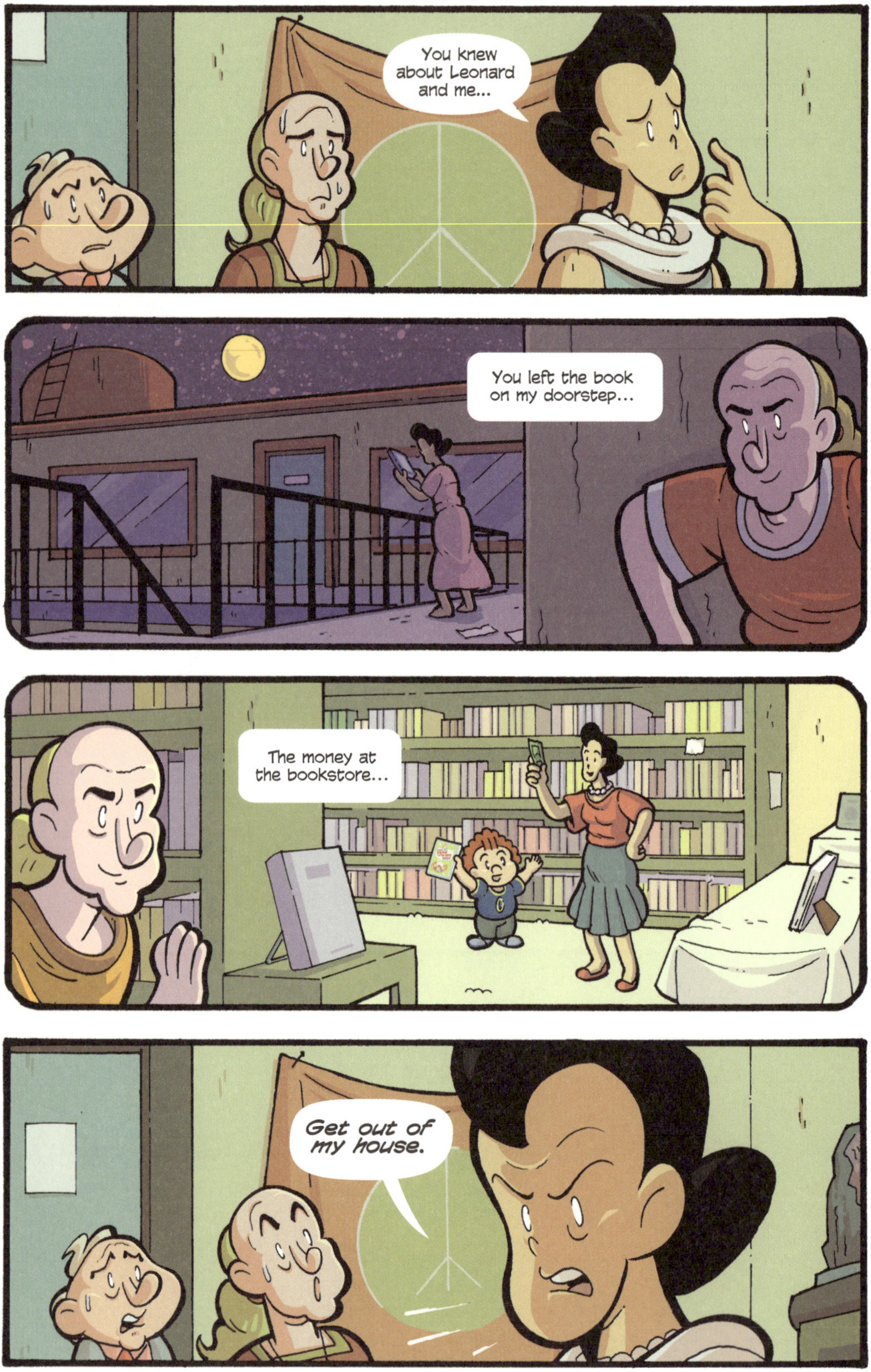
You knew about Leonard and me...
You left the book on my doorstep...
The money at the bookstore...
Get out of my house.

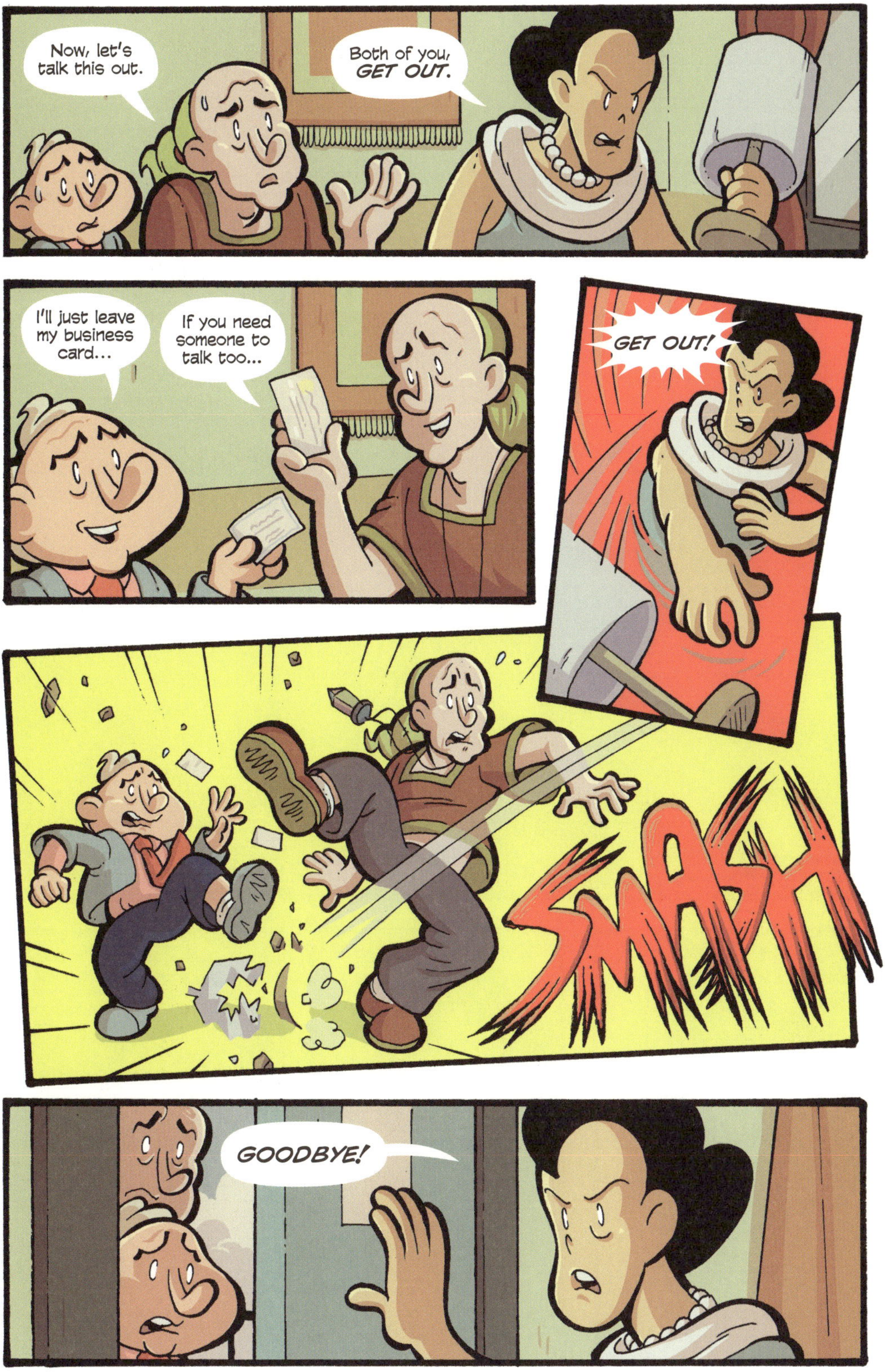
Now, let's talk this out.
Both of you, GET OUT.
I'll just leave my business card...
If you need someone to talk too...
GET OUT!
SMASH
GOODBYE!

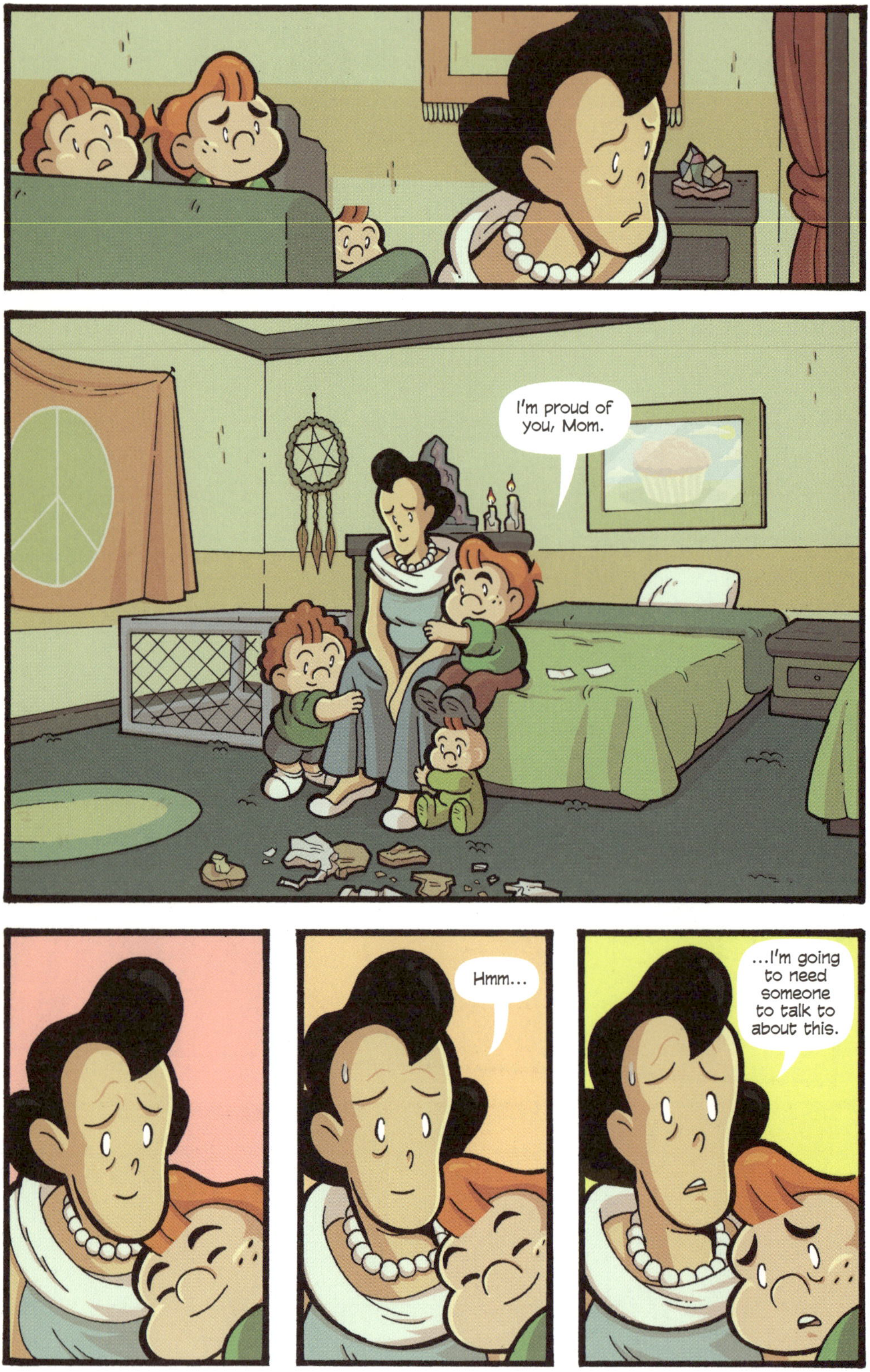
I'm proud of you, Mom.
Hmm...
...I'm going to need someone to talk to about this.

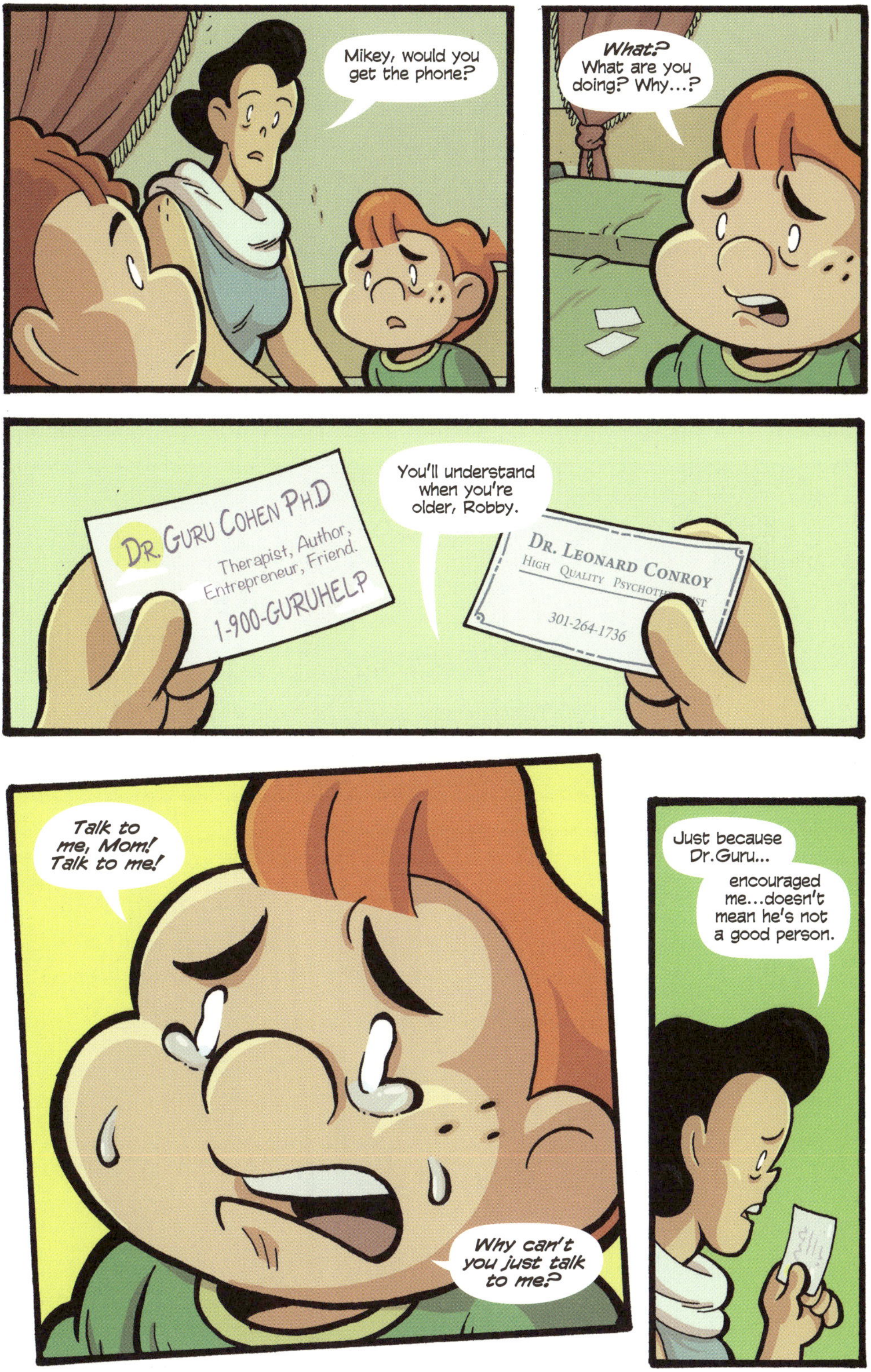
Mikey, would you get the phone?
What? What are you doing? Why...?
Dr. Guru Cohen Ph.D
Therapist, Author, Entrepreneur, Friend.
1-900-GURUHELP
You'll understand when you're older, Robby.
Dr. Leonard Conroy
301-264-1736
Talk to me, Mom! Talk to me!
Why can't you just talk to me?
Just because Dr.Guru...
encouraged me...doesn't mean he's not a good person.

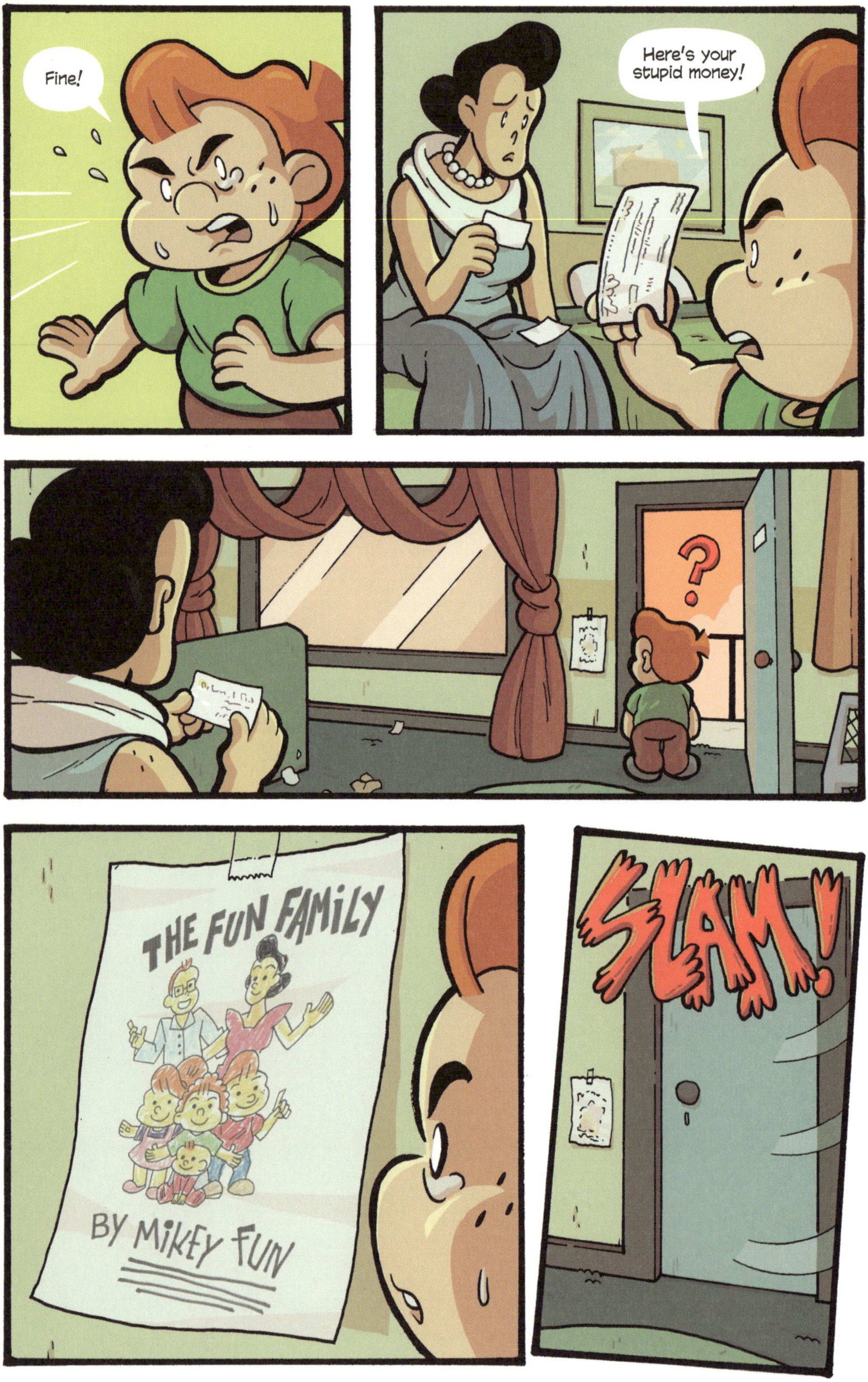
Fine!
Here's your stupid money!
?
THE FUN FAMILY
BY MIKEY FUN
SLAM!

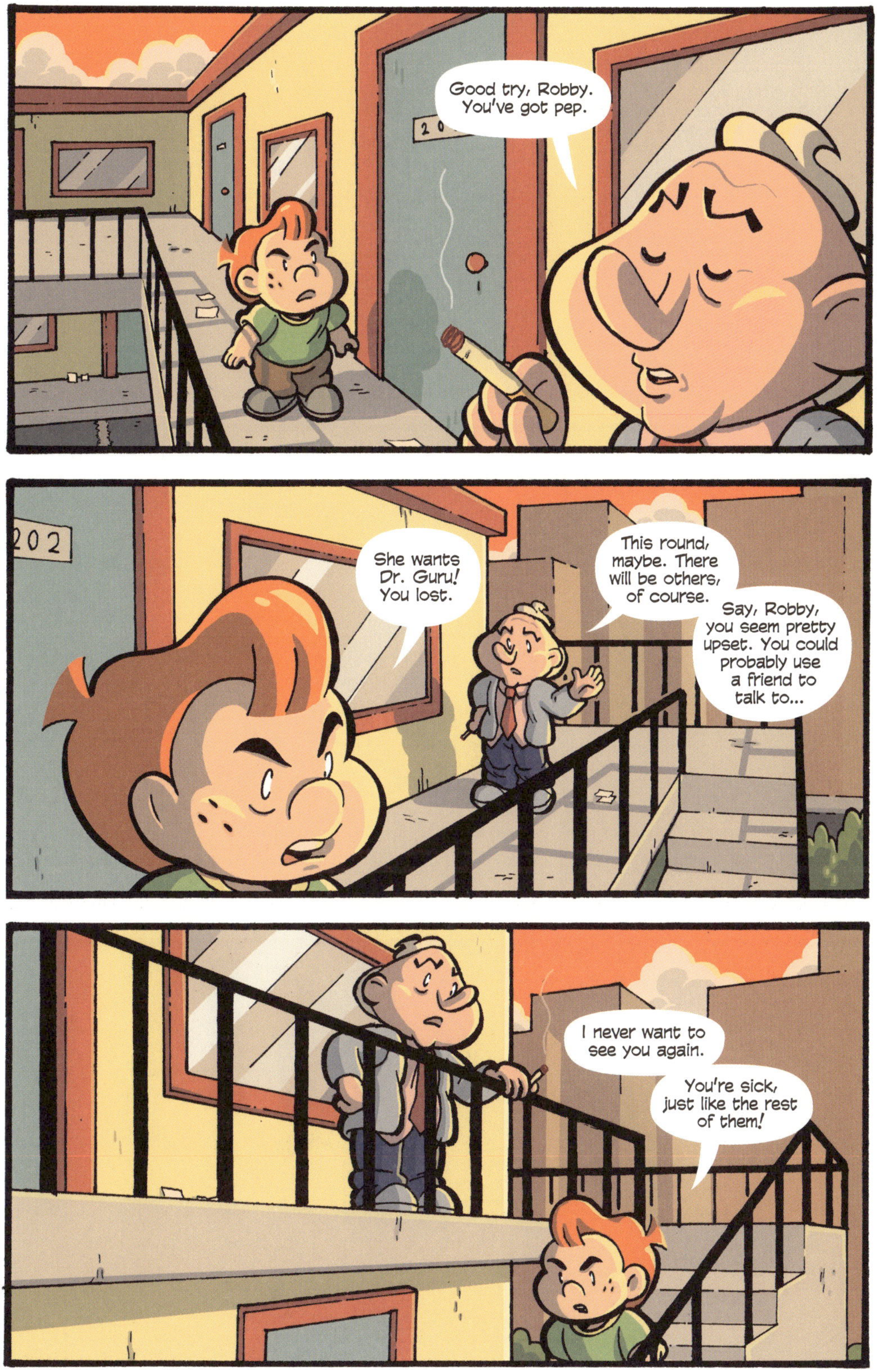
Good try, Robby. You've got pep.
202
She wants Dr. Guru! You lost.
This round, maybe. There will be others, of course.
Say, Robby, you seem pretty upset. You could probably use a friend to talk to...
I never want to see you again.
You're sick, just like the rest of them!

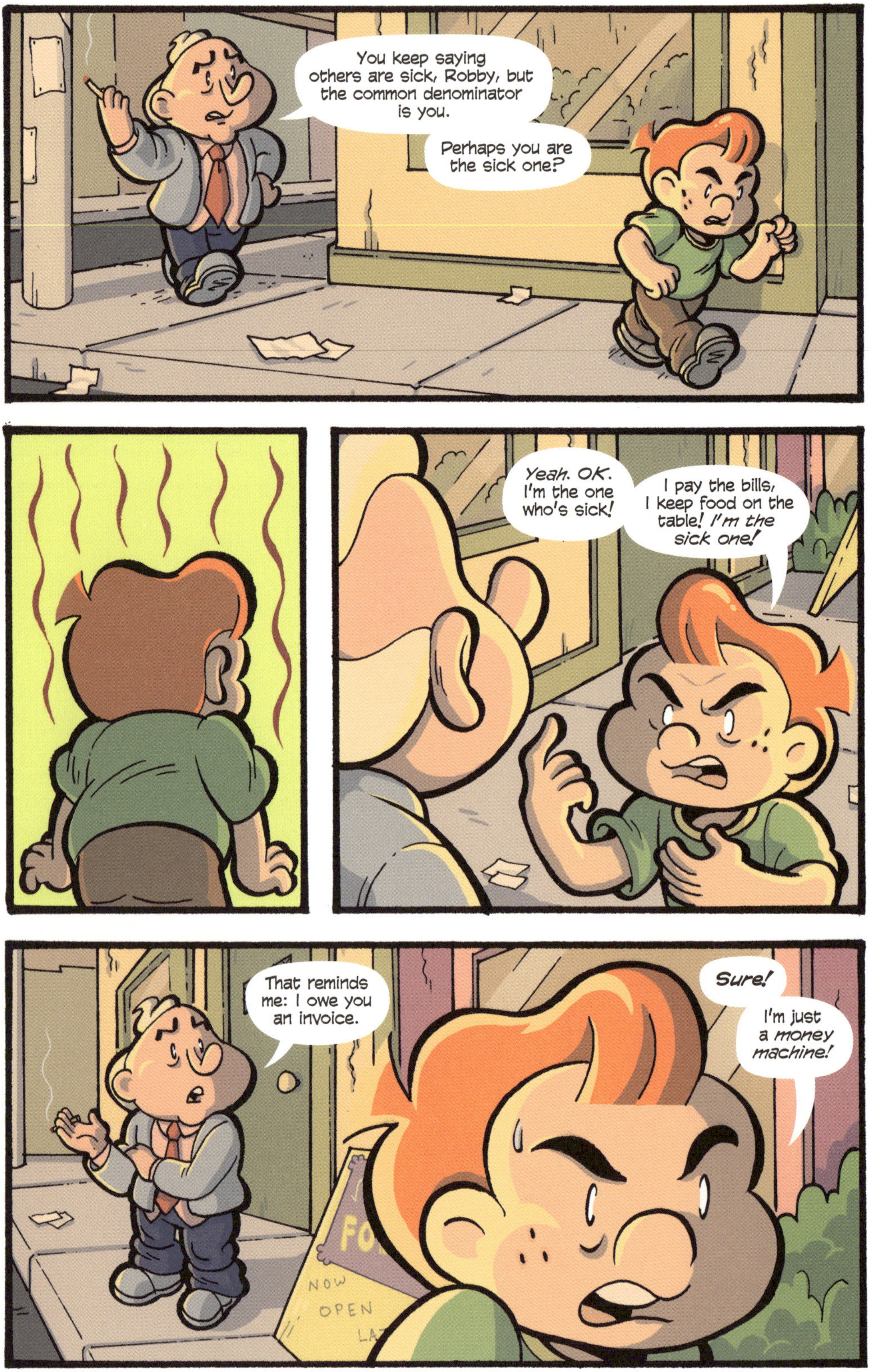
You keep saying others are sick, Robby, but the common denominator is you.
Perhaps you are the sick one?
Yeah. OK. I'm the one who's sick!
I pay the bills, I keep food on the table! *I'm the sick one!*
That reminds me: I owe you an invoice.
Sure!
I'm just a *money machine!*
NOW OPEN

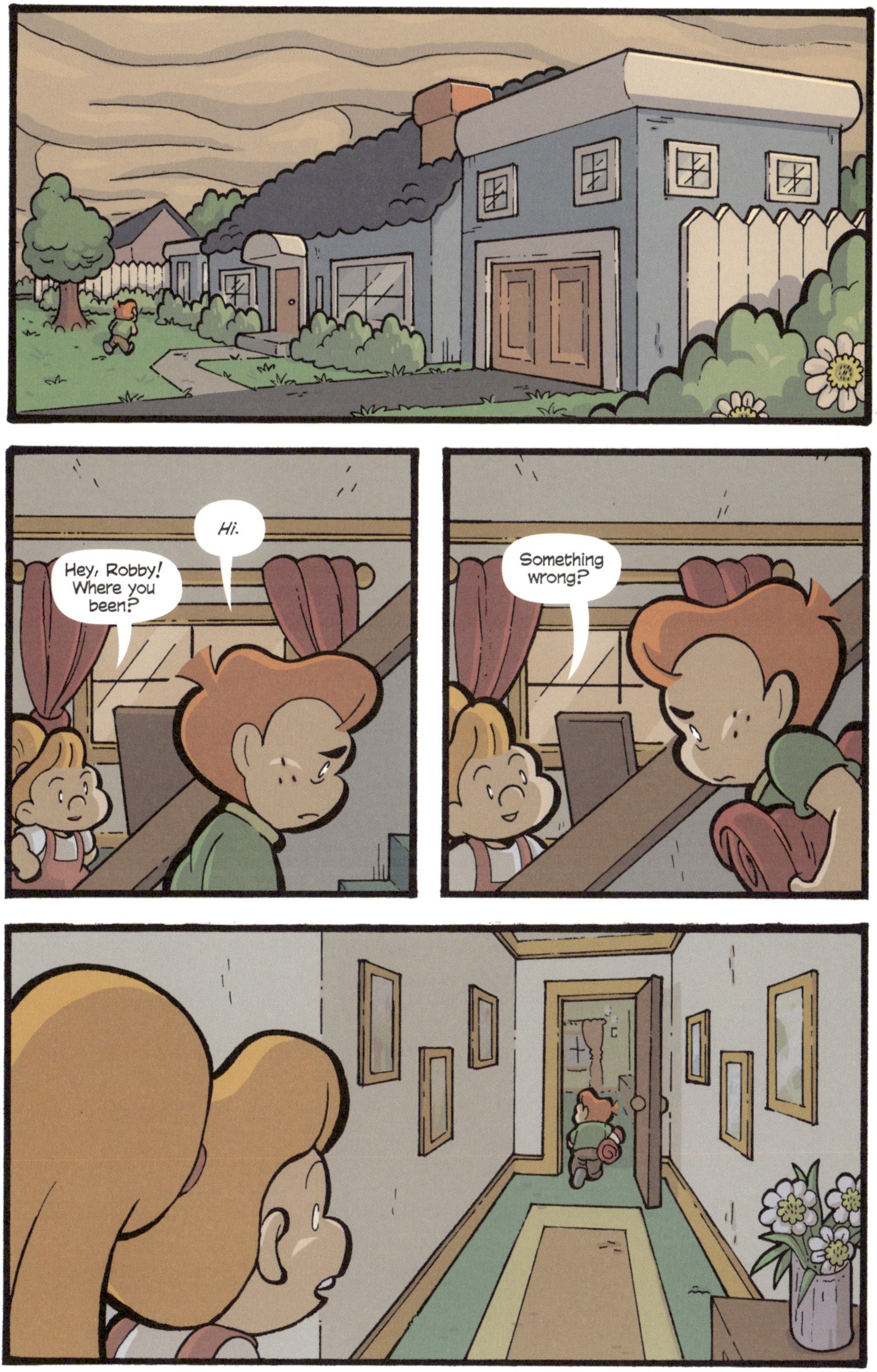
Hey, Robby! Where you been?
Hi.
Something wrong?

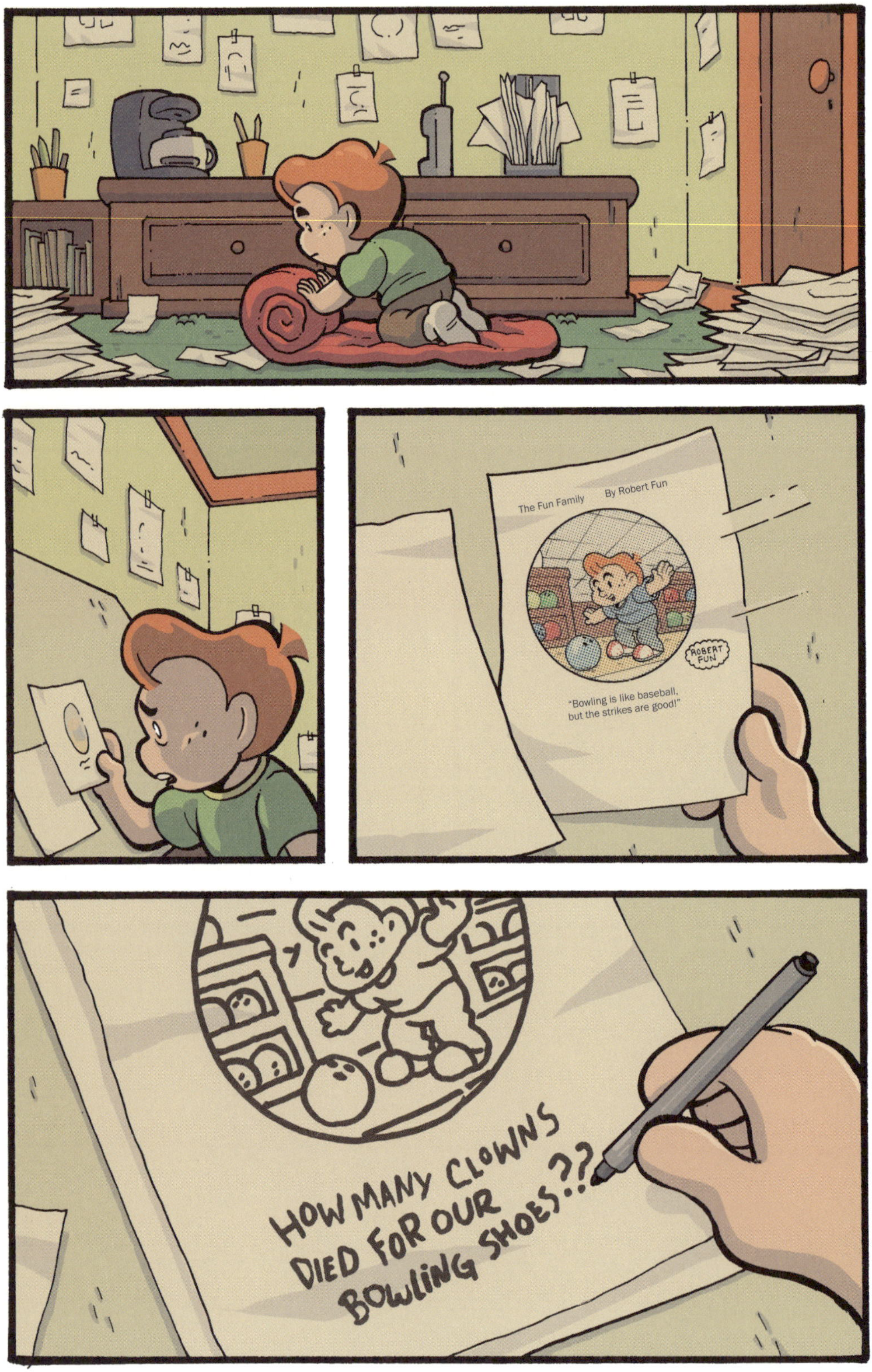
The Fun Family
By Robert Fun
ROBERT FUN
"Bowling is like baseball, but the strikes are good!"
HOW MANY CLOWNS DIED FOR OUR BOWLING SHOES??

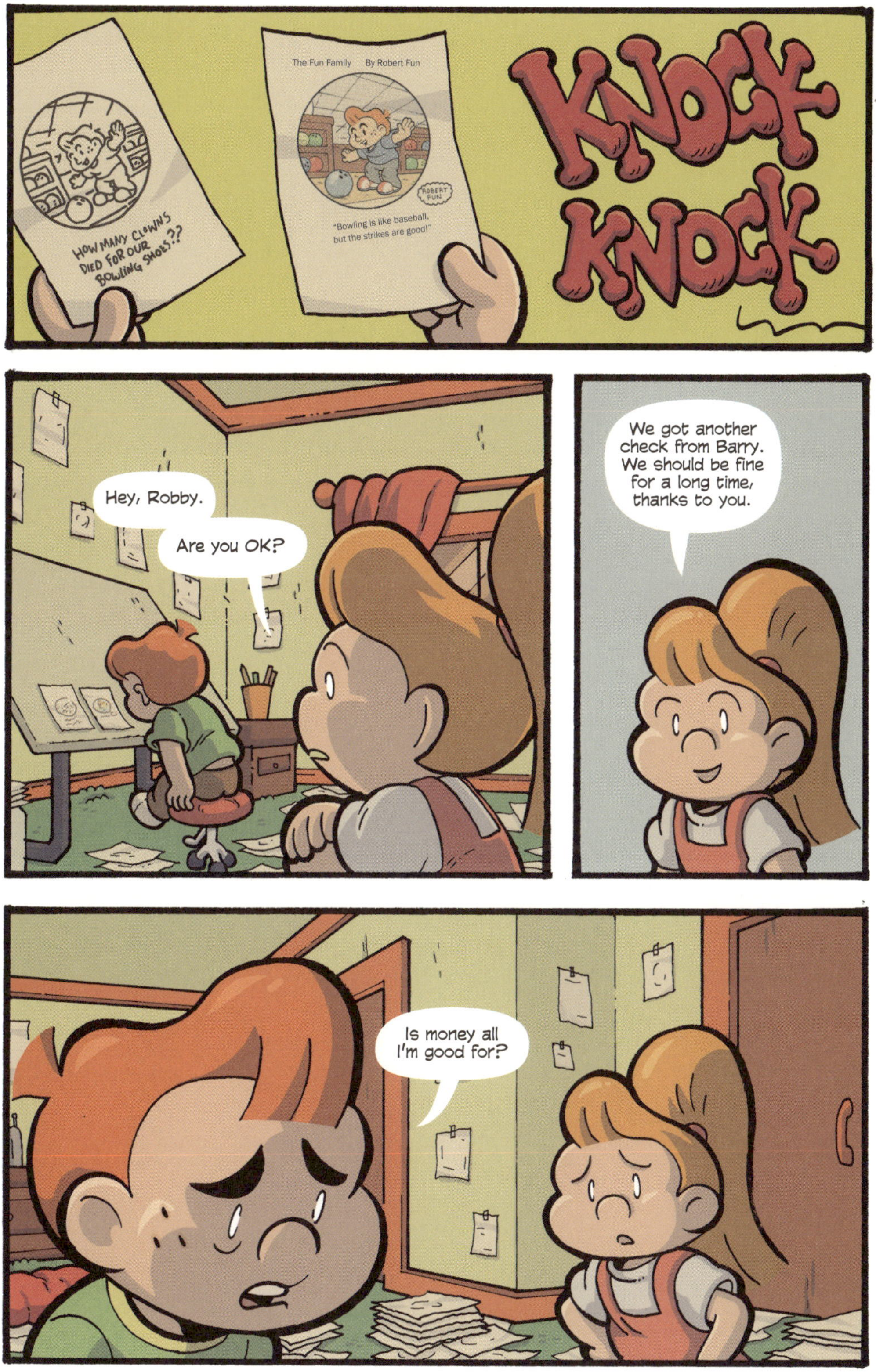
HOW MANY CLOWNS DIED FOR OUR BOWLING SHOES??
The Fun Family By Robert Fun
ROBERT FUN
"Bowling is like baseball, but the strikes are good!"
KNOCK KNOCK
Hey, Robby.
Are you OK?
We got another check from Barry. We should be fine for a long time, thanks to you.
Is money all I'm good for?

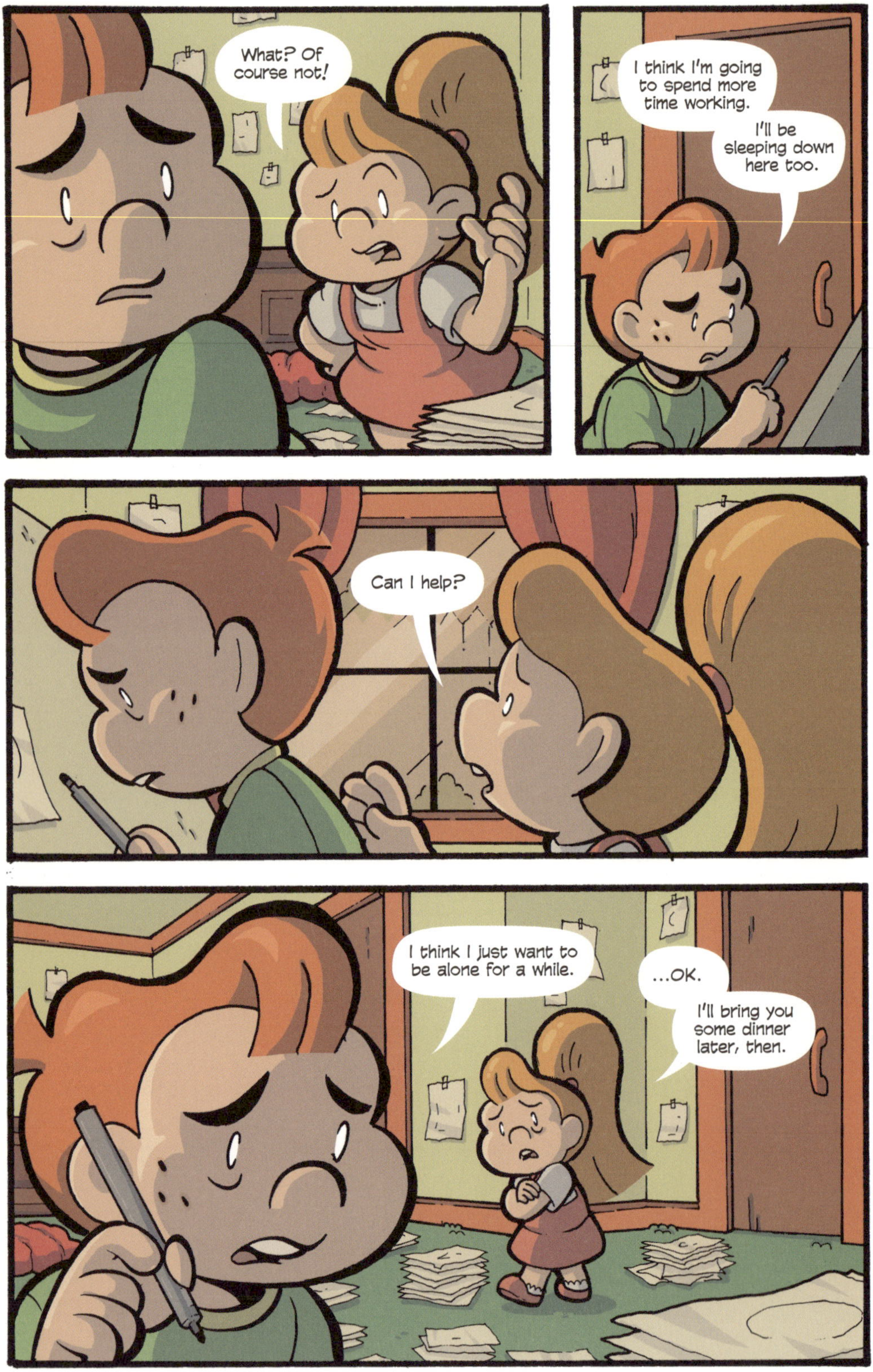
What? Of course not!
I think I'm going to spend more time working.
I'll be sleeping down here too.
Can I help?
I think I just want to be alone for a while.
...OK.
I'll bring you some dinner later, then.

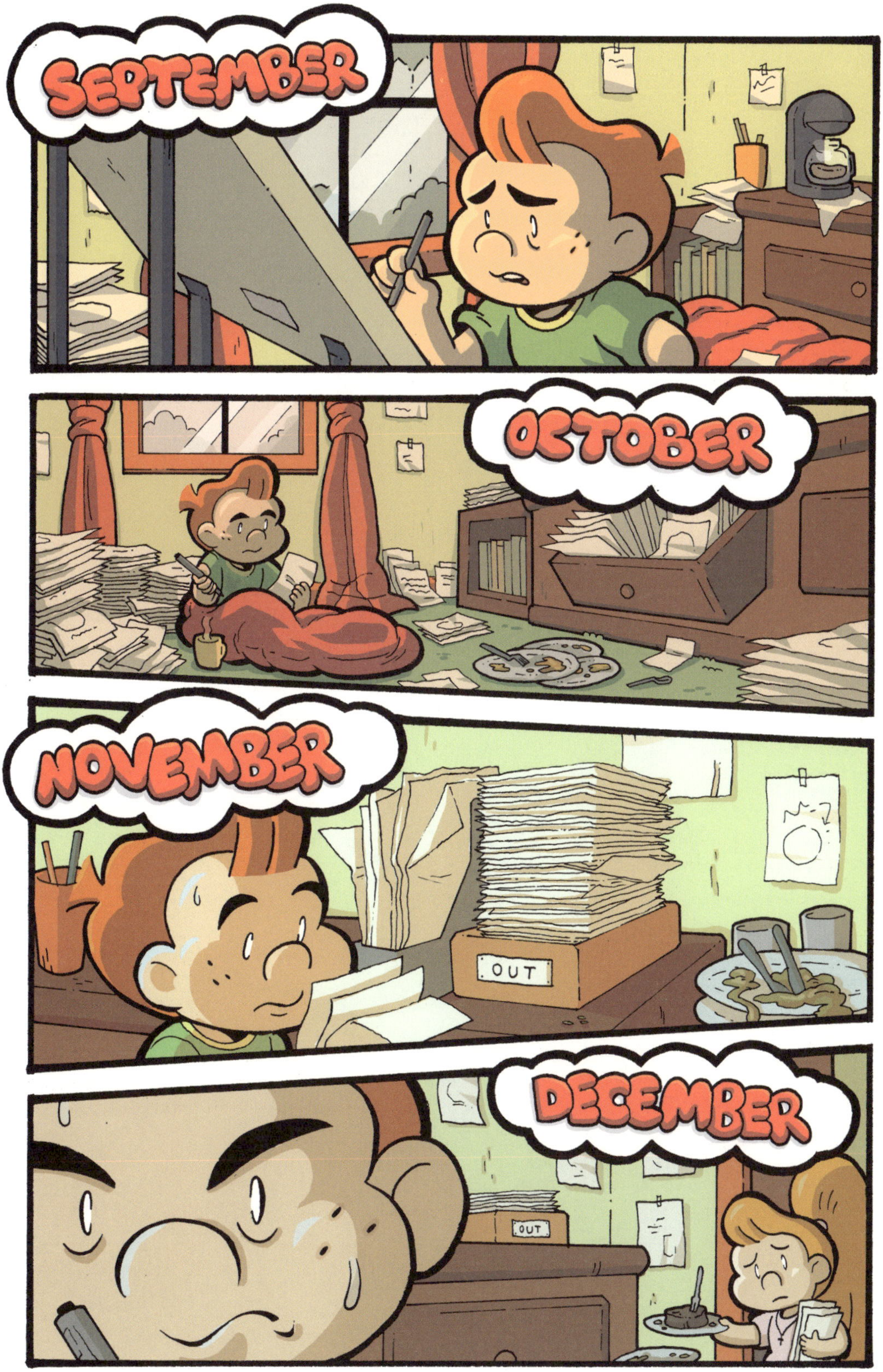
SEPTEMBER
OCTOBER
NOVEMBER
OUT
DECEMBER
OUT

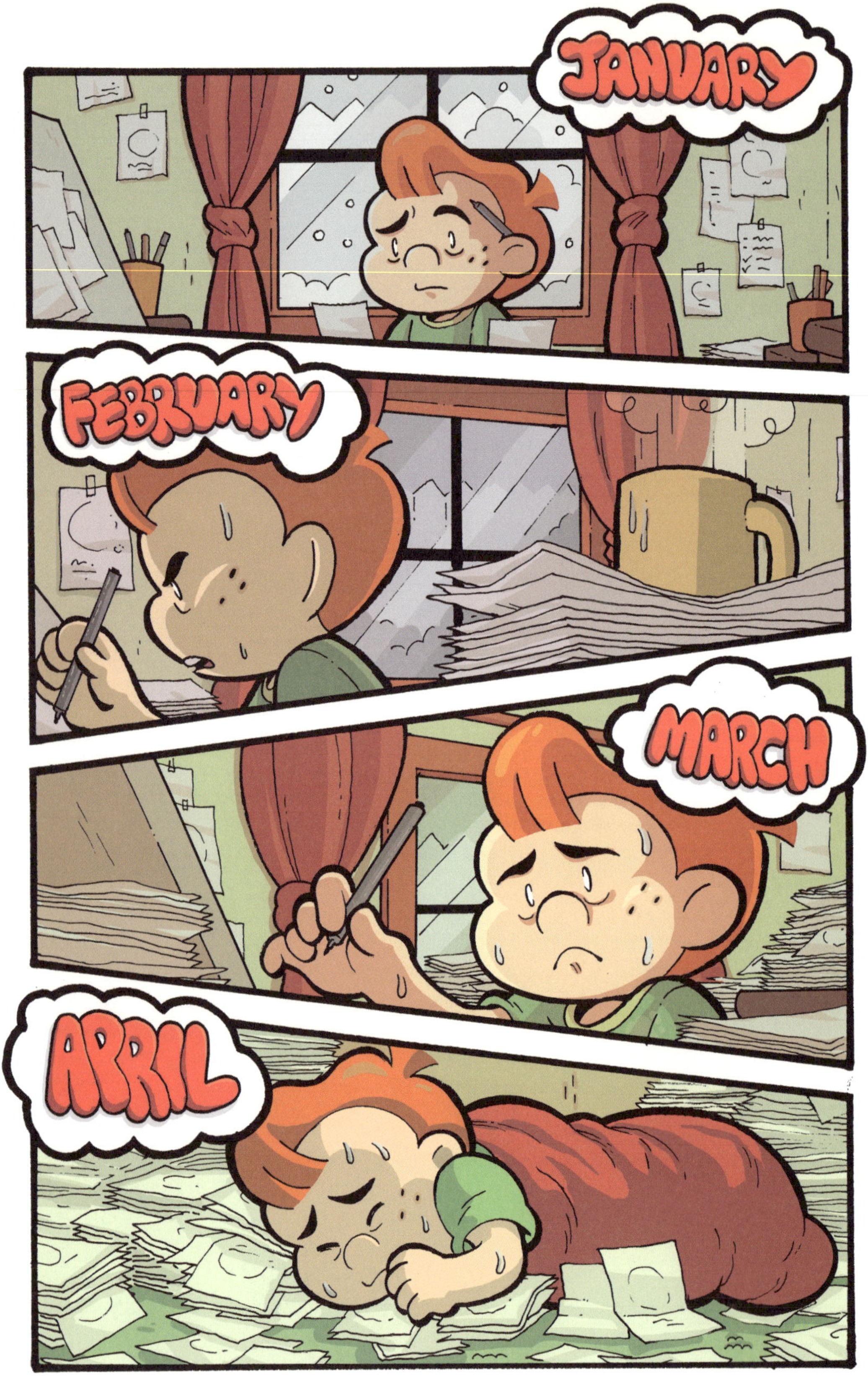
JANUARY
FEBRUARY
MARCH
APRIL

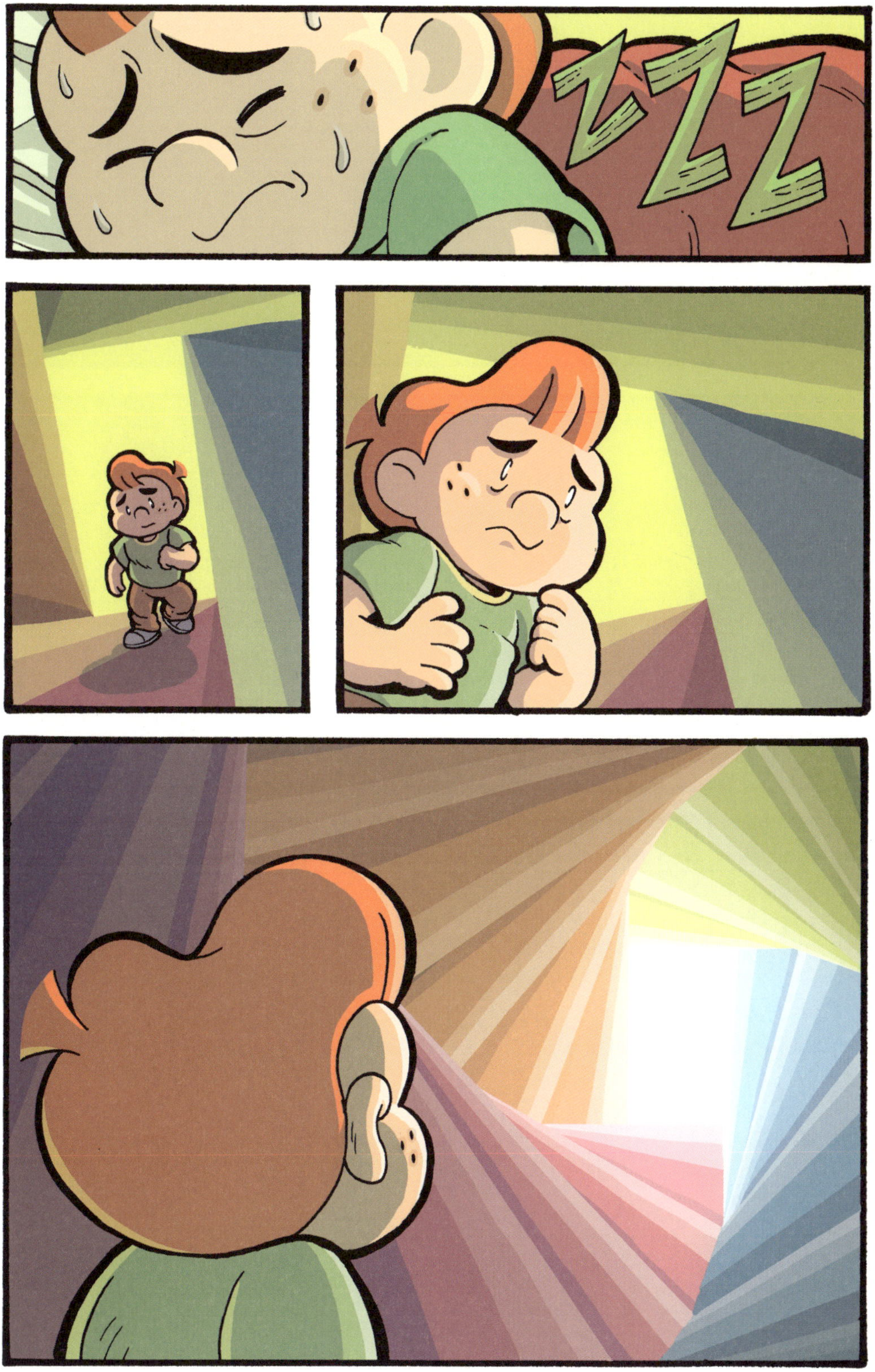
ZZZ

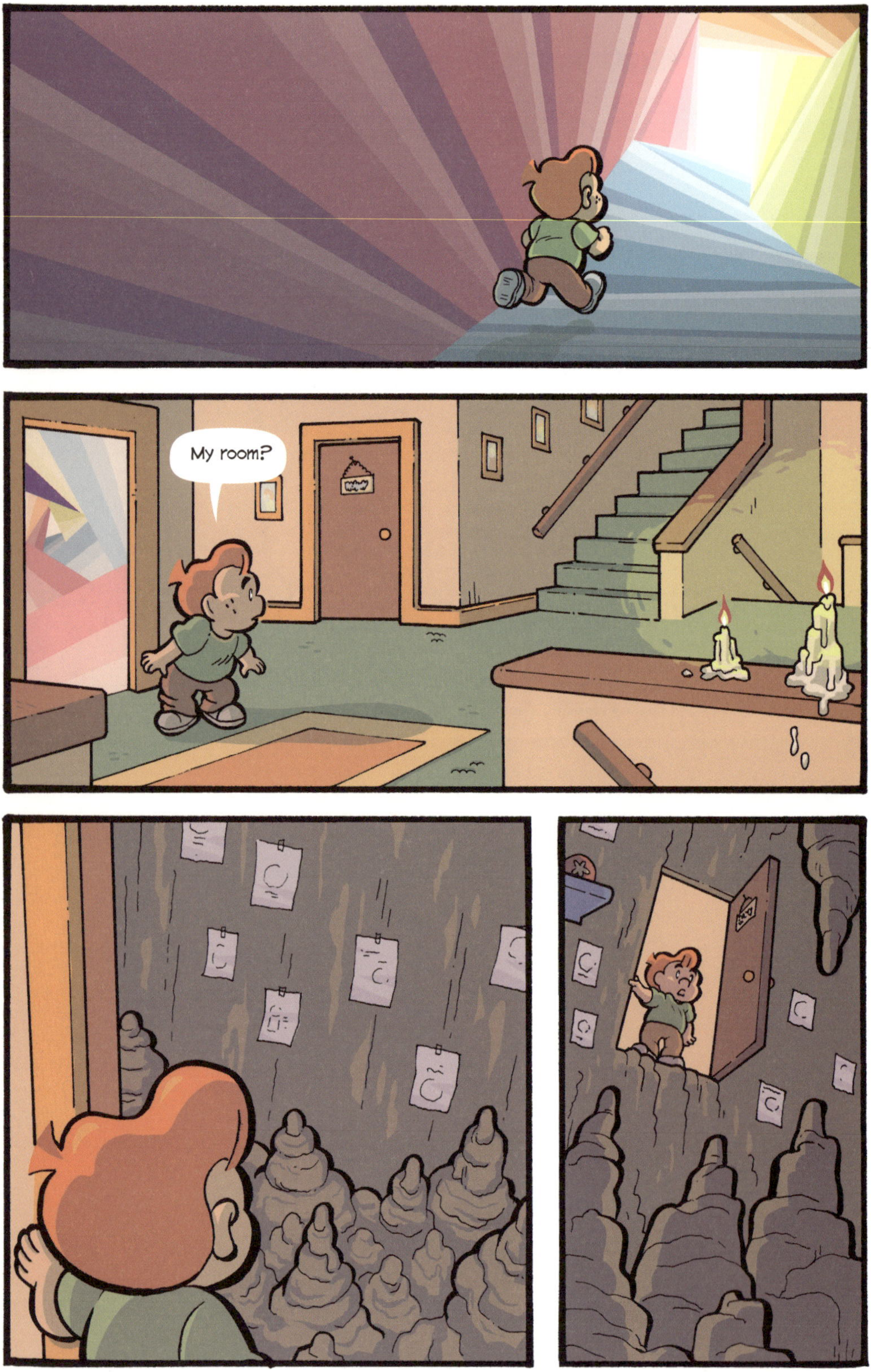
My room?

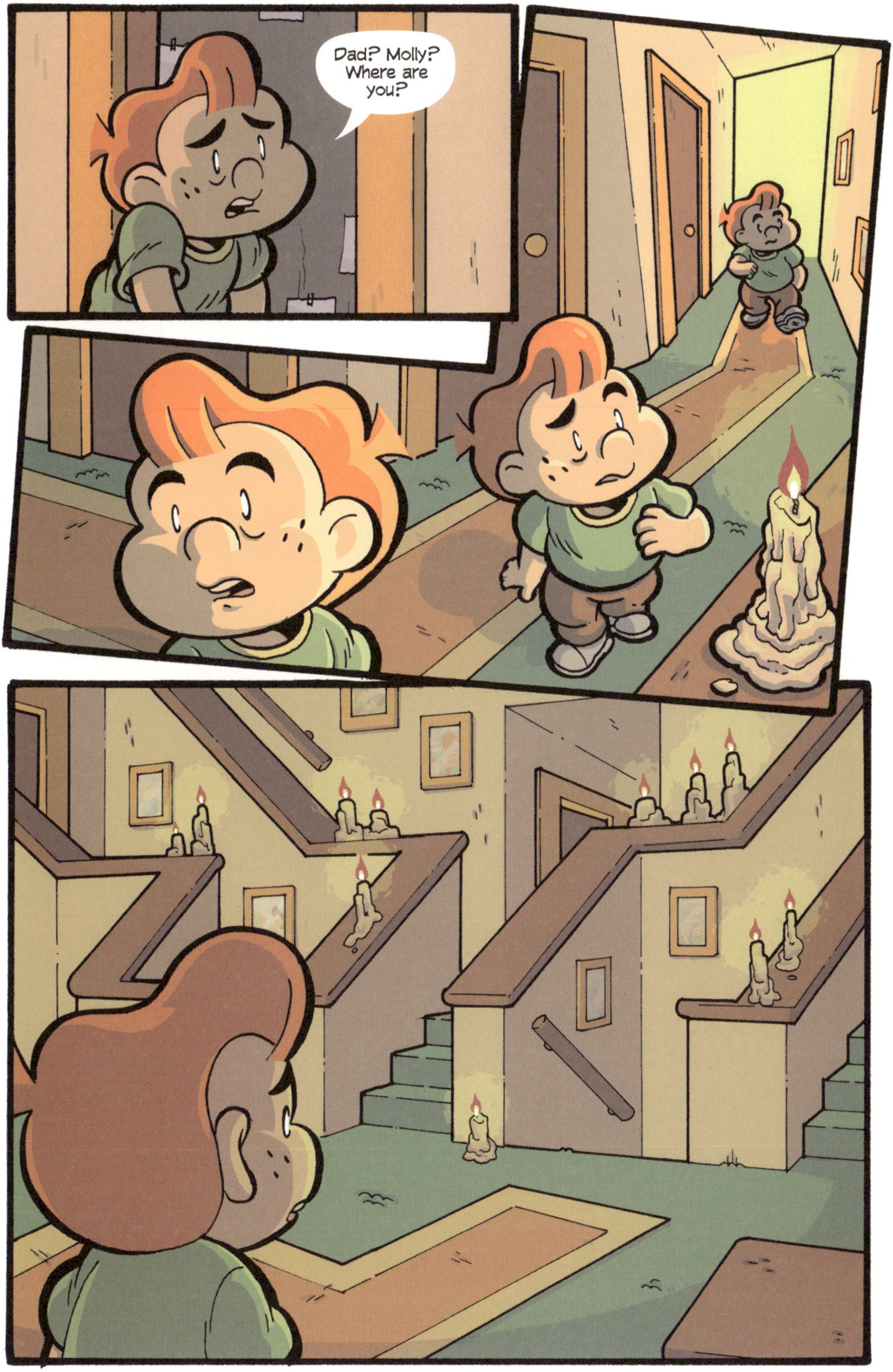
Dad? Molly? Where are you?

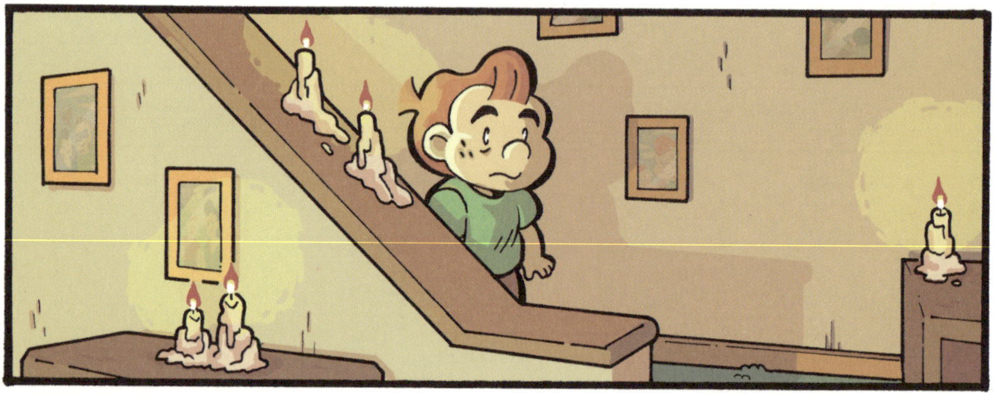

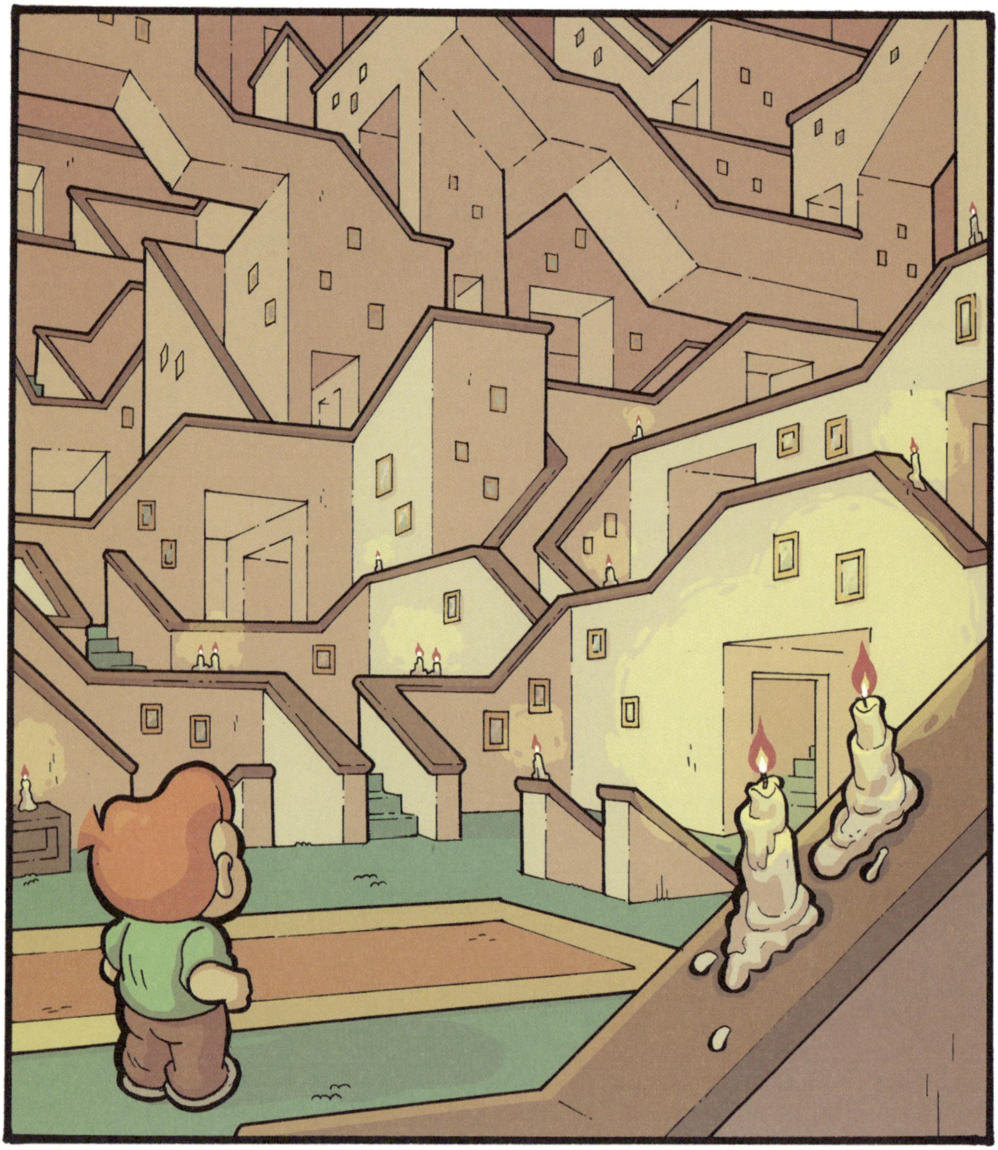

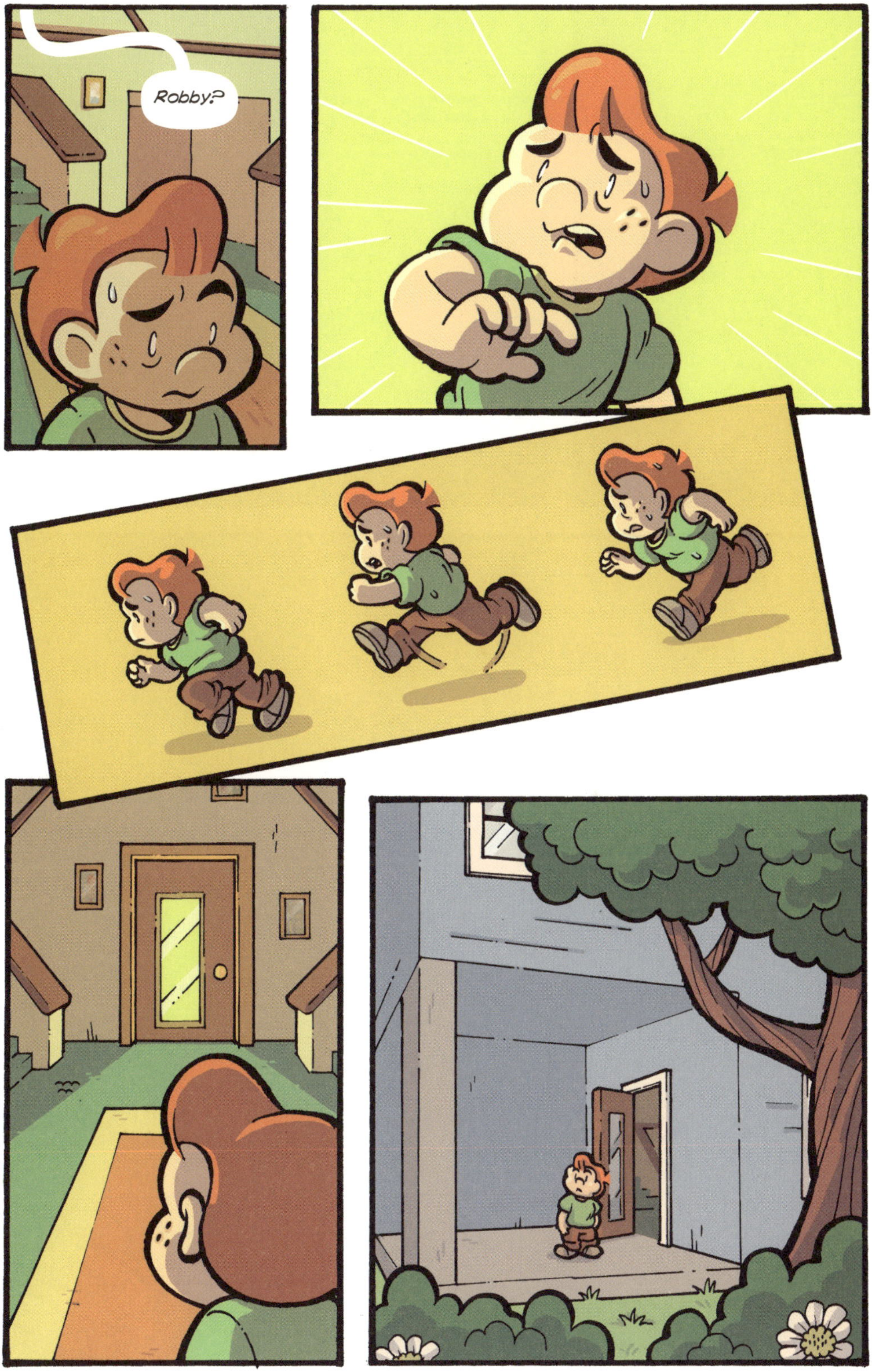
Robby?

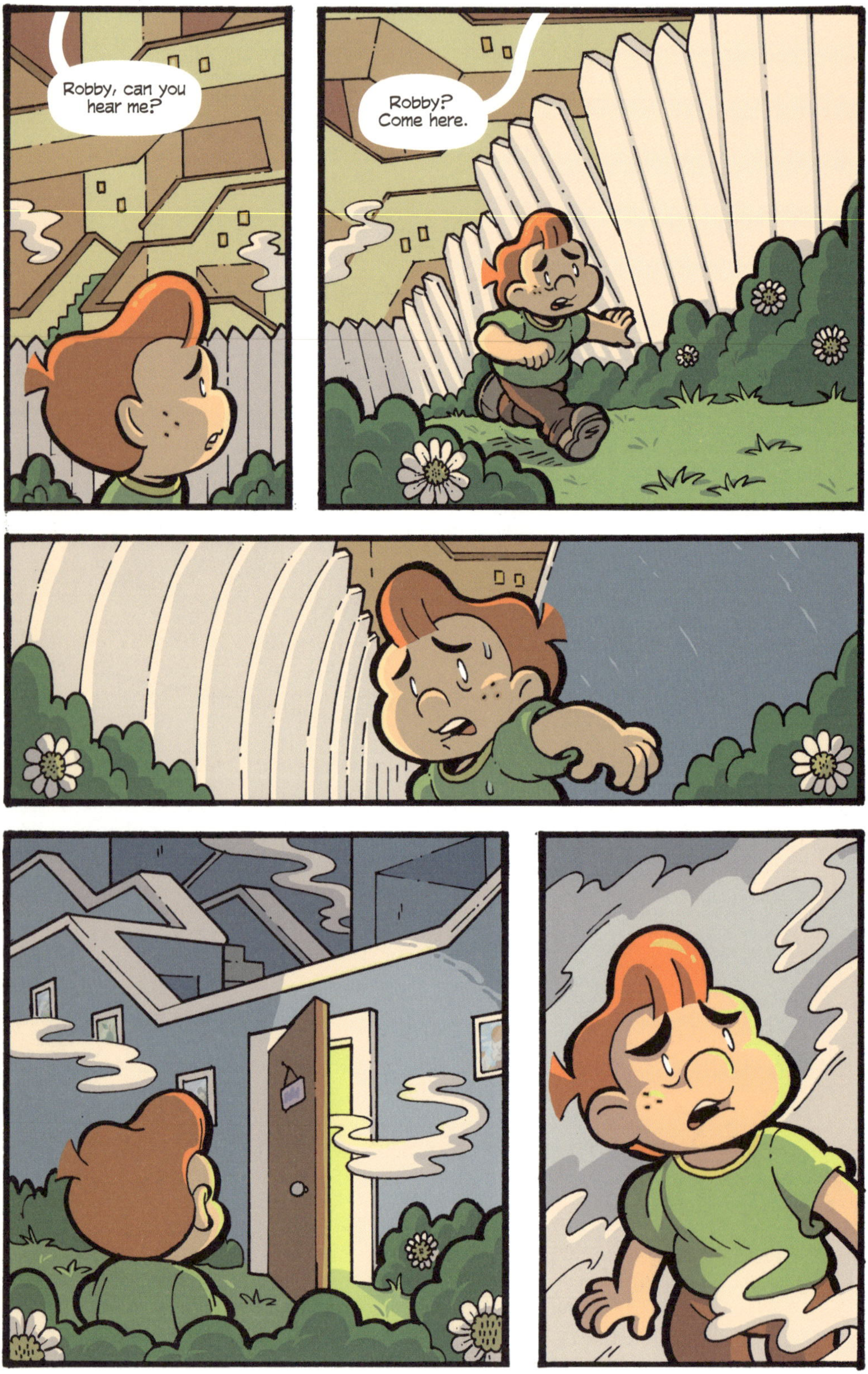
Robby, can you hear me?
Robby? Come here.

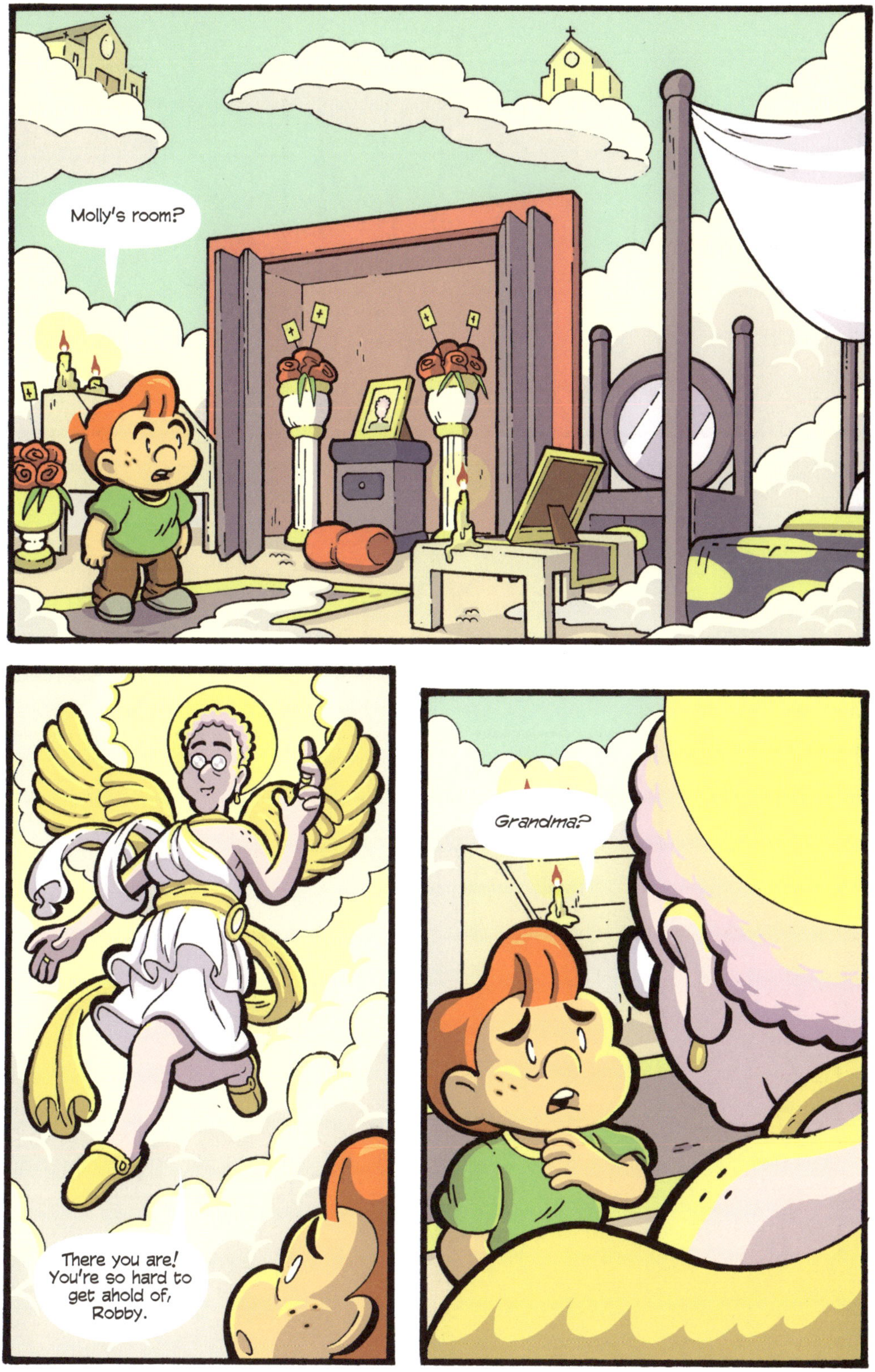
Molly's room?
There you are! You're so hard to get ahold of, Robby.
Grandma?

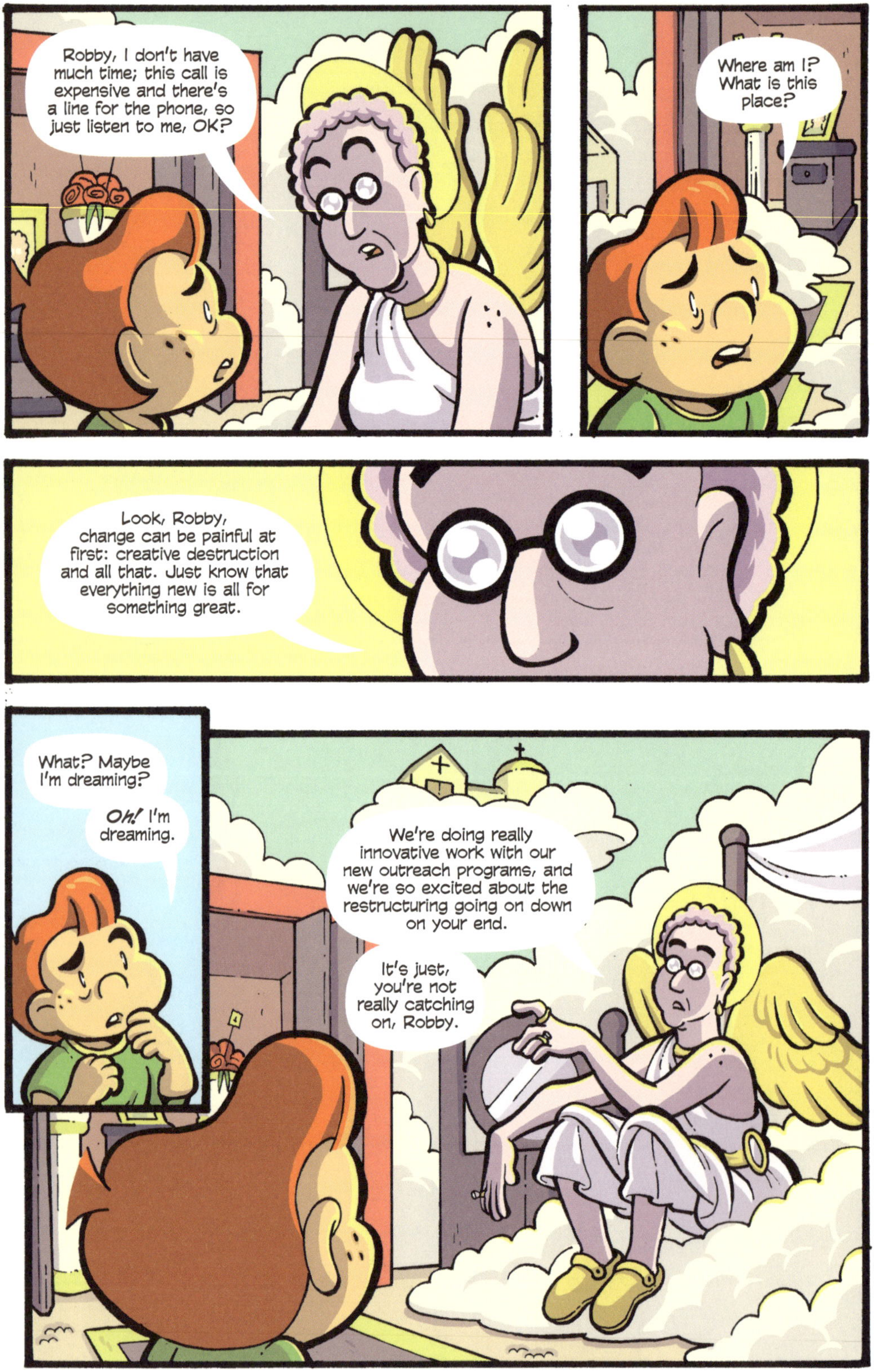
Robby, I don't have much time; this call is expensive and there's a line for the phone, so just listen to me, OK?
Where am I? What is this place?
Look, Robby, change can be painful at first: creative destruction and all that. Just know that everything new is all for something great.
What? Maybe I'm dreaming?
Oh! I'm dreaming.
We're doing really innovative work with our new outreach programs, and we're so excited about the restructuring going on down on your end.
It's just, you're not really catching on, Robby.

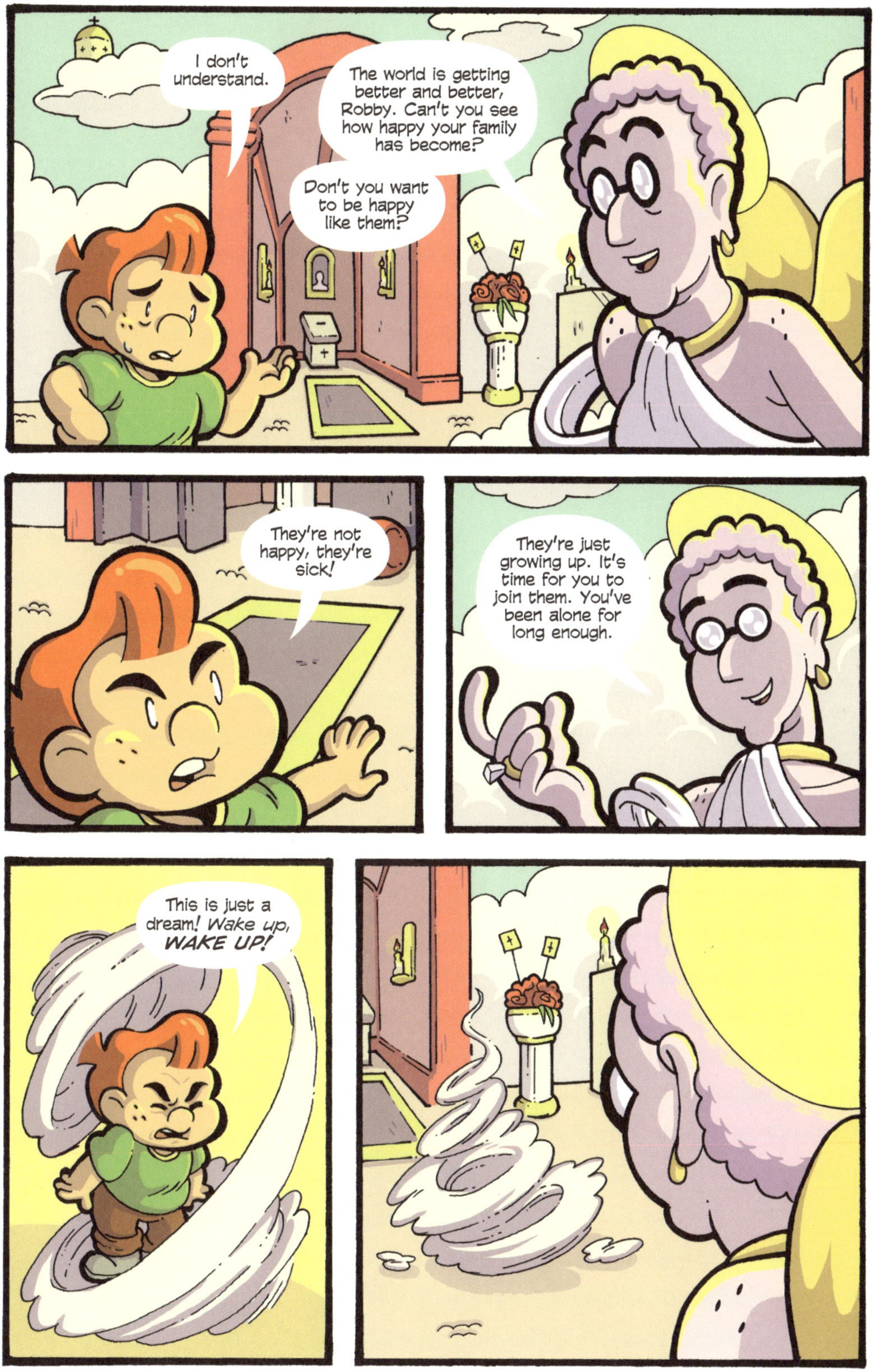
I don't understand.
The world is getting better and better, Robby. Can't you see how happy your family has become?
Don't you want to be happy like them?
They're not happy, they're sick!
They're just growing up. It's time for you to join them. You've been alone for long enough.
This is just a dream! *Wake up,* ***WAKE UP!***

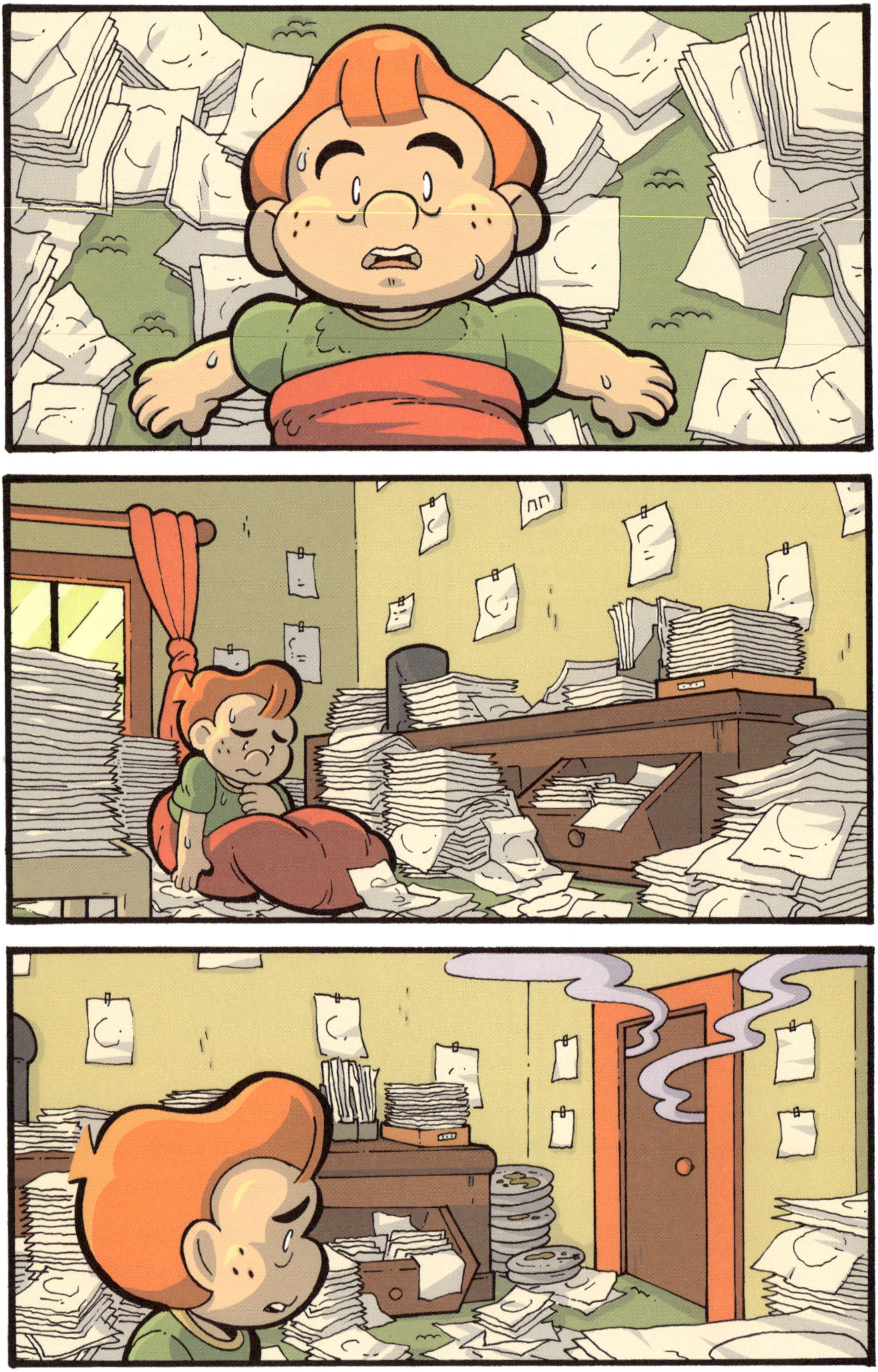

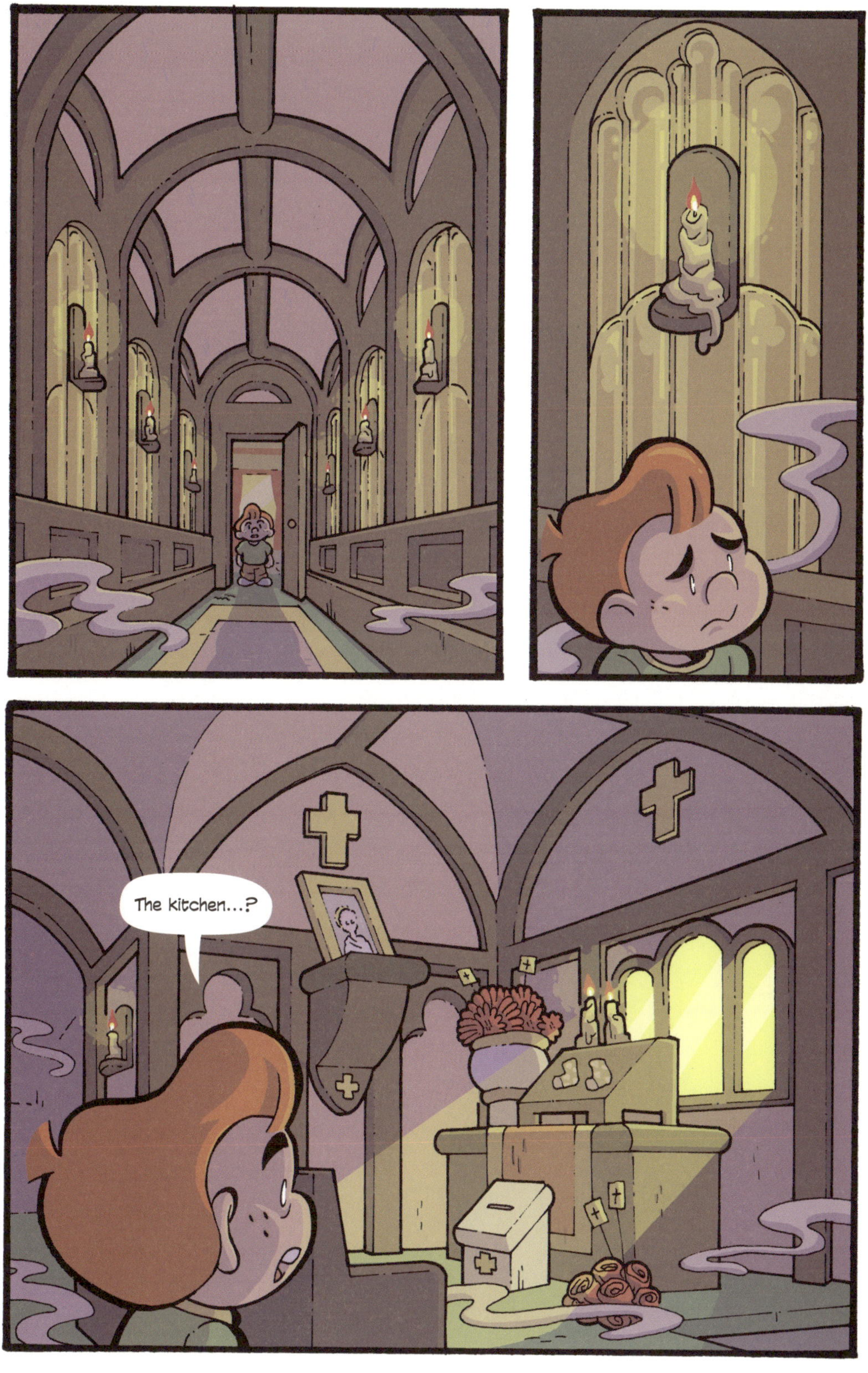
The kitchen...?

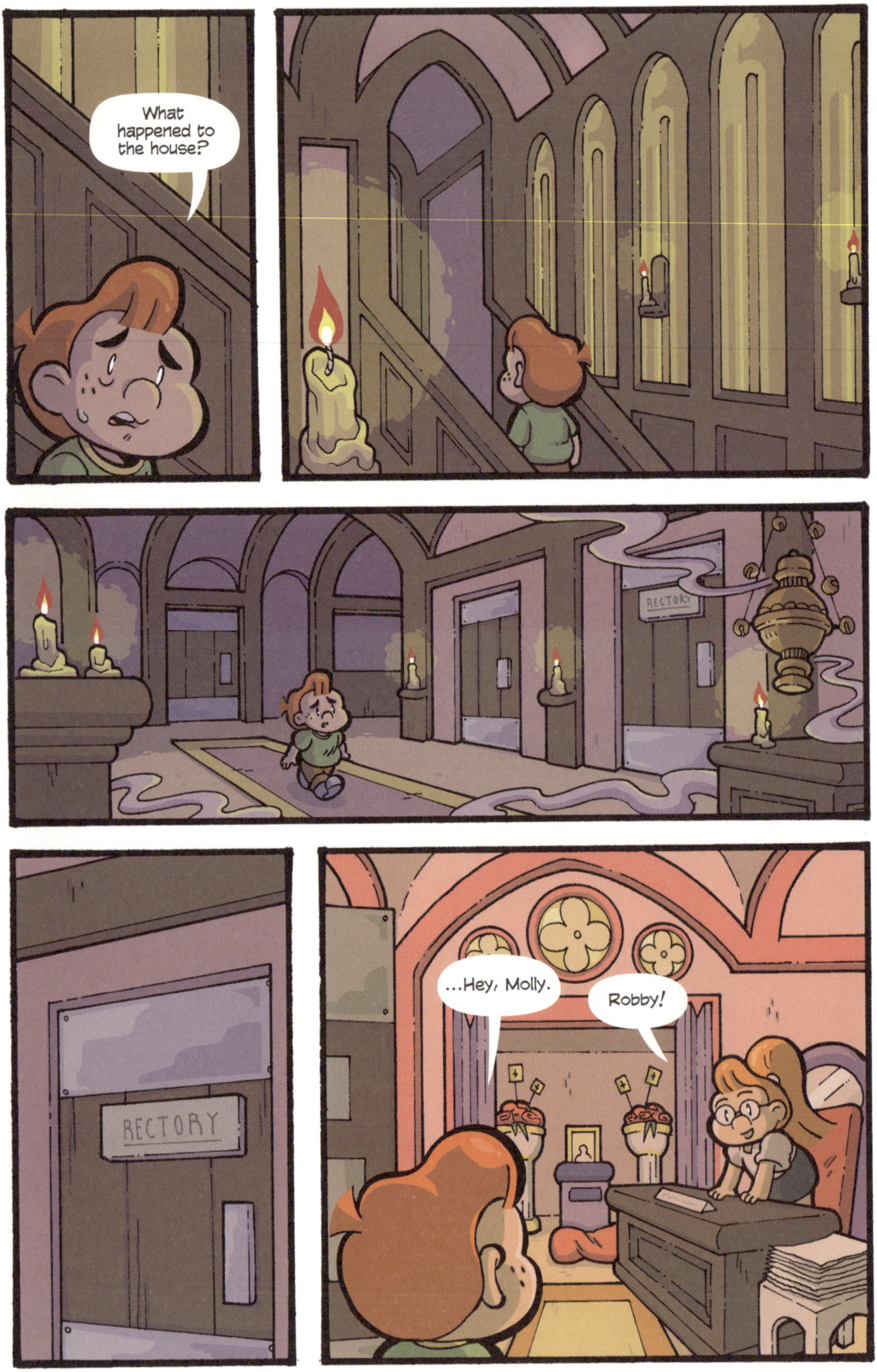
What happened to the house?
RECTORY
RECTORY
...Hey, Molly.
Robby!

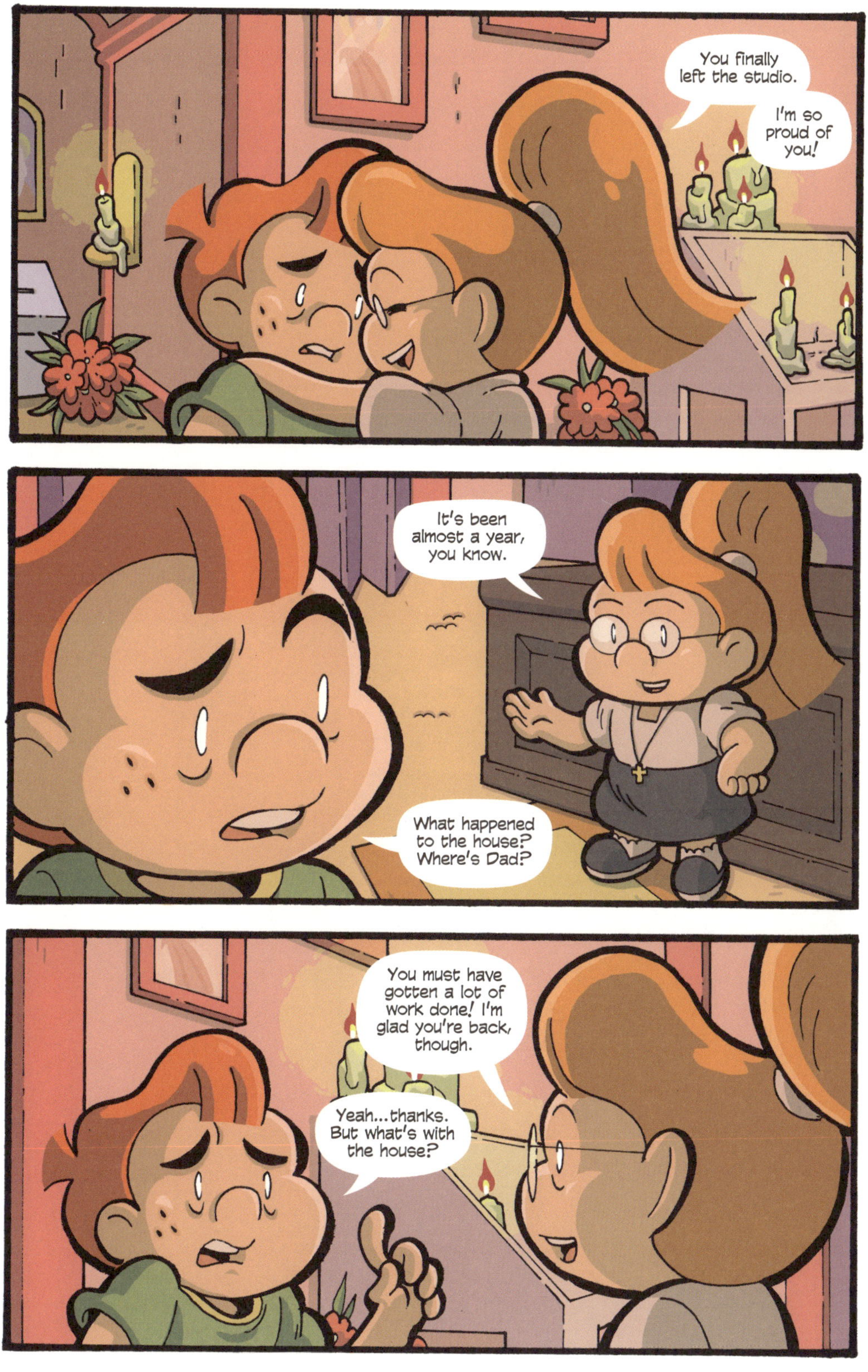
You finally left the studio.
I'm so proud of you!
It's been almost a year, you know.
What happened to the house? Where's Dad?
You must have gotten a lot of work done! I'm glad you're back, though.
Yeah...thanks. But what's with the house?

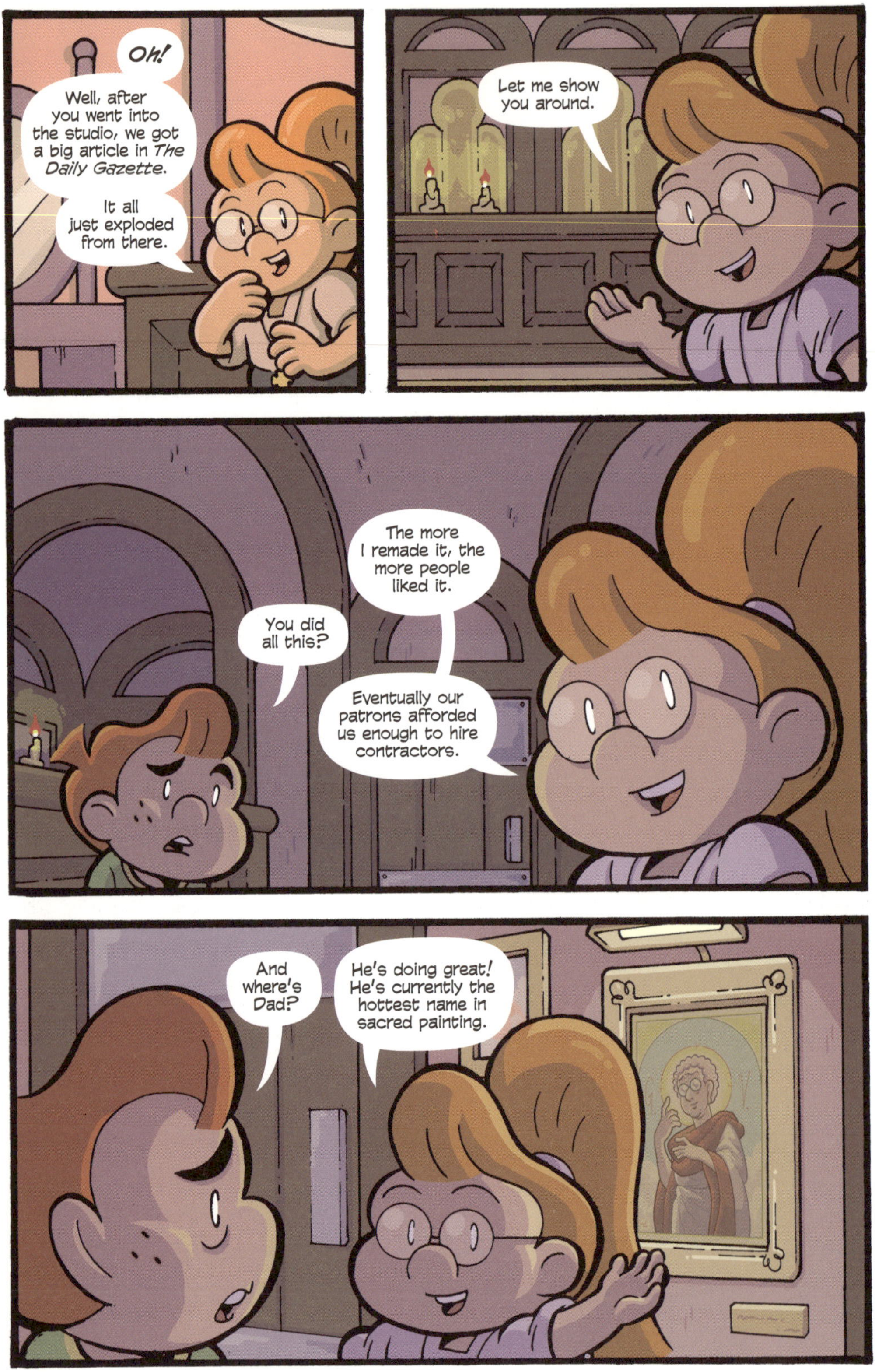
Oh!
Well, after you went into the studio, we got a big article in *The Daily Gazette*.
It all just exploded from there.
Let me show you around.
You did all this?
The more I remade it, the more people liked it.
Eventually our patrons afforded us enough to hire contractors.
And where's Dad?
He's doing great! He's currently the hottest name in sacred painting.

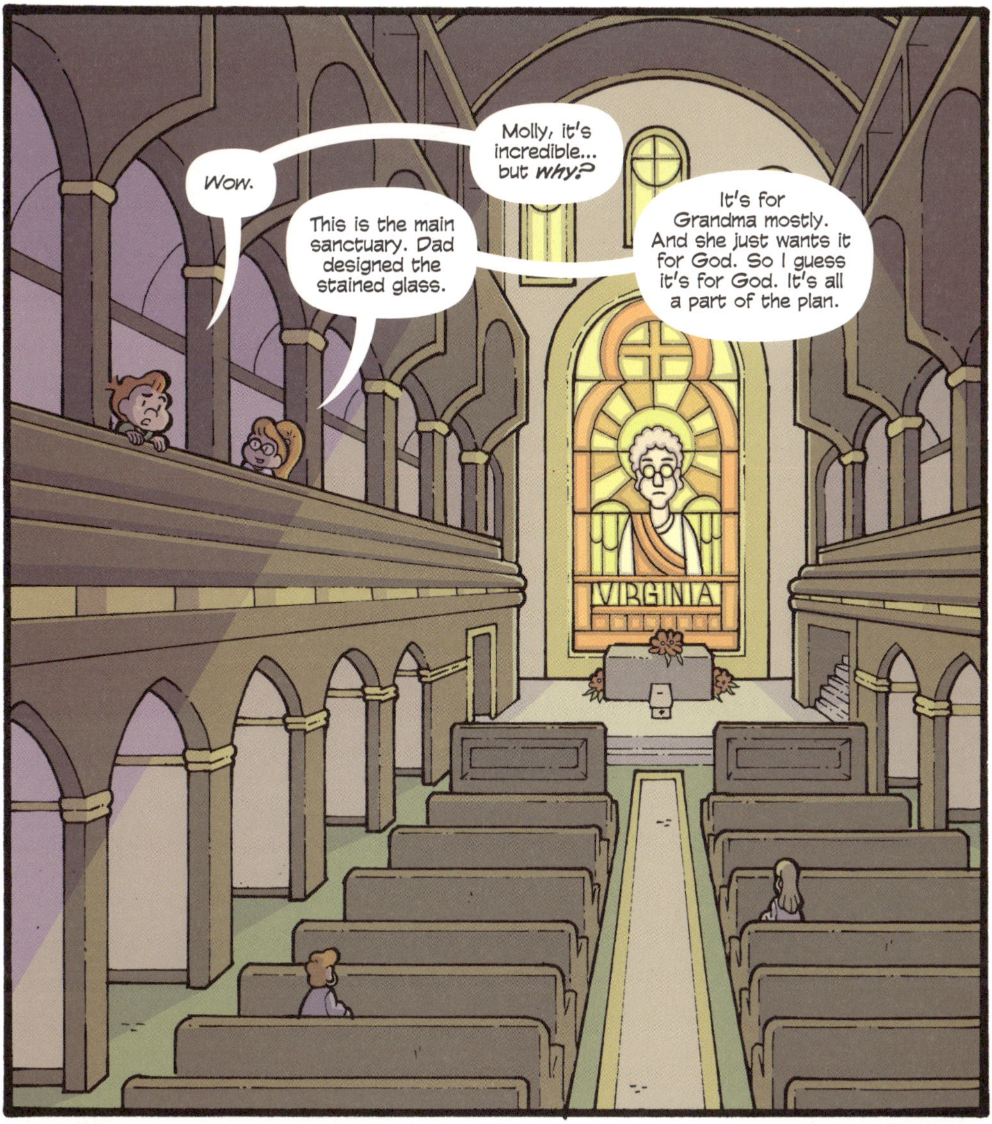
Wow.
Molly, it's incredible... but *why?*
This is the main sanctuary. Dad designed the stained glass.
It's for Grandma mostly. And she just wants it for God. So I guess it's for God. It's all a part of the plan.
VIRGINIA

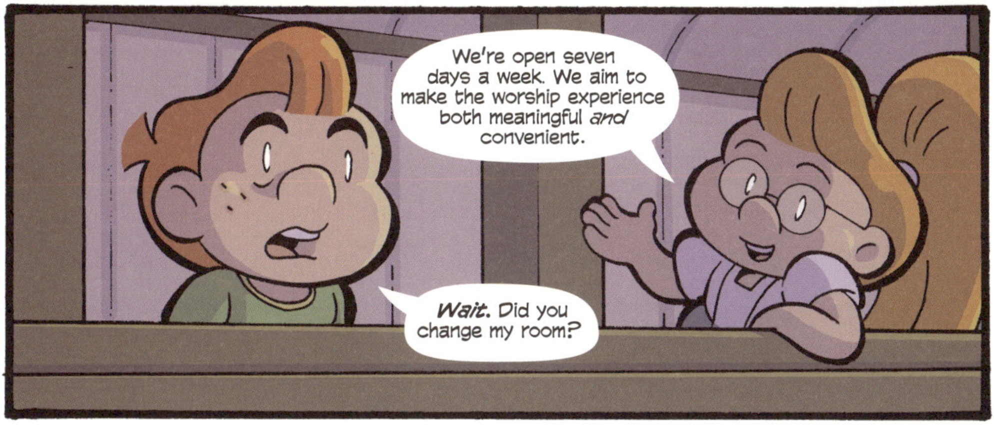
We're open seven days a week. We aim to make the worship experience both meaningful *and* convenient.
Wait. Did you change my room?

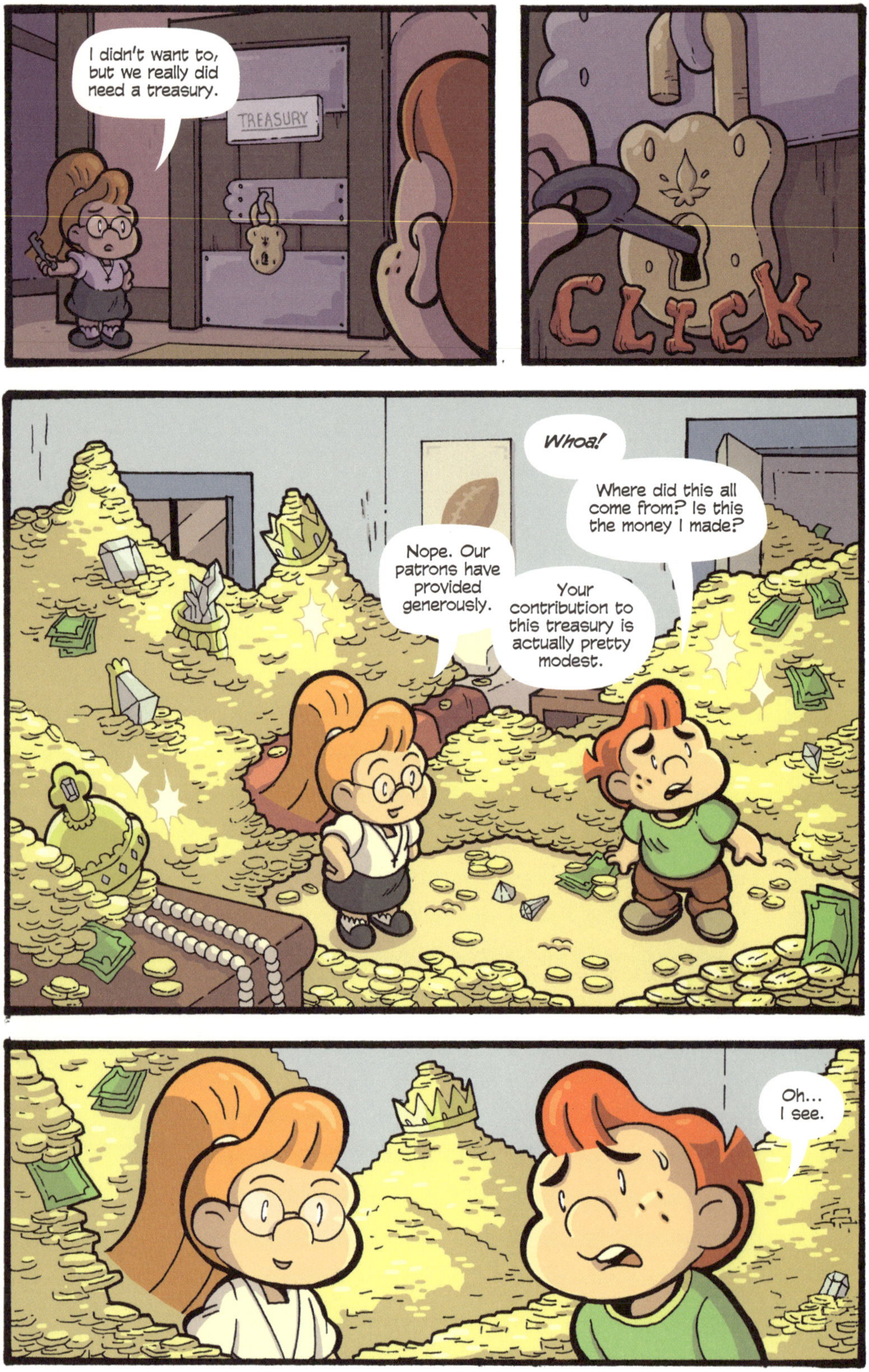
I didn't want to, but we really did need a treasury.
TREASURY
CLICK
Whoa!
Where did this all come from? Is this the money I made?
Nope. Our patrons have provided generously.
Your contribution to this treasury is actually pretty modest.
Oh... I see.

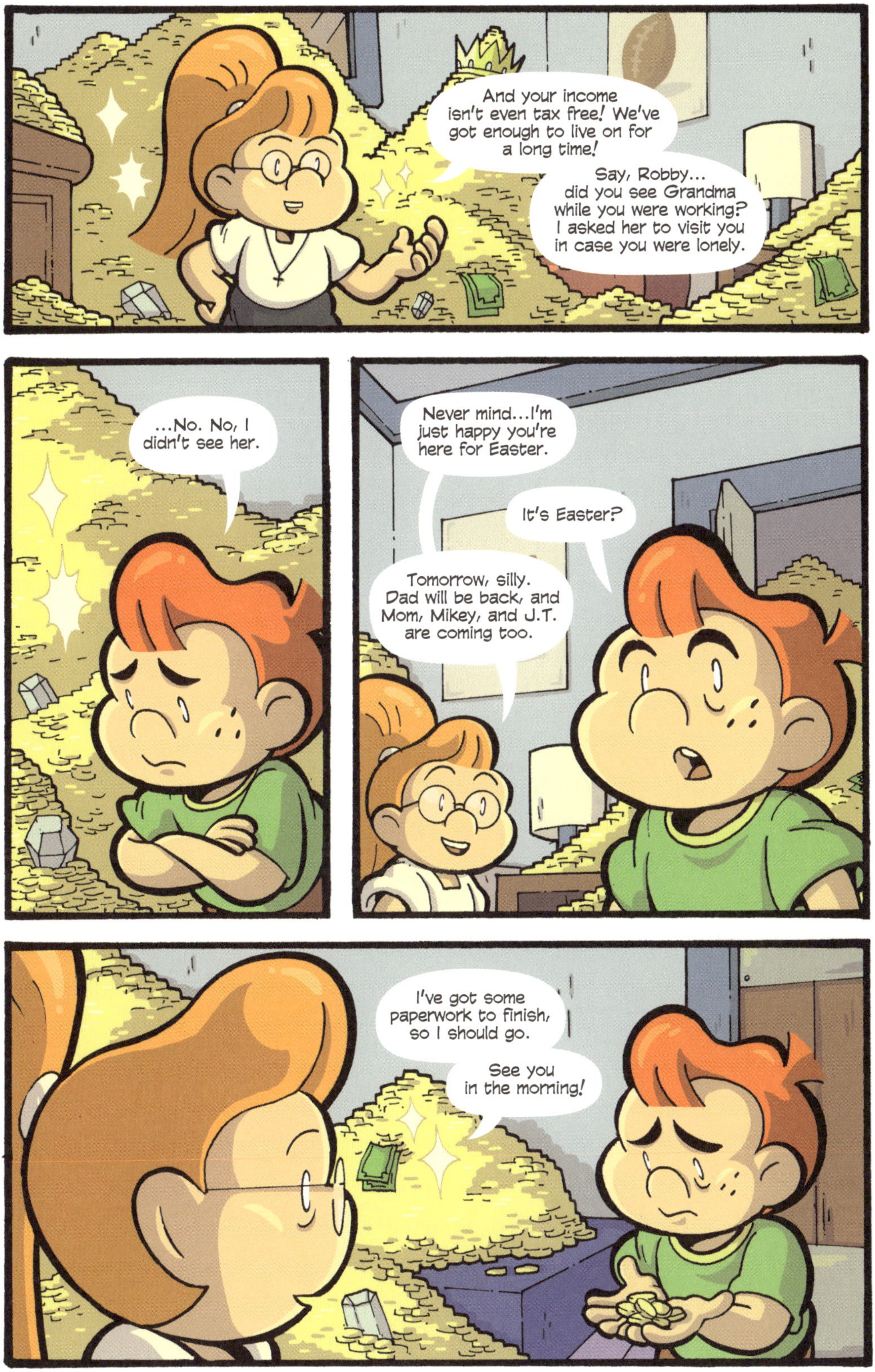
And your income isn't even tax free! We've got enough to live on for a long time!
Say, Robby... did you see Grandma while you were working? I asked her to visit you in case you were lonely.
...No. No, I didn't see her.
Never mind...I'm just happy you're here for Easter.
It's Easter?
Tomorrow, silly. Dad will be back, and Mom, Mikey, and J.T. are coming too.
I've got some paperwork to finish, so I should go.
See you in the morning!

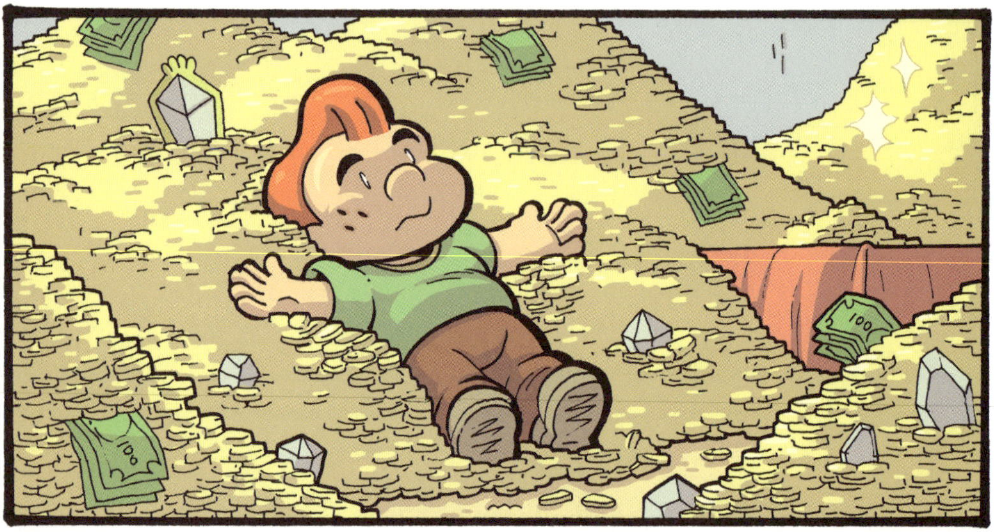

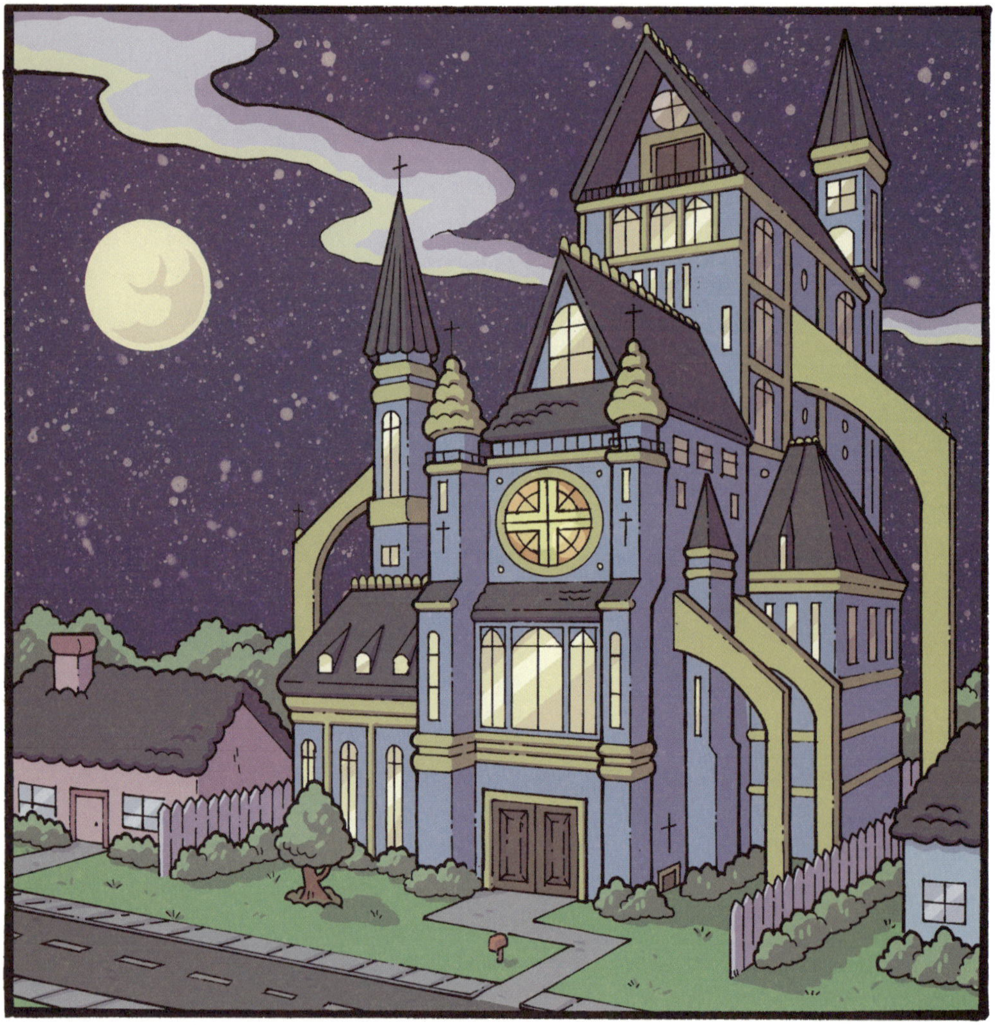

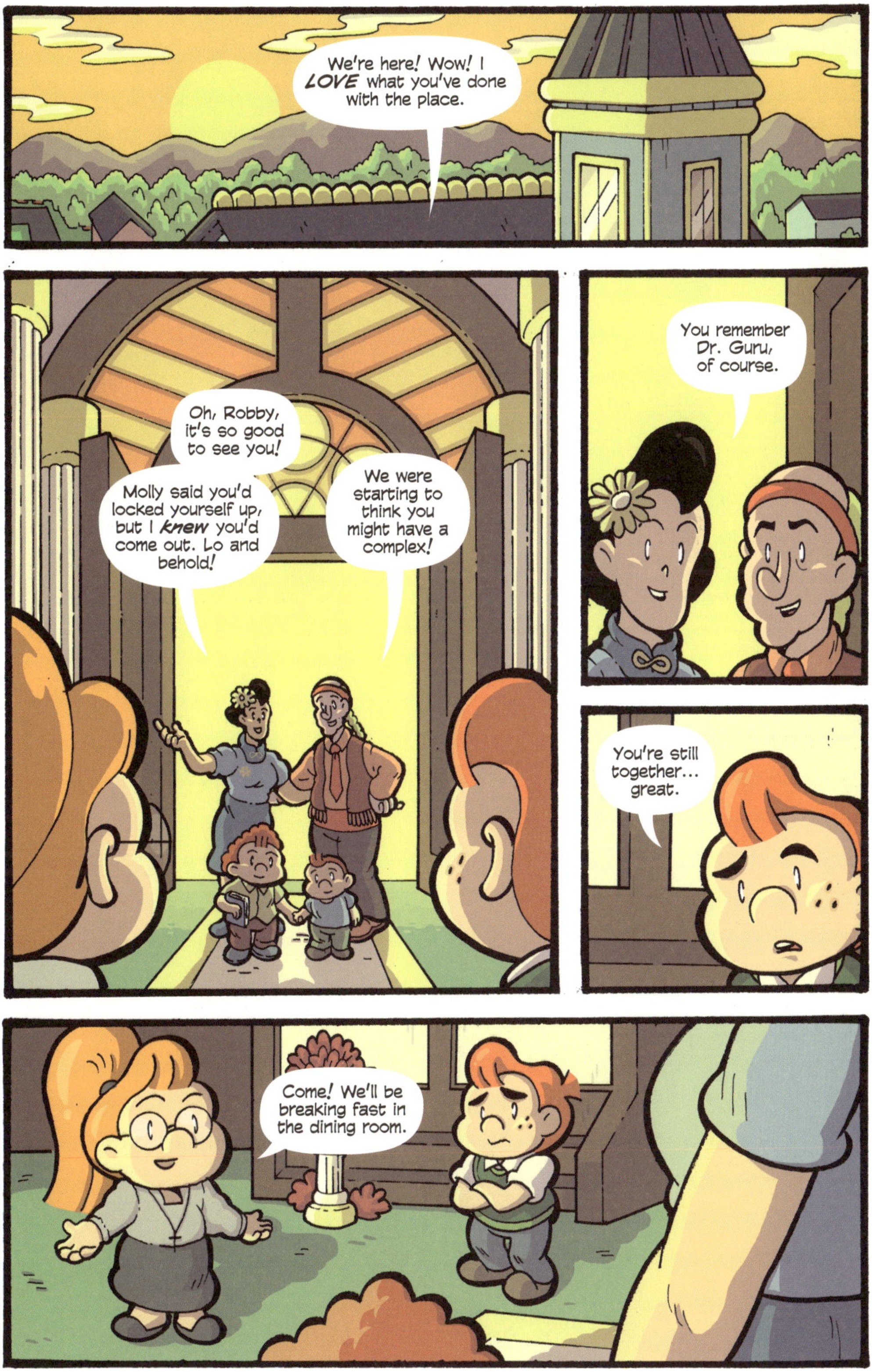
We're here! Wow! I *LOVE* what you've done with the place.
Oh, Robby, it's so good to see you!
Molly said you'd locked yourself up, but I *knew* you'd come out. Lo and behold!
We were starting to think you might have a complex!
You remember Dr. Guru, of course.
You're still together... great.
Come! We'll be breaking fast in the dining room.

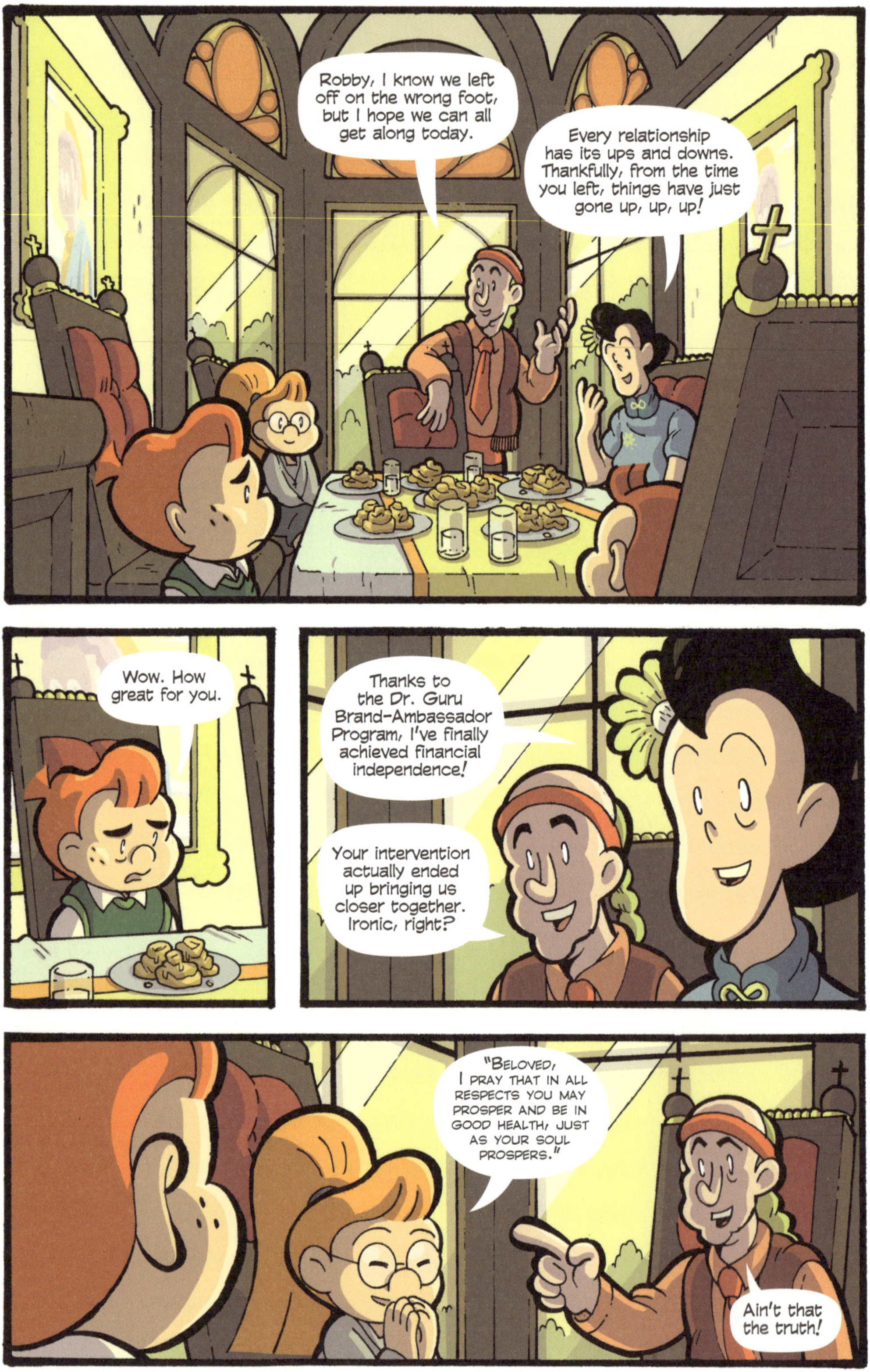
Robby, I know we left off on the wrong foot, but I hope we can all get along today.
Every relationship has its ups and downs. Thankfully, from the time you left, things have just gone up, up, up!
Wow. How great for you.
Thanks to the Dr. Guru Brand-Ambassador Program, I've finally achieved financial independence!
Your intervention actually ended up bringing us closer together. Ironic, right?
"Beloved, I pray that in all respects you may prosper and be in good health, just as your soul prospers."
Ain't that the truth!

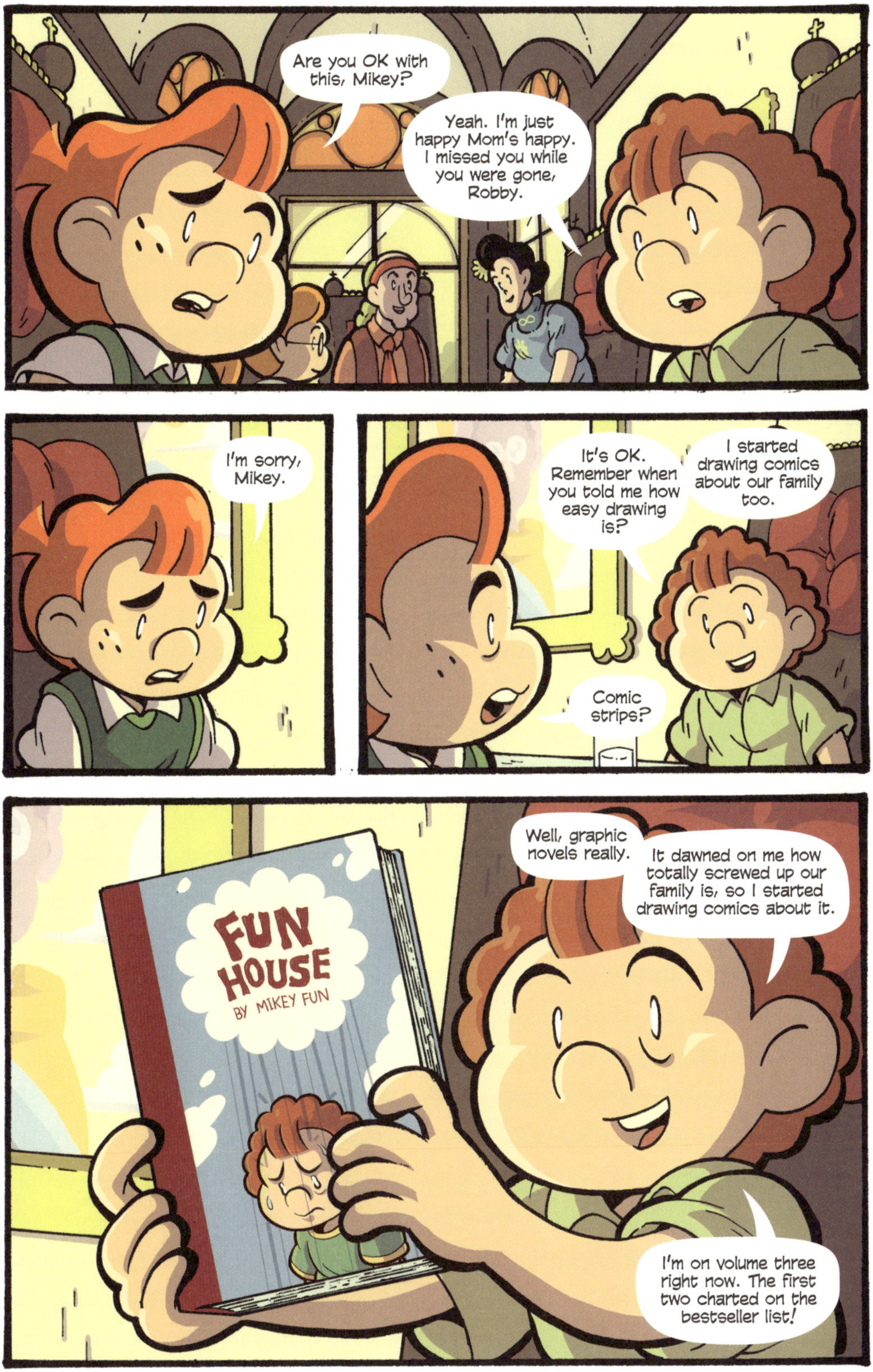

Are you OK with this, Mikey?
Yeah. I'm just happy Mom's happy. I missed you while you were gone, Robby.
I'm sorry, Mikey.
It's OK. Remember when you told me how easy drawing is?
I started drawing comics about our family too.
Comic strips?
Well, graphic novels really.
It dawned on me how totally screwed up our family is, so I started drawing comics about it.
FUN HOUSE
BY MIKEY FUN
I'm on volume three right now. The first two charted on the bestseller list!

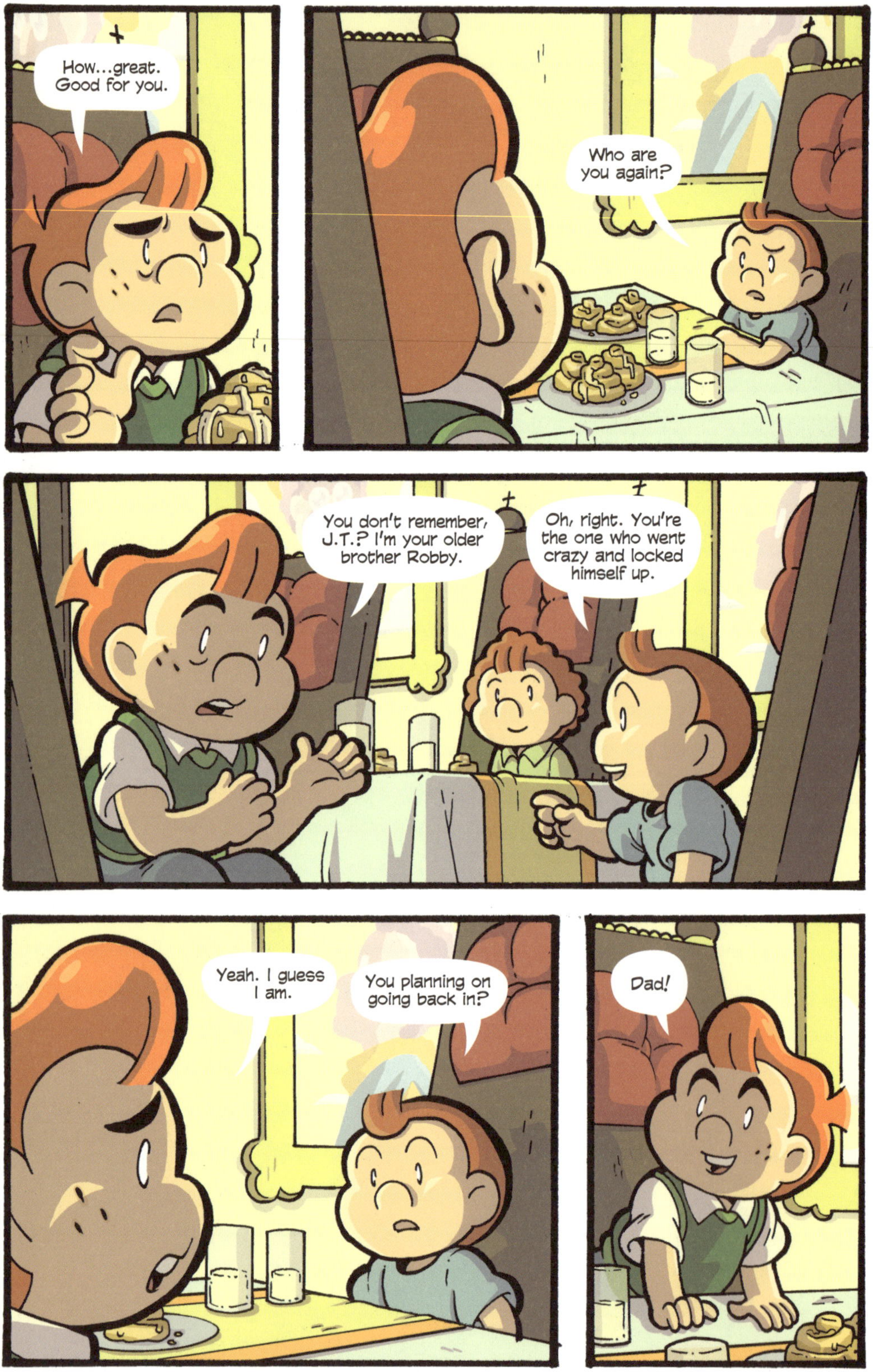
How...great. Good for you.
Who are you again?
You don't remember, J.T.? I'm your older brother Robby.
Oh, right. You're the one who went crazy and locked himself up.
Yeah. I guess I am.
You planning on going back in?
Dad!

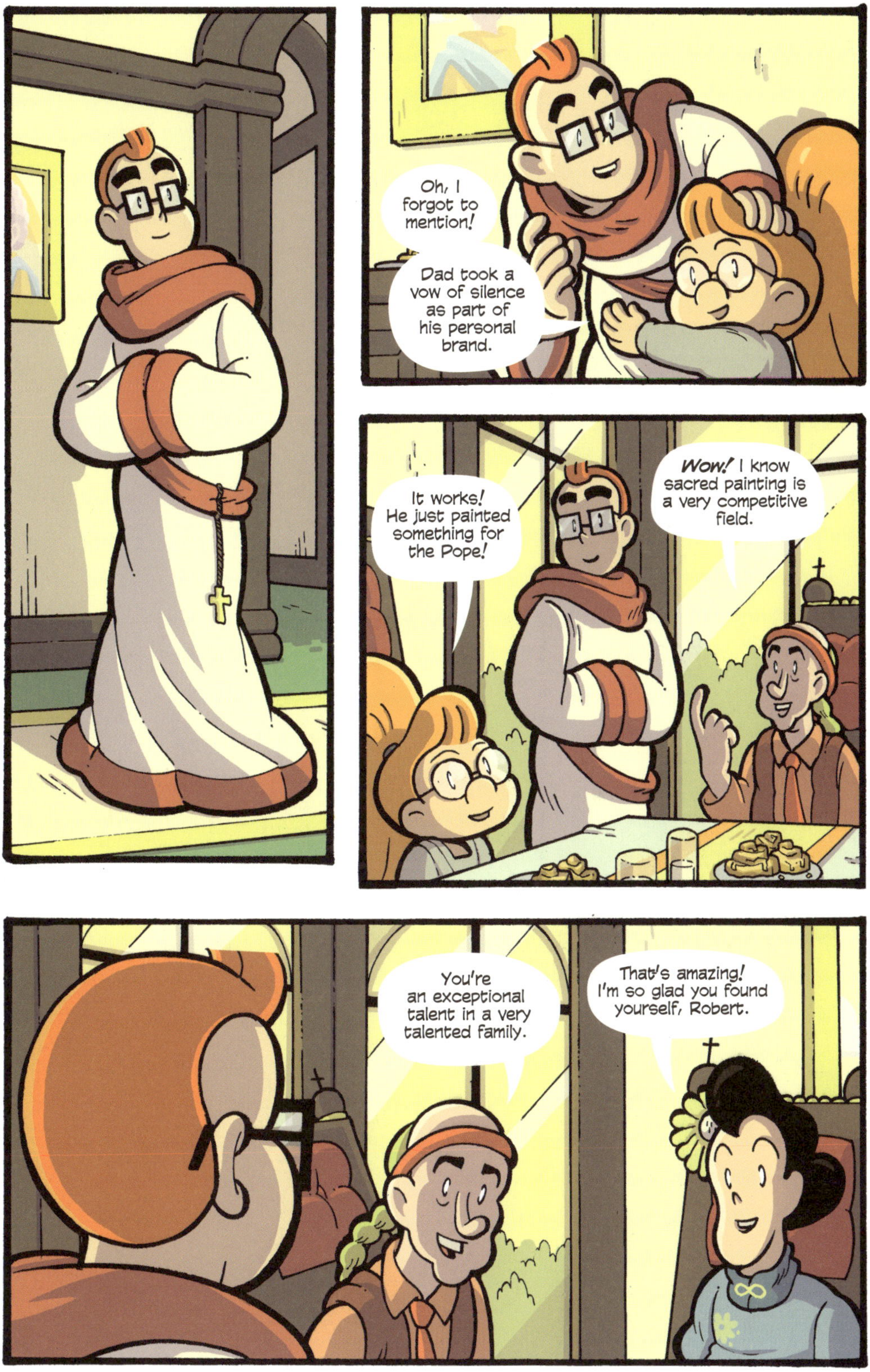
Oh, I forgot to mention!
Dad took a vow of silence as part of his personal brand.
It works! He just painted something for the Pope!
Wow! I know sacred painting is a very competitive field.
You're an exceptional talent in a very talented family.
That's amazing! I'm so glad you found yourself, Robert.

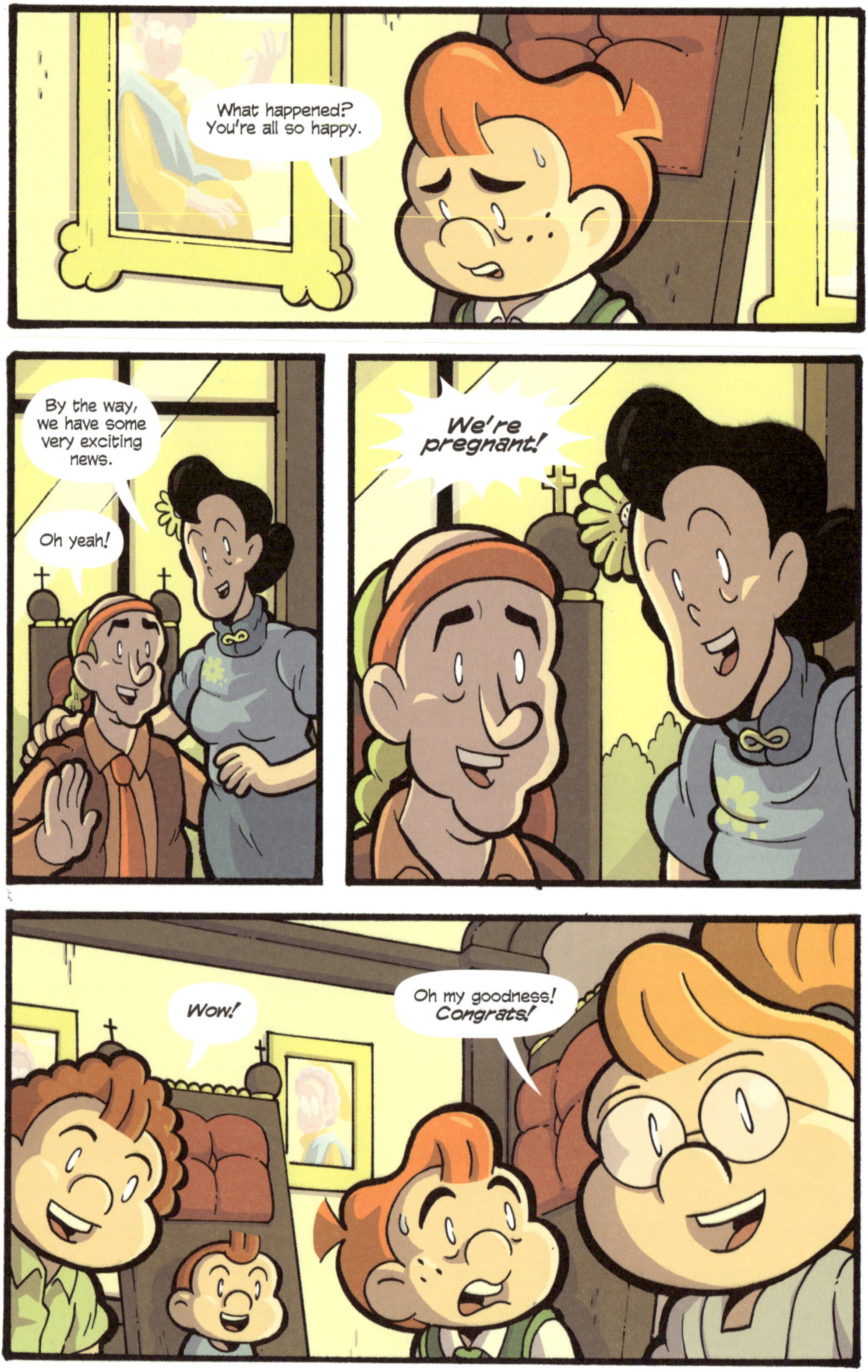
What happened? You're all so happy.
By the way, we have some very exciting news.
Oh yeah!
We're pregnant!
Wow!
Oh my goodness! Congrats!

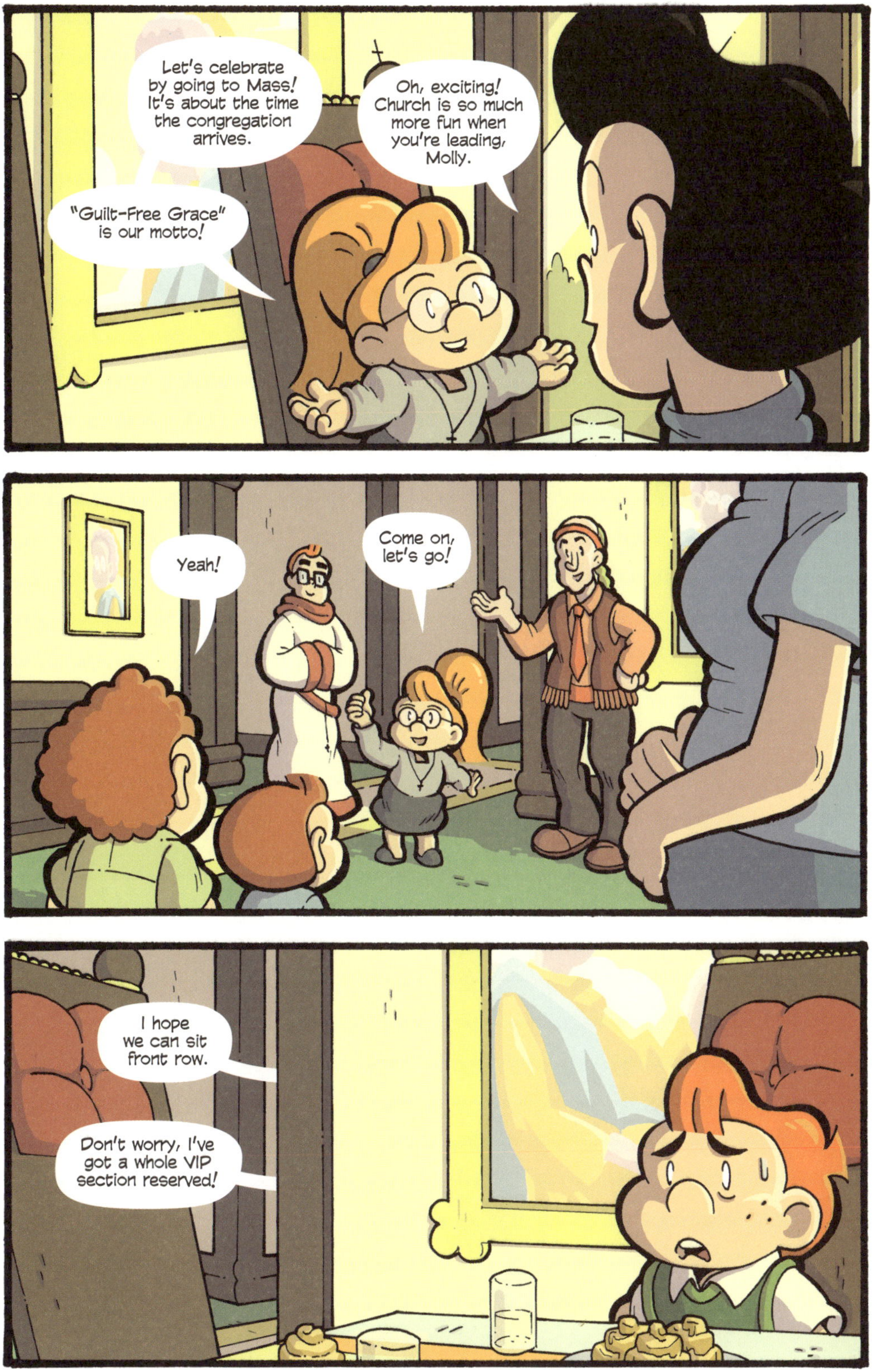
Let's celebrate by going to Mass! It's about the time the congregation arrives.
"Guilt-Free Grace" is our motto!
Oh, exciting! Church is so much more fun when you're leading, Molly.
Yeah!
Come on, let's go!
I hope we can sit front row.
Don't worry, I've got a whole VIP section reserved!

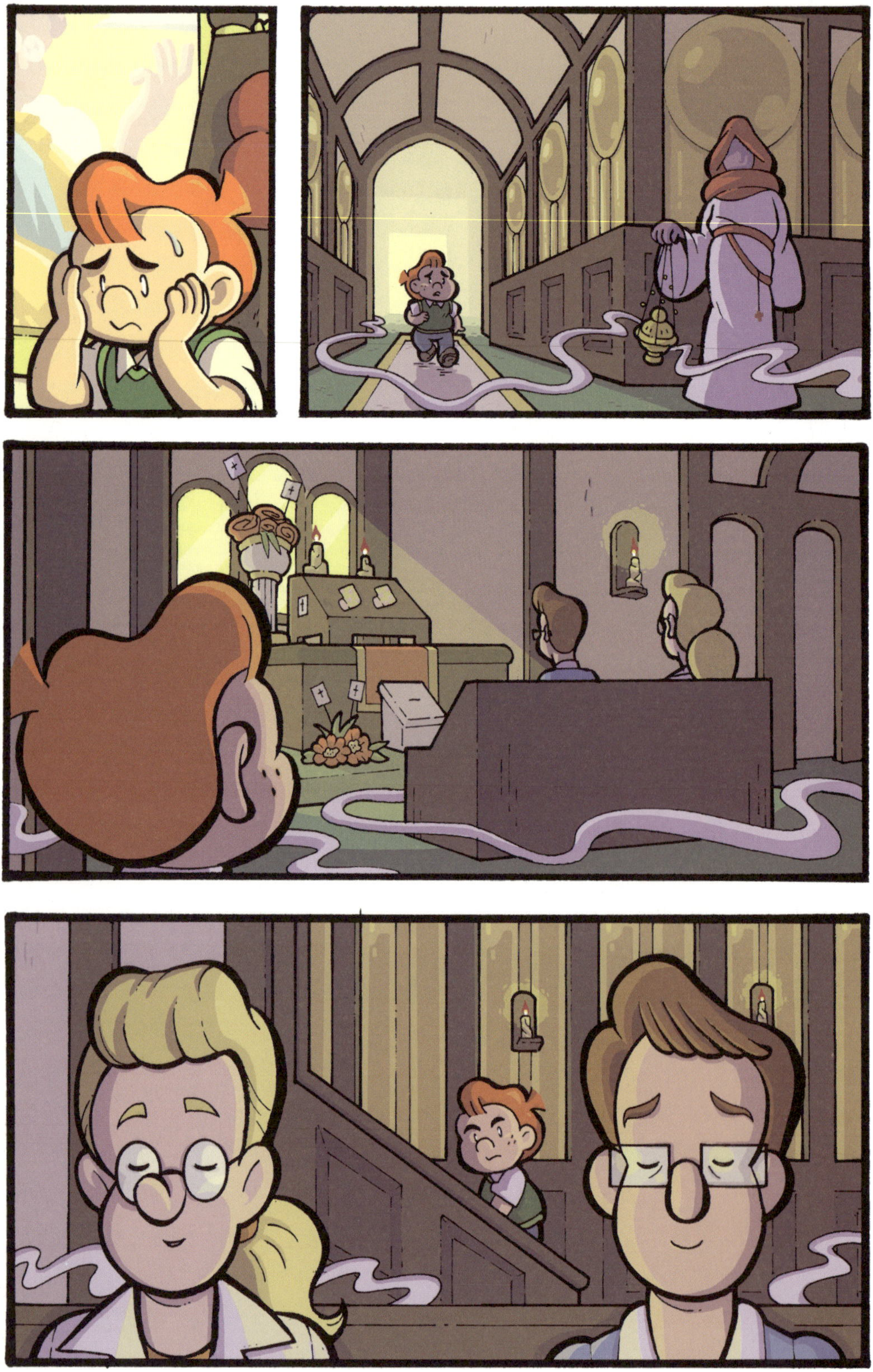

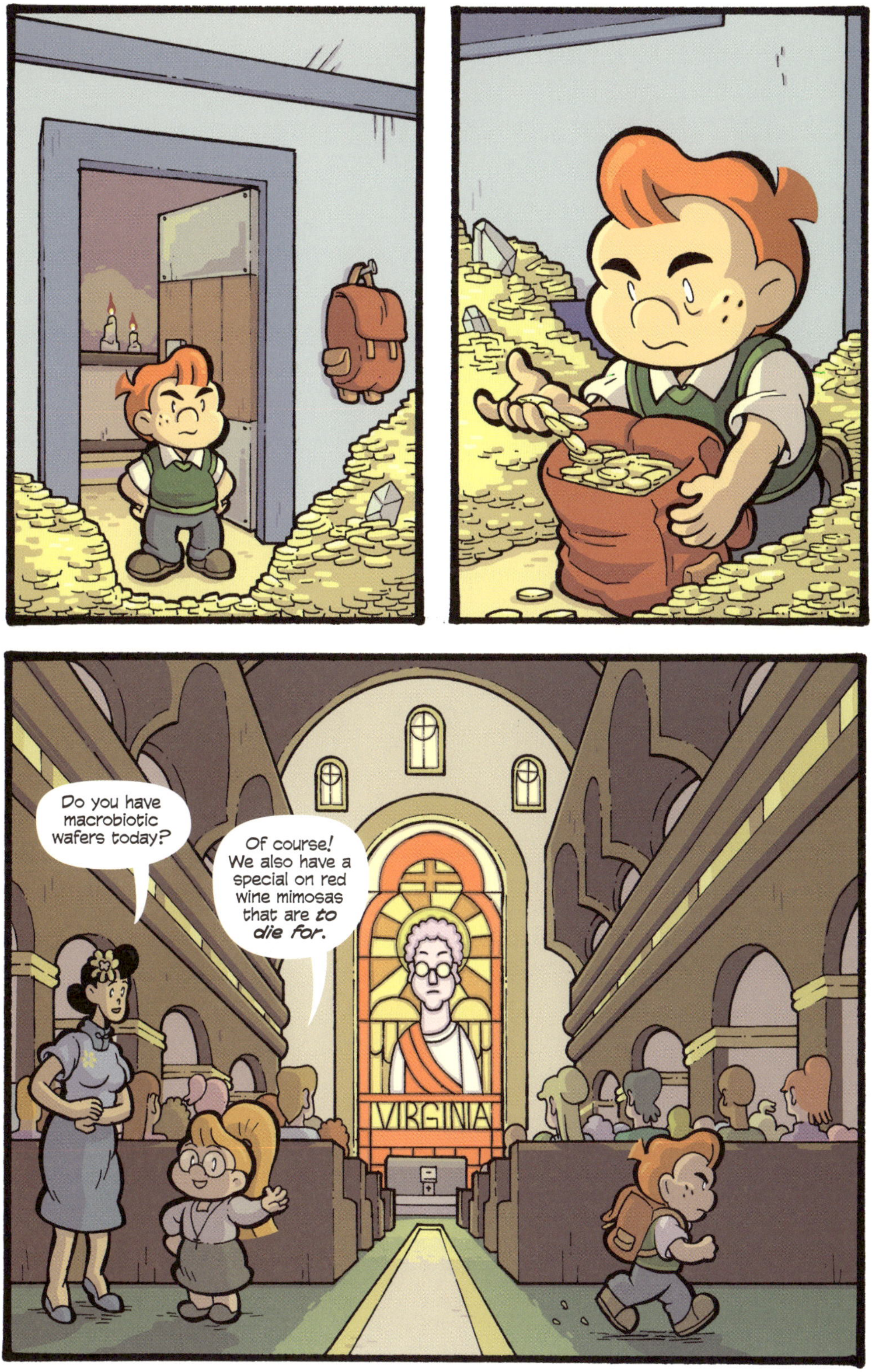
Do you have macrobiotic wafers today?
Of course! We also have a special on red wine mimosas that are *to die for.*
VIRGINIA

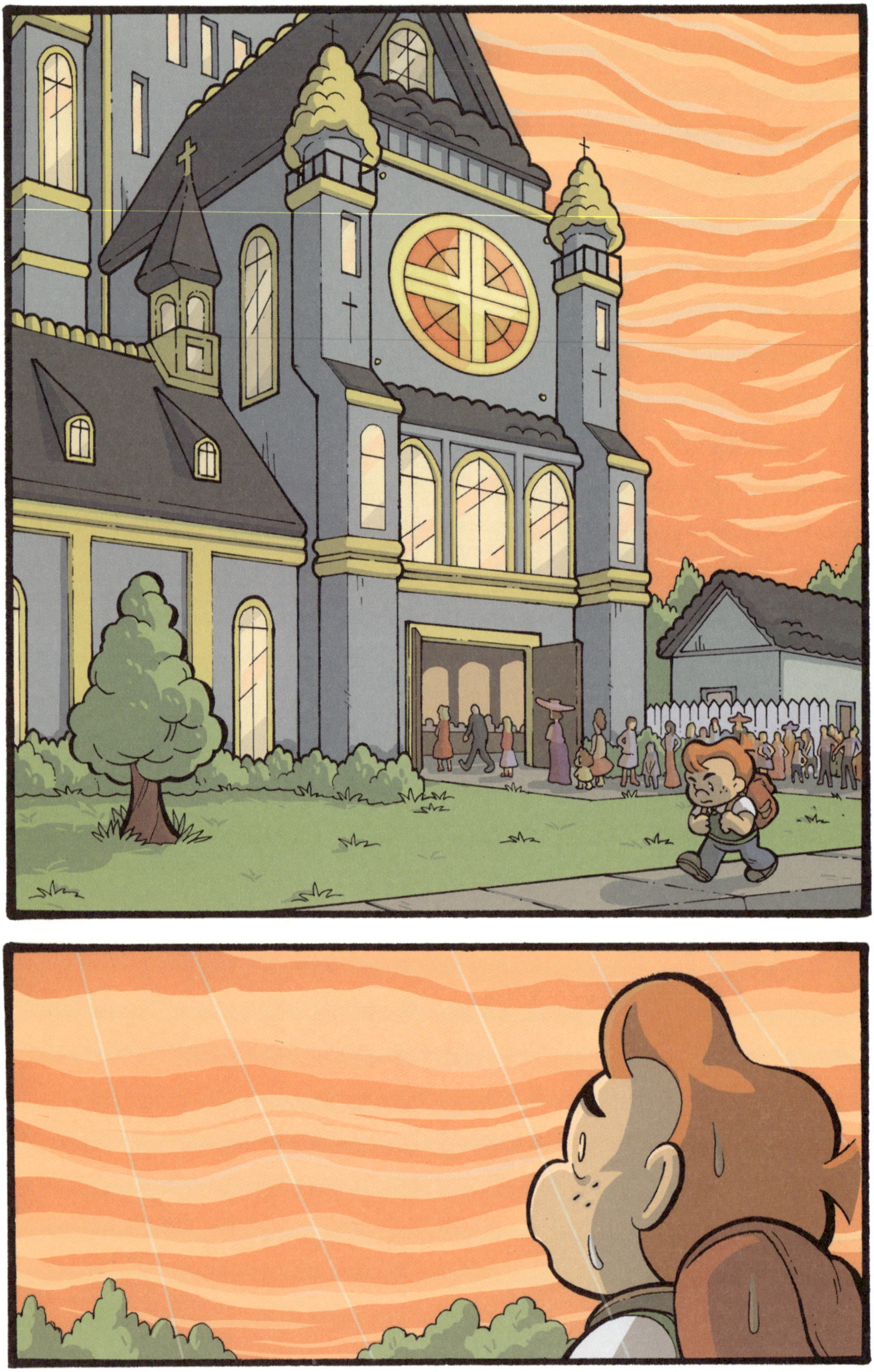

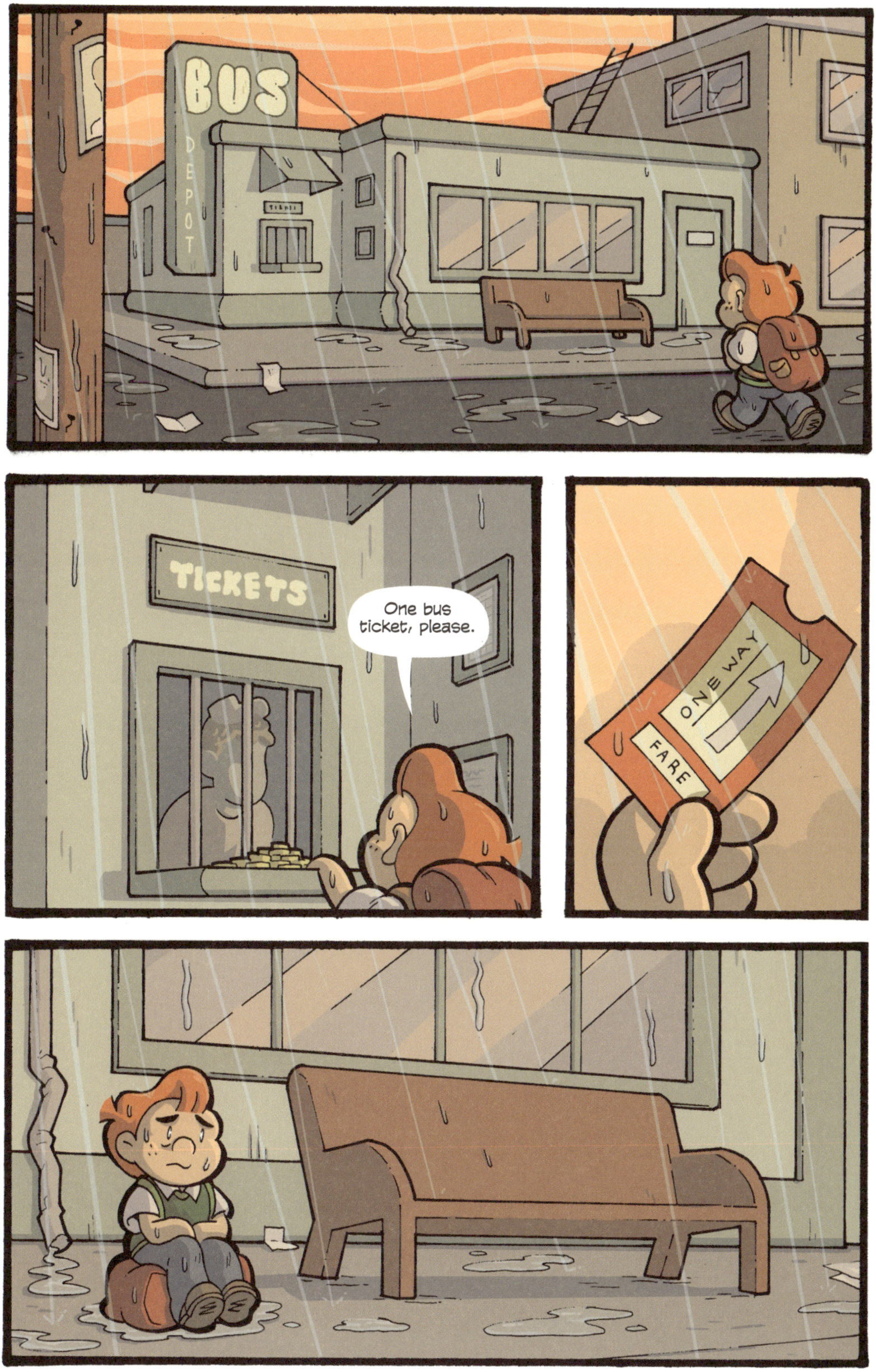
BUS
DEPOT
TICKETS
One bus ticket, please.
ONE WAY
FARE

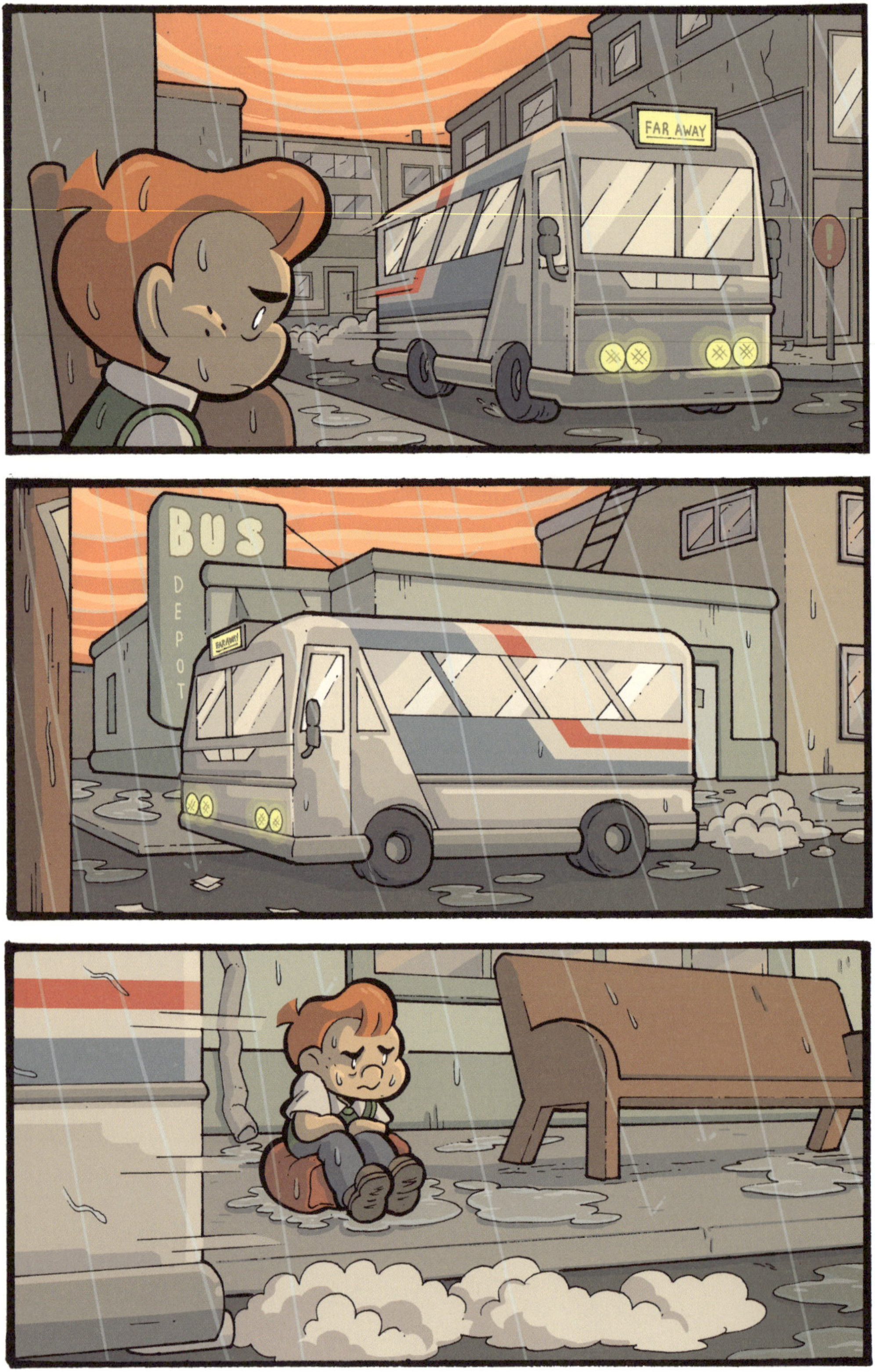
FAR AWAY
BUS
DEPOT
FAR AWAY

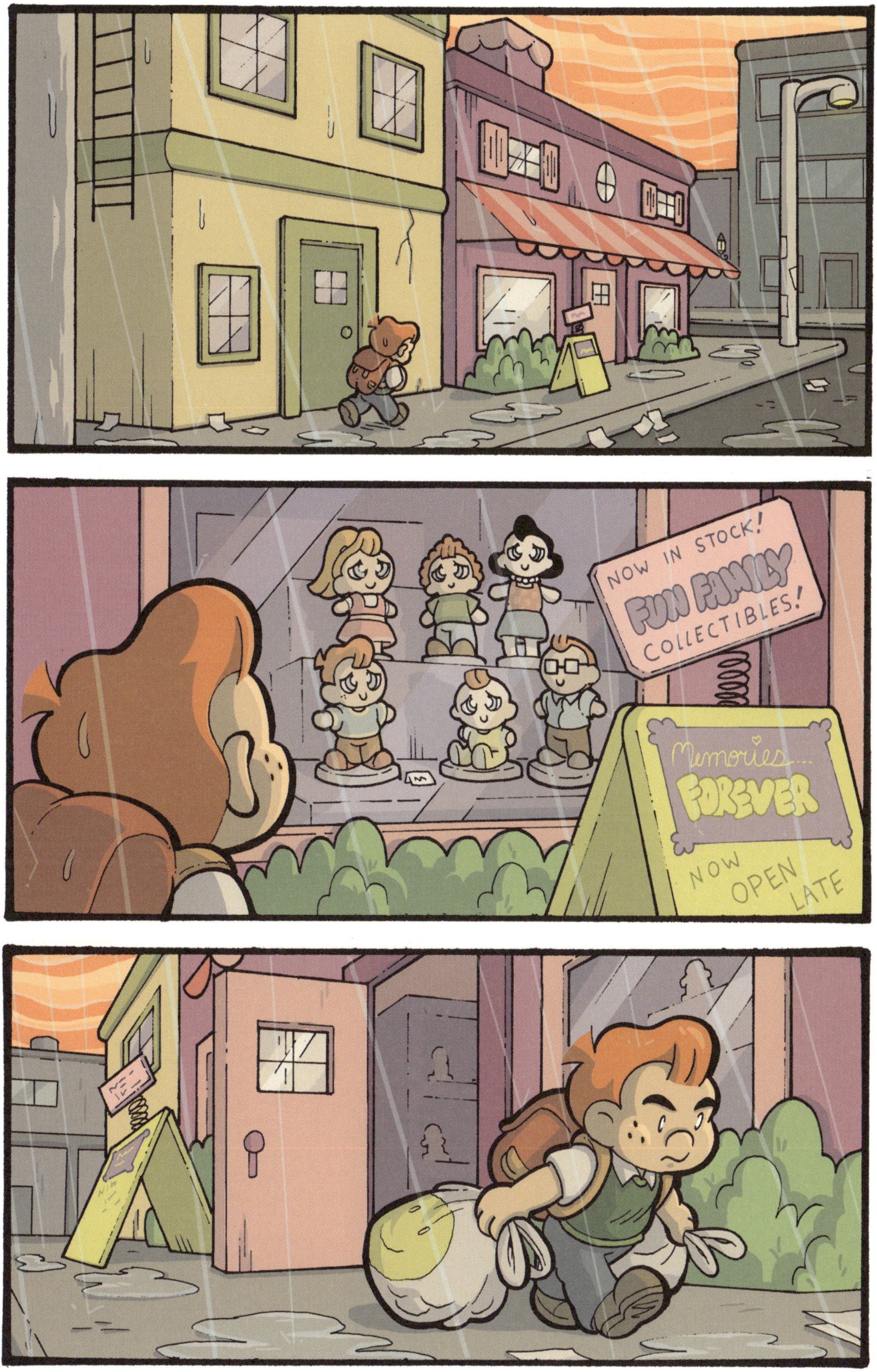
NOW IN STOCK!
FUN FAMILY
COLLECTIBLES!
Memories...
FOREVER
NOW OPEN LATE

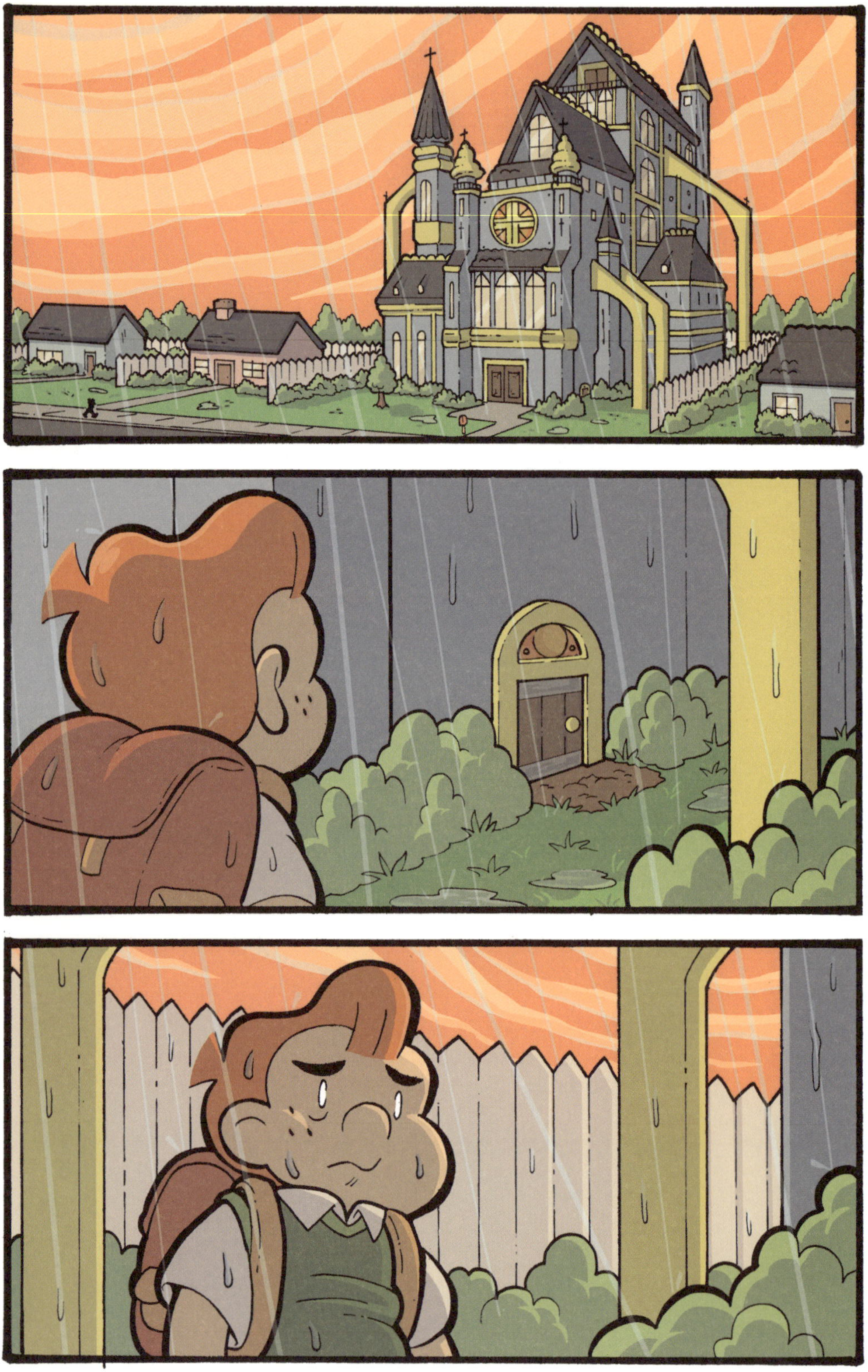

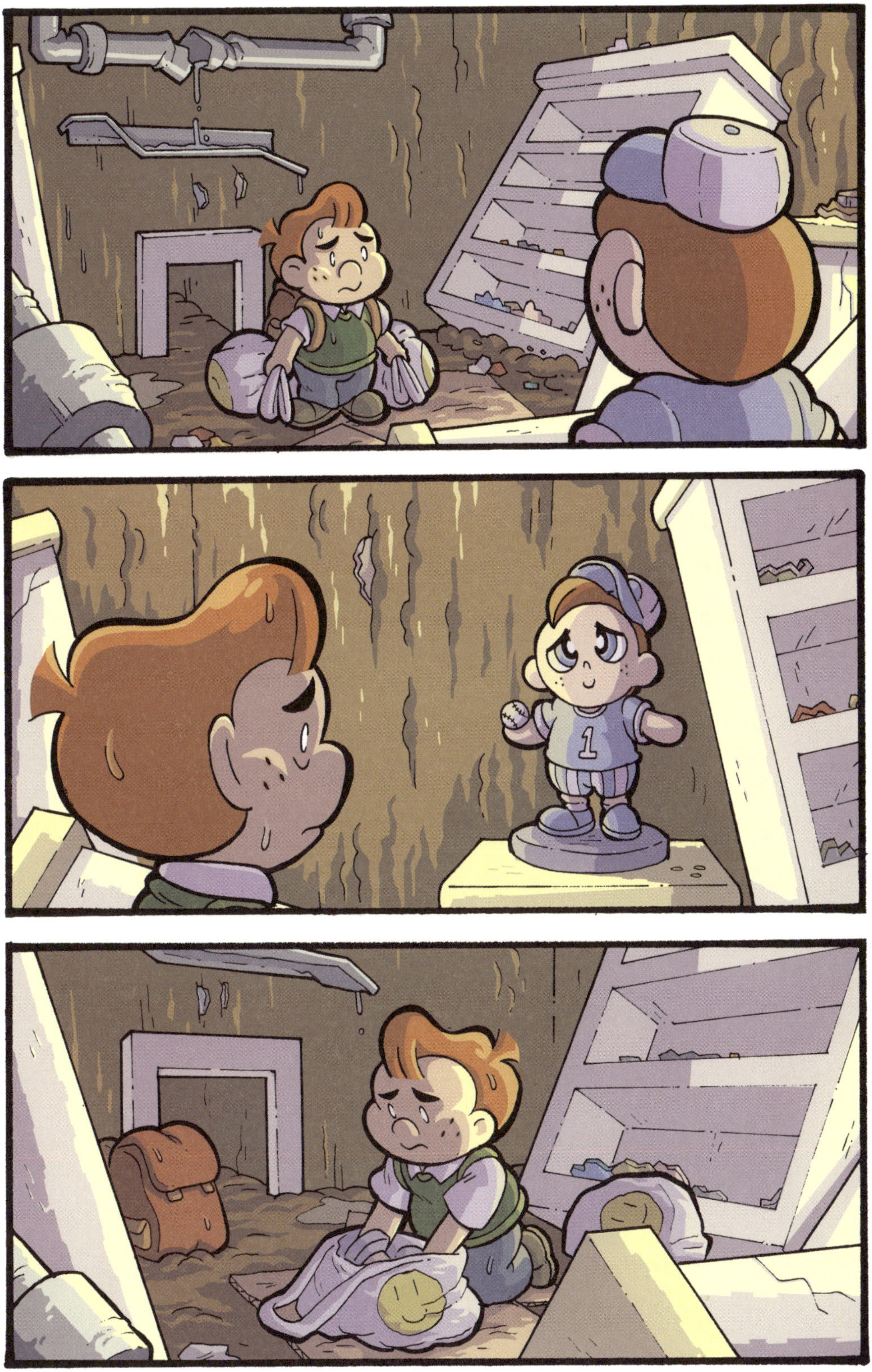
1

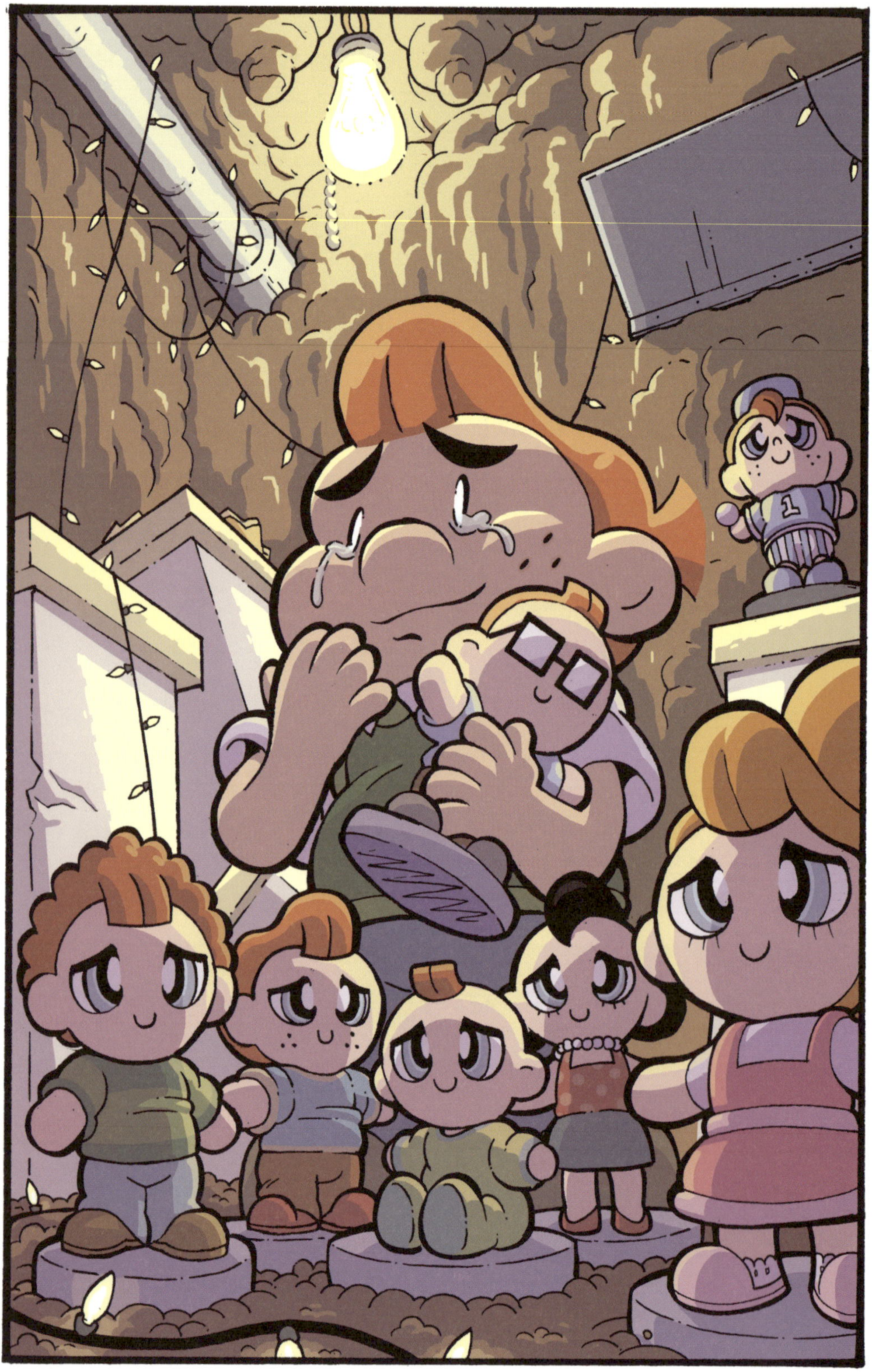

Benjamin Frisch is a cartoonist and storyteller from Williamsburg, Virginia. He has an MFA in Sequential Art from the Savannah College of Art and Design, and participated in the international artist residency program La Maison Des Auteurs in Angoulême, France. His work has appeared on the political satire site *Wonkette*, National Public Radio, and in the *Graphic Canon* comics anthologies.

The Fun Family is his first book.

BY: MIKEY FUN